MW00782980

MERIDIAN

Crossing Aesthetics

Werner Hamacher

Editor

Edited by
Bernhard Böschenstein and Heino Schmull
with assistance from
Michael Schwarzkopf and Christiane Wittkop

Translated and with a Preface by Pierre Joris

Stanford
University
Press

Stanford,
California

THE MERIDIAN

Final Version—Drafts—Materials

Paul Celan

Stanford University Press
Stanford, California

Printed in the United States of America

Library of Congress Cataloging-in-Publication Data

Celan, Paul, 1920-1970, author.
[Meridian. English]
The meridian : final version—drafts—materials / Paul Celan ; edited by Bernhard Böschenstein and Heino Schmull with assistance from Michael Schwarzkopf and Christiane Wittkop ; translated by Pierre Joris.
pages cm.—(Meridian, crossing aesthetics)
"Originally published in German under the title Der Meridian."
Originally presented as a speech to the German Academy for Language and Poetry on the occasion of Celan's acceptance of the Georg Büchner Prize for literature.
Includes bibliographical references and index.
ISBN 978-0-8047-3951-1 (cloth : alk. paper)—
ISBN 978-0-8047-3952-8 (pbk. :)
1. Celan, Paul, 1920-1970. Meridian. I. Böschenstein, Bernhard, editor. II. Schmull, Heino, editor. III. Joris, Pierre, 1946–, translator. IV. Title. V. Series: Meridian (Stanford, Calif.)
PT2605.E4M4713 2011
831′.914—dc22 2010043610

Typeset by Newgen North America in 9½ on 12 Life LT Std.

Contents

Translator's Preface ix
Editors' Preface xi
  The Origin of the Büchner-Prize Speech xiv
  Presentation and Transcription xviii

The Meridian, Final Version 1
Preliminary Stages 15
Drafts
  I. Main Section 48
  II. Main Section 55
  III. Main Section 74
Materials
  Darkness 84
  The Poem 96
  Breath 108
  Breathturn 123
  Encounter 132
  Hostility to Art 149
  Time Critique 161
  Notes on Büchner and K. E. Franzos 175
  Discarded Speech Parts 184
  Materials from Other Posthumous Writings 187
  Further Materials from *The Meridian*-Collections 199

Radio-Essay: *The Poetry of Osip Mandelstam* 215
Letter to Hermann Kasack of 16.5.60 222

Appendix 223

Notes 224
Editorial Comments
  On the Signature and Reference System 257
  On the Final and the Preliminary Versions of *The Meridian* Speech 257
  On the Drafts of the Büchner-Speech 258
  On the Materials for the Büchner-Speech 259
  On Materials from Other Archival Papers 261
Index of Names 263
Facsimiles 267

Translator's Preface

This translation took the best part of seven years to complete—and in that sense is probably the most epic endeavor in this discipline I have undertaken to date. In contrast, my translation of the four volumes of Celan's poetry starting with *Breathturn* took only about half this long. The reasons will be obvious: the difficulties of trying to render minute differences between four or more parallel German versions or drafts, while staying true to and rendering the typographical layout of the original transcriptions. These scholarly transcriptions of all the extant textual variants of Celan's Meridian speech include a complex apparatus to reproduce deletions, inserts, additions, and a further range of minuscule changes (capital to lower case, vice versa, etc.) which I tried to maintain as closely as possible in the English. I did, at times, make the decision to omit such an indication when what was obvious in German would have required an over-long explicatory addition in English that would not have added anything substantial to our understanding of the texts (for example, occasions when Celan corrected the spelling of a word or added initial caps to nouns, a basic grammatical rule in German but not in English). But wherever the change was in any way meaningful or enriching for the text I endeavored to find a way to make this visible in the English.

I have of course maintained the original typographical labels and special characters as inherited from the German version. The only addition are \backslashes\, which I use to indicate that the German word has also been retained and is framed by these markers. This happens when the original term does not have a satisfying equivalent in English, either because of its domain of etymological origin, or because Celan took it from a specialized vocabulary and the available English word would lose that specificity. When I felt that the German word was more accurate or detailed than any available English equivalent I would also give the original term; \backslashes\ are further used when an important aspect of the German term is untranslatable, as when, for example, Celan puns on meanings inherent in the image the German word presents and that are absent in the available English term. An example, among many others, would be the word \Gänsefüsschen\ which refers to quotation marks, though the literal meaning is "little goosefeet," a meaning which Celan foregrounds and plays on at length on a number of occasions.

The only section of the book I have taken the liberty to shorten is the "Editorial Comments" section in the Appendix, leaving out material relevant and of interest only to a scholar doing research on Paul Celan in the Marbach archives—which presupposes a knowledge of the German language and thus no need for this English version of *The Meridian*.

❖❖❖

I would like to thank, first and foremost, Werner Hamacher who approached me with the idea for translating the book, was able to convince me that it was possible, helped in innumerable ways over the years to create time and space for the project, and had enough confidence in my abilities to stand by me even when I was flailing about and ready to quit. I also want to thank my graduate students in the English department at the university at Albany, Sabine Seiler, whose "draft" translation of the preface of the German edition needed only the slightest revisions to become the final version, and Christopher Rizzo, who spent endless hours helping me straighten out the layout of the WordPerfect version. Helen Tartar, who was the Stanford editor at the start of the adventure, was and remains a friend and a prod—thanks are due to her too. During the fall of 2003 I was able to get a solid start on the translation, thanks to the Berlin Prize I was awarded by the American Academy in Berlin and which allowed me to work undisturbed and with all the needed German literary resources for three months in their beautiful residence on the Wannsee. Thanks are also due to Heino Schmull, the creator of the layout of the German edition, who provided me with the electronic version he had created and saved me much time. Last, but of course not least, I need to thank my family who put up with the long hours, the despondent, nay desperate monologues about the general impossibility of translation and the specific difficulties of this project—but who stood by, helped, and made finishing the job possible.

Of course, as they say, all remaining errors and mistakes are my own responsibility.

Pierre Joris
Bay Ridge, Brooklyn
February 7, 2010

Editors' Preface

The "Tübingen Edition"

By showing the layers of the genesis of Paul Celan's text, the *Tübinger Celan-Ausgabe* (TCA, Tübingen Celan edition) makes it possible to read them as poetic and historical documents and messages while also providing a vivid picture of the various stages of Celan's work on this text.

About This Book

This volume of Celan's notes to *The Meridian* can follow the editorial pattern of the poetry volumes only to a limited extent since the character of these texts is fundamentally different from that of the poetic works. The manuscripts and typescripts—most of them published here for the first time—can be considered working notes the author never intended for publication and never compiled systematically (or only partially). The material gathered here does not represent a strictly genetic corpus but is rather an extensive, heterogeneous collection of writings—Celan's attempts to write down his thoughts about his poetry —and shaped by the author's own needs. Celan had begun these attempts long before he received the news that the Büchner prize was to be presented to him, and then he completed the final version of the speech in a comparatively short time. Celan's notes trace the paths by which he arrived at the succinct formulations of his speech, formulations from which much has been omitted. The wealth of literary, philosophical, and political contexts and allusions in Celan's speech comes fully alive only against the background of these writings.

In organizing these papers for this edition, contradictory requirements had to be taken into account. On the one hand, presenting the texts as loosely ordered as they are in the file folders that make up the Celan collection of the German Literature Archive (Deutsches Literaturarchiv) in Marbach am Neckar, would have made this book unwieldy and difficult to read. On the other hand, systematizing them in any way destroys their original arrangement and the original context in which each text was placed.

We have tried to reach a compromise and balance these extremes—first, to make it possible for readers to become familiar with the situation in which the speech originated, and second, to make visible Celan's way of thinking. The writings gathered here do not reveal a linear progression; rather, there is a limited number of main themes Celan varied, interconnected, and developed. Our chosen method of presenting the material, especially in the largest section of the volume, the "Materials" for *The Meridian*, is designed to do justice to Celan's way of working on these notes. This will make possible a fruitful engagement with this wealth of complicated material.

The Structure of This Volume

The material in this volume is arranged in reverse chronological order—that is, the most recent text comes first—so that the development of the speech can be traced back from the finished final version through the *preliminary versions* of the speech as a whole and through the *drafts* of individual passages all the way to the initial notes and to text passages from earlier works that were taken up again in *The Meridian*.

Accordingly, this volume begins with the running text of the *final version* of the Büchner-prize speech. Its sections and paragraphs have been numbered consecutively, with the numbers printed in the margins. These numbers serve as references to the final version throughout the book.

The final version of the speech is followed by selected *preliminary versions* of the speech as a whole; in analogy to the TCA poetry volumes, these versions are presented in chronological sequence in four columns across a double page. The boldface numbers within the texts correspond to the numbering of the final version. Reading through the various preliminary versions reveals how Celan structured the text of his speech by means of line spaces and line breaks and how he focused his work. A direct comparison shows the last deletions, additions, and transpositions Celan made before finishing the speech.

However, the remaining, much larger part of the existing text cannot be presented in a similar synoptic fashion because the texts in this volume—unlike poems—are not versions of a limited number of clearly delimited individual texts. Here *drafts* prefiguring the wording of the Büchner–prize speech, are distinguished from notelike *materials*.

Roughly a sixth of these writings are *drafts* and can be linked to the individual passages in the speech they prefigure. The paragraphs of these texts are also numbered and keyed to the corresponding sections of the final version. For the sake of greater clarity, the speech has been subdivided into three main parts, corresponding to the phases of Celan's work on *The Meridian*. Within each part the texts are arranged in reverse chronological order, insofar as a chronological sequence could be determined. In all, this volume thus reconstructs the evolution of the speech.

Following Celan's usual method, all the other *materials*—most of them only fragments —are grouped under a limited number of main themes, for example, under "darkness" or "encounter," so that texts related in content are placed near each other. Though the transitions from one theme to the next are fluid, the subdivision of the material allows a clearer view of different aspects of the concepts and their interconnection and interpenetration with other concepts in Celan's thinking. When texts belong equally to two categories, they are printed under both headings.

Every text in the draft and materials sections is numbered sequentially. A system of cross-references keyed to these numbers allows readers to reconstruct the material's customary arrangement at any time. In addition, a system of references to parallel passages points out further connections.

Separating the drafts from the other writings clearly distinguishes between documents representing goal-oriented steps in the development of a fixed, firmly established text and more open notes not prefiguring a sharply defined final formulation. This separation also allows greater editorial latitude for the texts in the category materials as compared to the drafts and preliminary versions. As a result, readers can familiarize themselves with Celan's intellectual world by following the structure we suggest, and then, in a second step, with the help of the system of linked cross-references they can follow the notes in their customary arrangement. With the help of the signature markings, the introduction, and the appendix, readers can reconstruct the chronology, discover new connections and sources, and ultimately follow their own paths of interpretation.

Text Version

Celan's speech on the occasion of receiving the Büchner prize is his most important document on poetics. The speech, entitled *The Meridian,* was first published in 1961 as a monograph by S. Fischer in Frankfurt; it also appeared in that same year in the *Jahrbuch der Deutschen Akademie für Sprache und Dichtung.* The present edition includes that published text, selected preliminary versions, and, more important, the numerous drafts and materials, never before published, that preceded Celan's work on the speech.

Our text of the final version follows the first edition, which has been checked against Celan's corrections on the galley proofs (preliminary version "B"). The text of the preliminary versions, the drafts, and the materials is based on the unpublished papers relating to *The Meridian* in the Celan collection of the German Literature Archive in Marbach. These papers are kept in two simple file boxes (the binder with signatures "A" through "F" in one, and preliminary versions, galleys, etc. labeled "A" through "M" in the other).

Where necessary we have consulted additional writings: pages from other parts of the archive's Celan collection, such as his preliminary sketches for his radio-essay on Mandelstam with the initials "ÜR," Celan's notebooks and workbooks dating from 1960 as well as unpublished pages from the collection relating to *Niemandsrose* and the so-called "Dossiers—i ."

This volume also includes Celan's radio-essay *The Poetry of Osip Mandelstam* (pp. 215ff.). This essay was first published in a collection edited by Ralph Dutli (*Ossip Mandelstam: Im Luftgrab. Ein Lesebuch.* With essays by Paul Celan, Pier Paolo Pasolini, Philippe Jaccottet, Joseph Brodsky, ed. Ralph Dutli. Zurich 1988, pp. 69-81) but was not included in any of the existing editions of Celan's works. The text in the present volume follows Celan's last fair copy, the typescript ÜR 6.10, located among the Celan papers relating to Mandelstam.

Finally, this volume also includes the thank-you letter Celan wrote to Hermann Kasack, the president of the Deutsche Akademie für Sprache und Dichtung (German Academy for Language and Poetry), in response to a note informing him of the presentation of the Büchner prize (p. 222). Celan refers to this letter frequently in the speech and in his preparatory notes. The letter is located in the Kasack collected papers in the literary archive in Marbach.

The Origin of the Büchner-Prize Speech

The origin and evolution of *The Meridian* speech cannot be reconstructed with precision. If such a reconstruction is not to lapse into mere speculation, it must be based on dated writings. However, only very few of Celan's papers are dated, and therefore only a partial reconstruction is possible. Hypotheses about dates that are not noted on the papers themselves are out of the question—all the more so since Celan often wrote down the same texts more than once, sometimes with minor alterations, in different contexts and at different times.

The notes on *The Meridian*, which Gisèle Celan-Lestrange passed on to Bernhard Böschenstein, the editor, are combined into six binders and numbered consecutively. They are on loose-leaf sheets in simple file boxes and not uniform in character. Longer typescripts and single sheets with quick handwritten jottings are interspersed among sheets with various working notes that were written down with different writing implements and are separated from each other by a line or extra blank space. Typescripts and their carbon copies, fair copies and their preliminary versions, and other texts clearly belonging together are often spread over several binders (cf. the facsimiles, pp. 267ff.).

Of the six binders only three were compiled and given a title by Celan himself, namely, A: "On the Darkness of the Poetic," B: "Büchner" (that is, Büchner-prize speech), and F: "The Meridian." However, the pages in these three binders are not arranged in chronological sequence. Celan himself probably arranged them differently while working on them. The three remaining binders, C, D, and E, were compiled after Ceian's death by Gisèle Celan-Lestrange and a friend of the poet. These untitled binders contain the scattered papers that had been found in various pieces of furniture and books.

The oldest text of Paul Celan that already points to *The Meridian* is probably his "Address on the Occasion of the Presentation of the Literary Prize of the Free Hanseatic City of Bremen," which Celan gave on 26 January 1958. There we read: "Poems are also on the way in this manner: they are headed for something. For what? Toward something still open, still to be occupied, perhaps toward a responsive You" (GW 3,186). Toward the end of *The Meridian* speech we find a similar formulation in which the poet looks back on several "breathturns" in the speech; "Twice ... the breathturn seemed to happen. Perhaps also when I tried to set course toward that inhabitable distance which finally becomes visible only in the figure of Lucile" (43).

The notes to *The Meridian* compiled here include several passages that correspond to this or similar Versions of this phrase in Ceian's Bremen speech, for instance, that of being "on the way," of trying to "find a direction, get a bearing."

In August 1959 Celan wrote the *Gespräch im Gebirg.* (*Conversation in the Mountains*), and he mentioned its connection to Büchner's *Lenz* in his letter to Hermann Kasack dated 16 May 1960, the letter in which he responds to the notification of the Büchner-prize presentation.

In August 1959—that is, nine months before he received the letter notifying him of the prize award—Celan also wrote the earliest of the notes, namely, the bulk of binder A, which he entitled "On the Darkness of the Poetic." On 13 June 1960 Celan was still planning to develop these notes into an essay. Among his notes of that day is the following: "Essays: 1. Büchner-speech, 2. Darkness, 3. Mandelstam, 4. Translation of J. Parque into German" (Workbook II, 21, inserted sheet; sheet B 49, which is not reproduced here, has notes to Valéry's *Jeune Parque*, among them one that reads: "6/12/1960: All this to be developed in an essay on the translation of Jeune Parque!!"). The notes to *The Meridian* include jottings on all four of these projects.

Binder A was added later, probably by Celan himself, to binders B and F. On one of the two dated sheets in binder A Celan already wrote about the "constitutive, congenital darkness" of poetry (No. 64/102). His wording of this idea in the final version of the speech is: "This is, I believe, if not the congenital darkness, then the darkness attributed to poetry [...] from a [...] distance or strangeness" (27).

This core theme shows that the earliest binder of the poetological notes compiled here served as a draft for a text Celan later used in *The Meridian*. Probably the thirty-three sheets collected in this binder originally came from a single writing pad; thus, it is likely that not only the two dated sheets but also most of the others in this binder originated in August 1959. In addition, the notation "B-R" (Büchner-speech) does not appear on any of these sheets.

Several other sheets dating from August 1959, however, have been included in binder F, which Celan entitled "The Meridian." Of these, F14, F18, F 20, and F21 are dated; the related pages F 5-13, F 1547, F 19, and F 22 are not dated. Some of these texts reappear as undated copies near the end of binder F (F117-119). As a result, binder F—according to Gisèle Celan-Lestrange, compiled by Celan himself—seems to be chronologically and thematically a very varied collection, particularly since it also includes dated sheets from a later period, namely, the time between 28 September and 10 October 1960.

Celan's concentration on Mandelstam, specifically the translations from *Der Stein* (*The Stone*), *Tristia*, *Gedichte* (*Poems*) (in spring and summer 1958 and in early 1959) and Celan's composition of the note at the end of the first edition of these translations (9 May 1959), was significant for his Büchner-speech. While working on these themes, Celan probably also read Mandelstam's important prose works, and echoes of their main ideas appear in the preparatory notes and papers for *The Meridian*,

Mandelstam's prose works were found in Celan's library with underlining in his hand, among them, *Die Reise nach Arrnenien* (*The Journey to Armenia*), *Das Wort und die Kultur* (*The Word and Culture*), *Uber die Natur des Wortes* (*On the Nature of the Word*). His reading of Mandelstam's poetry and prose served Celan as his foundation in preparing his radio-essay, *Die Dichtung Osip Mandelstam's* (*The Poetry of Osip Mandelstam*), broadcast on 19 March I960. Two sections of that essay (numbered 33 and 36) have been included in *The Meridian.* It is likely that these passages, especially section 36, were transferred into the text of *The Meridian* only fairly late in the process, when Celan already felt pressed for time.

The letter from Hermann Kasack, the president of the academy, that announced the upcoming presentation of the Büchner prize to Celan is dated 11 May 1960. The draft of Celan's reply, which is included in the collection of his papers in the literary archive, was composed four days later. The final version of the letter was written one day after that, on 16 May 1960. The rough draft of the letter already contains an early version of a sentence from the speech: "Poems: the infinite speaking of mortality and pointlessness that is aware of its finiteness." Here, too, the connection between *Gespräch im Gebirg* (*Conversation in the Mountains*) and Büchner's *Lenz* is mentioned. Moreover, Celan reported in this letter that he had recently discussed Büchner with his students. Celan also participated in a seminar on Büchner's aesthetic views conducted by Hans Mayer, then a guest lecturer in Paris. Among others, the Büchner passages Celan later placed at the beginning of his speech were the subject of discussion and interpretation at that seminar.

Only one day after writing the above-mentioned letter, that is, on 17 May 1960, Celan jotted down important interconnections on sheet B 27 (nos. 135-138): the Pascal quotation about the "darkness we acknowledge," which he was to use in *The Meridian*, the Baudelaire quotation about the "sharp point of the infinite," which Celan's *Niemandsrose* was to echo (by way of Hofmannsthal who used the quotation several times, especially in his notes and drafts), the situation of St. Alexius "under the servants' stairs," which served Hofmannsthal to define the position of the poet in his speech *The Poet and Our Time* in analogy to Lenz, who wants to "walk on his head." This first passage from Büchner's work Celan wrote down was to remain the most important to him to the end of his life; his relationship to Büchner was primarily founded on this passage. Connecting the context of the Pascal quotation in Leo Schestow's essay, *La nuit de Gethsémani: Essai sur la philosophie de Pascal* (where Pascal's concept of the abyss is discussed) with Lenz's notion of walking on his head reveals that the idea of poetry as bottomless was on Celan's mind already as early as 17 May 1960. Celan links this bottomlessness—by way of 20 January, the date of the so-called Wannsee Conference, the 1942 conference about the implementation and coordination of the "final solution of the Jewish question"—to the move of poetry toward the dead of Auschwitz. Thus, a major part of *The Meridian*'s central idea and concept was already in place when Celan received the news of the Darmstadt academy's decision. As a conclusion to his speech Celan intended to use the quotation from Benjamin's essay on Kafka, which he in fact retained in the final version of the speech: "Attention is the natural prayer of the soul" (no. 51).

Celan's notes dating from the end of May 1960 deal with the significance of breath in poetry (nos. 262, 269, 579). This theme figures prominently in the materials for *The Meridian* but much less so in the final version of the speech (5b, 18c). Similarly, the theme "involution" (cf. nos. 375ff.), conceived of as the opposite of the maxim "Elargissez l'Art" —which M. N. Rosanov, quoted by Celan in reference to Lenz, attributes to Mercier —though frequent in the notes, is not even mentioned as a word in the final version of the speech. Instead, it appears there as the turning "into your innermost narrows" (42).

There are no dated sheets from the middle of June to the middle of August 1960 and none from the first two weeks of September. This may be because Celan traveled frequently during that time, meeting with Nelly Sachs both in Zurich and in Paris, going to Brittany and to Vienna to see Klaus Demus, and then taking a trip to Stockholm. The stress and strain Celan experienced as a result of Claire Goll's defamatory article in the Munich literary review *Baubudenpoet* (issue 5, March/April 1960) cast a shadow over the whole time in which he composed *The Meridian* ever since he read the article on 3 May 1960. Though not directly expressed in his work, Celan's anguish and concern are reflected in the strongly polarized juxtaposition of "poetry" and "art." While the notes contain numerous critical comments on this time, Celan left them out of the final text of the speech because they had been absorbed into Büchner's critique of art in the passages quoted at the beginning of *The Meridian*. It is by means of these quotations that the speech retains its political character; here Celan turns Büchner's hostility toward art—which he admits in his notes he shares—against those of his critics who brand him as a "second-hand metaphor dealer" (as Celan later ironically calls himself in a letter) and thus misunderstand the basis and direction of his poetry. For Celan, the critics denouncing his genitive metaphors were no different than those who sided with Claire Goll against him. In fact, at one time Celan even considered refusing the Büchner prize, as is clear from unpublished documents. This is important in the present context insofar as it illumines the connection between Celan's critical analysis of contemporary issues, hostility toward art, and the Goll affair. Even Celan's deletion of many personal and more direct formulations must be understood in this context. Büchner thus represented an opportunity for Celan to express very personal conflicts.

In the second half of August 1960 (August 19 and 22) Celan wrote in his workbooks mostly very short notes, only a few of which are related to the completed version of the Büchner-speech. Instead, most of these notes deal with Celan's view of poetry in a more general sense. A collection of notes on this topic Celan had jotted down earlier can be found in a series of typescripts dated 28 September 1960 (pp. 199ff.). These are the clearest reflection of the extreme tension between the smear campaign and Celan's understanding of his own poetry as directed toward the dead, as testifying to a unique individuation and hostile to any conscious artistry. Only four days later, on 21 May, Celan was already composing the beginning of the speech based on the *Lenz*; quotation in combination with the walk through the "mountains" on "January 20."

The last dated sheets, from 4 through 10 October and perhaps including the one from 14 October—in other words, the sheets written only a few days before the award ceremony —show that at that time there were still many options open to Celan, most of them differing from the final version of the speech. All in all, most of the texts that can be classified as drafts are in binder C, which includes mostly typescripts and only one dated sheet, the date being 9 October. The majority of these texts clearly dates from the days just prior to the completion of the final version.

From the fact that the parts of the speech not found in the handwritten notes in binders A, B, and F appear only on the typewritten sheets in binder C we can deduce that these sections probably were not formulated until just before completion of *The Meridian*. In particular, this is true for the Büchner passages quoted at the beginning, the central paragraph **36** about poetry as a dialog—which was taken from the radio-essay on Mandelstam—and most of the passage concluding *The Meridian*. Thus, the motif of the "meridian" was added only very late in the process. (The term appears for the first time in a letter from Nelly Sachs to Paul Celan, dated 28 October 1959. "Between Paris and Stockholm runs the meridian of pain and comfort," in *Paul Celan/Nelly Sachs: Correspondence,* ed. Barbara Wiedemann, translated by Christopher Clark, 1995, p. 14.)

According to contemporary witnesses, Celan completed die text of the speech only just shortly before the presentation of the prize, and the process of composition was accompanied by very intense inner struggles. Gisèle Celan-Lestrange described how Celan woke her up one night just a few days before the award ceremony to read her the final version of *The Meridian.* Celan also read it to Jean Bollack, asking him again and again, "Is it all right to say it like that?"

Presentation and Transcription

The first requirement of this transcription is to present the often very complex handwritten and typewritten material as legibly as possible while retaining its character as preliminary notes and drafts. At the same time, the writings' internal history, reflected in the many parts Celan crossed out, in numerous insertions and additions, should remain transparent. The present transcription is designed to strike a balance between these contradictory requirements.

Attempting to present the material as far as possible in its completeness would not have served our purpose. Limitation and selection were unavoidable, and consequently we more or less completely dispensed with a detailed breakdown of various layers of corrections and with a chronological presentation of internal variations. Peculiarities of the material used (such as different writing instruments, types of paper, etc.) are mentioned in the appendix only if the material was important in dating particular notes or establishing their context in the corpus as a whole.

When unambiguous, the numerous spelling errors have been silently corrected throughout. Punctuation marks have been reproduced as they were in the original. Missing punctuation marks were not supplied because punctuation often serves to accentuate meaning or clearly signals the inconclusive, open-ended nature of many of Celan's notes.

In this critical reproduction of the existing texts insertions and deletions are indicated; the text of the final version appears in the regular type size while deleted and corrected text is set in a smaller size. The distinction between a primary and a secondary textual layer (the latter set in a lighter typeface) has been maintained throughout. The secondary layer includes Celan's subsequent additions, comments, and elaborations. When shifts in the typescripts indicate a significant break in Celan's thinking, a notation in the text (<new start>) signals the new start. Markings by Celan, such as arrows, borders around words, carets, etc., are reproduced here to the extent possible. The same applies to the lines and crosses Celan often used to separate individual notes from each other. Even when these were inserted in the original just above the next note, here they are always placed directly below the preceding one since their function is to separate a note from what follows. The function of these markings becomes clear if one reads the text preceding and following the passage in question in the traditional arrangement of the material.

Typescript texts are labeled as such; however, further typographical differentiation—as in the TCA's poetry volumes—was not practicable because most of the material presented here consists of handwritten notes and drafts. Philological notes in the appendix supplement the transcriptions.

This edition would not exist without Gisèle Ceian-Lestrange (†) passionately working toward making it possible. Particularly in the early phases of the project, she tirelessly gave her help and accompanied the work with interest. We remember her with profound gratitude.

We sincerely thank Eric Celan for kindly granting us the rights to publish this complex, collection of his father's papers for the first time. Bertrand Badiou has earned our gratitude by providing additional material from other collections of Celan's papers.

The active support of the German Literary Archive in Marbach was indispensable to our work; in particular, we would like to thank Ute Doster, Jochen Meyer, Nicolai Riedel, and Reinhard Tgahrt.

We would also like to express our sincere thanks to the Fritz Thyssen Foundation for Its generous financial support of this project.

Many friends and colleagues have helped us with their advice either to clear up or reduce editorial difficulties or to track down little-known quotations. We wish to thank them all; the following list is representative though far from complete: Frank Bahr, Ernst Behler (†), Jean Bollack, Renate Böschenstein, Rosa-Maria Braun, Lucien Dallenbach, Gerhard Dette, Manfred Frank, Wolfram Groddeck, Christoph Horn, Karl and Luzie Krolow, Guido Naschert, Otto Pöggeler, Claus-Artur Scheier, Thomas Sparr, George Steiner, Martin Stern, Barbara Wiedemann, Werner Wögerbauer.

Jürgen Wertheimer and Markus Heilmann contributed valuable constructive suggestions to the editorial work on this volume.

Regarding Russian literature, we were fortunate to be able to count on the help of Annette Werberger. We thank her and Doris Grützmacher for their proofreading. The works of Christine Ivanovic on Celan's Russian library and in particular on Mandelstam proved highly valuable for our work.

The facsimiles on pp. 267ff. are reprinted here with the kind permission of the German Literary Archive, which holds the originals.

Typographical Labels and Special Characters

⌊Insertion into continuous text⌋
~~Deletion~~

{Overwriting, other deletions}	As a rule deletions are indicated as ~~crossed out;~~ if a group of letters was overwritten by another one, then the first group is {deleted} followed immediately by the new text, for ex.: "th{is}at" The crossing out of single letters or punctuation marks that cannot be represented as crossed out, as well as deletions within deletions, are also marked as {deleted}.
Invalid text	when (accidentally) not crossed out, is given in a smaller typeface; valid text, also when (accidentally) crossed out, in normal size. Occasionally Celan adds alternative formulations; both will be given in normal size type.
Deletion of complete passages	in a smaller typeface and with diagonal crossed lines.
⌊⌋⌈⌉	Word transpositions
Textual additions	Additions that cannot be fitted into the flow of the text, such as commentaries and alternative continuations (most often added in the margins or between paragraphs, often with a different pen) as well as text parts that are later supplements to an already formulated text, are marked as textual additions in a paler script. Corrections to the text (mainly between the lines) are, however, reproduced with ⌊insertion marks⌋.
Dotted underscore	is used by Celan both to mark a specific passage and to indicate the cancelation of a deletion.
~~Underscore deletion~~	is reproduced in the original and means mostly canceled deletion (in which case the text is in normal size), though on occasion also the deletion of a text passage previously marked by dotted underscore (as invalid text rendered in small typeface).

‖ Marks in the margins	are always indicated by double lines; especially conspicuous marks are described in the appendix.
Square and (round)	are imitated.
<new paragraph>	editorial annotation
<?>	undecipherable word
~	unreadable letter
•	marks the exact points of reference of an arrow reproduced alongside the text

Normal sized text indicates the last level of the editing process, while text without ⌊insertions⌋ and read with the ~~deletions~~ gives the original version of the text.
Other marks, such as cross-outs, are reproduced or else annotated in the text or the appendix whenever possible.
Page breaks are indicated only when they are consequential (for example for paragraph division). When a special textual order is present in the original, it will be clarified by an annotation in the appendix.
As Celan's (French) typewriter did not have an "ß," "ss" was changed into "ß," in the typescripts, following his manuscripts and the printed texts.
The following abbreviations are used in the headers; Ms. = manuscript, Ts. = Typescript, Cc, = carbon copy and Hw. = handwritten.

PAUL CELAN

THE MERIDIAN

Speech on the Occasion of Receiving the Georg-Büchner-Prize

Darmstadt, October 22, 1960

Ladies and Gentlemen!

1a Art, you will remember, is a puppet-like, iambically five-footed and—a characteristic mythologically vouchsafed for by the reference to Pygmalion and his creation—a childless being.

b In this form it is the subject of a conversation that takes place in a room, thus not in the Conciergerie, a conversation that, we sense, could be continued indefinitely, if nothing interfered.

c Something does interfere.

2 Art returns. It returns in another work by Georg Büchner, in *Woyzeck*, among other, nameless people and—if I may let a phrase Moritz Heimann meant for *Danton's Death* take this route—under even more "livid light before the storm." In this totally different era, the same art takes once again to the stage, presented by a carnival barker, no longer, as was the case during that conversation, linked to "glowing," "roaring," and "shining" creation, but set next to the creature and the "nothing" this creature "wears,"—art appears this time in the shape of a monkey, but it is the same art, we have recognized it immediately by its "coat and trousers."

3a And it comes—art comes—to us in yet a third work by Büchner, in *Leonce and Lena*, where time and lighting have become unrecognizable. For here we are "in flight toward paradise," "all watches and calendars" shall soon "be shattered," even "forbidden"—though just before that "two persons of the two sexes" are presented, "two world famous automatons have arrived," and a man who says of himself that he "may be the third and strangest of them all," and insists "with a growling voice," that we admire what's before our eyes: "Nothing but art and mechanics, nothing but cardboard and watch springs!"

b Art appears here in larger company than before, but clearly it is among equals: it is the same art, the art we already know.—Valerio is only another name for the barker.

4a Art, ladies and gentlemen, with everything that belongs to it and will yet belong to it, is also a problem, and as you can see, a mutable, tough and long-lived, I want to say, an eternal problem.

b A problem that allows a mortal, Camille, and someone who can only be understood from his death, Danton, to string together word upon word. It is easy to talk about art.

But whenever there is talk about art, there is also always someone present **5a**
who ... doesn't really listen.
More exactly: someone who hears and listens and looks ... and then doesn't **b**
know what the talk was all about. But who hears the speaker, who "sees him
speak," who perceives language and shape, and also—who could doubt this
here, in writing of this order?—breath, that is, direction and
destiny.
That person is—and you have known it all along, for she comes, often, and **c**
not by chance often quoted, she comes to you year after year—that person is
Lucile.

What had inserted itself during the conversation cuts through ruthlessly and **6a**
reaches Revolution Square with us as "the carts drive up and come to a halt."
The passengers are there, all of them, Danton, Camille, the others. Here too **b**
they all have words, many artful words, and they make them stick, there is
much talk—and here Büchner only needs to quote—talk of going-together-
into-death, Fabre even maintains that he can die "doubly," they are all at
their best—only a few voices, "a few"—nameless—"voices," find that "all of
this is old hat and boring."
And here, where it all comes to an end, in the long moments when Camille— **c**
no, not Camille himself, a fellow-passenger—as that Camille dies a theatrical
—one is nearly tempted to say: a iambic—death, which we can feel as his own
only two scenes later through a word foreign—yet so near—to him, when all
around Camille pathos and sententiousness confirm the triumph of "puppet"
and "string," then Lucile, one who is blind to art, the same Lucile for whom
language is something person-like and tangible, is there, once again, with her
sudden "Long live the king!"

After all the words spoken on the rostrum (the scaffold, that is)—what a **7a**
word!
It is the counterword, it is the word that cuts the "string," the word that no **b**
longer bows down before "the bystanders and old war-horses of history." It is
an act of freedom. It is a step.

Of course, one hears it—and that may not be by chance in the context of **8a**
what I dare to say about it now, that is today—one hears it first of all as a
declaration of loyalty to the "ancien régime."
But here—permit me, someone who grew up with the writings of Peter **b**
Kropotkin and Gustav Landauer, to emphasize this—here no monarchy and
no to be conserved yesterdays are being paid homage to.
Homage is being paid to the majesty of the absurd as witness for the presence **c**
of the human.

9 This, ladies and gentlemen, has no name fixed once and for all, but I believe that this is ... poetry.

10a "—oh, art!" I am stuck, as you see, on this word of Camille's.

b I am aware that one can read this word in different ways, one can give it different accents: the acute of today, the grave of history—literary history too, the circumflex—a sign of expansion—of the eternal.

c I give it—I have no other choice—I give it the acute.

11 Art—"oh, art": besides being mutable, has the gift of ubiquity—: it can also be found in *Lenz*, there too—permit me to insist on this—as in *Danton's Death*, only as an episode.

12a "At table Lenz was again in good spirits; the talk turned to literature, he was in his element ..."

b "... The feeling that what has been created has life, stands above these two and is the only criterion in matters of art ..."

13 I have picked out here only two sentences, my bad conscience about the grave bids me make you aware of this immediately—this passage has primarily literary-historical importance, one has to know how to read it together with the already quoted passage from *Danton's Death*; here Büchner's aesthetic conception finds expression, from here, leaving Büchner's *Lenz* fragment behind, one gets to Reinhold Lenz, the author of the "Notes on the Theater," and back beyond him, to the historical Lenz, to Mercier's literarily so productive "Elargissez l'Art." This passage opens up vistas, it anticipates naturalism and Gerhard Hauptmann, here we must look for and find the social and political roots of Büchnerian poetry.

14a Ladies and gentlemen, that I don't let this go unsaid does ease my conscience, if only for a moment, but it also shows you simultaneously, and thus disturbs my conscience anew—it shows you that I cannot get away from something that, for me, seems to have to do with art.

b I am looking for it here too, in *Lenz*—and permit myself to point this out to you.

c Lenz, that is Büchner, has, "oh, art" only disparaging words for "Idealism" and its "wooden puppets." He counters them—and here follow the unforgettable lines about the "life of the smallest," the "twitches," the "intimations," the "whole fine, nearly unnoticed pantomime"—he counters them with what is natural and creaturely. And he illustrates this conception of art with an experience:

"Yesterday as I was walking along above the valley, I saw two girls sitting on a **15**
rock: one was putting up her hair, the other helping her; and the golden hair was hanging free, and a pale, solemn face, and yet so young, and the black peasant dress, and the other one so absorbed in her task. The finest, most heartfelt paintings of the Old German School scarcely convey an inkling of this. At times one wishes one were a Medusa's head in order to turn a group like this into stone, and call everybody over to have a look."

Ladies and gentleman, please, take note: "One wishes one were a Medusa's **16a**
head" in order to ... grasp the natural as the natural with the help of art!
One wishes to does of course not mean here: *I* wish to. **b**

This is a stepping beyond what is human, a stepping into an uncanny realm **17a**
turned toward the human—the realm where the monkey, the automatons and with them ... oh, art too, seem to be at home.
This is not the historical Lenz, it is Büchner's Lenz who speaks thus, here too **b**
we have heard Büchner's voice: for him art retains something of the uncanny.

Ladies and gentlemen, I have given it the acute accent; I cannot hide from **18a**
you anymore than from myself that I took this question concerning art and poetry—one question among others—that I took this question of my own—if not completely free—will to Büchner, in order to locate his own question.
But you see it easily: Valerio's "growling voice" is unmistakable whenever art **b**
comes to the fore.
These are doubtlessly—and Büchner's voice invites the proposition—old and **c**
even ancient forms of uncanniness. That I worry these with such stubbornness today, probably is in the air—the air we have to breathe today.

Doesn't Büchner—I now must ask—doesn't Georg Büchner, the poet of the **19**
creature, propose a perhaps only half-audible, perhaps only half-conscious, but despite that no less radical—or perhaps exactly because of that, a truly radical calling-into-question of art, a calling-into-question from that angle? A calling-into-question to which all of today's poetry has to return, if it wants to question further? With other, perhaps too hasty words: may we, as happens in many places these days, start from art as something given and absolutely unconditional, should we before all, to put it most concretely, think—let's say—Mallarmé through to the end?

I have anticipated, reached beyond—not far enough, I know—I'll return **20a**
now to Büchner's *Lenz*, thus to the—episodic—conversation, that was had "at table" and that had Lenz "again in fine spirits."

b Lenz spoke for a long time, "now all smiles, now serious." And then, when the conversation had run its course, it is said of him, thus of the one preoccupied with questions about art, but at the same time also of the artist Lenz: "He had completely forgotten himself."

c I think of Lucile as I read this; I read: *He*, he himself.

d He who has art before his eyes and on his mind—I am with the Lenz narrative now—forgets himself. Art creates I-distance. Art here demands in a certain direction a certain distance, a certain route.

21 And poetry? Poetry which does have to tread the route of art? Then this would really be the route to the Medusa's head and the automaton!

22a Now, I am not looking for a way out, I am only pushing the question further in the same direction and, I believe, in the direction of the Lenz fragment.

b Perhaps—I am only asking—perhaps poetry, like art, moves with a self-forgotten I toward the uncanny and strange, and sets itself free again—but where? but in which place? but with what? but as what?

c Then art would be the route poetry has to cover—nothing less, nothing more.

d I know, there are other, shorter routes. But poetry too does hurry ahead of us at times. La poésie, elle aussi, brûle nos étapes.

23 I am taking leave of the man who forgot himself, the man preoccupied by art, the artist. I believe that I met poetry with Lucile and Lucile perceives language as shape and direction and breath—: here too, in this work by Büchner, I search for the same, I search for Lenz himself, I search for him—as a person, I search for his shape: for the sake of the place of poetry, for the setting free, for the step.

24a Büchner's Lenz, ladies and gentlemen, has remained a fragment. Shall we search for the historical Lenz to see what direction his existence takes?

b "He saw his existence as a necessary burden.—And so he lived on ..." Here the tale breaks off.

c But, like Lucile, poetry tries to see the direction shape takes, poetry hurries ahead. We know *toward* where he lived, how he lived *on*.

d "Death," we read in a work about Jakob Michael Reinhold Lenz published in Leipzig in 1909—written by a Moscow lecturer by the name of M. N. Rosanov—"death as final redeemer was not long in coming. In the night of 23 to 24 May, 1792, Lenz was found lifeless in a Moscow street. A nobleman paid for his burial. His last resting place has remained unknown."

Thus had he lived *on*. e
He: the true, the Büchnerian Lenz, Büchner's figure, the person we were able f
to perceive on the first page of the story, the Lenz who "on 20th January
walked through the mountains," he—not the artist, not the one preoccupied
with questions about art, he as an I.

Can we now perhaps locate the place where the strangeness was, the place 25a
where the person was able to set himself free as an—estranged—I? Can we
find such a place, such a step?
"... except sometimes it annoyed him that he could not walk on his head."— b
That's him, Lenz. That is, I believe, him and his step, him and his "Long live
the king."

"... except sometimes it annoyed him that he could not walk on his head." 26a
He who walks on his head, ladies and gentlemen—he who walks on his b
head, has the sky beneath himself as an abyss.

Ladies and gentlemen, it is common today to reproach poetry for its 27
"obscurity."—At this point permit me to quote somewhat abruptly—but
hasn't something opened up here, suddenly?—permit me to quote a line by
Pascal, a line that I read some time ago in Leo Shestov: "Ne nous reprochez
pas le manque de clarté puisque nous en faisons profession!"—This is, I
believe, if not the congenital darkness, then however the darkness attributed
to poetry for the sake of an encounter from a—perhaps self-created—distance
or strangeness.

But perhaps there are two strangenesses—close together, and in one and the same 28
direction.

Lenz—or rather Büchner—has here gone a step further than Lucile. His 29a
"Long live the king" is no longer a word, it is a terrifying falling silent, it takes
away his—and our—breath and words.
Poetry: that can mean an *Atemwende*, a breathturn. Who knows, perhaps b
poetry travels this route—also the route of art—for the sake of such a
breathturn? Perhaps it will succeed, as the strange, I mean the abyss *and* the
Medusa's head, the abyss and the automatons, seem to lie in one direction—
perhaps it will succeed here to differentiate between strange and strange,
perhaps it is exactly here that the Medusa's head shrinks, perhaps it is exactly
here that the automatons break down—for this single short moment?
Perhaps here, with the I—with the estranged I set free *here* and *in this manner*
—perhaps here a further Other is set free?

c Perhaps the poem is itself because of this ... and can now, in this art-less, art-free manner, walk its other routes, thus also the routes of art—time and again?

d Perhaps.

30a Perhaps one can say that each poem has its own "20th of January" inscribed in it? Perhaps what's new in the poems written today is exactly this: theirs is the clearest attempt to remain mindful of such dates?

b But don't we all write ourselves from such dates? And toward what dates do we write ourselves?

31a But the poem does speak! It stays mindful of its dates, but—it speaks. For sure, it speaks always only on its own, its very own behalf.

b But I do think—and this thought can hardly surprise you by now—I think that it had always been part of the poem's hopes to speak on behalf of exactly this *strange*—no, I cannot use this word this way—exactly *on another's behalf*—who knows, perhaps on behalf *of a totally other.*

c This "who knows," to which I see that I have now arrived, is all I can add, here, today, to the old hopes.

d Perhaps, I have to tell myself now—perhaps an encounter of this "totally other" kind with a not all too distant, with a very close "other" is—I am using here a familiar auxiliary verb—is thinkable—thinkable again and again.

e The poem tarries and tests the wind—a word related to the creaturely—through such thoughts.

f Nobody can tell how long the breath pause—the testing and the thought—will last. The "swift," which has always been "outside," has gained speed; the poem knows this, but heads straight for that "other," that it considers reachable, able to be set free, perhaps vacant, and thus turned—let's say: like Lucile—turned toward it, the poem.

32a Certainly, the poem—the poem today—shows, and this, I believe, has to do only indirectly with the—not to be underestimated—difficulties of word choice, the faster fall of syntax or the more lucid sense for ellipsis—the poem shows, unmistakably, a strong tendency to fall silent.

b It stands fast—after so many extreme formulations, permit me this one too—the poem stands fast at the edge of itself; it calls and brings itself, in order to be able to exist, ceaselessly back from its already-no-longer into its always-still.

This always-still can only be a speaking. But not just language as such, nor, **33a**
presumably, just verbal "analogy" either.
But language actualized, set free under the sign of a radical individuation that **b**
at the same time, however, remains mindful of the borders language draws and of the possibilities language opens up for it.
This always-still of the poem can indeed only be found in the work of the **c**
poet who does not forget that he speaks under the angle of inclination of his Being, the angle of inclination of his creatureliness.
Then the poem is—even more clearly than previously—one person's **d**
language-become-shape, and, according to its essence, presentness and presence.

The poem is lonely. It is lonely and *en route*. Its author remains added to it. **34a**

But doesn't the poem therefore already at its inception stand in the encounter **b**
—*in the mystery of the encounter?*

The poem wants to head toward some other, it needs this other, it needs an **35a**
opposite. It seeks it out, it bespeaks itself to it.
Each thing, each human is, for the poem heading toward this other, a figure **b**
of this.
The attention the poem tries to pay to everything it encounters, its sharper **c**
sense of detail, outline, structure, color, but also of the "tremors" and "hints," all this is not, I believe, the achievement of an eye competing with (or emulating) ever more precise instruments, but is rather a concentration that remains mindful of all our dates.
"Attention"—permit me to quote here a phrase by Malebranche, via Walter **d**
Benjamin's essay on Kafka—"Attention is the natural prayer of the soul."

The poem becomes—under what conditions!—the poem of someone who— **36a**
always still—perceives, is turned toward phenomena, questioning and addressing these; it becomes conversation—often a desperate conversation.
Only in the space of this conversation does the addressed constitute itself, as it **b**
gathers around the I addressing and naming it. But the addressed which through naming has, as it were, become a you, brings its otherness into this present. Even in this here and now of the poem—for the poem itself, we know, has always only this one, unique, momentary present—even in this immediacy and nearness it lets the most essential aspect of the other speak: its time.

c When we speak with things in this way, we are also always confronted with the question of their where-from and where-to: a question that "stays open," "does not come to an end," that points toward the open, empty and free—we are far outside.
d The poem, I believe, searches for this place too.

37a The poem?
b The poem with its images and tropes?

38a Ladies and gentlemen, what am I actually speaking about, when I speak from *this* direction, in *this* direction, with *these* words about poetry—no, about *the* poem?
b For I am talking about a poem which does not exist!
c The absolute poem—no, that certainly does not exist, cannot exist!
d But there is indeed in each real poem, even in the most unassuming poem, this irrecusable question, this outrageous claim.

39a And then, what would the images be?
b What is perceived and is to be perceived once and always again once, and only here and now. Hence the poem would be the place where all tropes and metaphors want to be carried ad absurdum.

40a Topos research?
b Certainly! But in light of what is to be searched for: in light of u-topia.
c And the human being? And the creature?
d In this light.

41a What questions! What claims!
b It is time to turn back.

42a Ladies and gentlemen, I am at the end—I am back at the beginning.
b *Elargissez l'Art*! This question comes at us with its old, with its new uncanniness. I took it to Büchner—and think I found it there again.
c I even had a ready answer, a "Lucilian" counterword; I wanted to counter, be ready with my own contradiction:
d Enlarge art?

No. To the contrary: go with art into your innermost narrows. And set **e**
yourself free.
I took this route, here too, in your presence. It was a circle. **f**
Art—thus also the Medusa's head, the mechanism, the automatons, the uncanny **g**
so difficult to separate out and which in the final analysis is perhaps only *one*
strangeness—art lives on.

Twice, with Lucile's "Long live the king," and when the sky opened as an abyss **43**
beneath Lenz, the *Atemwende*, the breathturn seemed to happen. Perhaps also when I
tried to set course toward that inhabitable distance which finally becomes visible
only in the figure of Lucile. And once, due to the attention given to things and
beings, we also came close to something open and free. And finally, close to
utopia.

Poetry, ladies and gentlemen: this infinity-speaking full of mortality and to **44**
no purpose!

Ladies and gentlemen, permit me, as I am back at the beginning, to ask once **45a**
more, in all brevity and from a different direction, the same question.
Ladies and gentlemen, a few years ago I wrote a small four-line stanza—here **b**
it is:
"Voices up from the nettle-route. / *Come to us on your hands.* / Whoever is **c**
alone with the lamp, / has only his hand to read from."
And a year ago, in memory of a missed encounter in the Engadine, I wrote **d**
down a little story, in which I let a man walk "like Lenz" through the
mountains.
On both occasions, I had written myself from one "20th January," from my **e**
"20th January," toward myself.
I had ... encountered myself. **f**

Does one take, when thinking of poems, does one take such routes with the **46**
poems? Are these routes only re-routings, detours from you to you? But they
are also at the same time, among many other routes, routes on which
language becomes voice, they are encounters, routes of a voice to a perceiving
you, creaturely routes, blueprints for being perhaps, a sending onseself ahead
toward oneself, in search of oneself ... A kind of homecoming.

Ladies and gentlemen, I am coming to the end—I am coming, with the acute **47**
accent I had to set, to the end of ... *Leonce and Lena*.

48a And here, with the last two words of this work, I must be careful.

b I must be careful not to misread, like Karl Emil Franzos, the editor of that "First Critical Complete Edition of Georg Büchner's Collected Works and Handwritten Posthumous Writings," which was published eighty-one years ago by Sauerländer in Frankfurt am Main—I must be careful not to misread, *like my countryman Karl Emil Franzos here rediscovered*, the "Commode" [the accommodating], we need now, as if it was "coming" ["Kommendes"]!

c And yet: isn't *Leonce and Lena* full of quotation marks, invisibly and smilingly added to the words, that want to be understood perhaps not as "Gänsefüßchen" [goose-feet], but rather as "Hasenöhrchen" [hare's ears], that is, something not completely fearless, that listens beyond itself and the words?

49a From here, thus starting from the "accommodating," but also in the light of utopia, let me now undertake some topos research:

b I am searching for the region from which Reinhold Lenz and Karl Emil Franzos, whom I met on the way here and in Georg Büchner, come. As I am back where I started from, I am also searching for the place of my origin.

c I am searching for all of this with a no doubt very imprecise because fidgety finger on the map—a child's map, I have to confess.

d None of these places can be found, they do not exist, but I know where, especially now, they should be, and ... I find something!

50a Ladies and gentlemen, I find something that consoles me a little for having in your presence taken this impossible route, this route of the impossible.

b I find what connects and leads, like the poem, to an encounter.

c I find something—like language—immaterial, yet terrestrial, something circular that returns to itself across both poles while—cheerfully—even crossing the tropics: I find ... a *meridian*.

51 With you and Georg Büchner and the State of Hesse I believe I have just now touched it again.

52a Ladies and gentlemen, today a high honor was conferred upon me. I will be able to remember that in the company of people whose persons and work mean an encounter for me, I am the recipient of a prize that is mindful of Georg Büchner.

b My heartfelt thanks for this distinction, my heartful thanks for this moment and this encounter.

I thank the State of Hesse, I thank the city of Darmstadt. I thank the German **c**
Academy for Language and Poetry.
I thank the President of the German Academy for Language and Poetry, I **d**
thank you, dear Hermann Kasack.
Dear Marie Luise Kaschnitz, I thank you. **e**

Ladies and gentlemen, I thank you for your presence. **53**

Preliminary Stages

Drafts (Nr. 1)

1a Art, you will remember, is a puppet-like, iambically five-footed and—this characteristic is also mythologically vouchsafed, a childless being; **b** it is the object of a conversation that ~~has~~ takes place in a room, thus not in the Conciergerie, a conversation that, we sense, could ~~go on~~ ⌞be continued⌟ indefinitely, if nothing interfered; **2** it ⌞, art,⌟ will return again later, at a certain distance, ⌞in another play,⌟ thus in another era, in "Woyzeck," presented by a market crier, no longer to be related to the glowing, roaring and shining creation, but besides the creature, in ~~the shape of a monkey~~ ⌞the shape of a monkey⌟ this time, and yet, ~~and in that it distinguishes itself fundamentally from the immediately recog~~ immediately recognizable by its jacket and pants. < ... >

Ts. "A"

<no title>

1a Art, you will remember, is a puppet-like, iambically five-footed and—this ⌞yet to be named?⌟ characteristic is also, ~~under~~ by the reference to Pygmalion and his ~~work~~—creature, {–}mythologically vouchsaved—childless being. **b** In this form it ~~is the~~ ⌞it constitutes⌟ the object of a conversation, that takes place in a room, thus not in the Conciergerie, a conversation that, ⌞we sense, could be continued indefinitely, if nothing interfered. **c** Something does interfere.

2 The ~~same art~~ will ~~then later~~ return ⌞.⌟ ~~vor,~~ ⌞It returns⌟ in another ~~play~~ ⌞work by Georg Büchner,⌟ in "Woyzeck," among other people, under even "a more livid light before the storm"—if I may let a phrase meant for "Danton's Death" ⌞by Moritz Heimann⌟ take this route—the same <u>art</u> is⌞,⌟ ~~there again,~~ in this totally different era too{,} ⌞there again,⌟ presented by a market crier, no longer, as was the case ~~in~~ ⌞during⌟ that conversation, to be related to the glowing, roaring and shining creation, but <u>besides</u> the creature and the "nothing," which this ⌞creature⌟ wears, art appears this time in the shape of a monkey, but it is the same, ~~about this no doubt is possible~~ we have recognized it immediately by its "jacket and pants."

3a ~~It returns, also~~ ⌞And also with a⌟ a third ~~play, in~~ ⌞work, with⌟ "Leonce and Lena," the time ⌞~~if, anyway we have time~~⌟ and the lighting ~~is completely different,~~ ⌞are ~~differ~~ here different than elsewhere,⌟ ~~from here it is even a~~ for here we are in "in flight to paradise," all watches and calendars shall ⌞soon⌟ be shattered,—though just before that "two persons of both sexes" are presented, "two world-famous automatons have arrived," and a ~~third~~ human being, who says of himself, that he "may be the third and strangest of them all," ~~leads them~~ ⌞insists,⌟ "with a growling voice ⌞"that we,⌟ ~~incidentally,~~ admire what's before our eyes: "Nothing but art and mechanics, nothing but cardboard and watch springs!"

Ts. "L"

⌊Paul Celan⌋

THE MERIDIAN

[1]⌊Büchner-speech 1960⌋

<new page>

[2]Ladies and gentlemen!

==

==[3]

1a Art, you will remember, is a puppet-like, iambically five-footed and—this [4] ~~yet to be named~~ characteristic is also, by the reference to Pygmalion and his creature, mythologically vouchsafed—a childless being. **b** ⌊In this form it constitutes the object of a conversation that takes place in a room, thus not in the Conciergerie, a conversation that, we sense, could be continued indefinitely, if nothing interfered. —**c** ⌊Something does interfere.

= ——

2 Art returns. It returns in another work by Georg Büchner, in [5]"Woyzeck," among other~~, un people, basically~~ nameless people and—if I may let a ~~phrase by Mo~~ phrase by Moritz Heimann meant for "Danton's Death" take this route —under even "a more livid light before the storm." The same art ~~is,~~ ⌊steps,⌋ even in this totally different era, once again onto the stage, presented by a market crier, no longer, as was the case during that conversation, to be related to the "glowing," "roaring" and "shining" creation, but besides the creature and the "Nothing," which this creature [6]"wears," art appears this time in the shape of a monkey, but it is the same one, we have recognized it immediately by its "jacket and pants."

<new page>

=

~~And~~ ——

3a And it also comes—art—to us through a third work by Büchner, "Leonce and Lena," where time and lighting are here ~~different than elsewhere~~ ⌊~~different than elsewhere~~ unrecognizable⌋, for we are "fleeing toward paradise," "all watches and calendars" shall soon be "shattered" even "forbidden,"—though just before that "two persons of both sexes are presented," "two world famous automatons have arrived," and a ~~third~~ human being, who says of himself that he "may be the third and strangest of them all," insisting "with a growling voice" that we admire what's before our eyes: "Nothing but art and mechanics, nothing but cardboard and watch springs!"

Further Variants

[1] ~~Büchner-speech 1960~~
Speech on the occasion of receiving
the Georg Büchner Prize 1960. <Dsl. "I">

[2] <in the yearbook without this salutation>

[3] <in proofs and first edition only a single space>

[4] <Ts. "L": in left margin, marked: "+">
this characteristic <Ts. "D">
this ~~yet to be named~~ characteristic <Dsl. "I">

[5] "Woyzeck"<yearbook>

[6]"wears"{.}⌊,—⌋ <corrected in proofs>

Drafts (Nr. 1) | Ts. "A"

b Art ~~is not alone here,~~ appears here in larger company, but clearly it is among equals, it is the ~~same, well known.~~ art, which we already know. Valerio—is here only another name for the market crier.

<...> **4a** ~~Art~~ ~~This art~~ This creature is also a problem, and, as you can see, a tough and long-lived, I want to say, an eternal problem. A problem that allows one mortal, Camille, and one who can only be understood through his death, Danton, to string words together. It is easy to talk about art.

4a Art, ladies and gentlem e n, is , ~~with all of that, also~~ with everything that belongs to it also a problem, and, as you can see, one subject to transformation, a tough and long-lived, I want to say, an eternal problem. **b** A problem that lets one mortal, Camille, and one to be understood only through his death, Danton, to ~~put together~~ string together. It is easy to talk about art.

5a But whenever there is talk about art, there is always someone present who doesn't listen. **b** More exactly: someone who hears and listens and looks—and then doesn't know what the talk was all about. Someone, however, who hears the one who speaks, who sees him speak, who has become conscious of language and of shape, and at the same time also, who could doubt this, of direction, that means breath.

5a But whenever there is talk about art, there is always also someone who is there present and ... doesn't listen. **b** More exactly: someone who hears and listens and looks—and then doesn't know what the talk was all about. Someone, however, who sees him speak, who has become conscious of language and of shape, and at the same time also, who ~~would~~ could here, in the realm of such writing, doubt it, ~~of direction~~ ~~and fate~~, ~~that means~~ breath{.} , that means direction and fate.

c That is, you ~~have known~~ know it, she comes, the often ~~cit~~ and not by accident so often cited, with each in this one too new year To you,—that is Lucile.

<new page>

c That is, you have known it all along, for she comes, the so often and ~~probably not because of that~~ not by accident cited, with each new year to you,—that is Lucile.

6a What had inserted itself during the conversation ~~sets itself~~ ruthlessly cuts through , it ~~goes,~~ ~~leads~~ reaches Revolution Square with us, as the carts drive up and come to a halt. **b** The ~~prisoners are~~ passengers are ~~there~~ ~~have come along~~ , they are there, all of them, Danton, Camille, the others. They ~~all~~ have , here too, words, artful words, they make them stick, there is, Büchner needs only to quote here, talk about ~~shared death~~ together-into-death, Fabre can ~~do that~~ wants even to die "doubly," everyone is at their best —on top of the scaffold,—only ~~some~~ ~~a few~~ some voices , — ~~a few~~ "some" nameless " voices " {—}, find, that all of this is " old hat " and " boring ".

<new page>

6c And ~~then,~~ at the end, when Camille, surrounded by the others, not he himself, but only ~~one~~ a similar one among among ~~others~~ all similar ones—**(b)** For Fabre can even die doubly— , when Camille theatrically—one is nearly tempted , although the metrical is missing, to say: dies a iambic

c And here, at the end where everything comes to an end , when Camille, ~~surrounded by the others~~ no, not he , not he himself, but ~~one am~~ a ~~similar one among all similars~~ ~~,,going-together-into-death~~ ~~Not dying alone~~ "passenger", theatrically—one is nearly tempted to say: an iambic death—which only two scenes later we, through a word foreign to him ,

Ts. "L" | Further Variants

b Art appears here in larger company than before but clearly it is among equals, it is the same art{,}⌊: an art,⌋ we already know.—Valerio is only another name for the market crier.

=

[7]**4a** Art, ladies and gentlemen, with everything that belongs to it and will yet belong to it, is also a problem and as you can see, one subject to transformation, a tough and long-lived, I want to say, an eternal problem.

<new page>

[8]**b** A problem that lets one mortal, Camille, and one who can only be understood through his death, Danton, string together words.—It is easy to talk about art.

[7,8] <Paragraph marked in Ts. "D">

= ——

[9]**5a** But whenever there is talk about art, there is always someone present who ... doesn't truly listen.

[9] <Paragraph marked in Ts. "D">

b More exactly: someone who hears and listens and looks ... and then doesn't know what the talk was all about. Someone, however, who hears the one who speaks, who "sees" him speak, who has become conscious of language and of shape, and at the same time—who could doubt this here, at the place of such writing?—, and at the same time also of breath, that means of direction and fate.

c That is, and you have known it all along, for she comes, the so often and not by accident so often quoted one, she comes to you with each new year—that is Lucile.

=

6a What had inserted itself during the conversation cuts through ruthlessly and ~~it reaches~~ ⌊~~we reach~~⌋ ⌊reaches⌋ Revolution Square ⌊with us⌋ as "the carts drive up and come to a halt."

——

[10]**b** The passengers are there, all of them, Danton, Camille, the others. Here too they all have words, artful words, and they make them stick, there is much talk—and here Büchner only needs to quote—talk of going-together-into-death, Fabre even maintains that he can die "doubly," they are all at their best, ~~at their best~~⌊,⌋ even on the scaffold, [11]at their best,—only a few voices "some"—nameless—"voices," find, that all this is "old hat and boring."

[10] <space deleted in Dsl. "I">

[11] ~~also on the scaffold,~~ at their best, <Dsl. "I">

c And here, where it all comes to an end, in the long moments when Camille—no, not he, not he himself, but a fellow-passenger—, as that Camille dies a theatrical—one is nearly tempted to say: an iambic—death, which we can feel as his own only two scenes later through a word foreign—yet ⌊so⌋ near to him—, when all around Camille pathos and

Drafts (Nr. 1)

death, ~~of~~ which we can experience as <u>his</u>, through a foreign word, only two scenes later, as all around him, ~~the sententientiousness and~~ pathos and sententiousness confirm the triumph of puppet and string,—then Lucile, one who is blind to art, for whom language has something person-like and tangible, is there with that ~~counte~~ shattering "Long live the king!"

7b It is the counterword{.}, ~~**8a** One hears it first as a declaration of loyalty to the "ancien régime" **b** This is no declaration of loyalty to the monarchy. Here no monarchy is being paid homage to. **c** Homage here is for the majesty of the absurd as witness for the human. **9** This is ... poetry.~~ The word that cuts the string{.}, the ~~word, that does not, like art, have consequence~~ is an act of freedom.

8a One hears it first of all as a declaration of loyalty to the "ancien régime," **b** but here no monarchy and no yesterday is being paid homage to; **c** homage is being paid here ~~for the among~~ for the majesty of the absurd as witness for the human. **9** This, ladies and gentlemen, has no name, but I believe it is ... poetry.

=

11 "—oh, art!": in *Lenz* too it is there, as it has, besides being mutable and able to split, also the gift of ubiquity.

=

12a "At table Lenz was again <u>in good spirits:</u> the talk turned to literature, he was in his element ...

b ~~The feeling that what has been created has life, possibility for being, and then it's all right, then we don't have to ask if it is beautiful or ugly.~~ The feeling that what has been created has life,

Ts. "A"

as <u>his</u> own, as all around Camille pathos and sententiousness confirm the triumph of puppet and string,-then Lucile, one who is blind to art, the same Lucile, for whom language has something person-like and ~~visible~~ tangible, is there once again with her sudden "Long live the king!"

7a ~~What a word~~ After all the words spoken on the rostrum—it is the guillotine!—what a word! **b** It is the counterword that cuts the string the string, the word that no longer bows down before "the bystanders and old war-horses of history," it is an act of freedom.

8a Of course, one hears it—and that ~~has~~ may, in relation to what I dare say about it now, that is <u>today</u>, {is} not by chance—, one hears it first as a declaration of loyalty to the "ancien régime." **b** But here—permit me, that is someone who grew up not least with the writings not least because he also grew up with also with the writings of Peter K Peter Kropotkin and Gustav Landauer also with G. L.'s words for becoming human beings to emphasize this—, here no (t any) monarchy and not to be conserved yesterdays are being paid homage to. **c** Homage is being paid to the majesty of the absurd as witness for the presence of the human!

9 This, ladies and gentlemen, has no name fixed once and for all, but I believe that this is ... poetry.

=

10a "—oh, art!" I ~~know~~ am stuck, as you see, on this word of Camille's. **b** I am aware that one can read this word in different ways, one can give it different accents: the acute of today, the grave of history—literary history too—, the circumflex—a sign of expansion—of the ~~Eternal. I give it the acute~~ Eternal.

c I give it ~~with the guilty conscience that goes with it~~ —I have no other choice— the acute.

11 Art—"oh, art": it ~~is, i have to set this right, in the end it doesn't seem to be a childless being~~[16] ~~seems~~ has, besides being mutable, also has the gift of ubiquity: it can also be found in *Lenz* ~~again~~ there too, ~~in the interval.~~ As in *Danton's Death* as an episode —, there too there too—permit me to insist on this— as a problem,✲ split this time into into literature and painting.

12a "At table Lenz was <u>again in good spirits</u>: the talk turned to literature, he was in his element ...

b The feeling that what has been created has life, stands

Ts. "L"

sentententiousness confirm the triumph of "puppet" and "string,"—then Lucile, one who is blind to art, the same Lucile for whom language has something person-like and tangible, is there, once again, with her sudden "Long live the king!"

=<?>[12]

7a After all the words spoken on the rostrum[13]—it is the guillotine—what a word!

b It is the counterword, the word that cuts the "string," the word that no longer bows down before the "bystanders and old war-horses of history,"—it is an act of freedom. It is a step.

<new page>

[14]**8a** Of course, one hears it—and that may not be by chance in the context of what I dare say about it now, that is today—, one hears it first of all as a declaration of loyalty to the "ancien régime."

b But here—permit me, that is someone who grow up with the writings of Peter Kropotkin und Gustav Landauer{,} ~~to emphasize~~ ⌊, to emphasize this—, here no monarchy and no to be conserved yesterdays are being paid homage to.

c Homage is being paid here to the majesty of the absurd as witness for the presence of the human!

= <?> [15]

9 This, ladies and gentlemen, has no name fixed once and for all, but I believe that this is ... poetry.

=

=

10a "—oh, art!" I am stuck, as you see, on this word of Camille's.

b I am aware that one can read this word in different ways, one can give it different accents: the acute of today, the grave of history—literary history too, the circumflex—a sign of expansion—of the eternal.

c I give it—I have no other choice—, I give it the acute.

<new page>

11 Art—"oh, art": besides being mutable, has the gift of ubiquity—: it can also be found in *Lenz*{-} ⌊,⌋ there too—permit me to insist on this—, as in *Danton's Death*, only as an episode{.}. ⁂ ~~as a problem split into literature and painting.~~

=

12a "At table Lenz was again in good spirits : the talk turned to literature, he was in his element ... ⌊"⌋

Further Variants

[12] <½ space in Ts. "L">

[13] {—} ⌊(⌋ it is ~~the guillotine~~ ⌊the scaffold⌋{—}⌊)⌋ <corrected in proofs>

[14]<Paragraph marked in Ts. "D">

[15]<1/2 empty space in Ts. "L">

[16]<Ts. "A": Here Celan starts an insertion between lines, but then continues to write on directly.>

Drafts (Nr. 1; 2)

stands above these two and is the only criterion in matters of art.⌞..”—⌟

from: Nr. 1 (C 34/35)

13 I know, this passage has literary-historical importance, ~~here, concerning the author of “Soldiers,” talks~~ it has to be read ⌞ read together⌟ with the already quoted passage in *Danton*, it concerns, and I don’t want to question this in any way here, it concerns Büchner’s ~~interpretation~~ aesthetic conceptions, it concerns Mercier’s “Elargissez l’art!,” ~~the a an the problem~~ an anticipation of naturalism, it concerns the social and political aspects and roots ~~of Büchner’s~~ of the büchnerian opus.

from: Nr. 2 (C 4,2)

Ts. “A”

above these two and is the only criterion in matters of art ...”

13 I have picked out? here? only two sentences, ~~my alreasdy mentioned bad conscience~~ ⌞—my bad conscience about the grave? forbids? it? me, ~~to overlook this~~ make you ⌞not ⌞not immediately⌟⌟ aware of this, ⌞—⌟ this passage has, before all else, literary-historical importance, one has to know how to read it together with the already quoted passage in *Danton’s Death*, here ~~it concerns Büchners~~ Büchner’s aesthetic conception finds expression, ~~this then leads to,~~ ⌞from here ⌞ leaving Büchner’s *Lenz* fragment, ⌞one gets to⌟ Reinhold Lenz, the author of the “Notes on the Theater,” and back beyond him, the historical Lenz, ⌞further back⌟ to Mercier’s literarily so ~~fruitful~~ ⌞productive⌟ ⌞ ⌞—⌟ and also applicable to today’s art problems ⌞—⌟⌟ “Elargissez l’Art” Mercier’s, it ⌞this passage⌟ opens up vistas, it anticipates naturalism and Gerhard Hauptmann, here we must ~~find~~ look for the social and political ~~aspects~~ roots of the büchnerian ~~opus~~ ⌞poetry⌟ and ⌞find⌟.

14a Ladies and gentlemen, that I don’t let this go unsaid, does ease my conscience ⌞—⌟ ⌞ if only⌟ for a moment ⌞—⌟,—it shows you, and that is perhaps ⌞~~perhaps only~~⌟ ~~as it bears on those things I myself try to write, {from some} informative,~~—⌞that has its ~~unsurveyable~~ not surveyable subjective limits⌟ it shows you that I cannot get away from something that, for me, seems to have to do with art. **b** I am looking for it here too, in *Lenz*,—and permit myself to point this out to you.

c ⌞Lenz, that is Büchner, ~~utters~~ ⌞has⌟, “oh, art,” only disparaging words for idealism and its “wooden puppets”{:}. {e} He counters them, and here follow the unforgettable lines about the “life of the humblest person,” the “twitches,” the “winks, the “subtle, barely noticed play of facial features,”—he counters ~~the~~ them with what is natural and creaturely. And he illustrates this conception of art with an experience:

<new page>

15 “Yesterday as I was walking along above the valley, I saw two girls sitting on a rock: one was putting up her hair, the other helping her; and the golden hair was hanging free, and a pale, solemn face, and yet so young, and the black peasant dress, and the other so absorbed in her task. The finest, most heartfelt paintings of the Old German School scarcely convey an inkling of this. At times one wishes one were a Medusa’s head in order to turn a group like this into stone, ~~and call everybody over to have a look.~~ ⌞”⌟

Ts. "L"

Further Variants

b "...The feeling that what has been created has life, stands above these two and is the only criterion in matters of art ..."

=

[17]**13** I have picked out here only two sentences, my bad conscience about the grave forbids me not to make you aware of this immediately,—this passage has primarily literary-historical importance, one has to know how to read it together with the already quoted passage from *Danton's Death*; here Büchner's aesthetic finds expression, from here, leaving Büchner's *Lenz* fragment behind, one gets ⌊,⌋ ~~back,~~ ⌊—⌋ to Reinhold Lenz, the author of the "Notes on the Theater," and back beyond him[18], the historical Lenz, to Mercier's literarily so productive "Elargissez l'Art." This passage opens up vistas, it anticipates naturalism and Gerhard Hauptmann, here we must look for and find the social and political roots of Büchner's poetry.

=

[19]**14a** Ladies and gentlemen, that I don't let this go unsaid does ease my conscience, if only for a moment, it also shows you[20] at the same time, and ~~in that~~ ⌊~~to be sure~~⌋ ~~it has its subjective limits that cannot be surveyed~~ ⌊and thus disturbs it ~~one more time~~ my conscience anew⌋,—it shows you that I cannot get away from something that, for me, seems to have to do with art.

b I am looking for it here too, in *Lenz*,—and permit myself to point this out to you.

c Lenz, that is Büchner, has, "oh, art" only disparaging words for "Idealism" and its "wooden puppets." He counters them, and here follow the unforgettable lines about the "life of the humblest person," the "twitches," the "winks," the "subtle, barely noticed play of facial features," —he counters them with what is natural and creaturely. And he illustrates this conception of art with an experience:

<new page>

=

[21]**15** "Yesterday as I was walking along above the valley, I saw two girls sitting on a rock: one was putting up her hair, the other helping her; and the golden hair was hanging free, and the pale, solemn face, and yet so young, and the black peasant dress, and the other one so absorbed in her task. The finest, most heartfelt paintings of the Old German School scarcely convey an inkling of this. At times one wishes one were a Medusa's head

[17] <paragraph marked in Ts. "D">

[18] to\ ~~jenem~~ ⌊dem⌋ <corrected in proofs>
\

[19] <paragraph in Ts. "D">

[20] but also <Ts. "D">

[21] <double space in Dsi. "i" marked once>

Drafts (Nr. 11; 16)

• Uncontrived
most natural
16-17 p. 95: one ⌊= I, Lenz⌋ this "one" here has clearly an ~~I Acc~~ I-value wishes one were a Medusa's head, i.e. one—Lenz—would like to venture into the no-longer-human, that is, however, ~~projected outw~~ turned toward the human ⌊{as} in its most •"uncontrived"⌋; that, and not that which is said {to} about "art," carries the I-accent. And that's why, after this excursus, it goes on accurately:
20b,d •p. 96: "he had completely forgotten himself"

from: Nr. 11 (C 17/18,3)

✻ With that I have ventured far away, respectively repeated ⌊rather awkwardly⌋ some things Günter Eich said here a year ago and some things ~~perhaps~~ still to be said? ⌊vaguely ⌊enough⌋⌋ anticipated.<...>

from: Nr. 16 (F 2/3 [C 1])

Ts. "A"

16a Ladies and gentlemen, please, take note: "One wishes one were a Medusa's head" ⌊...⌋, to capture the natural ⌊as the natural⌋ in art!

b "One wishes to," does of course not mean here: I wish to.

17a This is a stepping beyond what is human, a stepping into a/n/ ~~not g~~ ⌊turned toward the human⌋,⌋ ~~and~~ ⌊ ~~at least as not to be described as totally canny~~ ⌊uncanny⌋ realm ⌊that for him is no <t canny>⌋—the realm where the automatons also and thus ~~also,~~ ... oh ⌊, also⌋ art seems to be at home.—**b** ~~That is~~ ⌊This is⌋ not the historical Lenz, it is Büchner's Lenz who speaks thus, here too we have heard Büchner's voice: for him art retains something of the uncanny.

18a Ladies and gentlemen, ⌊I have given it the acute accent;⌋ I cannot hide from you anymore than from myself that I had to take this question,? ⌊with⌋ one ⌊~~one among many others~~⌋ question⌊s⌋ concerning art and poetry ⌊—one question among others—⌋ to Büchner ⌊in order to locate his own question⌋{:}, ⌊I⌋ ⌊~~I gave~~ but I had to give it the acute!⌋ **b** ~~But you see:~~ But you <see> it easily:⌋ Valerio's ⌊"⌋ growling voice⌊"⌋ is unmistakable whenever art comes to the fore.— **c** These are doubtlessly, and Büchner's voice ⌊, ~~the voice of the poet of the creature,~~⌋ invites the proposition, old and even ancient forms of uncanniness. That I worry them today with such ~~stubborness~~ ⌊persistence⌋, ⌊cannot let them be <?>⌋— probably is in the air—the air we ~~breathe~~ have to breathe.✻ An acute question~~—who knows, perhaps it {cocnerns} has,~~ ⌊it has, I suppose, and⌋ ⌊already⌋ very far back, to do with the misgivings Günter Eich spoke of here a year ago ⌊so frankly⌋. **19** I want to be even clearer, I ask: Doesn't Büchner, the poet of the creature ⌊that is⌋, propose something like a ⌊a perhaps only half-conscious, but despite that ⌊—or perhaps exactly because of that—⌋⌋ no less radical calling-into-question of art? A calling-into-question of art, ~~from which all poetry~~ ⌊to which all poetry has to ~~return~~ ⌊especially today⌋ ~~again and again~~⌋ ⌊if it⌋ ~~wants to go on~~ questions ~~has~~ ⌊and wants to question further⌋? Or—I ~~now anticipate~~ ⌊now skip over⌋ some things—, may we, as happens these days ⌊in many places ~~and unde~~⌋, start from ~~all~~ art as something given, should we, to put it most concretly, think Mallarmé through to the end ⌊—i.e. ~~to death~~—perhaps to death—⌋? ~~More explicitly—now I am put myself in danger of,~~

Ts. "L"

Further Variants

in order to turn a group like this into stone, and call everybody over to have a look."

=

16a Ladies and gentlemen, please take note: "One wishes one ⌊were⌋ a Medusa's head," in order to ... grasp the natural as the natural with the help of art!

b One [22]wishes to does of course not mean here: I wish to.

[23]**17a** This is a stepping beyond the human, a stepping into an uncanny realm turned toward the human—the realm where the monkey, the automatons and with them ... oh, art [24]seems to be at home.

[25]**b** This is ⌊(⌋ ~~not the historical Lenz~~ ⌊)⌋, this is ⌊//⌋ the Büchnerian ⌊~~Lenz~~⌋ who speaks, here we have heard Büchner's voice: for him art ~~keeps~~ ⌊~~safe~~⌋ ⌊retains⌋ something of the uncanny.

<new page>

[26]**18a** Ladies and gentlemen, I have given it the acute accent; I cannot hide from you any more than from myself that I took this question concerning art and poetry—[27]one question among others—, that I took this question ~~to Bü~~ of my own ⌊, if not free⌋ will to Büchner, in order to locate his own question.

b But you see it easily: Valerio's "growling voice" is unmistakable whenever art comes to the fore.

---

[28]**c** These are doubtlessly—and Büchner's voice invites the proposition—old and even ancient forms of uncanniness. That I worry these with such stubbornness today, probably is in the air—the air we have to breathe today.

✻ ~~An acute question it has, I suppose, and already very far back, to do with the misgivings Günter Eich spoke of so freely here a year ago.~~

19 ~~I want to be even clearer, I ask:~~ Doesn't Georg ⌊—~~I~~ [29]I now must ask—⌊doesn't Georg Büchner⌋ ⌋, the poet of the creature ~~that is,~~ [30]propose a perhaps only half-loud, perhaps only half-conscious, but despite that no less ⌊radical⌋—or perhaps exactly because of that (—) ⌊so⌋ a truly radical calling-into-question of art(?)—a calling-into-question from that angle?—A calling-into-question to which all of today's poetry has to return, if it wants to question further? With other words, words that ~~anticipate~~ skip over some things: may we, as happens in many places these days, start from art as something given and absolutely unconditional, should we before all, to put it most concretely, think—let's say—Mallarmé through to the end~~—i. e. Perhaps even to death—~~?

[22] wish to, <Yearbook>

[23] <para only in Dsl. "I" empty space marked>

[24] seem ⌊s⌋ <make-up "C">; seems <yearbook>

[25] <para. marked in Ts. "D">

[26] <para. only in Dsl. "I," blank line marked; para. in Ts. "D">

[27] one <yearbook>

[28] <erased blank line in Dsl. "I">

[29] so I have to ask myself now <Ts. "D">

[30] a perhaps only half-loud, perhaps only half-conscious, ⌊and half-loud⌋ <Dsl. "I">
a perhaps only half-loud, perhaps only half-conscious ⌊,⌋ ~~and half loud~~ <proof correction>

Drafts (Nr. 11)

20b,d p. 96: "he had completely forgotten himself"

↙

Self-forgetfulness allows the treatment of art as a problem—~~crea~~ produces the distance which lets art become an object; art has at least a tendency toward I-distance. **22b-c** Poetry ~~carries the I to the other; it~~ moves with the I toward the other and strange, brings it across, ⌞is, with it, the alienating,⌟ ... and sublates itself with it ⌞again⌟.—picks itself up ⌞again⌟ with it. Art, that is the route ~~to be rushed through~~ to be traveled by poetry.—

from: Nr. 11 (C 17/18,3)

Ts. "A"

20a I have anticipated, I'll return to Büchner's *Lenz*, thus to the ⌞—episodic—⌟ conversation that was had "at table" and that had Lenz "in fine spirits." **b** Lenz spoke for a long time, "now all smiles, now serious." And then ~~it is said~~, when the conversation has run its course, it is said of him, thus the one preoccupied with questions about ~~aestheti~~ art ~~Lenz~~ ~~Reinhold Künstler~~ Lenz: "He had completely forgotten himself." **c** I read this, the way Lucile would have read it: he, he himself.

d He who has art before his eyes, forgets himself; art creates I-distance. <new take> Art demands distance{.} ⌞~~un art~~, in any case.⌟

21 And poetry? Poetry, which ~~isn't separable from art?~~ ⌞Which does have to tread the route of art?⌟ ⌞ Then one could really say, to tread the routes ~~of~~ ⌞to⌟ the automaton and Medusa's head!⌟ **22a** I try to continue my questioning. Perhaps—I am only asking now—⌞I am ⌞not⌟ looking for a way out, I only push the question further, in the same direction⌟, **b** perhaps poetry⌞, like art,⌟ moves with a ⌞self-forgotten⌟ I toward that other and strange, brings it, this strange, across, is, with it, the alienating, and sets itself free again with it ... ⌞: as an alienated I.⌟ **c** Then art would be the route poetry has to cover—nothing less, but nothing more either. **d** I know, there are shorter routes. But poetry too does hurry ahead of us at times. La Poésie, elle aussi, brûle nos étapes.

=

Ts. "L"

20a I have anticipated ⌊, reached beyond, ⌊—⌋ ⌋—not far enough, I know—, I'll return now to Büchner's *Lenz*, thus to the—episodic—conversation, that was had "at table" and that had Lenz "again in good spirits."

b Lenz spoke for a long time, "now all smiles, now serious." And then, when the conversation had run its course, it is said of him, thus of the one preoccupied with questions about art, ⌊but at the same time also of the artist⌋ Lenz: "He had completely forgotten himself."

c I think of Lucile as I read this; I read: *He*, he himself.

[31]**d** He who has art before his eyes and on his mind, forgets ~~himse~~—I am with the Lenz{-}narrative now—, forgets [32]himself; Art creates I-distance. Art demands ⌊here⌋ ⌊in a certain direction⌋ a certain distance{.}⌊, a certain route.⌋

21 [33]And {the} poetry? Poetry, which does have to tread the route of art? Then [34]we'd really have here the route to the Medusa's head {(}and the automaton{)} ~~sketched out for us to walk!~~!

22a Now, I am not looking for a way out, I am only pushing the question further in the same direction, ⌊and, I believe, also⌋ in the ⌊~~perhaps also~~⌋ ⌊~~also~~⌋ direction of the Lenz-fragment.

b Perhaps—I am only asking—, perhaps poetry, like art, moves with a self-forgotten I toward the uncanny and strange, ~~brings it, this strange, across,~~ and sets itself—but where? but in which place? but with what? ⌊but as what?⌋—free again?

[35]**c** Then art would be the route poetry has to cover—nothing less, nothing more. ~~We can, like Lucile~~

d I know, [36]there are other, shorter routes. But poetry does hurry ahead of us at times. La Poésie, elle aussi, brûle nos étapes.

23 I am taking my leave of the self-forgotten man, the one preoccupied by art, the artist. I believe that I met poetry with Lucile and Lucile perceives language as shape and direction and breath—: here too, in this work by Büchner, I search for the same, I search for Lenz himself, I search for him—as a person, I search for his shape, for the sake of the place of poetry ⌊,⌋ ~~the sake~~ for the "setting free"⌊,⌋ ~~the sake~~ of the "step."

Further Variants

[31] <two deleted spaces in Dsl. "I">

[32] self-forgotten{;}. <Dsl. "I" and proof corrected>

[33] And the poetry? <Ts. "D">

[34] we'd really have the <Ts. "D">

[35] <para. in Ts. "L" marked with a circle>

[36] there are shorter routes. <Ts. "D">

Drafts (Nr. 6/73; 17; 20/695)

(13,24) But this fragment is not to be read as a report on the author of the soldiers and the tutor or, what makes ⌊it⌋ clearer: the author of the "Notes on the Theater"—what is to be read here is the fatefulness of a man named Lenz, of whom one knows—without having learned it—what kind of burden his existence is to be ⌊found by⌋ read ⌊ing⌋ from it ~~sh~~<?> here, that he under the burden ⌊the Büchnerian Lenz like the historical one,⌋ collapsed under the burden{,} of his existence, is picked up on a Moscow street—

from: Nr. 6/73 (C 30,1)

25b "...except sometimes it annoyed him that he could not walk on his head." Now that is the line so well-known to you, so often quoted—: I believe that I may, that I must pick up the thread from this. <...>

from: Nr. 17 (C 36-39 [F 4])

✻ Abyss: poetry—it did not, like Camille ⌊—oh art—⌋ mock; it is consequence—~ : **26b** he who thinks about walking on the head, knows that he then has the sky beneath him as an abyss.

↙

30 To wr.<ite> under such dates.—

from: Nr. 20/695 (C 52b,2)

Ts. "A"

24a Büchner's Lenz, ladies and gentlemen, has remained a fragment. Do we have to, in order to understand it, have ~~consul~~ consulted other books, to learn ⌊know<?>⌋, what else has happened to this man? **b** "He saw his existence as a necessary burden.—And so he lived on{:}: ⌊"⌋ {h} Here the tale breaks off ... **c** But poetry ~~sees~~ ⌊tries⌋, like Lucile, ⌊the person and the ~~and~~⌋ direction and breath{,} ⌊to see.⌋ {d} Poetry hurries ahead—: that Lenz has to collapse under the burden ⌊of his existence⌋, that we know, when we ~~see look at and~~ when we ~~pere~~ look at and perceive Lenz, Lenz's shape, Lenz himself.—**d** "Death," we read in ~~the~~ ⌊a⌋ a work about Jakob Maria Lenz published in Leipzig in 1909—the work of the Moscow lecturer M. N. Rosanov,—"death as redeemer was not long in coming. In the night of 23 to 24 May 1792, Lenz was found lifeless on a Moscow street. A nobleman paid for his burial. His last resting place has remained unknown."—**e** Thus had he lived on.

f He: the true, the Büchnerian Lenz, Büchner's figure, the person we were able to perceive on the first page of the story, the Lenz, who "on 20th January walked through the mountains," the poet.

[41]✻ The poet—the one who~~, seeks the other~~ ⌊, with his own most I⌋ goes <the> route of art ⌊~~—at times al~~ sometimes perhaps also a shorter one—⌋, toward the "other," who brings it, the other and the strange, across, and returns with him, ~~the estran~~ as the estranged and sets himself free with it?

25b "...except sometimes it annoyed him that he could not walk on his head." That's him, Lenz.✻ Here is, if it is a place, ~~all of Lenz's~~ the place of this poetry. And this place is a, like the place of the Medusa's head, a strange place. A place in the direction of this figure.

26b He who walks on his head, ladies and gentlemen, has the sky beneath him as an abyss.

<new page>

Ts. "L"

24a Büchner's Lenz, ~~ladies and gentlemen,~~ has remained a fragment. Shall we, search for ~~what happened to him in~~ the historical Lenz to see what direction his existence takes?

[37]**b** "He saw his existence as a necessary burden.—And so he lived on~~to~~ ..."

Here the tale breaks off.

[38]**c** But, like Lucile, poetry tries to see ~~direction~~ the direction shape takes, poetry hurries ahead. We know toward where he lived, toward where he lived, how he lived on.

<new page>

d "Death," we read in a work about Jakob Michael Reinhold Lenz published in Leipzig in 1909—written by ⌊~~a Russian~~ ⌊a Moscow⌋ [39]lecturer by the name of⌋ M. N. Rosanov{s}—, "death as redeemer was not long in coming. In the night of 23 to 24 May 1792, Lenz was found lifeless on a Moscow street. A nobleman paid for his burial. His last resting place has remained unknown."

—<..>[40]

e And so he lived on.

{ }+

f He: the true, the Büchnerian Lenz, Büchner's figure, the person we were able to perceive on the first page ⌊of the story⌋, the Lenz who "on 20th January walked through the mountains," he—not the artist, not the one preoccupied with questions of art, he as an I.

25a Can we now ⌊perhaps⌋ find the place where the strangeness was, the place where the person was able to set himself free, as an—⌊~~arguably~~<?>⌋ estranged—I? Can we find ~~the~~ ⌊this⌋ place ⌊,⌋ ~~and the~~ ⌊this⌋ step?

[42]**b** "... except sometimes it annoyed him that he could not walk on his head."

26b ~~He who walks on his head, ladies and gentlemen, has the sky beneath him as an abyss.~~

25b—That's him, Lenz. That is, I believe, him and his step, him and his ↘

~~(9)~~ For that too, as for Lucile's "Long live the king" ⌊.⌋ There is no name fixed once and for all, but I believe ... here too there is, if it ~~is a place~~ can even be named so, a place of poetry—of this poetry.

<new page>

And this place too is, ~~as it is to be looked for in the direction of this figure,~~ like the one of the Medusa's head, a strange place. And a place in the direction of this figure!

25b "... except sometimes it annoyed him that he could not walk on his head."

Further Variants

[37,38] <deleted spaces in Dsl. "I">

[39] lecturer by the name of Rosanow <Ts. "D">
by the name of M. N. Rosanov <corrected in proofs>

[40] <Hyphen or dash after "unknown.">
Unknown." {—} <Dsl. "I">

[41] <Ts. "A": Paragraph marked with a circle>

[42] <Ts. "L": marked with three lines; Dsl. "I": deleted space>

Drafts (Nr. 17; 16)

<...> **27** Therefore also, I believe, the ⌊so easy⌋ maligning of poetry ~~today~~ for its darkness and strangeness: it comes no doubt from that direction. Perhaps I may ⌊here⌋, somewhat abruptly, but perhaps not without justification, quote a line by Pascal, that I recently read in Leo Shestov: "Ne nous reprochez pas le manque de clarté puisque nous en faisons profession." This is, if not the congenital darkness, then however the ⌊"⌋ darkness ⌊"⌋ attributed to it ⌊self-created for the sake of an encounter⌋ from ~~a~~ ⌊this⌋ distance. In this direction the poem is surely en route, and from that direction it returns—as poem. <...>

from: Nr. 17 (C 36-39 [F 4])

<...>✻ I now must return to the poem and at the same time to a line—a line by Büchner—, with which for weeks, even months, as ⌊usually happens⌋ with lines of poetry, I've kept company against my will, a line that, like so much of what is part of a poem, already just because of the irrefutability and imperiousness of its presence, knew how to become significant; <...>

from: Nr. 16 (F 2/3 [C 1])

Ts. "A"

27 Ladies and gentlemen, it is common today to reproach poetry for its "obscurity."—At this point permit me to quote somewhat abruptly thus—but ⌊hasn't⌋ something ~~has indeed~~ here opened up suddenly ⌊?⌋—to quote a line by Pascal, a line that I recently read in Leo Shestov{:}. Here is this line: "Ne nous reprochez pas le manque de clarté puisque nous en faisons profession!"—This is, I believe if not the congenital darkness, then however the "lightlessness," attributed to the poem, ~~which~~ for the sake of an encounter from a—perhaps self-created—distance. **28**—But there are probably two strangenesses and others and is—here the uncanny probably lies—difficult to differentiate

29a Lenz ⌊—or rather Büchner—⌋ has here gone a step further than Lucile: his ~~word is a gesture~~ "Long live the king" is no longer a word, it is a ⌊terrifying⌋ falling silent, it takes away his—and our—breath and words. **b** The poem ~~is~~ ⌊can be⌋ a breathturn. Perhaps—I'll risk the question—it is thus also a sort of reversal. Perhaps this reversal will also differentiate between strange and strange. **d** ⌊Perhaps.⌋

"....................

✻ "except sometimes it annoyed him that he could not walk on his head, ~~that he could not walk on his head.~~" ⌊I do not need to⌋ I ~~have to admit to you here, that~~ ⌊first bring to your attention that⌋ I cannot tear myself loose from this line. It has been on my mind—no, it has pursued me for some time now. Perhaps we are confronted ⌊here⌋, I have to ask myself, with one—if not the most basic figure of poetry.

Ts. "L" | Further Variants

26b He who walks on his head, ladies and gentlemen, [43]⌊—He who walks on his head,⌋ has the sky beneath him as an abyss.

=[44]

27 Ladies and gentlemen, it is common today to reproach poetry for its "obscurity." At this point permit me to quote {-} somewhat abruptly—but hasn't something opened up here, suddenly?—, permit to quote a line by Pascal, a line that I read ~~recently~~ ⌊some time ago⌋ in Leo Shestov: "Ne nous reprochez pas le manque de clarté [45]puisque nous en faisons profession!"—This is, I believe, if not the congenital, then however the ~~darknesse~~ "lightlessness" attributed to poetry for the sake of an encounter from a—perhaps self-created—[46]distance or strange-ness.

28 ⌊{(}⌋ But ~~certainly~~, ⌊perhaps there are two strangenessess—close together ⌊and⌋⌋ in ⌊one and⌋ the same direction. ⌊{)}⌋

29a Lenz—or rather Büchner—has here gone a step further than Lucile. His "Long live the king" is no longer a word, it is a terrifying falling silent, it takes away his—and our—breath and words.

<new page>

[47]~~The poem~~

b[48] Poetry⌊~~, that~~⌋ can mean a breathturn. Perhaps it travels the route—~~the route~~ also the route of art—for the sake of such a breathturn? Perhaps it will succeed, as the strange, ⌊I mean⌋ the abyss and the Medusa's head, the abyss and the automatons, seem to lie in this direction,—perhaps it will succeed ⌊here⌋ to differentiate between strange and strange,—perhaps it is exactly here that the Medusa's head shrinks, perhaps it is exactly here that the automatons break down—for this single short moment? Perhaps here, with the I—with the estranged I ⌊set free⌋ here and in this manner,—perhaps here a further other is set free{?} ⌊~~—an other, that has to be searched for again and again?~~⌋ ⌊?⌋

c Perhaps the poem is ~~only the news~~ itself because of this ... and can now, in this art-less, art-free manner, walk its other routes, thus also the routes of art time and again?

d Perhaps.

=

[43] ~~—he who walks on his head,~~ <Dsl. "I">

[44] <only paragraph in Dsl. "I," single space marked>

[45] car <yearbook>

[46] lightlessness attributed.{"} <Dsl. "I"; Sentence marked with serpentine lines in left and right margins.>
~~lightlessness~~ ⌊darkness⌋ attributed.
<corrected in proofs>

[47] <In Ts. "L" at this place these notes "14–16 tighten! Reread!". Meant are the pages 14–16 with paragraphs 29b to 32b.>

[48] Poetry can mean a breathturn <Ts. "D">
~~The~~ Poetry{,}⌊: that⌋ can <Dsl. "I">

Drafts (Nr. 17; 18)

<...> **30a** Again and again we write the 20 January, "our" 20 January.

30b Under such dates do we write, from such dates we write ourselves today—✻ perhaps most clearly in the poem. Most clearly: that means with all the clarity we owe—or believe we owe—to what we have experienced both on the outside and the inside, and thus to what still needs to be reckoned with under this or that figure.

from: Nr. 17 (C 36-39 [F4])

31a I speak, as I am permitted to speak of poems, in matters concerning me. **b** Whereby I, and this seems to me to have always belonged to the hopes of the poem, speak perhaps also in matters of the strange—who knows, perhaps even in the strangest matter. **c** This "who knows" is the only thing I am able to add here, today to these hopes, as resembling hope. **d** Perhaps even an ~~concordance~~ ⌞encounter⌟ of this "strangest" with the just plain "strange" ⌞and "other"⌟ is thinkable—~~e~~ **e** the poem tarries or rather tests the wind—a word to be related to the creaturely—through such thoughts. **f** Nobody can tell how long the ~~pause~~ breath pause—and with it the testing—will last; ⌞the "swift," which has always been outside, has gained speed;⌟ the poem knows this; ~~with all its~~ it heads straight for a strange and a strangest, that it thinks as being ⌞reachable,⌟ vacant and ⌞let's say: like Lucile⌟ turned toward it, the poem. <...>

from: Nr. 17 (C 36-39 [F4])

32a The poem shows, and this has, I believe, in no way to do with the—not to be underestimated—difficulties of word choice, the faster fall of syntax or the more lucid sense for ellipsis—, the poem shows, unmistakably, a strong tendency to fall silent.

Ts. "A"

30a Ladies and gentlemen, we write it again and again, the 20 January, this 20 January.

30b Under such dates do we write, from such dates we write ourselves,—who knows toward what dates we write ourselves.—✻ Poetry, for me that does not mean only lyric poetry; the novel, the play, they all ~~arguably write~~, ⌞~~are~~ ⌞can⌟ arguably, in their own manner,⌟ like the poem, be written{.}under such dates{.}

<new page>

✻ But what is ~~"new"~~ new in the poem—I do not mean the so-called "modern lyric poem," what is new in the German poem—I am focusing before all on this—, what's new in this poem is arguably (**30a**) that this is the clearest attempt to remain mindful of such dates. The clearest: that means with all the clarity we owe—or believe we owe—to what we have experienced both on the outside and the inside, and thus to what still needs to be reckoned with under this or that figure.

31a I speak, as I am permitted to speak of poems, I speak, I know, in matters concerning me:✻ thus poems are indeed: mono-tone; "nobody becomes what he is not." **b** But I do think—and this thought can hardly surprise you anymore at this point—, I think that it has always been—part of the poem's hopes to speak exactly ~~in ali~~ also in an alien⌟, i.e. in an other's⌟ matter—who knows, perhaps in ~~strangest~~ the matter ⌞of a totally other⌟. **c** This "who knows"—it is ⌞arguably⌟ related to what has preceded it ~~once already~~—, this "who knows" is the only thing that I am able to add, here, today to ⌞the old hopes⌟ ~~as resembling hope~~ ⌞~~hopeful~~⌟. **d** Perhaps even an encounter of this "~~strangest~~ ⌞totally other⌟"—I am using here a ⌞familiar⌟ auxiliary verb—with the not all too distant "other" is thinkable, **e**—the poem tarries and tests the wind—a word to be related to the creaturely—through such thoughts. **f** Nobody can tell how long the breath pause—and with it the testing—will last{.}; {T}the "swift," which has always been outside, has gained speed; the poem knows this; it heads straight for that other, that it thinks as reachable, ⌞as to be set free,⌟ vacant and—let's say: like Lucile—turned toward it, the poem.

32a Certainly the poem—the poem today—shows, and this, I believe, has ~~in no way~~ to do ⌞only indirectly⌟ with the—not to be underestimated—difficulties of [50] word choice, the faster fall of syntax or the more lucid sense for ellipsis,—the poem shows, unmistakably, a strong tendency to fall silent.

Ts. "L"

30a Perhaps one can say that each poem has its own ⌊"⌋ 20th January ⌊"⌋ inscribed in it? Perhaps what's new in the poem ⌊s⌋ ⌊written⌋ today is exactly this: theirs is the clearest attempt to remain mindful of such dates?

<new page>

b But don't we all write ourselves from such dates? And toward what dates do we write ourselves?

=

=

=

=[49]

31a But the poem does speak! It stays mindful of its dates, but—it speaks. For sure, it always only speaks on its own, ~~perhaps~~ its very own behalf. ✻ ~~It is monotone: "Nobody becomes what he is not": this line by Hofmannsthal~~

b But I do think—and this thought can hardly surprise you at this point—, I think that it has always been part of the poem's hopes to speak on behalf of exactly this "strange"—no, I cannot use this word this way~~—that in the matter~~ exactly on an other's behalf—who knows, perhaps on behalf ~~of the~~ of a totally other.

c This "who knows"—to ⌊which⌋ I see that I have now arrived at—, is all I can add, here, today to old hopes.

d Perhaps, I have to ~~think now~~ ⌊tell myself now⌋,—perhaps an encounter~~, an agreement~~ of this "totally other" with a not all too distant, with a very close "other" is—I am using here a familiar auxiliary verb~~—, is perhaps even~~ thinkable—thinkable again and again.

e The poem tarries and tests the wind ~~a~~—a word related to the creaturely—through such thoughts.

f Nobody can tell how long the breath pause—the testing and the thought—will last. The "swift," which has always been ⌊"⌋ outside ⌊"⌋, has gained speed; the poem knows this; but it heads straight, arguably, for that "other"⌊,⌋ that it considers reachable, able to be set free, perhaps vacant, and turned—let's say: like Lucile—toward it. ⌊~~—or only—~~⌋,

32a Certainly, the poem—the poem today—shows, and this, ~~most prob~~ I believe, has to do though only indirectly with the—not to be underestimated—difficulties of ~~syntax~~ word choice, the faster fall of syntax or the more lucid sense for ellipsis,—the poem shows, unmistakably, a strong tendency to fall silent.

Further Variants

[49] <four spaces in Ts. "L"; three in Dsl. "I," here one is marked>

[50] <Ts. "A": unreadable hw. note in top margin>

Drafts (Nr. 18;17; 16; 82)

b It stands fast—⌞via⌟ some experience and conceptions, whose subjective limitations I ask not to be overlooked—~~let me~~ ⌞I now arrive⌟ at this extreme formulation arrive at—, the poem stands fast at the edge of itself. In its self-sublation ⌞it⌟ sees its —perhaps only—chance; it calls and brings itself, in order to be able to exist, ceaselessly back from its already-no-longer into its always-still. ✲ In this in between, in the moment of its becoming free and having been set free, in this state of floating and drifting away ~~is seen~~ the ground of the poem—this, its own bottomlessness, the poem sets as its ground. **7b** the poem ⌞—born in distress—⌟ ~~thinks~~ ⌞understands⌟ itself as an act of freedom. <new attempt> ~~The medium, in~~ It is a step. The medium in which this step ~~is so happens~~ occurs, is language

from: Nr. 18 (C 33)

<...> **33a-c** ~~But~~ ⌞Rather⌟ in the poem as the poem of the one who knows that he speaks under the angle of inclination of his Being, that the language of his poem is neither "analogy" nor just language as such, but language <u>actualized</u>, simultaneously voiced and voiceless, set free in the sign of a radical individuation that at the same time, however, remains mindful of the borders language draws and of the possibilities language opens up for it. **d** The poem is one person's language-become-shape, it has objectivity, presentness, presence; it stands into time. <...>

from: Nr. 17 (C 36-39 [F4])

<...>✲ Poems ~~want to~~ ⌞exclude⌟ everything they are not by themselves,—the one who has written them they include ~~and keep captive for a long time;~~ ⌞(**34a**)—he is added to it;⌟ <...>

from: Nr. 16 (F 2/3 [C 1])

✲ The poem gives itself into the hand of the one, you, who stand ~~in~~ therewith in (**34b**) the mystery of the encounter—into what hand does it give itself! It gives itself into your hand? ⌞by the most strange illuminated⌟ as if it were its own!

from: Nr. 82 (C 12)

Ts. "A"

b It stands fast—⌞after so many extreme formulations,⌟ permit me this ~~extreme formulation~~—, the poem stands fast at the edge of itself; it calls and brings itself, in order to be able to exist, ceaselessly back from its already-no-longer to its always-still{,} ✲ ~~in the moment of its becoming free and having been set free, in statu nascendi and in statu moriendi at the same time, it sees its chance{;}. Such movements, I believe, are most deeply inscribed in the poem, they are acts of freedom, but they too can only be documented in the medium of language~~

33a This always-still is a speaking. It is not just language as such, nor should it be "analogy." **b** It is <u>actualized</u> language, ~~simultaneously voiced and unvoiced~~, set free in the sign of a radical individuation that at the same time, however, remains mindful of the borders language draws and of the possibilities language opens up for it. **c** It is the poem of the one who does not forget that he speaks under the angle of inclination of his Being, the angle of inclination of his mortality; **d** it is one person's language-become-shape, it has ~~objectivity,~~ presentness, presence. <new attempt> **34a** ~~It~~ ⌞The poem⌟ is lonely and en route. b ⌞but stands ⌞is⌟, here already, in the encounter—in the mystery of the encounter.—⌟ <...>

Ts. "L" | Further Variants

b ~~Permit me,~~ It stands fast—after so many extreme formulations, permit me this one too—, the poem stands fast at the edge of itself; it calls and brings itself, in order to be able to exist, ceaselessly back from its already-no-longer into its always-still.
<new page>

33a This always-still can only be a <u>speaking</u>. But not just language [51]as such and ⌊presumably⌋ | nor | ~~indeed~~ | ~~no~~ word-based "analogy" [52]⌊either⌋.

[53]**b** But language <u>actualized</u>, set free under the sign of a [54]necessary individuation that at the same time, however, remains mindful of the borders language [55]sets and of the possibilities language opens up for it.

c This always-still of the poem can indeed only be ~~the~~ found ⌊in the⌋ work of the poet who does not forget that he speaks under the angle of inclination of his Being, the angle of inclination of his ~~mortality~~ creatureliness.

d Then the poem is—even more clearly than previously—one person's language-become-shape,—and, according to its essence, presentness and presence.

=

34a The poem is lonely. ⌊It is⌋ {L}lonely and en route. Its author remains added to it.

b But doesn't the poem therefore already at its inception stand in the <u>encounter</u>,—in the <u>mystery</u> <u>of the encounter</u>?

[56]=

[51] as such, <yearbook>

[52] <Ts. "L": Fair copy of corrected sentence in top margin>

[53] <Dsl. "I": paragraph 33b marked in margin with serpentine lines.>

[54] ~~necessary~~ radical, <corrected in proofs>

[55] borders language sets <Ts. "D"; marked in left margin: "?">
~~sets~~ ⌊draws⌋ <corrected in proofs>

[56] <double space in Dsl. "I" and first edition, in yearbook, single space>

Drafts (Nr. 17)	Ts. "A"
<...> **35a** The poem wants to head toward some other, it needs this other; it ~~bespeaks itself to it~~ needs an opposite; it seeks it out; it bespeaks itself to it. **b** Each thing is, for the poem heading toward this other, a figure of this other. **c** The attention the poem tries to pay to everything it encounters, its sharper sense of detail, outline, structure or color is not, I believe, the achievement of an eye competing with ever more precise instruments—it is a form of concentration. **36a** The poem becomes the poem of someone who perceives~~, and is attentive~~ is turned toward phenomena, questioning and addressing these; ~~they are~~ ⌊~~it is~~⌋ ⌊it becomes, going through so much that is no longer addressable,⌋ conversation. **b** And only in the space of this conversation does the addressed constitute itself, does it presence itself, as it gathers ⌊around⌋ the I addressing and naming it. But the addressed which ⌊through naming⌋ has become a you, brings its other- and strange-ness into this present; in this here and now of the poem—the poem itself has only this one, unique ⌊,momentary⌋ presence—, even in this immediacy and nearness it lets its most essential aspect speak: its time. <new paragraph> **c** When we talk in this way with things, we are always also at the question of their where-from and where-to: at a question that "stays open,""does not come to an end," that points toward the open, empty and free—we are far outside: ✻ every strange time is other than ours; we are ⌊far outside, but⌋ in any case only at the edge of our own time; the perceived things are also there with us: they stand there where we stand at last: the things in the poem somehow partake of such "last" things ⌊could be, one never knows, the "last" things⌋. ~~Each poem~~ *from: Nr. 17 (C 36-39 [F4])*	<...> **35a** It wants to head toward some other, it needs this other, it needs an opposite; it seeks it out, it bespeaks itself to it. **b** Each thing ⌊, each human⌋ is, for the poem heading toward the other, a figure of this other. **c** The attention the poem tries to pay to everything it encounters, its sharper sense of detail, outline, structure or color ⌊but also of the "tremors" and "hints"⌋—all this is not, I believe, the achievement of an eye competing with ever more precise instruments—it is a form of concentration. **d** "Attention"—permit me to quote here a phrase by Malebranche, via Walter Benjamin's essay on Kafka—, "Attention is the natural prayer of the soul." **36a** The poem ~~tries~~ ⌊becomes⌋ the poem of someone who perceives, is turned toward phenomena, questioning and addressing these; it becomes conversation. **b** {In}Only in the space of this conversation does the addressed constitute itself, does it presence itself, as it gathers around the I addressing and naming it. But the addressed which through naming has become a you, brings its other~~—and strangeness~~ ⌊-ness⌋ into this present; even in this here and now of the poem—for the poem itself, we know, has only this one, unique ⌊, momentary⌋ presence—, even in this immediacy and nearness it lets its most essential aspect: its time, speak. **c** When we talk in this way with things, we are always also at the question of their where-from and where-to: at a question that "stays open," "does not come to an end," that points toward the open, empty and free—we are far outside. **d** The poem searches for such a place.

Ts. “L”

35a The poem wants to head toward some[57] other, it needs this other, it needs an opposite. It seeks it out, it bespeaks itself to it.

b Each thing, each human is, for the poem heading toward the other, a figure of this other.

<new page>

c The attention the poem tries to pay to everything it encounters, its sharper sense of detail, outline, structure or color, but also of the “tremors” and “hints,”—all this is not, I believe, the achievement of an eye competing with ever more precise instruments—it is rather a ~~form of concentration~~. a concentration that remains mindful of all our dates.

=

d “Attention”—permit me to quote here a phrase by Malebranche, via Walter Benjamin’s essay on Kafka—, “Attention is the natural prayer of the soul.”

=

36a The poem becomes—under what conditions!—the poem of someone who—always still—perceives, is turned toward phenomena, questioning and addressing these; it becomes conversation—often ~~also~~ ⌞~~it is~~⌟ ⌞it is⌟ a desperate conversation.

=

b Only in the space of this~~—today’s—~~conversation does the addressed constitute itself, as it ~~presences~~ ⌞gathers⌟ around the I addressing and naming it. But the addressed which through naming has become a you, brings its other-ness into this present. Even in this here and now of the poem—for the poem itself, we know, has only this one, unique, momentary presence—, even in this immediacy and nearness it lets the most essential aspect of it, [58]⌞the Other⌟ speak: its time.

=

c When we talk in this way with things, we are always also at the question of their where-from and where-to: at a question that “stays open,” “does not come to an end,” that points toward the open, empty and free—we are far outside. **d** The poem, I believe, searches for this place too.

=

=

=[59]

Further Variants

[57] Ander~~n~~ ⌞en⌟ <corrected in proofs>
Andern <make-up “C”>

[58] essential aspect of it <Ts. “D”>
essential aspect of it, the other, <Dsl. “I”>
essential aspect of it, the {o} ⌞O⌟ther <corrected in proofs>

[59] <three spaces also in Dsl. “I” but note.: “2 spaces”>

Drafts (Nr. 66; 6/73)

Ts. "A"

37 And the images, the metaphors of the poem? ~~They are indeed~~

38a Ladies and gentlemen, what am I talking about, when I talk thus of the poem, of the poem? **b** I am talking about a poem which does not exist! **c** The absolute poem—no, that doesn't exist, cannot exist! **d** But there is ⌐indeed¬ in each real poem, this irrecusable question about it.

39a What would the images be? **b** What is perceived and is to be perceived once and only now and only here. And the poem would then be the place ⌐,¬ where all tropes are ⌐want to be¬ carried ad absurdum.

✻ ~~Please permit me to repeat this:~~

40a Topos research{,}? **b** {c}Certainly! But in light of what is to be searched for: in light of Utopia!

✻ These are extreme formulations, perhaps also formulations in extremis. {D} They thrust through the approaches of the poem, they do not oversee it. **40a** Topos research? **b** Certainly, but in light of what is to be searched for, the ~~no place~~ ⌐placeless,¬ in light of u-topia

=

39a ~~Images:~~ The image? The metaphor? ✻ They are the seen, the perceivable, they have the aspect of the phenomenal. **b** The poem is the ⌐singular¬ place, where all tropes are carried ad absurdum—

Nr. 66 (C 45)

41a What questions! What claims! **b** It is time to turn back.

42a I am at the end—I am back at the beginning.

b Elargissez l'Art! This question comes at us with its old, already in Büchner's poetry ~~speaking~~ ⌐audible¬ uncanniness, from a new ⌐,much more uncanny¬ direction. **c** I have searched for ~~a counterword~~ ⌐a counter-thought¬, no, I had gone to it with this ~~counterword~~ ⌐thought¬.

d-e Elargissez l'Art? ⌐I wanted to answer:¬ ⌐reply¬ ⌐"Enlarge art? No¬ No, to the contrary, go with art into your ⌐innermost¬ narrows!

42b,e "Elargissez l'art"? No: ~~rétrécissez-le!~~ Go with art into ~~the~~ ⌐your¬ narrows!

from: Nr. 73/6 (C 30,1)

Ts. "L"

37a The poem?

b The poem with its images and tropes?

=

=

38a Ladies and gentlemen, what am I actually talking about when I talk from this direction, in this direction, with these words about poetry—no, about the poem?

b For I am talking about a poem which does not exist!

c The absolute poem—no, that ~~God knows~~ ⌞certainly⌟ doesn't exist, cannot exist!

d But there is in each real poem, even in the most unassuming poem, there is [60]this irrecusable question, this outrageous claim.

<new page>

[61]**39a** And ~~thus~~ ⌞then⌟, what would ~~for example~~ the images be?

b ⌞~~They would be~~⌟ What is perceived and is to be perceived once and only now and only here. **c** And the poem would ~~thu~~ then be the place where all tropes and metaphors want to be carried [62]ad absurdum

=

[63]**40a** Topos research?

b Certainly! But in light of what is to be searched for: in light of u-topia.

c And the human being? And the creature?

d In this light ⌞!⌟ ~~standing~~

=

=

41a What questions! What claims!

b It is time, [64]to turn back.

=

=

[65]**42a** Ladies and gentlemen, I am at the end—I am back at the beginning.

=

[66]**b** Elargissez l'Art! This question comes at us with its old, ~~also~~ with its new [67]uncanniness. I took it to Büchner—and think I found it there again. **c** I even had an answer ready, a "Lucilian" counterword; I wanted to ~~reply~~ counter{:}⌞, be ready with my own contradiction.⌟

d Enlarge art?

e No, to the contrary. Go with art into your innermost narrows! And set yourself free!

=

Further Variants

[60] <Ts. "L": dotted underlining>

[61] <para. only in Dsl. "I," single space marked>

[62] <Ts. "L": dotted underlining>

[63] <double space in Dsl. "I," single space marked>

[64] that I turn back. <Ts. "D">

[65,66] <para. in Ts. "D">

[67] uncanniness ⌞,⌟ <corrected in proofs>

Drafts (Nr. 16; 87; 82; 80)

✻ There are routes, relations and context for which, it seems to me, the criteria of the literary do not suffice; **42f** I took this way with that line—such a route did this line take with me. This route describes a circle

from: Nr. 16 (F 2/3 [C 1])

44 P<oems>: oh this infinity-speaking full of mortality and to no purpose!

from: Nr. 87 (E 4,2)

45b Seven years ago, I was far from Büchner, —but there are communicating vessels— I wrote these lines: **c** Voices up from the nettle-route:/ Come to us on your hands. / Whoever is alone with the lamp / Has only the hand to read from. <...>

from: Nr. 82 (C 12)

46 The poem is the detour from you to you; it is the route. It is also the route of language toward itself, its becoming visible and mortal: wherewith the poem becomes the raison d'être of language.

Nr. 80 (C 6,4)

Ts. "A"

f ~~I went~~ ~~only~~ ~~with it into my narrows.~~ I took this route, here too and <in> your presence. **g** But art—thus also ×/ the Medusa's head—lives on. ×/ the mechanism, ~~d u the~~ the watch springs, the Medusa's head, the uncanny so difficult to separate out, perhaps only one strangeness—, art so mutable, so ubiquitous lives on. **43** Twice, with Lucile's "Long live the king" and ~~when Lenz~~ when the sky opened as an abyss beneath Lenz, the breathturn ~~was~~ seemed to be there. Perhaps also, when I tried to set course toward ~~that distant~~ that ~~strangest~~ distant you, that in the end becomes visible ~~only in the~~ again only in the figure of Lucile. And once we also came close to something open and close to utopia.

44 ~~Poems~~ Poetry—: ~~the~~ oh this infinity-speaking ~~full of~~ ~~so much~~ mortality and to no purpose!

42f ~~I had tried to take a route—it was a circle.~~

✻ ~~So what was it?~~ The route of poetry: the breathroute.

45a Permit me, please, as I am back at the beginning, to ask once more, in all brevity, but from a different direction, that question.

b Ladies and gentlemen, a few years ago I wrote a small four-line stanza—here it is: **c** "Voices up from the nettle-route:/ Come to us on your hands. / Whoever is alone with the lamp / Has only the hand to read from."

d And in August ~~of last year~~ of this past year I wrote, in memory of a ~~sojourn~~ missed encounter ~~in the mountains~~ in the Engadine, a little story, in which I let a man walk "like Lenz" through "The mountains"...

e ~~I had last~~ I had written myself, on both occasions, I realized it only much later, from a 20th January. ~~Is it any surprise if I~~ **f** I had ~~, today too, only~~ ... encountered myself. **46** Does one take, when thinking of poems, such routes? Are these routes only re-routings, detours from you to you? But then it is indeed ~~the~~ route, ~~that~~ also one of the routes one ~~has to~~ can take, to be, as voice, perceived , seen by a you, for then it is, again and again, a route to a ~~every~~ you(!): thus a creaturely route! And a homecoming at the same time!

Ts. “L”

[68] **f** I Took this route ⌞,⌟ here too, in your presence. It was a circle.

=

g Art, ~~the unca~~ thus also the Medusa’s head, the mechanism, the automatons, the uncanny so difficult to separate out and which in the final analysis is perhaps only one strangeness—~~this~~ ⌞~~mutable~~⌟ art lives on.

=

43 Twice, ~~when~~ with Lucile’s “Long live the king,” and when the sky opened as an abyss beneath Lenz, the breathturn seemed to be there. Perhaps also when I tried to set course toward [69]that distant ⌞—occupiable—⌟ you, that ~~does~~ finally does become visible only in the figure of Lucile. And once, given the attention to things and beings, [70]we also came close to [71]something open and free. And finally, close to utopia.

[72] =

44 Poetry, ladies and gentlemen:
this infinity-speaking full of mortality and to no purpose!
<new page>

=

[73]**45a** Ladies and gentlemen, permit me, as I am back at the beginning, to ask once more, [74]in all brevity, and from a different direction, ~~after~~ ⌞the same question⌟.

b Ladies and gentlemen, a few years ago I wrote a small four-line stanza—here it is:

c “Voices up from the [75]nettle-route / Come to us on your [76]hands / Whoever is alone with the lamp / has only his hand to read from.”

d And a year ago, ~~I had back then missed an encounter~~ ⌞in⌟ ~~in Engadine~~ memory of a missed encounter in Engadine, I wrote down a little story, in which I~~, I let~~ a man walk [77]“like Lenz” through the mountains ~~and meet himself.~~

e On both occasions, I had, [78]written myself from a 20th January ⌞“, [79]from my “20th January”⌟. ⌞~~I have returned to it~~⌟

↕ ~~No wonder, that I also~~
~~If thus one encounters, through the written,~~

f I had ... encountered myself.

46 Does one take, when thinking of poems, does one take such routes with poems? Are these routes only reroutings ⌞re-routings⌟, detours from you to you? But ~~then I~~ they are also at the same time, among many other routes, routes on which language becomes voice, they are encounters, routes of a voice

Further Variants

[68]<space deleted and crossed-out space mark in Dsl. “I”>

[69]that distant and occupiable you <Ts. “D”>
that ~~distant occupiable you~~ ⌞distant and occupiable⌟ <Dsl. “I”>

[70]we came close <Ts. “D”>

[71]an ⌞~~—perhaps the same—~~⌟ <Dsl. “I”>

[72]<1½ blank lines in Ts. “L”>

[73]<In Dsl. “I” single space, note.: “2 spaces.” Para. in Ts. “D”>

[74]in all brevity and from a different direction, <make-up “C”>

[75]nettle-route ⌞:⌟ <corrected in proofs>

[76]hands⌞.⌟ <corrected in proofs>

[77]“like Lenz {“} through the mountains{”} <Dsl. “I”>

[78]without knowing it, <Ts. “D”>

[79]—from my <Dsl. “I”>

Drafts (Nr. 81)

47-48 ~~We~~ I am at the end here and must be careful, like my ⌊half-Asian⌋ countryman Karl-E-<mil> Franzos, to reinterpret the fundamentally accommodating⌊⌋, that we use—or used—as something⌋ as something to come. (But: there are, as in Leonce and Lena, quotation marks smilingly added to the words, thus also given to take along, that do not necessarily want to be "Gänsefüßchen," [goose-feet] but perhaps "Hasenöhrchen," [hare's ears] i.e. as something that listens ⌊not completely fearless⌋ wants to be understood beyond itself and the ~~words~~ ⌊⌋, that means also that which they signify⌊⌋.) ✲ I will give you therefore, in contrast to my so uncritical, though simultaneously ⌊—something mentioned ~~much less~~ ⌊much more rarely⌋—⌋ such a rat-hating, ⌊⌋, manuscript-loving⌋ ⌊~~half Asian~~⌋ countryman) when all is well and done a second, ⌊hopefully⌋ right⌊er⌋ interpretation. Who knows, perhaps I say ⌊this way too once again⌋ the same thing. ⌊(but let's keep silent about hermeneutics)⌋

from: Nr. 81 (C 8/9)

Ts. "A"

47 Ladies and gentlemen! I ~~am coming now to the end~~ am coming to the end—to the end of *Leonce and Lena*. **48b** I will be careful, like my countryman Karl Emil Franzos—~~I encou~~ him too ⌊~~, the forgotten one,~~⌋ I encounter, after all these detours, ~~also~~ only ~~now~~ ⌊~~in~~ Büch in {~~~} Büchnerian<?> ⌋—, I will be careful, not to read the "accommodating," that is used now, as if it was a "to come." **c** And yet: Isn't *Leonce and Lena* full of quotation marks, smilingly added to ⌊these⌋ the words, that do not necessarily want to be understood as "Gänsefüßchen," [goose-feet] but ⌊perhaps⌋ as "Hasenöhrchen," [hare's ears], that is as something not completely fearless, that listens beyond itself and the words? ~~I ask one more time from here, I ask about the encounters on this route and detour, which I was allowed to travel with poems. I did, and that too {I owe to} I have to thank for today, encounter so many people and names: Georg Büchner,~~

49a From here on, thus starting from the "accommodating," but also ~~in the~~ in light of utopia, ~~I~~ let me now ~~search~~ ⌊~~research~~⌋ ⌊~~for~~⌋ ~~{a} the topos for~~, undertake some topos research: **b** I am searching for ~~the birthplace of those, whom I? and because of that I will~~ now ~~have to thank~~ ⌊from Karl Emil Franzos and my own⌋ ⌊~~the places, where where Karl Emil Franzos~~⌋ ⌊~~the place where~~ those I encountered⌋ ⌊the region from which Karl E. F. und R. L., whom I met in ⌊Georg⌋ Büchner come;⌋ As I am back where I started from, I am also searching for where I ~~started~~ ⌊begun⌋, for my; ⌊place of my ⌊own⌋ origin;⌋ **c** I am searching for all this ⌊, with a barely ~~uncertain~~ trembling ⌊imprecise⌋ ⌊with a ⌊No doubt⌋ imprecise because slightly fidgety,⌋ finger,⌋ on the map—a ~~small~~ ⌊child's-⌋map, I have to ~~acknowledge~~ ⌊confess⌋. **d** None of these places ~~is inscribed,~~ ⌊can be found,⌋ ⌊they do not exist,⌋ but I know where ~~they are, approximately—~~ ⌊especially now⌋ they should be⌋, and—I find something!

Ts. "L"

to a perceiving you,—creaturely routes ⌊,—⌋ blueprints for being perhaps, a sending oneself ahead—toward oneself, in search of oneself ... A kind of homecoming.

~~And a finding oneself again~~

=

=

[80]**47** Ladies and gentlemen, I am coming to the end—I am coming, with the acute accent I had to set, to the end of⌊...⌋ *Leonce and Lena.*

=

48a And here, with the last two words of this work, I must be careful.

b I must be careful not to misread, as Karl Emil Franzos, the editor ~~who eighty one years ago here in Frankfurt of that~~ of that [81]First Critical Complete Edition of Georg Büchner's Collected Works and Posthumous Writings,~~ that was~~ published[82] eighty-one years ago by Sauerländer in Frankfurt am Main, did—I must be careful not to misread, like my ~~mine~~ countryman Karl Emil Franzos here rediscovered, the [83]"Kommode"[accommodating], we need now, [84]as a "Kommendes" [a coming thing]!

c And yet: isn't *Leonce and Lena* full of quotation marks, invisibly and smilingly added to the words ⌊~~perhaps~~⌋, that ~~want to be read~~ want to be [85]understood ⌊perhaps⌋ not as "Gänsefüßchen," [goose-feet] ~~but perhaps~~ ⌊but rather⌋ as "Hasenöhrchen" [hare's ears]? ⌊that is, something not completely fearless that listens beyond itself ⌊and the words⌋?

<new page>

[86] **49a** From here, thus starting from the [87]⌊"⌋ accommodating ⌊"⌋, but also~~, and this time probably no longer at, and this time certainly not~~ in the light of utopia, [88]let me now undertake, one last time, some topos research:

b I am searching for the region from which Reinhold Lenz and Karl Emil Franzos, whom I met ~~in such incomprehensible on this present Büchner route~~ ⌊on the route here and in Georg Büchner⌋, come. As I am back where I started from, I am also searching for the place of my origin.

c I am searching for all this with a no doubt very imprecise, [89]because ~~a little trembling~~ ⌊fidgety⌋ finger on the map—a child's-map, I have to confess.

d None of these places can be found, they do not exist, but I know where ⌊⌊, especially⌋ now,⌋ they should be, ~~even now~~ and ... I find something!

=

Further Variants

[80] <paragraph in Ts. "D">

[81] <title underlined in Dsl. "I," in the "B" proofs a note: "no cursive!! But quotation marks!">

[82] published—<yearbook>

[83] "{K}⌊C⌋ommode" <Dsl. "I">

[84] for the <Ts. "D">

[85] to be read as. <Ts. "D">

[86] <Ts. "L": in top margin the deleted note "~~last but one page~~">

[87] "{K}⌊C⌋ommoden" / original has "Kommoden" / <Dsl. "I">

[88] let me undertake, ~~one last time,~~ ⌊—now—⌋ some topos research <corrected in proofs>

[89] because ~~a~~ ⌊~~little~~⌋ fidgety <Dsl. "I">

Drafts (Nr. 81; 86; 89)

50b-c What does connect what was quoted at the beginning with the last quote, what connects your present Büchner-prize winner with that Reinhold Lenz? Something that is at bottom not there. Something like the totally sensual speech etc. ... ___: a meridian.

from: Nr. 81 (C 8/9)

50c Perhaps ⌞Something, that today and here may look for and take one of these names enlivened by this opposite;⌟

Something invisible, in no way enriching the "totally sensual speech," ⌞something immaterial, not available, early⌟ ⌞cybernetically irrelevant⌟ ⌞, indifferent⌟ but earthly, terrestrial, ⌞compass-like-⌟ round, ⌞that returns over its poles⌟ {I}in{-}it{-}self{-} while cheerfully even crossing the "tropics" /Tropen/ ⌞—I don't say: the tropics /die Wendekreise/—⌟" links me—imprecisely!—with it ⌞—something ⌞equally⌟ immovably sun-distant⌟: a meridian.

from: Nr. 81 (C 8/9)

a ... meridian.

51 With you and the State of Hesse I have just now touched it.

from: Nr. 86 (C 26,1)

52 My heartfelt thanks to the German Academy for Language and Poetry, to the State of Hesse and the municipal authorities of the city of Darmstadt for awarding me their prize: the prize that carries the name of a giant, the name of Georg Büchner. Permit me

from: Nr. 89 (C 40)

Ts. "A"

50a ⌞Ladies and gentlemen,⌟ I find something which consoles me a little for having ~~with you, ladies and gentlemen~~ in your presence taken this ~~route~~ impossible ⌞~~improbable?~~⌟ route—this route of the impossible.

b ~~What do I find it to be?~~ I find ⌞~~something~~ <?>⌟ what connects{,} ⌞and⌟ leads to an encounter.

c ⌞I find⌟ {S}something~~ like language ~~⌟, that resembles ~~language and perhaps also the {poem} route of the poem;~~ ⌞resembles the poem ~~res~~ and its route:⌟ something⌟ immaterial{.}⌞,⌟ ~~the "pe~~ but ~~terrestrial~~ ⌞at the same time also⌟ earthly, ⌞~~sublunar~~⌟ terrestrial, circular ⌞describing a circle⌟, that returns to itself over ⌞both⌟ poles, ~~and thus~~ while—cheerfully—even crossing the tropics—I find ... a meridian.

51 With you ⌞~~Bü (Büchner)~~⌟ ⌞and Georg Büchner⌟ and the State of Hesse I have ~~today~~ ⌞~~in this hour~~⌟ ⌞just now⌟ been allowed to touch it ⌞again.⌟

<½ empty page>

52a Ladies and gentlemen, today a high, a unique ~~award~~ honor was conferred upon me. I will be able to reflect that ~~as the b~~ in the company of people whose ⌞person and whose⌟ work{,} mean ~~the~~ an encounter for me, I am the recipient of ~~the Georg Büchner~~ ⌞a⌟ prize{.}⌞, that is mindful of Georg Büchner.⌟

b My heartfelt thanks for this distinction, my heartfelt thanks for this moment{,} ⌞and⌟ this encounter.

c I thank the State of Hesse. I thank the city of Darmstadt. I thank the German Academy for Language and Poetry.

d I thank the President of the German Academy for Language and Poetry, I thank you, dear Hermann Kasack.

e Dear Marie Luise Kaschnitz, I thank you.

═

53 ⌞~~Honored~~⌟ Ladies and gentlemen, I thank you all.[92]

Ts. "L"

50a Ladies and gentlemen, I find something which consoles me a little for having in your presence taken this ~~route~~ impossible route, this route of the impossible.

b I find what connects and leads, like the poem, to an encounter.

c I find something—like language—immaterial, yet earthly, terrestrial, circular ⌊~~round~~⌋, that returns to itself across both poles while—cheerfully—~~also~~ ⌊even⌋ crossing the tropics —: I find ... a meridian.

51 With you and Georg Büchner and the State of Hesse I ~~have been permitted to touch it~~ believe I have just now touched it again.

<new page>

[90]**52a** Ladies and gentlemen, today a very high honor, ~~a unique~~ was conferred upon me. I will be able ~~to reflect that~~ ⌊~~to remember~~ to remember that⌋ in the company of people, whose person and work [91]mean an encounter for me, I am the recipient of a prize that is mindful of ~~Georg B~~ ~~the poet~~ Georg Büchner.

b My heartfelt thanks for this distinction, my heartfelt thanks for this moment and this encounter.

c I thank the State of Hesse. I thank the city of Darmstadt. I thank the German Academy for Language and Poetry.

d I thank the President of the German Academy for Language and Poetry, I thank you, dear Hermann Kasack.

e Dear Marie Luise Kaschnitz, I thank you.

53 [Ladies and gentlemen, I thank ~~you all.~~ ⌊~~Your~~⌋ ⌊you for ⌊your⌋ presence.—⌋

Further Variants

[90] <only paragraph in Dsl. "I," double space marked. ½ space in Ts. "D">

[91] mean ⌊s⌋ <corrected in proofs>

[92] When your breath grows through it, you are given over to your poem,

<Note on the back page of the last sheet of Ts. "A":>

Drafts

Drafts of the 1st Main Section (Paragraphs 1–24)

a. Last draft of the opening before first redaction of the complete speech

18◂▸17 *1* *C 34/35* *Ts., C 35 pag.: -2-*

1a Art, you will remember, is a puppet-like, iambically five-footed and—a characteristic mythologically vouchsafed for, childless being; **b** it is the subject of a conversation that ~~too~~ takes place in a room, thus not in the Conciergerie, a conversation that, we sense, could ~~go on~~ ⌞be continued⌟ indefinitely, if nothing interfered; **2** it ⌞, art,⌟ does reappear later on, at some distance, ⌞in another play,⌟ in another time, thus, in *Woyzeck*, presented by a carnival barker, no longer linked to glowing, roaring, and shining creation, but set next to the creature, this time in ~~the shape of a monkey~~ ⌞the shape of a monkey⌟, but yet, ~~and in this it is fundamentally different form the immediately recogni~~ by its coats and trousers. **4a** ~~Ar~~ ~~This art~~ ⌞This being⌟ is ⌞also⌟ a problem, and, as you can see, a tough and long-lived, I want to say, eternal problem. **b** A problem, that lets a mortal, Camille, and someone who can only be understood from his death, Danton, string together word upon word. It is easy to talk about art.

5a But whenever there is talk about art, there is always someone around who doesn't really listen. **b** More exactly: someone who hears and listens and looks—and then doesn't know what the talk was in fact all about. But who hears the one who talks, who sees him talking, who perceives language and shape, and at the same time also, who could doubt it, direction, that means breath.

c That person is, you ~~have~~ know it, she comes, the often ~~quo~~ and not by chance often quoted, with each ⌞in this⌟ new year ⌞also to you⌟,—that person is Lucile.

<new page>

6c And ~~then,~~ at the end, when Camille, surrounded by the others, not <u>he</u> ⌞himself⌟, but only ~~someone~~ ⌞someone similar⌟ among ~~other~~ ⌞all similars—(**b**) Fabre can even die doubly—⌟, ⌞as Camille⌟ dies a theatrical—one is nearly tempted{,} to say⌞, although the metrical is missing,⌟: an iambic—death, ~~of~~ which we ⌞can⌟ feel as <u>his own</u> only two scenes later ⌞, through a foreign word,⌟, as all around him ~~sententiousnesses and~~ pathos and sententiousness confirm the triumph of puppet and string,—then Lucile, ⌞one who is blind to art,⌟ for whom language is something person-like and visible, is there once again with that ~~counte~~ shattering "Long live the king!"

7b That is the counterword, ~~**8a** One hears it first of all as a declaration of loyalty to the "ancien régime"~~
4/696, 20/695 ~~**b** It is not a declaration of loyalty to the monarchy.~~ ⌞~~Here no monarchy is being paid homage to~~⌟ ~~paid homage.~~ ~~**c** Here homage is being paid~~ ⌞to⌟ ~~the majesty of the absurd as witness to the human. **9** That is ... poetry.~~ ⌞The word that cuts the string{.}⌟ ⌞, the ~~word that does not, unlike art, have consequences~~ is an act of freedom.⌟

8a One hears it first as a declaration of loyalty to the "ancien régime," **b** but here no monarchy and no yesterday is being paid homage to; **c** homage is being paid here to the ~~to the under /among/~~ for the majesty of the absurd as witness for the human. **9** This, ladies and gentlemen, ⌞has no name, but I believe that this⌟ is ... poetry.

694 **11** "—oh, art!": in *Lenz* too it is there, for it has, besides being mutable ⌞and the ability to split⌟, also the gift of ubiquity.

12a "At table Lenz was again <u>in good spirits:</u> the talk was of literature, he was in his element ... **b** ~~The feeling that whatever's been created, life, the potentiality of existence, and that's that; we need~~

~~not then ask whether it be beautiful or ugly.~~ The feeling that whatever's been created possesses life outweighs these two and should be the sole criterion in matters of art. ⌊..."—⌋ *398, 534*

❖❖❖

b. Preceding and parallel drafts of individual paragraphs.

Ts., pag. -3- *C 4,2* *2* *658◄►311*

---

13 I know, this passage has its literary-historical importance, ~~here speaks, concerning the author of the "Soldiers"~~ it has to be read ⌊together⌋ with the already quoted passage from Danton, what's at stake, I don't want to question this in any way here, is Büchner's ~~interpretation~~ aesthetic conceptions, is Mercier's "Elargissez l'art!," is ~~the a problem anti~~ an anticipation of naturalism, are the social and political aspects and roots ~~of Büchner's~~ of the Büchnerian opus.

❖❖❖

Ms. *C 51,1* *3/693* *480◄►694*

5a But there is always someone present and who doesn't listen, **b** i.e., who hears and then doesn't know what the talk was all about; and has heard something, that wasn't ~~exac~~ talked about. Who hears the one who talks, who /~~ge~~/ has perceived language{,} and shape, and, who could doubt this, direction, i.e. breath.—
c That is, you know, the woman who comes toward you each time from a different direction; it is Lucile

---

❖❖❖

Ms. *C 52b,3-52a,4* *4/696* *20/695◄*

22c Perhaps poetry is a consequence of art—one of its consequences; perhaps ⌊art⌋ is the route poetry has to cover again and again. **d** There are, I know, shorter routes. Mais la Poésie, elle aussi, brûle nos étapes *1, 20/695*

✻ The one leads to the other, but: a leap is needed *68/384*

Ms. *C 52a,1* *5/697* *►698*

Vive le Roi
7b that is the <u>counterword</u>.—**9** This, ladies and gentlemen, is poetry = an ⌊invisible,⌋ dependent being{,}(a being belonging to a person.—

❖❖❖

8◄►743 *6/73* *C 30,1* *Ms.*

(**13,24**) But this fragment is not to be read as a report on the author of the Soldiers and the Tutor or, what makes ⌊it⌋ even clearer: the author of "Notes on the Theater"—what is to be read here is the fatefulness of a man named Lenz, of whom one knows—without having learned it—what kind of burden his existence is to be ⌊found by⌋ read ⌊ing⌋ from it ~~sh~~ <?> here, that he under the burden ⌊the Büchnerian Lenz like the historical one,⌋ collapsed under
35, 51 the burden{,} of his existence, is picked up on a Moscow street—

90, 320, 700 **42b,e** "Elargissez l'art?" No: ~~rétrécissez-le!~~ Go with art into ~~the~~ ⌊your⌋ narrows!

❖❖❖

14◄ *7* *C 29,1* *Ts.*

6c,7b Lucile, who, you remember, with the word "Long live the king" knows how to take a step into freedom, the one who in "art," **1a** a puppet-like, (iambically-) five-footed and childless half-being—**2** we meet him, in the shape of a monkey, but in ⌊~~the same~~⌋ coat and trousers immediately recognizable, in the market stall scene in *Woyzeck*—, **5a-b** Lucile is the one who doesn't see or hear art, who only hears ~~the one~~ that person talk who with another

►6/73 *8* *C 29,2* *Ts.*

1a Art, you will remember, is a puppet-like, iambically five-footed and, that is ⌊this characteristic is⌋ also mythologically verifiable ⌊vouchsafed for⌋, a childless being; **b** it is the subject of a conversation that takes place in a room, i.e. not in the Conciergerie, a conversation that, we sense, could go on endlessly, if ~~something~~ nothing interfered; **2** it takes only later, ⌊at a certain distance⌋ in another play, ⌊and in a different era,⌋ once again to the stage, in *Woyzeck*, in the shape of a monkey this time, ⌊and in a show booth,⌋ but ~~clearly~~ immediately recognizable by its coat and trousers. <new paragraph> **4a-b** Art is a ⌊is a tough, I want to say eternal⌋ problem, that ~~concerns Camille,—and that Lucile, though the one fatefully associated with Camille, doesn't hear~~ makes a mortal, Camille, and someone who has also to be understood from his death, Danton, lose words that ~~of~~ let themselves be strung together seamlessly ⌊.⌋ It is easy to talk about art.

❖❖❖

90◄►545 *9* *C 42* *Dsl., pag. -6-*

17, 543 ✻ You miss something here, I know, you miss the questions about poetry as questions about the art of poetry.—

1b, 10a "—oh, art!" This ~~is~~ ⌊are⌋, you will remember, the ~~sentence~~ ⌊not really enthusiastic⌋ words of Camille, during a conversation, more exactly: a conversation that did not ⌊yet⌋ take place in the Conciergerie, but in a room. **b** I know, one can read this with different emphases, mark it with different accents: with the ~~grav~~ acute of the ~~modern~~ ⌊contemporary⌋, the grave of the ~~literary-~~historical (literary history too), with the circumflex—a sign of expansion—of the eternal.—**c** I give it the acute. (**18c**) If I do this, I see ~~art radically~~
330 ~~put into question~~ art questioned not in view of its renewal and rejuvenation, thus in view of some Mercier'ian "Elargissez l'art" now to be completed by my very own latest attain-

ments, but radically, from the ground up, as phenomenon.

<new formulation> *638*

1a "... If someone carves a puppet, with the string it dangles from and jerks about on visible for all, with joints that bang out each each step in five-footed iambs ..." I won't quote more—You will certainly remember the ~~further~~ ⌊other⌋ characteristics of the five-footed ⌊and childless⌋ **2**—it takes the stage ~~by the way~~ ⌊also⌋ ⌊—"You now see the art!"—⌋, presented by the carnival barker, ~~also~~ in Woyzeck, we recognize it by ~~the~~ coat and ~~the~~ ⌊its coat and its⌋ trousers~~, it wears~~{.}⌊: oh art, the same art.⌋

Against it, made so contemptible, Camille sets creation

❖❖❖

Ms.	*B 5,2-B 7*	*10*	*750◄►93*

✻ "What's on the lung, put on the tongue," my mother used to say. The poem, even if it *264*
doesn't ~~exactly~~ ⌊always⌋ resemble that which comes on doves' feet, still comes on breathroutes—and, if it wants to remain the poem, will never take different routes. The poem is a constant, even if in the most painful manner, intermittent congress with language:
a congress with the invisible, the invisible-near; ~~it is—why not call it by its name—a sort of belief.~~ *82, 241*
22b-c ⌊And⌋ art, that is ⌊, I believe,⌋ is only the route the poem covers again and again—a route, this seems unmistakable to me, full of old and new uncanninesses. **1-2** ~~Art, ha carries, with Büchner too~~ Art, that is, ⌊directly ⌊, thus not from its literary-historical perspective⌋ considered,⌋ already in Büchner—remember the conversation between Camille and Danton, ⌊~~it is~~ ⌊it takes place, significantly, in a room and not in the Conciergerie—⌋ remember the market stall scene in *Woyzeck*—something ⌊Art, that is something⌋ puppet-like, ⌊(iambically) ⌋ five-footed and childless ⌊something monkey-like, ~~and Un~~⌋ ⌊, ~~Un-free and Un-human~~⌋ ⌊~~Not~~= ⌊not- completely or only half-⌋ human⌋; **16a** ~~in *Lenz* too Lenz, for whom ⌊, as for Büchner,⌋ it's a matter of {a} the natural, confronts, ⌊as⌋ someone self-forgotten ⌊admittedly⌋, the natural with a "Medusa-like" gaze, in order to ... grasp it as the more natural ...~~ **5** Lucile, who is so close to Camille, doesn't hear what he has to say about art, she only sees him speak—~~she~~ sees ~~him~~ ⌊only his talking⌋, she doesn't ⌊hear and⌋ see the "problems of art." **7-8** And it is exactly she, who ~~irresistible {toward} everything—one is tempted to say: most artfully~~ ⌊automatically⌋ ~~—with the call pits herself against~~ ⌊in the decisive moment finds ~~the~~ that liberating ~~counterword~~⌋ "Long live the king!," ~~she sets herself free.~~ ⌊does find the counterword. For that is what it is, a counterword, and⌋ ~~This is certainly no homage~~ no homage addressed to an "Ancien Régime"—easily transferred to the situation today, and also to ~~the situation~~ ⌊that of⌋ poetry—"Ancien;" ~~it is~~ homage is being paid ⌊there⌋, face-to-face with the inhuman, ~~the~~ the majesty of the absurd as witness for ~~the creature~~ the ~~human~~ ⌊mortal⌋. "Long live poetry!", ~~that is~~ this ~~call~~

❖❖❖

c. From a binder of nested double sheets (C 14–28) and one later sheet (C 31). Excerpts and elaboration of the examples from Büchner. Reproduced in the sequence of the signatures.

707◂▸709 *11/708* *C 17/18,3* *Ms.*

Hostility to Art

p. 96, Lenz

12a p. 94: "At table Lenz was again in fine spirits; the talk was of literature, he was in his element. The era of ideal ... etc.—

Digression on art

•most unaffected

most natural

16-17 p. 95: At times one = I, Lenz this 'one' here has clearly an ~~I-acc~~ I-value wishes one were a Medusa's head, i.e. one—Lenz—wishes to ~~project in~~ step into the no-longer-human, although turned toward the human {as} in its • "most unaff{ec}ted;" that, and not what is said {to}about "art"carries the I-accent. And so, after this digression, it is stated, logically:

20b,d •p. 96: "he had completely forgotten himself"

Self-forgetting permits to treat art as a problem—/~~crea~~/ creates the distance that makes art into an object; art has at least a tendency toward I-distance. **22b,c** Poetry ~~carries the I toward the other; es~~ moves with the I toward the other and strange, brings it over , is, with it, the uncanny, ... and sublates itself Again with it.—

Art, that is the route poetry ~~has quickly to trav~~ has to cover.—

❖❖❖

709◂▸711 *12/710* *C 18,2* *Ms.*

Lucile

5 It is significant that Lucile, the one turned ~~most essentially~~ fatefully-mute toward him, ~~indeed the~~ dedicated ... and closest —not with words—, sees him speak, hears him too, but doesn't know what he says, when he speaks about art.—

6-8 It is the same Lucile, who in the end takes the only ~~still possi~~ possible step and who, with her 'long live the king' call does not pay homage to the monarchy and the Ancien Régime, but to the majesty of the absurd as witness for the creature—She, Lucile, takes the real step: her death is a freedeath /Freitod = suicide/; the others obey the bystanders of history (and have words for art—

❖❖❖

373◂▸69 *13* *C 25,1* *Ms.*

7b Lucile 'Vive': It is, at the supreme moment, the absurd {m}- and counter-meaning, it is an act of freedom.

❖❖❖

Ms. *C 28* *14* *692◄►7*

6c,5b Lucile: who despite the distance is so near to him (Camille), who thanks to ⌊through⌋ all distance is the one close to him, ~~and~~ listening to him, the listening /Zuhörende/ and belonging /Zugehörende/one: **7b** That is also why she takes the only free step: the step outside

•Congruence

8a the call 'Vive le Roi' in no way means ⌊is heard as⌋ a declaration of loyalty to some • Ancien Régime (or nouveau régime or monarchy) *444*

7b it means ~~the~~ an act of freedom: **8c** here homage is paid, in the face of two executioners, to the for you, ⌊~~dissonant~~:• absurd⌋ majesty of the absurd {,} as producer of the human,

✻•1606 Kepler: dreamed of a new star

❖❖❖

Ms. *C 31,4* *15* *718◄►419*

22d Poetry too hurries ⌊can⌋ ⌊hurry⌋ ahead of us

La Poésie, elle aussi, brûle nos étapes— *457*

❖❖❖

d. Earlier beginning of the speech, probably as pages -1- and -2- of Nr. 17 (C 36ff.), later replaced by Nr. 1 (C 34/35).

►17

Ts.(Ms.) [Dsl.] *F 2/3 [C 1]* *16* *[►91]*

✻ I am, and that is truly somewhat comforting, not the first who has to recognize how difficult it is for him to speak of poetry and poems: for poems distinguish themselves exactly because they try to speak for themselves, want to begin and end with themselves—each poem in its own, as imperfect as tyrannical, manner. Poems ~~want to~~ ⌊exclude⌋ everything, that is not themselves,[1]—the one who has written them they include [2]~~and keep him prisoner a long time;~~ *586* ⌊(**34a**)—he is added to them;⌋ they only open up ⌊—no, ~~they show~~ step before the eyes and become an event⌋ for the one who ~~knows~~ ⌊is ready,⌋ ~~to step~~ to stand in front of them as a You, alone as they are, excluding everything that does not completely belong to them. [3]~~Thus, at bottom, poems are just {once} there, when they meet someone; that happens only once and—each time—once more~~

✻ ⌊Whoever writes poems, is⌋ Only "for the length of the poem" we are ~~the~~ ⌊a⌋ true familiar /Mitwisser/ ~~of our~~ ⌊of one's⌋ own poems; if ~~we~~ ⌊he⌋ ~~were~~ was that for more than the length of *133, 484* its creation, then ~~our~~ ⌊his⌋ poem would lose the secret of that which meets us—we are, ~~that~~ also *44/472, 483,* as ~~its~~ ⌊their⌋ I, the first You of our poems—, it would, given that it wouldn't come toward us *508* anymore, it would be producible for us and thus all the time—and would thus no longer be a poem.—[4]As long as synthetic ⌊man⌋ does not yet exist—I have few insights into the already *302* obtained results in this field—, as long there is no synthetic poem either.

635 (I know, there do exist—probably collaborating—pioneers in that field.)

✻ No synthetic—one is tempted to say: no “art-poem.” ~~The~~ ⌊For the⌋ word “art” has been enriched, {by} in this context too, by a connotation, in which it threatens to go up or—perhaps ⌊one⌋ still can formulate it this way—go under completely and which it renders in fact taboo for the one who tries to preserve the word “poetry.” In Büchner already this word has the
376/530, 718 sound effect connotation of the noises and silences of the automatic—thus of the un-human and un-free, because un-souled—so difficult to describe in language. In any case I believe that there the human, even if not as ⌊the⌋ language-power /Sprachgewaltige/ is set against it, even if not as ⌊the⌋, then however as that which ⌊—with its word too⌋ shows the way toward the free.

602 ✻ With that I have ventured far away, respectively repeated ⌊rather awkwardly⌋ some things Günter Eich said here a year ago and ⌊vaguely ⌊enough⌋⌋ anticipated some things ~~perhaps~~ still to be said. I now must return to the poem and at the same time to a line—a line by Büchner—, with which for weeks, even months, as ⌊usually happens⌋ with lines of poetry, I've kept company against my will, a line that, like so much that is part of a poem, already just because of the irrefutability and imperiousness of its presence, knew how to become significant; it was—please ⌊,⌋ do not overlook{,} the infantile ⌊~~linearily single track~~ ⌊artlessness⌋⌋ of this statement—always there again when I thought of this place here and this present hour.

There are routes, relations and contexts for which, it seems to me, the criteria of the literary do not suffice; **42f** I took this route with that line—such a route did this line take with
357 me. This route describes a circle.

❖❖❖

Drafts of the 2nd Main Section (Paragraphs 25–36)

a. Largest draft of the middle section before the first redaction of the whole speech

			1◄►89
Dsl./Ts.(Ms.), pag. -3-, -4-, -5-	*C 36–39 [F 4]*	*17*	*[16◄►385/505]*

✻ Where ~~is~~ does the poem stand today, how does it relate to ~~the~~ its time, to the problems of
lyric poetry?—I do not know. *9, 543*
1 **25b** "... except sometimes it annoyed him that he could not walk on his head." That is the
often quoted line you know so well—: I believe that I may, that I must pick up the thread from
here. **30a** Again and again we write the 20th January, "our" 20th January.

30b We write under such dates, from such dates we write ourselves today—✻ perhaps
most clearly in the poem. Most clearly, that means, with all the clarity we owe—or believe we
owe, to what we have experienced both on the outside and on the inside and thus to what still
needs to be reckoned with under this or that figure. *25, 38, 40–47*
2 ✻ In the poem: that, I believe, does not mean—or no longer means—, [3]n'en déplaise à
Mallarmé, in one of those phonetically, semantically and syntactically over-differentiated
language structures assembled from "words" / "Worten" bzw. "Wörtern"/{;}. Not in the
poem that sees itself as "wordmusic"; not in any "mood poetry" woven from various *25, 38, 45, 53, 70*
"timbres"; ~~and neither~~ ⌊not⌋ in the poem as the result of word-creations, word-concretions,
word-destructions, word-games; not in any new "expressive art form"; nor in the poem as in a *53*
"second" reality that would heighten the real symbolically.—**33a-c** ~~But~~ ⌊Rather⌋ in the poem
as the poem of the one who knows that he speaks under the angle of inclination of his Being,
that the language of his poem is neither "analogy" nor language as such, but language
actualized, voiced and voiceless at the same time, set free under the sign of a radical
individuation that at the same time, however, remains mindful of the borders language draws
and of the possibilities language opens up for it. **d** The poem is one person's language-
become-shape, it has objectivity, presentness and presence; it stands into time. ✻ There is a
lyric *koine*. And there is the poem as singular, [4]breath-carried, heart- and sky-grey language in
time.

31a I speak, as [5]I am allowed to speak of poems, on my own behalf. **b** Whereby, and that,
it seems to me, seems to belong to the poem's hopes [6]since always, I perhaps also speak on
behalf of an alien,—who knows, perhaps even of a totally alien matter. **c** This "who knows" is *669*
the only thing resembling hope that I am able to add today and here to the old hopes.
d Perhaps ~~a correlation~~ ⌊an encounter⌋ of this "totally alien" with the plain "alien" ⌊and *282*
"other"⌋ is thinkable—**e** the poem tarries or rather tests the wind—a word related to the
creaturely—through such thoughts. Nobody can tell how long the ~~pause~~ breath pause—and
with it the testing—will last; ⌊the "swift", which has always been outside, has gained speed;⌋
the poem knows this; ~~with all its~~ it heads straight for an alien and a totally alien, that it considers
as ⌊reachable,⌋ vacant and turned ⌊let's say: like Lucile⌋ toward it, the poem. [7]**27** ~~Therefore~~
also, I believe, the ⌊so easy⌋ maligning of poetry ~~today for its~~ darkness and strangeness: this
comes no doubt from that ~~direction.~~ Perhaps I may ⌊here⌋, somewhat abruptly, but [8]perhaps
~~not without~~ justification, quote a line by Pascal that I recently read in Leo Shestov: "Ne nous

reprochez pas le manque de clarté puisque nous en faisons profession." This ~~is, if not the~~ congenital darkness, then however the ⌞"darkness⌟"⌟ ~~attributed to it~~ ⌞self-created for the sake of an encounter⌟ from ~~a~~ ⌞this⌟ ~~distance~~. In this direction the poem is surely en route, and ~~from this direction~~ it returns—as poem. **35a** The poem wants to head toward some other,
683 it needs this other; it ~~bespeaks itself to it~~ needs an opposite; it seeks it out; it bespeaks itself to it. **b** For the poem, each thing is a figure of this other toward which it is heading. **c** The attention the poem tries to pay to everything it encounters, its sharper sense of detail, outline and structure, or color, is not, I believe, the achievement of an eye competing with ever more precise instruments,—it is a form of concentration. **36a** The poem becomes the poem of someone who perceives~~, and is attentive~~ is turned toward phenomena, questioning and addressing these; ~~they are~~ ⌞~~it is~~⌟ ⌞it becomes, through so much that is no longer addressable,⌟ conversation. **b** And only in the space of this conversation does the addressed constitute itself, presence itself, gather itself ⌞around⌟ the I addressing and naming it. But the addressed which ⌞through naming⌟ has become a you, brings its otherness and alienness into the present; in the here and now of the poem—the poem itself has only this one, unique ⌞, momentary⌟ presence—, even in this immediacy and nearness it lets its own most essential aspect speak: its time. <new paragraph> **c** When we talk in this way with things, we are always also at the question of their where-from and where-to: a question that "stays open,"
56 "does not come to an end," and points toward the open, empty and free—we are far outside: ✻ each alien time is another time than our own; we are ⌞far outside, but⌟ in any case
119, 182, 520 nevertheless only at the edge of our own time; with us the perceived things are also there: they stand there where we stand at last: the things in the poem share something with such "last" things ⌞could be, one never knows, the "last" things⌟. ~~To each poem~~

~~The time of the poem Despite all the tension between the "singular" times, simultaneity {is} prevails in the poem.~~

❖❖❖

b. Precursory and accompanying drafts and notes for individual passages.

18 *C 33* *Ts.*

⌞12—~⌟

31a I speak, as I speak of poems, in matters concerning me. **b** Whereby I, and this seems to ~~me to have~~ always belonged to the truest, because most painful hopes of the poem, ~~speak perhaps~~ also in matters of the strange—of the strange, who knows, perhaps of ~~the strangest~~ matter. **c** This "who knows" is the only thing I myself am able to add ~~here today~~ in this context.

32a The poem shows, and that has, I believe, in no way to do with the—not to be underestimated—difficulties of word choice, the faster fall of syntax or the more lucid sense of ellipsis—, the poem shows, unmistakably, a strong tendency to fall silent. **b** It stands fast—⌞above⌟ some experiences and conceptions, the subjective limitations of which I ask you not to overlook—~~let me~~ ⌞I come to⌟ this extreme formulation come to—, the poem stands fast at the edge of itself. In its auto-sublation ⌞it⌟ sees its—perhaps only—chance; it calls and brings itself, in order to be able to exist, ceaselessly back from its already-no-longer into its always-still. ✻ In this in-between, in the moment of its becoming free and having been set free, in this state of floating and drifting ~~is seen~~ lies the ground of the poem—this, its own bottomlessness, the poem sets as its ground. **7b** The poem ⌊—born in distress—⌋ ~~thinks~~ ⌊understands⌋ itself as an act of freedom. <new paragraph> ~~The medium, in~~ It is a step. The medium, in which this step ~~is so happens~~ occurs, is language *24, 26, 27, 32/74*

❖❖❖

Ms. *F 37* *19* *220◄►601*

---

speaks

✻ ... across the alienated {H}human un-land to the—perhaps originally—most alien, perhaps turned toward him. *30, 31*

36b—the perhaps addressable, occupiable,—or just to be named—, by your naming raised to the state of a You (opposite)—

❖❖❖

Ms. *C 52b,2* *20/695* *694◄►4/696*

✻ Abyss: poetry—it has not, like Camille mocks ⌊—oh, art—⌋; it is consequence—~ : **26b** whoever thinks about walking on his head, knows that then he has the sky beneath him as abyss. *1, 4/696, 168*

↙

30 To wr.<ite> under such dates—

❖❖❖

10.10.60, Ts. *M 1,1* *21* *►186*

BR

10.10.

30b ... from such dates and moments we write ourselves, the poem writes itself. ✻ This cannot be read off calendars and horologes, (**7b**) the bystanders and old war-horses of history do not notice it, are not witnesses—are not present—only the victims of what the bystanders call history know something about it; and also, perhaps you yourself are in touch with it, when the hourglass tips over. *23, 24*

❖❖❖

c. Group of typescripts in separate double sheet C 53–59.

Ts. *C 56* *22* *25◄►24*

31a I speak, when I speak of poems, in matters concerning me. **b** Whereby I ~~also~~, and that has, it seems to me, since always belonged to the truest, because most painful hopes of the poem, perhaps also speak in matters of the strange—~~who knows~~ of the strange, who knows, perhaps in the strangest matter. **c** This "who knows" is the only thing resembling hope which in this context I am able to add here today. **e** I ~~test the~~ tarry ⌊—⌋ with the poem—for a time in the company of this thought. **f** Nobody can tell how long a "reprieve" the "swift," "swifter" by some degree of uncanniness, which even today is outside, will grant this thought.

❖❖❖

700◂▸25 *23* *C 53* *Ts.*

25b "... except sometimes it annoyed him that he could not walk on his head."

30b I believe that I may pick up from here: from such dates and moments we write ourselves, the poem writes itself. ✻ These dates and moments, they cannot be read off the
21, 24 calendars and clocks, (**7b**) the "old war-horses and bystanders of history" miss them; only the victims of what appears from the perspective of that ~~history~~ "bystander" as history, know something about it; and you too—you yourself—are at times in touch with it, when you tip over the hourglass. The poem: again and again it writes its "20th January."

31a I speak, as I am permitted to speak of the poem, in matters concerning me; **b** whereby I, and that, it seems to me, has belonged since always to the most true, because most painful, hopes of the poem, speak ~~also in~~ perhaps also the strange—of the strange, who knows, perhaps ~~eve~~ of the strangest matter. **c** This "you know" is the only ~~thing resembling hope~~ thing resembling hope which I, in this context, can add on my own here and today. **31e** I test the air—in all the ⌊conscious⌋ creatureliness added to this word ⌊with me⌋ by that name in whose proximity you permit me to stand—with this thought. **f** Nobody can tell how long a reprieve the "swift, that ⌊(⌊today too⌋)⌋ is outside, will grant this thought.

❖❖❖

22◂▸468 *24* *C 57/58* *Ts.(Ms.)*

25b "... except sometimes it annoyed him that he could not walk on his head."

30b I believe that I may pick up from here: from such dates and moments we write ourselves, the poem writes itself. ✻ These dates and moments, they are not readable (cannot
21, 23, 457 be read) off calendars and horologes, (**7b**) the "old war-horses and bystanders of history" have ⌊blinkers,⌋ no eyes for it; only the victims of what, under <the> perspective of those bystanders, appears as history, know something about it; and you too, you yourself are at times in touch with it, when you tip over the hourglass. ⌊The poem:⌋ {A} ⌊a⌋gain and again ~~we~~ ⌊it⌋ write⌊s⌋ the "20th January."

31a I speak, as I speak of the poem, in matters concerning me; **b** whereby I, and that has, it seems to me, since always belonged to the hopes of the poem, perhaps also speak in matters of the strange—of the strange, who knows, perhaps of the strangest matter. **c** This "who knows" <new attempt> is the only thing resembling hope which I can add on my own today too, here too. **e** I test the wind ⌊—with all the creatureliness ~~added~~ ⌊to be added⌋ by Büchner to this word—⌋ with this thought. **f** Nobody can tell, ~~how long the~~ ⌊what reprieve⌋ the "swift, that ⌊today too⌋ is outside," will grant this or similar thoughts. ✻ The poem ⌊~~—not only the~~
616 ~~Geiger counters—~~⌋ ~~knows~~ ⌊thinks⌋ at all times that ~~it—that~~ we {—} ⌊perhaps⌋ already ⌊tomorrow⌋
30, 31, 33/111 ⌊will come to⌋ lie beneath ⌊the⌋ ruin{s} of the scales, on which we could have been weighed{.}; {M}may they be, so ~~the hope~~ ⌊to such a hope it rises⌋, the ruins of a scale!

✻ What I am trying to say here bypasses much that should be ~~weighed scale~~ weighed and pondered: it only wants to hold on to the direction of the just named hope **32a** ~~Hence~~ The poem shows, and this has, ~~in no way~~ I believe, in no way to do with the—not to be underestimated—difficulties of word choice, ⌊and image-choice⌋ ~~and with the manifesting itself also in the German poem~~ ⌊, the faster fall ⌊language-fall⌋ of syntax today{,} or the more lucid⌋ sense for ellipsis, but with ~~the language~~ the poem as manifestation of language—, the poem shows an unmistakable tendency to fall silent. **b** The poem stands fast—⌊some⌋ experience and conception, whose subjective limitations I ask not to be overlooked, {tempt} me / lead me/ to this extreme {A} formulation—, the poem stands fast at the edge of itself. In its auto-sublation ⌊it⌋ sees its—perhaps only—chance; it calls and brings itself, in order to be able to exist, ceaselessly back from its already-no-longer into its always-still. ✻ In this in-between, *18, 26, 27, 32/74*
in the moment of its becoming free and being set free, in this drifting lies the ground of the poem—the poem sets this ⌊its own⌋ groundlessness as its ground. **26b** He who also thinks of walking on his head knows that then he has the sky beneath him as abyss.

✻ This opposition is, I believe, even if nourished by innumerable ⌊different⌋ near and ~~distant sources~~, ~~even though infintely~~ ⌊somewhat⌋ the only ~~variable "theme"~~ of the poem *516*

✻ ~~This opposition is, I believe,~~
With this opposition, I believe, the ground situation of the poem is: ~~given—allegorically—given: finite and infinite, fatefully the first, the human,~~
given.

❖❖❖

Ts., C 55 pag. -2- *C 54/55* 25 *23◄►22*

25b "... except sometimes it annoyed him that he could not walk on his head."

Permit me to pick up from here.

30a We write, in a falling-, ⌊yes nearly⌋ fallen-silent and speech-less way, i.e. with all the due clarity experienced from inside and outside and therefore in this or that shape ⌊perhaps⌋ still to be reckoned with, again and again the ⌊"Lenz"ian⌋ 20th January, <u>this</u> 20th January. *17, 38, 40–47*

b Under such dates we write, from such dates we ⌊contemporaries⌋ write ourselves ✻—most clearly⌊,—and that doesn't always mean: most eye catchingly—⌋no doubt in the poem.

In the poem: not in this or that structure assembled ⌊from⌋ "word material," responding *17, 38, 45, 53, 70*
phonetically and semantically ⌊and syntactically⌋ to itself and its ⌊"⌋world⌊"⌋ ⌊and its "things," *38, 40–47*
for which this name seems to offer itself; **33b** but in the poem as under ~~this and no other~~ the unique angle of inclination of a language actualized through Being. ⌊In the actuality of this language there is an act⌋

With the poem, then, with language set free under the sign of an individuation as intransigent as it is conscious of its limits and its possibilities, ✻ with the poem that remains most painfully mindful of all the experiences and convulsions of its language we write ourselves *39/342, 40–47*
toward a necessary, an inalienable reality. By the word-shape—what else could it be? By it we are recognizable—, open on all sides, world- and time-permeable, we venture, and that is, given all the exaltation that at times informs us, at times unpleasant—and at times also truly uncanny—, ~~we venture~~ into the ⌊perhaps⌋ word- and answerless.

40, 43 ✻ That is the route—more exactly: that is what most deeply gives direction and meaning. It
is the color of what is ascribed and prescribed to ~~ourselves~~ us; even there where we ⌜ourselves,⌝
47 precipitate it out of language with begging heart, it bears the stamp of that which befalls us—
from afar. **2** The light that rules above all of this, is ⌜often⌝—if I may use a word by Moritz
742 Heimann, meant for "Danton," ⌜(**4b**)—someone ⌜represented and⌝ to be understood—from
his death⌝—"livid light before the storm." ✻ ⌜It must have penetrated deeply into the poem's
55 darkness if it is to ~~illuminate.~~ light up and illuminate.⌝

✻ ~~The~~ ⌜Thus⌝ is the route, that we travel with the poem. The route the poem travels with us. Certainly much accretes along the way—no, had already accreted before ~~we~~ this ⌜—voiced-voiceless—⌝ route began. We are lonely—we are not alone. We are those who have come, come into the world and into language—we remain for a time. There is much to be done; much speaks, in a manner peculiar to it, to us; we don't get through there all that easily; we don't free ourselves ~~there~~ ⌜here⌝ all that easily.

The point is such a freeing; the point is, anticipating on the far ⌜or the near⌝, this moment, this situation, this face-to-face; the point is, **26b** he who walks on his head has the sky beneath him as an abyss.

291, 715 [Poems pull a hippocratic face]

❖❖❖

d. Further preliminary drafts

402◂▸242 *26* *C 5,2* *Ts.*

32a The poem shows, and that, I believe, is connected not to speechlessness, but in the highest
sense to language itself, an unmistakable tendency to fall silent; **b** it maintains itself—experience
and reflection ~~cause~~ ⌜lead⌝ me to this extreme formulation—at the edge of itself. In its
auto-sublation it sees its—perhaps only—chance; it calls and brings itself, in order to exist, from
18, 24, 27, its ⌜Already-⌝{N}no-longer into its Always-Still. ✻ In this in-between, the space of its becoming
32/74; 27, 239 free, its being set free and floating free, in statu nascendi thus and simultaneously also in statu
moriendi, lies the ground of the poem. This groundlessness the poem takes as its ground (sets as
its ground). **26b** But he who walks on his head, has the sky below him as an abyss

❖❖❖

448◂▸445 *27* *F 23* *7.10.60, Ms.*

7.X.

⌜**30,25** .... 20th January: on his head ....:⌝

601 **32a** the poem shows—not a tendency to speechlessness, but to fall silent; **b** it maintains
itself—the situation of the poem compels ⌜experience and reflection compel m⌝ me to
this ~~not to be understood as rhetorical,~~ ⌜extreme⌝ formulation—at the edge of itself. In
893 its auto-sublation it catches ⌜sees⌝ its chance; it ⌜calls and⌝ brings itself ⌜sometimes⌝,

as it ⌊does⌋ still exist, ⌊in order to exist,⌋ from its already-no-longer ×/• into an always-still.—

✻ By this movement, by these vibrations that can in no way be measured with instruments, it can be recognized—⌊Cilia, ciliary movements—⌋

✻ ×/ In this in-between: of floating free—• statu moriendi—is the ground of the poem: the *18, 24, 26, 32/74,*
poem takes its groundlessness as ground. **26b** He who walks on his head, has the sky ××/ beneath *257; 30*
him— *132, 704, 711*

✻ ××/ the sky—those are les espaces infinis—// If it is true that, that ~~the~~ ⌊also from the⌋ sky ~~it~~ there is yearning for mankind, then that ~~may~~ ⌊can⌋ indeed be welcome for him.—

✻ To fall silent: as clear ⌊unmistakable⌋, as ... *132*
Sounding of language amidst the information system— *249; 602*

✻ • More solidly than ever the poem remains tied to its here and now.

• Movement: by this ciliary ⌊sense-⌋ movement, which is able to communicate itself to us not *212, 344*
through this or that instrument, but directly through our thought and Being, we recognize the poem: We are the medium in which ⌊it happens⌋..

❖❖❖

from 7.10.60, Ms. *F 24,3* *28* *446◄►182*

×××

✻ ... in this groundlessness lies—archaically enough—the ground {a} and the principle of the poem—

❖❖❖

Ms. *F 104* *29* *376/530◄►343*

BR

35d Attention, as quoted by W<alter> Benj<amin>—is, according to Malebr<anche>, the natural prayer of the soul; ✻ we have to add: the attention experienced in a matter of seconds—and thus, ~~as~~ exactly because of its short duration, felt as bliss—in the face of darkness =

❖❖❖

5.10.60, Ms., F 41 pag. -2- *F 40–42* *30* *553◄*

B-R
5.X.60

25b "... except sometimes it annoyed him that he could not walk on his head."
30a I believe that I may pick up the thread from here: we write, each according to his own ⌊and given⌋ way, ~~always still~~ again and again the 20th January. **b** We write ourselves from such dates, we write ourselves toward such dates; the poem does the same.

31a I speak, as I speak of the poem, in matters concerning me. **b** Whereby I, and this seems to me to have always belonged to the hopes ⌞—arising at some distance from its origins—⌟ of the poem, speak perhaps also in matters of the strange—of the strange, who knows, if not in the strangest matter. **c** This "who knows" is the only hope-like thing I am able to add here and now to the previously ~~surmised supposed~~ ⌞mentioned⌟ hopes. **31e** + I test the wind—in Georg Büchner's vicinity I dare to appropriate this word, ⌞used by hunters⌟, thus by those who bring death,⌞⌟ related to the creaturely, for myself—, I tarry and test the wind with this thought. **f** Nobody can tell how long this ~~pausing~~ pause ⌞—for that is what it is, despite all—⌟—and with it the thought, ~~it awakens~~ ⌞that belongs to it⌟ ⌞that it makes possible⌟—will last. ~~The "swift outside" knows how to infest the poem~~ ✲ The poem is in a hurry; it ~~keeps~~ ⌞must⌟, ~~to~~ ⌞when it⌟ it ⌞~~will~~ try should in the strangest matter as in matters most concerning it ⌞~~to~~⌟ speak ~~know how to,~~ hurry through ~~all~~ the human un-land ~~Est~~ estranged ⌞all over⌟; **31f** it has to ⌞head straight⌟ for
19, 31 ~~a~~ ⌞~~the~~ that⌟ strangest matter, ~~the poem for The poem for the longest time is no longer there where we were in the habit of finding it; it presupposes much~~ which it ~~for itself~~—always still—⌟ thinks (not: imagines) as accessible, occupiable, at least nameable. ✲ The poem, despite the restraint that characterizes it, is in a hurry{:},—like all of us, when we are ⌞~~by ourselves~~ truly⌟
24, 31, 33/111 alone: ~~we know~~ ⌞the presentiment,⌟ that we already ⌞now could⌟ lie beneath the ruins of the scales, on which we could have been weighed{.}⌟, is shared by many of us. And⌟ the thought, that we will come to lie at least under ~~this~~ these ruin{s}—and not far outside {—} {in} into the free {—}and uncanniest—, is the farthest, that ~~we still~~ ⌞the poem in human terms⌟ ⌞still⌟ dare{s} to think. ⌞I admit:⌟ {O}one of the routes ~~the poem~~ ⌞it⌟ takes, leads ~~probably also~~ ⌞doubtlessly⌟ thither.

27, 123, 151 ✲ One of the routes: others ~~lead~~, arising from the bottomless, lead{ing} back into the bottomless; the abyss is their homeland; their language is their being under way; nothing more.

◄475

[134◄►663] 31 F 43/44 [F 88] 4.10.60, Dsl./Ts.[Ts.(Ms.)]

B-R

4 October 60.

25b "... except sometimes it annoyed him that he could not walk on his head."

I believe that I may pick up the thread from here.

⌞**30a** 20th January → Poems—⌟ **31a** I speak, as ~~I do in fact write poems,~~ ⌞speak of the poem,⌟ in matters of my own; **b** whereby I, and that seems to me to belong from always to the hopes of the poem, to speak ~~also perhaps I suppose~~ also in matters of the strange—in matters of the strange,
407, 534 who knows, perhaps of the strangest matter. **c** This "who knows" is the only hope-like thing, which I ⌞on my own⌟ can add to the previously mentioned hopes here ⌞and now⌟; **e** I test the wind ~~with this thought~~ <new attempt>—I choose, ~~the~~ in Büchner's nearness this word to be related to the creature—with this thought. **f** Nobody can tell, how long the breath pause—and with it the thought that belongs to it—will last. ~~The poem is in a hurry~~ There is something
683 "swift" in the ⌞The "swift outside" is also in the po⌟ poem: it heads, in order to be able to speak in this matter as in its most own, toward a most strange; ✲ it hurries through{,} the estranged, ⌞everything that estranges itself from us,⌟ which separates it from that unknown; ⌞through all
19, 30, 863 that densely settled human un-land⌟ something uncommonly ~~impatient~~ ⌞~~Impatiently~~ restless⌟— not: impetuous—is ⌞, despite all restraint,⌟ with the poem, as with us all: we lie beneath the
24, 30, 33/111 ruins of the scales, on which we could have been weighed.

It is ~~not~~ no longer a matter of ⌊aesthetic⌋ economy, it is a matter of the most essential: it is a matter of direction.—⌊Here direction is doubtlessly one of the carriers of meaning—⌋

31f Therefore: from this heading-toward-the-strangest, which thinks itself as vacant ⌊and accessible, thus ⌊based on this claim⌋ occupiable, there also comes, I think, the estranging and *321, 500, 817* darkness of the poem. ×/ **27** Here now also, abruptly, ⌊dictated by the soul⌋ ~~thus in some measure~~ ⌊~~perhaps dictated by the soul not without its own~~ and thus perhaps in some mea<sure>⌋ justified, a word by Pascal can come to stand, which I, raising the abruptness, quote following Leo Shestov: Ne nous reprochez pas le manque de clarté puisque nous en faisons profession. This is, if not a congenital, then however a darkness born to the poem from a distance ⌊the strange⌋.

✻ ×/ which is in no way linked to a representation of a relation beyond the personal— *33/111*

❖❖❖

Ts.(Ms.) *C 7,4* *32/74* *559◂▸81*

✻ Seen from the point of view of the poem, practice nearly always means exercitium and asceticism.—There are psychograms. And there is ~~the~~ ⌊the poem as⌋ gift{.} ⌊for the ensouled one⌋ *553*
There is, in the small ⌊•narrow⌋ space ⌊~~and the bare second~~⌋, where poetry happens, a-becoming-free, not only of language, but also of the one who speaks ⌊—through that which *18, 24, 26, 27,* speaks itself toward him.⌋ Poetry ⌊, thus what connects ultimately,⌋ is an act of freedom; to this *239, 259* freedom belongs, if not ⌊however⌋ ~~grace~~ ⌊rarely⌋ always grace, then however certainly goodwill.
✻ (An impossible word ⌊today—but not here!—⌋, I know, ⌊think of it this way: as Tyche⌋ → *482* but where are we, when we speak of poems, if not with the impossible coming into language)
Poems are not first of all written records, ⌊do not begin with being written down⌋; they are gifts to the attentive. **35d** Attention is, here I quote a word by Malebranche—I quote it following Walter Benjamin's Kafka essay first published in the Jüdische R—<und>schau—, attention, that is the natural prayer of the soul.

42b,e •narrowing // ⌊Mercier's word, broadened by cybernetics:⌋ Elargiss{ons}ez l'art— *451, 536/712; 9*

❖❖❖

e. Single drafts from adjacent groups of inserted double sheets. F 93 is linked with F 102, F 56,4/57,1 with F 65,2 and F 69,1.

Ms. *F 102,1* *33/111* *172◂▸112*

✻ •... speaks in the strangest matters. Danton (who finds ~~into~~ death by his own grace) projects brotherliness into irreality: "~~Thou~~ You cannot prevent that in the basket" = You see, it is a borrowed ⌊quotation⌋ and a mortal word exiled into infinity: the poetics ~~are~~ ⌊,that is the place⌋ *84* ~~that are~~ the ⌊in the darkness⌋ scattering quotation marks.—

✻ •The strangeness ⌊the darkness,⌋ of poetry comes ~~out~~ from this: from the direction, in which it ~~moves.~~—the estranged around it •hurrying through, directed toward what's strangest.×/

✲ •hurrying through—something impatient,—not: impetuous—inheres ⌊probably⌋ in all of
24, 30, 31 us—: we do lie beneath the ruins of the scales on which we are weighed.—

27 ×/ Here now, in this context, i.e. abruptly, can stand a word by Pascal, which I, even more abruptly, quote following Shestov: ne nous reprochez pas le manque de clarté ... This is, if not the congenital, then however the darkness born to the poem. It has nothing to do with
60/582 obscurantists, even academic ones.—•

31 ✲ • whereby I do not believe I have to mean ~~a~~ the fabrication of a suprapersonal relation.—
×

❖❖❖

656◂▸571 *34/493* *F 93* *Ms.*

31a I speak, ~~as I~~ given that I write poems, in my own and most own matters. **b** Whereby I, and that seems to me to belong to the last ⌊, because oldest⌋ ~~and still to be defended~~ hopes of the poem, ⌊also⌋ hope to promise in matters of the strange. ✲ In the strangest matters: in You-distance. At the perihelion of poetry.—The poem has, ~~I am afraid~~, entered the phase of total You-Darkness: it speaks in the strangest matters!—

I speak now in the first now in the second person; by naming now the one now the other, I mean the same.—~~The possib~~ In the You-Darkness too the possibility of the self-encounter ×/remains
82 possible
I have to prove this—I quote (Büchner): "..."

×/mystic motive

❖❖❖

498◂▸408 *35* *F 69,1* *Ms.*

30a The 20th of January = in this finitude: the tension—⌊toward⌋ the infinite—**24d** the street in
51 Moscow, on which

❖❖❖

324◂▸326 *36/325* *F 65,2* *Ms.*

(**34a**) -i- The poet is added to the poem as person—

❖❖❖

404◂▸625 *37* *F 56,4/57,1* *Ms.*

31a I speak, as I speak of poems ⌊—and that ⌊this speaking⌋ is connected to the writing of poems⌋, in matters of my own. **b** Two years ago I believed exactly in this way also to speak in matters of the strange—my experiences ⌊since then⌋ let me intensify the strange: I hope to speak in the strangest matters. ✲ The strangest, as the unknown, is the plainly friendly; and in the poem also becomes the nearest, abruptest, by stepping into the strangest, to the very closest. Solve et coagula.

❖❖❖

f. Group of drafts F 124–133, that all start from the quote "except sometimes it annoyed him ...", reproduced in the sequence of the signatures.

Ts. *F 124* *38* 657◄

B

25b "... except sometimes it annoyed him that he could not walk on his head."
Allow me to pick up the thread from here.
30a We write, ~~still always~~ with all that was experienced from the outside and the inside and thus in this or that shape the owed clarity ~~yet~~ to be expected, again and again the 20th January, our 20th January. *17, 25, 40–47*
b We write under such dates, we write ourselves from such dates, ✻ most clearly—and that ~~also~~ means ⌊at times⌋: most reticently ⌊,because most deeply moved⌋—probably in the poem.
✻ In the poem: not in this or that structure of a language artfully assembled from "word material," and which understands itself as "expression" or "communication," thus as a responding to itself and to the ⌊phonetic-semantic⌋ standing opposite it; **33b-c** but in the poem as the ⌊, world-creating language ⌊language that says itself to the ⌊questioning⌋ individual—⌋ actualizing itself ~~again and~~ again under the ~~angle of inclination~~ unique angle of inclination of a Being. *17, 25, 45, 53, 70* *25, 40–47*

Ms. *F 125* *39/342*

25b Except sometimes

30a We write—~~our~~ ⌊the⌋ poem writes—always still the 20th January, <u>this</u> 20th January. **b** It writes itself from such dates—✻ ~~it~~ writes ⌊itself⌋ toward the horizons that become visible from there: it writes itself toward ~~the necessary~~ certainly not the imaginary, it writes itself toward the ~~necessary~~ ⌊needed⌋ and inalienable ⌊real⌋; it is on the way there; from that direction its meaning opens up for it—opens up for us. *25, 40–47*

Ts. *F 126,1* *40*

B

25b "... except sometimes it annoyed him that he could not walk on his head."
Permit me to pick up from here.

30a We write, in a reserved, ⌊speechless⌋ falling- and fallen-silent way, that is with all the experienced, experienceable and yet to be experienced ~~shocks~~ ⌊⌊the from outside

17, 25, 38, 43, ~~the~~ experienced and thus in this or that shape the owed clarity ~~to~~ yet to be expected⌋, ~~always still~~
45, 46, 47 ⌊again and again⌋ the 20th January, <u>this</u> 20th January.
b We write ourselves from it and from other dates of this kind, we write ourselves, with the
poem—⁂ whereby in this context something else is to be understood than those more or less
25, 38, 43, 46, unconcerned language structures sent to meet the phonetic or semantic responding, resp. "ready-
47; 530/376 to-receive" in this or that way, for which this name seems to offer itself—, with the <u>poem</u>
therefore, the poem remaining most painfully mindful of all the experiences and shocks we write
25, 39/342, 43, ourselves toward a necessary, inalienable reality—: in word-shape—what else could it be?—,
46, 47 open on all sides, we venture, and that is at times unpleasant, into the word- and answerless.
⁂ That is {a}the route, more exactly: that is what most deeply gives direction and
25, 43 meaning. Much, certainly, accretes along the way—no, had already accreted even before
we got under way. We are lonely—we are not alone. We are those who have come—we
remain that for a while. There is much to be done; ~~we do not escape~~ so easily{.} ⌊we are not set
free.—⌋

41 *F 126,2* *Ms.*

---

336 The poem: the voice

▸291 *42* *F 126,3* *Ms.*

---

336 Form—problems of style: co-extensive, not co-substantial with the poem—

❖❖❖

291◂ *43* *F 128,1* *Ts.*

25b "... except sometimes it annoyed him that he could not walk on his head."
30a We write, in a reserved ⌊, falling and having fallen silent way⌋ i.e. with all the experienced,
experienceable and still to be experienced shocks of owed clarity, always still the 20th January, <u>this</u>
20th January. **b** We write ourselves from it, we write ourselves, with the poem—⁂ whereby in this
context something else ~~must be~~ ⌊is to be⌋ understood than those more or less unconcerned
25, 38, 40, 46, 47 language structures sent to meet the ⌊in this or that⌋ sound- and meaning-ways responding, for
which this name offers itself ⌊habitually⌋—, we write ourselves with the poem remaining ~~mindful~~
25, 39/342, 40, 46, 47 most painfully mindful of such experiences toward a necessary, an inalienable reality—: in word-
shape, ⌊—what else could it be?—,⌋ open to all sides, we venture, (**26b**) ~~walking on our heads,~~
⌊and that is sometimes annoying,⌋ into the ~~wordless.~~ word- and answerless.

25, 40; 343 ⁂ That is the route, more exactly: that is what ⌊most deeply⌋ gives direction and meaning. Much
accretes along the way{.}—no, has ⌊had⌋ already accreted, even before we, having reached word-
nearness, got under way. We are lonely—we are not alone. We are those who have come—we
remain that{,} for awhile. There is much to be done{.}; we do not escape so easily.

Ms. *F 128,2* *44/472*

✻ Not this or that message addressing that other's "erogenous{"} zone"—should one not say here "message ⌊messägsch⌋" = (**35b**) but what stands ~~tow~~ opposite the shape-like shape of the other; (**34b**) it is an encounter, accompanied by the secret of friendship and love.

Ts. *F 129* *45* *►302*

B

25b "... except sometimes it annoyed him that he could not walk on his head."
Permit me to pick up the thread from here.
30a We write, with all the owed clarity that has been experienced from inside and outside, that
has to be presenced in this or that shape, again and again the 20th January, our ⌊in each case⌋ 20th *17, 25, 38, 40,*
January. *43, 46, 47*
b Under such dates we write, from such dates we write ourselves, ✻ most clearly—and that means
at times: most speechlessly, because most affected—no doubt in the poem.
In the poem : not in this or that—from "word-material" artfully and self-righteously constructed *17, 25, 38, 53, 70*
structure of a ~~language~~ ⌊—come what may—⌋ expression- and communication-friendly
⌊denotation-friendly⌋ language

❖❖❖

Ts. *F 132* *46* *515◄*

B

25b "... except sometimes it annoyed him that he could not walk on his head."
30a We write, reservedly, i.e. with all the experienced ⌊~~and~~ experienceable and still to be
experienced⌋ shocks owed clarity, always still the 20th January, <u>this</u> 20th January{.}; **b** we write
ourselves from it, write ourselves with the poem—✻ whereby in this context those ~~homely, thus-~~
~~domestic, stanza- and rhyme-friendly language structures cannot be meant~~ language structures that *25, 38, 40, 43, 47*
unconcernedly reflect consonance and harmony cannot be meant
✻—whereby in this context something else has certainly to be understood than the ⌊more or
less⌋ structure unconcernedly turned toward the rhyme, to which one habitually gives this *25, 39/342, 40,*
name—, we write ourselves with the poem toward a necessary, an inalienable reality *43, 47*

Ts. *F 133* *47* *►367*

25b "... except sometimes it annoyed him that he could not walk on his head."
30a We write ⌊, reservedly, i.e. with all clarity,⌋ always still the 20th January, <u>this</u> 20th January; *17, 25, 38, 40,*
b we write ourselves from it, we write ourselves, with the poem—✻ whereby a ⌊particular *43, 45, 46*
"typogenic"⌋ language structure dictated only by stanza- and rhyme-constraints is in no ways to
be understood—, toward an ~~inalienable real~~ a necessary, an inalienable real, each in his— *25, 39/342, 40, 43, 46*

do I need to add? mortal—way.

25, 258 ✻ We write: we speak, hewn from the

❖❖❖

g. Earlier exploratory work for single sections of the middle part. B21 is probably the first sketch for a Büchner-speech upon reception of the news of the impending prize presentation.

214◄

=770 *48* *workbook II, 15 [8]* *from 19.8.60, Ms.*

25b "except sometimes it ..."

≡I believe, I may pick up from here

❖❖❖

672◄►753 *49* *B 38* *Ms.*

---

30 We write always still _, today too,_ the 20th January, this 20th January, to which, _since then_ so much iciness /Eisiges/ has added itself.
✻ We are, thanks to the poet G. Büchner, with the poet Reinh. Lenz, in the mountains; we are with the poem.

Büchner-speech

❖❖❖

362◄►49 *50* *B 35* *Ms.*

Büchner—
35d Permit me to clothe my thanks _in a _borrowed_ word_ to become a word in a borrowed word; a ~~word~~—I think, "close to Büchner," that I find in the essay by W.<alter> B<enjamin> first published in the Jüdische Rundschau from ... **38.** It is a word by Malebranche. It says: 'Attention, that is ...

❖❖❖

511◄►920 *51* *B 21* *21.5.60, Ms.*

21.V.60. Büchner-speech

Dear friends of the poem

Beginning:

134, 409, 704, **25b** "Except sometimes it annoyed him ...
805 **30a** We write _still always, we write today too_ the 20th January. ✻ Let's look around—we are in
406, 737 (walk through) the mountains—we walk through the poem—×/

(24d) ×/ some day⌊, when we are only the written,⌋ we, like Lenz, will be picked up on the
street—it does not have to be a Moscow street. *35, 360, 736*

End: **(53)** I thank you for your attention, on both counts—

35d Attention, that is—I quote a word by Malebranche, I quote it according to the Kafka *84*
essay by Walter Benjamin first published in the Jüdische Rundschau of ... publ.—, "Atte-<ntio>n that is the natural pray-<er> of the soul—

❖❖❖

h. From the exploratory work for the radio-essay on Osip Mandelstam

Ms.	*ÜR 6.12,23a [5]*	52

(27) The <u>darkness: "congenital" (Pascal)</u> || *121, 136, 153, 825*

❖❖❖

Ts (Ms.) pag. -2-	*ÜR 6.12,13r [Auszug]*	53

1. Speaker: ✻ The twenty poems from the volume "The Stone" disconcert. *194, 486*
They are not "word-music," not "mood poetry," ⌊~~in assonance and~~ ⌊indulging in *17, 25, 38, 45, 70*
~~on~~ "tone colors"⌋ no ~~symbolically overextended sensuous~~ ⌊overextending of the real⌋ ⌊impressionistic⌋⌊, tone color solicitous⌋ symbolically transfigured, ⌊no⌋ higher or deeper ⌊"second"⌋ reality emblematically ciphered; they are free of neologisms, word-concretions, word-destructions, they are not a new "expressive art"{.} ⌊(as it arises ~~back then~~ ⌊at that time also⌋ in ~~Rus~~ Russian Futurism)⌋
⌊Symbol and⌋ image ⌊is not metaphor, it⌋ has phenomenal character.
33a-c The poem in this case is the poem of the one who knows that he is *354, 501, 556*
speaking under the angle of inclination of his existence, that the language of his
poem is neither "analogy" nor ~~"a more originary" language or even~~ just plain *68/384*
language, but <u>actualized</u> language, voiceful and voiceless at the same time, set free under the sign of an indeed radical individuation remaining mindful of ~~its~~ limits, but ⌊At the same time remaining mindful of the limits imposed on it by language and the possibilities language has opened up for this individuation⌋.
(50c) The place of the poem remains a human place, "a place in the cosmos," *488*
certainly, but here, down here, in time; the poem, with all its horizons, remains a sublunar, a terrestrial, a creaturely phenomenon. **33d** It is one person's language become form, it has objectivity \Gegenständlichkeit\, oppositeness \Gegen<u>ständig</u>keit\, substance \Gegen<u>wärtig</u>keit\, and presence. It stands into time.

❖❖❖

54 *ÜR 6.12,8 [1]* *Ms.*

M.:

(**32**) the fall \Gefälle\ of language ⌊language-fall⌋ becomes faster, the figure is the hyperbole ⌊the tone abrupt⌋ ⌊the ~~declarative sentences line up~~⌋

55 *ÜR 6.12,8 [2]* *Ms.*

Beginning:
✻ language is, ⌊at least in its intention on,⌋ no longer word-music, **33a-c** the poem is the poem
340, 422 of the one who ~~un~~ knows that he speaks under the angle of inclination of his existence, that the
language of his poem is not plain language, but language that is ⌊set {setting itself} free and is⌋
25, 259 language actualizing itself, ⌊| voicefull | and voiceless | at the same time⌋ ~~the result of a radical indi that this language only~~ ⌊but under the sign of an as modest as⌋ as radical individuation ~~becomes poem~~. ⌊Is a language that sets free and actualizes itself.⌋
The place where this comes about is a human place—"a place in the cosmos," certainly, but here, on earth, in time.×/
(**50c**) ×/ The poem: a ~~phenom~~ ⌊~~cre~~⌋ terrestrial, a creaturely phenomenon, ⌊it stands into time, a
61/103; 305, 870 porous thing, open to time, by men and spoken by a human mouth in their direction, ⌊bodily and ~~un~~ bodyless at the same time,⌋ discoverable~~—not always~~ discovered when?⌋
728 ✻ ~~The metaphoric o~~ The symbolic and the metaphoric recede, ~~the Here~~ poetry ~~dispenses with~~ is an earthly, terrestrial phenomenon, the hieratic begins to yield to the demotic, the poem opens up to time.

❖❖❖

56 *ÜR 6.12,11* *Ms., pag. -3-*

36a-b The poems of Osip Mandelstam ⌊are the poems of someone who perceives⌋ ~~of someone~~ ⌊attentively⌋ turned toward what appears, ⌊~~of someone~~⌋ questioning and addressing what appears; they are conversation. In this conversation ~~this~~ what is addressed constitutes itself, ~~gathers~~
306, 341, 486 ~~itself around the addressing I, takes on form by gathering around the addressing I.~~ Gathers around the ~~speaking~~
508 addressing ~~I~~ and thus naming I. But into this present, ~~(the present of the poem—, the named brings~~ into this Here and Now of the poem what has been addressed and by naming become a You brings ~~its other its most own~~ its otherness and strangeness along; ⌊yet⌋ in the immediacy and nearness of the poem it lets its distance have its say too. It guards what is it most own: its time.
17 ✻ It is this tension between the times, one's own and the foreign, which lends that pained-mute vibrato to the Mandelstam poem by which we recognize it. ×/ (This vibrato is everywhere: in the
59 ⌊intervals ~~between the~~ ⌊between⌋ ⌊words ~~just as, betw~~ and the stanzas, in the "courtyards," where the rhymes ⌊and assonances⌋ stand, in the punctuation. All this has semantic relevance.) **36c** Things come together, ~~yet they remain incommensu~~ yet even in this togetherness resounds the question of their Wherefrom and Whereto—a "yet to be decided"question, | Pointing to the open and occupiable into the empty and the free, "| That does not come to an end" | ~~One to the one that by the poet—a mortal—, And~~

~~Therefore In the In this space~~
~~In {this space} space of such poems~~
✻ This question is not only made good in the “thematics” of the poems; it also takes shape—and that’s exactly why it becomes a “theme”—in the language of the poems. The word ⌞—the name—⌟ shows a tendency to the noun-form, ~~the adjective in the domain~~ the “infinite forms” <underline struck out>, the nominal forms of the verb dominate: ~~Time joins in, Time participates.~~ The poem remains open to time, time can join in, time participates. *59, 70, 94*

❖❖❖

Ms. *ÜR 6.12,3r [1]* *57/485*

—M—

(**36a-b**) Here the poem is the place where what is looked at and perceived through language—the named—enters in terms of its time into a relationship of tension with the one who looks and speaks. ✻ The strange remains strange, it does not “correspond” ⌞and respond⌟ completely, it retains its opacity ⌞which lends it relief and appearance (phenomenality)⌟

36b—to let the incommensurable of the other have its say:
the time that is the other’s own, ✻ the space that is his own, the nearness and distance in time and space, the unknown, from which {he} it comes toward you—like you toward ~~him~~ this other.—

❖❖❖

Ms. *ÜR 6.12,21 [3]* *58*

Death
✻ ⌞It is⌟ what is ~~looked at~~ ⌞perceived ⌞in its nakedness; the perceived⌟⌟ with its ~~unknown,~~ ⌞strange and⌟ **36c** ~~Where from~~ standing open, ⌞with its strange and⌟ ⌞with its⌟ “empty” ⌞and free⌟ Where-from and Where-to.
:—The sail—

❖❖❖

Ts. (Ms.), pag. -3- *ÜR 6.12,9 [excerpt]* *59*

~~are S~~ (**36a**) perceptions in language, conversation with the one standing opposite, standing in opposition, conversation with the other and the strange, conversation with humans and with things, conversation with what appears, at times also conversation ⌞, questioning conversation⌟ with oneself—in the midst of exactly that which appears to him.

2. Speaker: (**36b**) This appearing has, like the one who perceives it with his language, its ~~time~~ own time. ~~In the poem these—different—times clamp together It has both, nearness and distance, it comes toward one~~ Thus it comes toward one: even in its nearness its distance has its say, its own time has its say; ✻ in the poem these—different—times clamp together, the hour and the aeon speak, the heartbeat and the world clock. *824*

1. Speaker: ✻ They speak together, come together—they remain incommensurable. Because of this there comes to be in the poem that turbulence and tension by which we recognize: still always time joins in, participates. ⌞In such a⌟

~~2. Speaker: In such a~~ time-yard \Zeit h o f\ stand the poems of Osip Mandelstam. ~~Thus his—for which the critics~~ ⌞later⌟ ~~accused him of being “hostile to progress”—tendency toward substantives, toward those~~ Thus even in the ~~stu~~ substantival *104, 280, 518*

56, 70, 94; 59, arrays this word vibrato that has (also) semantic relevance. Thus even in the lapidary—and more
512; 196 than a few of these poems have the character of an inscription—the trembling of the mortal hand. Mandelstam's poem carries its hope with it into this "petrification," this hope for the—near or distant—eye.

❖❖❖

i. From and around binder A (August 1959).

114◂▸583 *60/582* *A 23/24* *Ms.*

Ladies and gentlemen,

31a I speak ⌞, as I do write poems,⌟ in matters of my own; **b** ~~permit me this addition: exactly because of that{,} I believe, and~~ indeed in more than one aspect, to speak in matters of the strange." ⌞whereby, and that is also connected to the writing of poems, I hope to speak ⌞at least⌟ in some pieces also in matters of the strange.⌟

✻ I speak ⌞of the poem, of the poem today. I do not speak of "modern lyric poetry"⌟ of the darkness of the poem. ×/ I say poem and understand with that ~~something~~, ⌞a language structure,⌟ that is enlisted by poetry \Dichtung\ as well as by the lyric poem \Lyrik\.

"Lyric poetry"\ "Lyrik"\ and "lyric poet" \ "Lyriker"\, are both early 19th century coinages.

Relation of tension etc.

There is, I think, ~~beyond~~ this side and beyond all esotericism and hermeticism, this side and beyond secret- and revelation-knowledge, a darkness of the poem.

"Writing as a form of prayer," we read ~~in~~<?>—deeply moved—in Kafka. This, however, does not mean that praying comes first, writing does: one cannot do it with hands folded.

✻ ×/ And I do not speak either of those darknesses that a "Philology,"—I wish one could, in this context, spell that word with a small initial letter—that triumphs under the applause of the dilettantes, spreads over the poem; a philology that babbles for ex. about ⌞genitive⌟ metaphors, without ever having given a thought to what a m. is, where it is to be found in the text, and how many genitives there are. Of these, the tracts and tractlets of the philologically accredited
33/111 cultural attachés, nothing will be said here. There are ⌞~~such~~ ⌞these⌟ highly cultured⌟ obscurantists, ~~certainly, even among the poets: Hölderlin~~ have always existed: let me remind you, that the description "metaphysical" for Donne, Marvell was originally meant contemptuously

❖❖❖

162◂▸104 *61/103* *A 15,1* *Ms.*

✻ There is⌞,⌟ ~~, believe a~~ this side and beyond ~~all~~ esotericism, hermeticism, etc. a darkness of the poem. The exoteric too, the most(") open poem too—and I believe that today ⌞, before all in
55 German,⌟ such, in places even ⌞extremely porous,⌟ completely light-porous poems are written—has its darkness, has it qua poem, ~~will—I underline: qua poem—~~⌞comes,⌟ because it is a poem, ~~is born~~ dark ⌞into the world⌟. (**27**) A congenital, constitutive darkness, then{.}, that belongs to today's poem.

✻ This today that—permit me this discrimination—mine, yours, and ~~the more spacious one, which we~~ have in common: ~~when~~ I ~~cannot conceal~~ from you (and from me) that I don't know how I

❖❖❖

Ms. *A 13,2* *62/542* 541◂▸425

31a I speak ~~here~~, as I do write poems, in matters of my own; **b** permit me to attach to this statement the hope that in this respect I do also speak in matters of the strange. *108, 471*

✻ First this, I do not speak of "modern lyrical poetry"{.}, ~~In parenthesis~~ I speak of the poem today. *474*

(~~Moreover~~ ⌊Incidentally⌋, and this does indeed ⌊already⌋ belong to this "today": it would be, I believe, ~~the investigation~~ not uninteresting to investigate the conditions under which the nouns "Lyrik" [lyrical poetry] and "Lyriker" [lyrical poet], coined at the beginning of the 19th century,—before then one speaks of "lyrische Poesie" "lyrical poetry"—have gotten into that relationship of tension with "Dichtung" [poetry] and "Dichter" [poet]—designations that have their own fortune{.}, {)} in which ~~toda~~ they certainly stand)

❖❖❖

19.8.59, Ms. *F 15,1* *63/332* 502◂▸123

(**33b,d**) The poem: ~~tha~~ a self-realization of language through radical individuation, i.e. the single, unrepeatable speaking of the individual.

❖❖❖

Ms., 17.8.59 *A 6/7* *64/102* 207◂▸380

✻ ~~I renounce~~ ⌊From experience I promise myself to make do without all too many borrowed concepts. Furthermore I will try,⌋ {(}here and in what follows) in view the of the poem's contemporaneity to renounce all and any etiology. I keep the poem in front of me.

Imagination and experience, experience and imagination make me think, in view of the darkness of the poem today, of a darkness of the poem qua poem, a constitutive, (**27**) thus a congenital darkness. ✻ In other words: the poem is born dark; it comes, (**33b**) as the result of a radical individuation, into the world as a language fragment, thus, {with} i.e. as far as language manages to be world, freighted with world.

17.8.

❖❖❖

Drafts of the 3rd Main Section (Paragraphs 37–53)

a. For paragraphs 37–40 ("Tropes and Images")

358◂▸301 65 *C 47,3* *Ms.*

Who believe in ambulant metaphors.

40a Topos research, ⌜friend?⌝ **b** {c}Certainly—But in light of what is to be searched for, in light of *u*-topia

---

❖❖❖

305◂▸591 66 *C 45* *Ms.*

✻ These are extreme formulations, I know, maybe also formulations in extremis. {D}They thrust through the approaches of the poem, they do not oversee it. **40a** Topos research? **b** Certainly, but in light of what is to be searched for, ~~place-less~~ ⌜the placeless,⌝ in light of u-topia

39a ~~Images~~ The image? The metaphor? ✻ They are the seen, the perceivable, they have phenomenal character. **b** The poem is the ⌜single⌝ place where all tropes are carried ad absurdum—

❖❖❖

590◂▸98 67 *C 3,5* *Ms.*

---

40 Topos-research, certainly—but in light ⌜of what is to be searched for, in light of⌝ utopia!

❖❖❖

86◂▸715 68/384 *C 26,2* *Ms.*

240/410, 338 **39b** The poem is the place where all synonymy ⌜and ~~all resemblance~~⌝ ends; where all tropes
⌜and everything improper⌝ is led ad absurdum; ✻ the poem has, ~~a~~ I believe, even there where it is
most graphic, an anti-metaphorical character; ~~it is untranslatable;~~ the image has a phenomenal
53 trait, intuitively recognizable.—What separates you from it, you will not bridge; you have to
4/696 make up your mind to jump.

❖❖❖

13◂▸310 69 *C 25,2* *Ms.*

---

40 Topos research ⌜in poetry⌝ takes place in light of what is to be searched for: in light of utopia

❖❖❖

637◂▸87 70 *E 4,1* *Ts.(Ms.)*

---

338 ✻ ⌜Poems, n'en déplaise à Mallarmé, are not ⌜made⌝ built of <u>words</u> ⌜neither, n'en déplaise à
17, 25, 38, 45, 281 certains autres, are they made of word-material⌝ **39b** In the poem all synonymy and tropes

\Tropik\ are led ad absurdum; in the poem language repeats itself, in • the single and finite, as spiritual shape.

❊ • In the single and finite the ~~poe~~ word becomes name—nomen, tendency toward the noun x/ 305
It is assigned to a name that is unpronounceable. 56, 59, 94

x/ perhaps it is from there that a certain tendency toward the nominal can be explained—

❖❖❖

Ms. *F 118,1* *71* *355◄►227*

❊ There is no word that, once pronounced, doesn't carry along its figurative \übertragenen\ meaning; and yet the words in the poem believe themselves to be untranslatable \unübertragbar\;
39b the poem appears as that place where all metaphoricity is led ad absurdum. *598*

❖❖❖

Ms. *F 112,1* *72* *483◄►893*

---

re "image":
40 -i- Topos-research happens here in light of utopia—

❖❖❖

b. Re speech section 42 ("Élargissez l'art"—"Narrows")

Ms. *C 30,1* *73/6* *8◄►743*

(13,24) But this fragment is not to be read as a report on the author of the Soldiers and the Tutor or, what makes ⌊~~it~~⌋ even clearer: the author of "Notes on the Theater"—what is to be read here is the fatefulness of a man named Lenz, of whom one knows—without having learned it—what kind of burden his existence is to be ⌊found by⌋ reading it ~~se~~<?> here, that he under the burden ⌊the Büchnerian Lenz like the historical one,⌋ collapsed {,} under the burden of his existence, is picked up on a Moscow street— *35, 51*

42b,e "Elargissez l'art?" No: ~~rétrécissez-le!~~ Go with art into ~~the~~ ⌊your⌋ narrows! *90, 320, 700*

❖❖❖

Ts.(Ms.) *C 7,4* *74/32* *559◄►81*

❊ Seen from the point of view of the poem, practice nearly always means exercitium and ascesis. *553*
—There are psychograms. And there is ~~the~~ ⌊the poem as⌋ gift{.} ⌊for the ensouled one⌋ There is, in the small ⌊•narrow⌋ space ⌊~~and the bare second~~⌋, where poetry happens, a becoming-free, not only of language, but also of the one who speaks{;} ⌊—through that which speaks itself toward *18,24,26,27, 239,259*

him.⌋ Poetry ⌊, thus that which connects ultimately,⌋ is an act of freedom; to this freedom belongs, if not ⌊however⌋ ~~grace~~ ⌊rarely⌋ always grace, certainly goodwill. ✻ (An impossible word ⌊today—but not here!—⌋, I know, ⌊think of it this way: as Tyche⌋ - but where are we, when we
482 speak of poems, if not with the impossible coming to language) Poems are not first of all written records, ⌊do not begin with being written down⌋; they are gifts to the attentive. **35d** Attention is, here I quote a word by Malebranche—I quote it following Walter Benjamin's Kafka essay first published in the Jüdische R–<und>schau—, Attention, that is the natural prayer of the soul.

42b,e •Narrowing # ⌊Mercier's word, broadened by cybernetics⌋ Elargiss{ons}ez l'art—

451, 536/712; 9

❖❖❖

c. Re speech sections 45–50 (Final part, The Meridian)

357◂▸396 | 75 | C 46,4 | Ms.

47 There are four conclusions—I choose, (**3**) because ~~calendars I would—~~ ⌊I have nothing against⌋ the shattering of certain clocks and the prohibition of certain calendars, the last one. Leonce

❖❖❖

284◂ | 76 | C 22,1 | Ms.

(**45**) I would like to ask myself the question, what is it that forced me to walk this ⌊nettle-⌋ route from that place in Lenz to the quotation about hands

❖❖❖

77 | C 22,2 | Ms.

(**50c**) Let me, given that the accommodating is valid ⌊as conclusion⌋, find a name for that from the Valerio-perspective.

❖❖❖

▸560 | 78 | C 22,3 | Ms.

(**50c**) the cybernetically presumably irrelevant

❖❖❖

743◂▸716 | 79 | C 30,3 | Ms.

50c ⌊something immaterial<?>,⌋ something, like language, not present,

❖❖❖

9. 10. 60, Ts. *C 6,4* *80/303* *257◂▸659*

---

46 The poem is the detour from you to you; it is the route. It is also the route of language to itself, its becoming visible and mortal: whereby the poem becomes the raison d'être of language.

❖❖❖

Ts.(Ms.) *C 8/9* *81* *32/74◂▸338*

B-R

Final sentence:

50c •Perhaps ⌊Something that today and here may look for a name enlivened by this opposite;⌋

Something invisible, in no way enriching that "perfectly sensual speech," ⌊something immaterial, not present, early⌋ ⌊cybernetically irrelevant⌋ ⌊, something indifferent⌋ yet earthly, something ⌊compass like⌋ round, something {R}returning{-}to{-}itself{-} ⌊across its poles⌋ and thus cheerfully crossing even the "tropics" \"Tropen"\ ⌊—I do not say: the two tropics \Wendekreise\—⌋ connects me—imprecisely!—with it ⌊—something ⌊very⌋ very far from the sun and unmoveable⌋: • a meridian. *558*

• At noon

• ~~{rushing from pole to pole} to be searched for between pole and pole~~

• May I ~~name~~ find a name for it from the ⌊Valerio- ~~and~~ i.e.—⌋ stargazer's vantage point?— something with the same distance from the sun: a meridian—

• sun-distant in the same way—

• Is it a ⌊a sort of⌋ spirit? ⌊Should it be a kind of spirit?⌋ It is a meridian.—

✻ Permit this year's and today's prize recipient—for Büchner is also the author of Leonce and Lena—this correlation

48c Can one explain this ⌊Could one give another explanation here⌋? Perhaps as in Leonce and Lena, where the quotation marks ~~invisibly~~ smilingly ⌊added to⌋ the words should not be considered as goose-feet \Gänsefüßchen\, but as hare's ears \Hasenöhrchen\:

✻ •What is it?

Permit me—Poetry ~~does have something to do with wants to~~ ⌊I said it<?> at the beginning, knows, that it ⌊lives⌋ by its⌋ {a}Auto-sublat{ing}ion—{-} from the Valerio- and stargazer's vantage p. name it ⌊thus⌋: it is a meridian.

48c This is so—how come? Permit me to find a name for it, permit me, as I remember the Leonce- and- Lena-language, where the quot—<ation>marks, smilingly added to the words, are not to be understood as g—<oose>f<ee>t, but as hare's ears, thus as something that listens above and beyond itself (the words), permit me to search here for a few words to repeat once more what I have already said :

50c Something ~~not present~~ ultimately not present connects me to Lenz. Something invisible, the sensuous, et cetera.

47-48 ~~We~~ I am coming to the end and must beware not to reinterpret, like my half-Asian countryman Karl-E-<mil> Franzos, the fundamentally accommodating , which we need—or needed—as a as a coming. (But: there are, as in Leonce and Lena, quotation marks, smilingly added to the words, thus with added quotation marks that do not necessarily want to be understood as goosefeet, but perhaps as hare's ears, i.e. as something not completely fearless that listens above and beyond itself and the ~~words~~ , that means also that which they refer to)
✻ I give you, then, in contrast to my ~~half-Asian~~ countryman, supposedly so uncritical, yet at
83 the same time —something mentioned ~~much less~~ much more rarely — also such an enemy of
rats , such a friend of manuscripts) finally\zu guter Letzt\ a second, hopefully more accurate version. Who knows, maybe I say this way too one more time the same thing. (but let's not talk about hermeneutics)
50b-c So what connects the beginning quote with the final quote, what connects today's prize recipient with that Reinhold Lenz? Something fundamentally not present. Something the perfect sensuous speech etc. ... ___: a meridian.

❖❖❖

386◂▸516 *82* *C 12* *Ts.(Ms.)*

B-Rede

End:

✻ The distance, that which has been crossed, that which returns from the infinite, from what is
385/505 farthest, finite-infinite, **44** the infinitely spoken {E}M mortality and no purpose -------:
34/493 ✻ Selfencounter (mysticism, see Ernst Bloch, Spirit of Utopia)
478 ✻ The poem gives itself to you, into the hand of the one who therefore (**34b**) stands in the secret
497 of the encounter—in what a hand does it give itself thus! It gives itself into your hand that the strangest illuminates as into the own hand!
45b Seven years ago, I was far from Büchner, —but there are communicating vessels— I wrote these lines: **c** Voices up from the nettle-route: / Come to us on your hands / Whoever is alone with the lamp, / Only has his hand to read from. / Permit me, the one granted the Büchner
10, 239; 282; Prize, to stand by Lenz and his hands{!}: **50c** Something invisible and earthly and sublunar,
824 terrestrial , that may today ~~light up in the transitory,~~ search for a name leads there, ~~i.e. up the mountain~~ connects me with it: a meridian.•
(Something round, returning to itself?) ~~and isn't it cheerful?~~—something and at that ~~even~~
584 ~~the "tropics"~~ enjoyably cheerfully crossing even the "tropics"
connects me (approximately) with him: a meridian. •à quelques "world-minutes" près

❖❖❖

645◂▸267/605 *83* *E 7* *Ms.*

✻ Let me me with thanks come to you on a route that shares it with the poem, thus ultimately with the written, into-the-world-written and the readable ~~that wants-toward-the-other—~~ , in the unsuspectedly revealed ~~to let be~~ to recognize from afar and invisibly what is allotted to him \Zugewiesene\ or meant for him \Zugedachte\ as ~~there~~ present and true—: **49b** ~~I come~~ I come thus to you on an often and unsuspectingly traveled street of my ~~as one for me~~ for me by now as a nameless - near ~~to be named birth town~~{.—}

~~This street, {it} which long ago changed names.~~ ⌊, I⌋ come via the detour along
Franzos-alley, I come with the thanks of a painful thought: the route to the rather close forester's
house, where Karl-Emil Franzos, in every, even the most bitter, sense my countryman, ~~started~~
~~a life in which one day the manuscripts of the man the rats~~ never walked and probably ~~never~~ again *81, 743*
could walk. And yet it is, unwalked, a route.

❖❖❖

28.9.60, Ts. *F 48,2* *84* *400◄►643*

✻ Do not speak so much of the Jewish ⌊of the poem⌋—you barely know it. Look at it, take it in; *418*
be attentive. **35d** Attention, I quote a word by Malebranche, I quote it after Walter Benjamin, *617, 941*
"Attention, that is the natural prayer of the soul."

48b-c When you—permit me, as a countryman of the so uncritical Büchner-publisher Karl *743*
Emil Franzos, ⌊in what follows⌋ this ⌊so⌋ completely uncritical manner of reading—, when you
don't consider each of the quotation marks invisibly and smilingly added to the word as
goosefeet \Gänsefüßchen\, when you know that it can be a hare's ear \ Hasenöhrchen\, then you *33/111, 650/748*
hear in the accommodating, on which Leonce and Lena ends ⌊toward which Büchner brings you *534, 650/748*
jokingly⌋, even if not something coming, but perhaps something that has a resemblance to this
natural prayer.

❖❖❖

Ms. *F 46,3/47* *85* *236◄►400*

Discursive Thinking *755*
Intuitive thinking: (**45d,49**) ~~Lenz~~ that, in a piece called Conversation in the Mountains, I saw Lenz
come, unconsciously, not unwittingly; and when then, in May, my countryman Karl-Emil Franzos,
with some forgetting, entered into this context ... *746*
✻ There are secrets. Poem and secret, today too, and despite all the malice and all the treason of
the poet{ry} ⌊-producers⌋ and the ~~poetry~~ accents-exploiters, are allied.

❖❖❖

d. Re speech sections 44 and 51–53 (Thank-yous)

Ms. *C 26,1* *86* *374◄►68/384*

---

a ... meridian.
51 With you and the State of Hesse I have just now touched it.

❖❖❖

70◄►264 *87* *E 4,2* *Ts.*

---

44 P<oems>: oh this infinity-speaking full of mortality and to no purpose!

❖❖❖

184◄►206 *88* *E 3,2* *10.10.60, Ts.*

---

51 ..... a ... meridian. The State of Hesse touches it just now. ⌊has touched it just now⌋

❖❖❖

17◄ *89* *C 40* *Ts.*

---

52 My heartfelt thanks to the German Academy for Language and Poetry, to the State of Hesse, and the mayor of the city of Darmstadt for awarding me their prize: the prize that carries the name of someone great, the name of Georg Büchner. Permit me

►9 *90* *C 41* *Dsl.*

---

44 "Poems—: oh this infinity-speaking full of mortality and to no purpose!" (**52**) I entrusted these words months ago, because of the immediate joy, ~~to my thank you letter to~~ to the letter that tried to thank Hermann Kasack, of the German Academy for Language and Poetry, the State of Hesse, and the city of Darmstadt.

✻ With these words I return today—even the "oh,"~~—I know, a vocable that is lyrically untimely, and yet, don't you agree, Büchnerian, is~~ ⌊that ~~I, out of respect~~ the repression of which from the point of view of modern poetry I had brought up, has, you hear it⌋ come along, and with it, from the same direction, thus, my heartfelt thanks.

✻ ~~To come with poems into the vicinity of a name, that means to write poe~~ I do not have, concerning mortality and purposelessness, too bad a conscience: I ⌊have or at least I⌋ had, as far as I remember—I belong ~~not to my readers—~~only since yesterday evening, after a rather long interruption, to my readers again—, nearly exclusively to do with that. Though in what concerns the infinity-speaking, thus the poems qua poems, I do unhappily no longer know exactly where I situate myself, or rather where the poem situates itself in relation to me. Two years ago I wrote a
700 poem called "Stretto"\"Engführung"\ i.e. I let this poem lead me into the narrows, I am,
320 although I continue to write in relation to my conceptions of the poetic, that means of poetry as not only a personal⌊, even private,⌋ problem, ~~still in these ⌊in similar⌋ narrows—with one word: I ask myself, as you do ⌊too⌋, if there is a way forward there, and if, given the kinds of things I write, there is a sense~~

❖❖❖

92◄►922
[16◄►97] *91* *D 3 [C 2]* *Dsl.[Ts.], pag. -2-*

---

750 Permit me, please, therefore, to say only a few things—about the poem.

52 Permit me, the youngest ⌊and at a loss for words not only in his poems⌋ of all Büchner-Prize recipients so far, to give ~~thanks. I~~ my heartfelt thanks to the State of Hesse, the German Academy for Language and Poetry, for the high honor bestowed upon me now.
This thank you is

Ts. *D 2* *92* *720◂▸91*

---

44 Poems—: this infinity-speaking full of mortality and to no purpose—: **52c** those were, ⌊months ago,⌋ because of the immediate joy, the words, with which I accompanied my <thanks> to Hermann Kasack and beyond him ⌊to⌋ the German Academy for Language and Poetry, ~~the~~ ⌊to the⌋ State of Hesse, and ~~the city~~ ⌊to the⌋ <city> of Darmstadt.

❖❖❖

Ms. *B 8/9* *93* *10◂▸751*

Ladies and gentlemen!

44 ‘Poems—: oh this infinity-speaking full of mortality and to no purpose’: ✻ those were,
months ago, the words, that I sent along with my thanks, my heartfelt thanks, to Hermann
Kasack, ~~the President of the Academy~~. With ~~such~~ these words I now come{,} ⌊~~anaphorically~~⌋
⌊also⌋ ~~a second time~~ ⌊~~today~~ now⌋ back—even the -oh, -which I thought of repressing ~~because~~,
mindful of \Understatements\ appropriate for the ~~contemporary~~ ⌊modern⌋ poet, has, you hear *752*
it, come along. That gives you a first insight into the conditions prevalent ⌊at this moment⌋ in
my study.
Here I have to quote a further word, revealing in terms of my ideas of the world and of things, from that letter: I had ~~asked~~ ~~Hermann Kasack~~ the President of the German Academy for Language and Poetry, to give my—not less heartfelt—thanks also to the State of Hesse, asking that all the trees be included too—

❖❖❖

▸521

28.9.60, Ts. *F 86,5* *94* *=860*

---

44 The poem: oh this infinity-speaking full of mortality and to no purpose! ✻ This ~~belief~~
⌊momentary belief⌋ in the ~~infinite-infinite~~ noun and participle, this conspirational devotion *56, 59, 70, 843*
\Ver- und Zugeschworensein\ to the ~~Infinite~~, infinite forms of the temporal! This naming and naming of the most transient! (**52a**) I thank you for this prize, the prize that carries the name, open to time, steadfast in time: Georg Büchner.

❖❖❖

Ms. *F 74,3* *95* *476◂▸522*

Last sentence:
52a I thank you for this prize which carries the name: Georg Büchner.— *859*

❖❖❖

30.5.60, Ms. *E 14,3* *96* *262◂▸754*

---

44 Poems—: oh this infinity-speaking full of mortality and to no purpose.— *287, 737*

❖❖❖

Additional Notes to the Text of the Speech

91◄►381	*97*	*C 3,1*	*Ms.*

(**30**) One could date this anew—⌞and, why not—~~even~~ in ~~Portug.~~<?> Spanish—not only in German—⌟ and from ⌞a⌟ 30th January—

❖❖❖

67◄	*98*	*C 3,6*	*Ms.*

(**31c**) This "who knows"—it is ⌞~~has to~~⌟ be related to the first—

◄658	*99*	*C 3,7*	*Ms.*

(**30b**) Under such dates we write today
Who knows toward what we have to write ourselves.—

❖❖❖

311◄►402	*100*	*C 4,4*	*Ms.*

(**49c**) I have a son who is five and a half, he is interested, like his father, in the earthly: he owns a globe

❖❖❖

Materials

Darkness

The congenital darkness of the poem

►*661* *101* *A 1* *(Folder caption), Ms.*

O{f}n the darkness of the poetic

❖❖❖

~~*207*◄►*380*~~ *102/64* *A 6/7* *17.8.59, Ms.*

~~I renounce~~ ⌞From experience I promise myself to make do without all too many borrowed concepts. Furthermore I will try to here and in what follows) in view of the todayness of the poem to renounce all and any etiology. I have the poem before me [[in front of me]].

313, 339 Imagination and experience, experience and imagination, in view of the darkness of the poem today, make me think of a darkness of the poem qua poem, thus of a constitutional, a congenital darkness. In other words: the poem is born dark; it comes, as the result of a radical individuation, into the world as a piece of language, thus, i.e. as far as language manages to be world, laden with world.

17.8.

❖❖❖

162◄ *103/61* *A 15,1* ~~*Ms.*~~

55, 305, 234/615 There exists⌞,⌟, ~~believe a~~ on this and on the far side of all esotericism, hermeticism, et cetera, a darkness of the poem. Even the most exoteric, the most {"}open poem—and I believe that today ⌞, particularly in German,⌟ such, in places even ⌞distinctly porous,⌟ totally translucent poems are being written—has its darkness, has it qua poem, will—I underline qua poem—⌞comes,⌟ because it is the poem, dark born. ⌞into the world⌟. A congenital, constitutive darkness, then{.}, that belongs to the poem today.

This today which—permit me this distinction—my, yours and the more spacious one, which we have in ~~common: when I cannot conceal from you (or from me), that I do not know~~, how I

104 *A 15,2* *Ms.*

59, 280, 518 —the morrow—

Timestead

takes the

►*422* *105* *A 15,3* *Ms.*

|| The poem coming into the world comes laden with world into ~~the~~ it, the world.

❖❖❖

Ms. *A 17,2* *106* *300◄►318*

~~An~~ even the most "exoteric," the most open poem is dark; and, permit me this maybe not totally superfluous indication: if any {bo} one poet was a vir clarus, it was Hölderlin.

❖❖❖

Ms. *A 18* *107* *319◄►607*

We have more than one—bitter—reason, to put what around us has achieved importance ⌞and
which has achieved rank and name⌟, between quotation marks; the poem is the place where
⌞all⌟ these words that, without making allowance for any supposed originality ⌞thus achieved⌟,
rather, laden also with this load, hope to find refuge once more as words .—We live in an era
where one legitimizes oneself lengthily to the outside, so as not to have to justify oneself to
oneself. In that sense, poetry, in its present mode, preserves for itself the darkness of the
"illegitimate"; it presents itself without references, ⌞without indications⌟ thus without quotation 648
marks.

❖❖❖

Ms. *A 20* *108* *561◄►543*

I{m}do not speak of the "modern" poem, I speak of the poem today. And to the essential aspects
of this today—my today, for I do speak on my own behalf—belongs its lack of a future: I cannot 471
keep from you that I do not know how to answer the question, toward what ⌞in the direction⌟ of
which morrow the poem is moving; if the poem borders on such a morrow, then it possesses
darkness. The poem's hour of birth, ladies and gentlemen, lies in darkness.~~And there is little to
suggest that~~ ⌞Some claim to know that⌟ it is the darkness just before dawn; I do not share this
assumption.

hold it to be congenital, or better, constitutive. The poem is dark qua poem.

❖❖❖

19.8.59, Ms. *F 17,3* *109* *689◄►882*

Why the poems of earlier times seem more "comprehensible" to us than those of our contemporaries? Maybe also because qua poems, i.e. taken together with their darkness, they have already volatilized ...

❖❖❖

Ms. *F 62,2* *110* *327◄►461*

Congenital darkness of poetry

(... Born-to dreaming / "Zugebornes Träumen"/ "songes naturels"/ Valéry -i- born-to from the poem

❖❖❖

172◄ *111/33* *F 102,1* *Ms.*

240/410, 401, 747, 843; 704, 747 84, 650/748 • ... speak on the strangest matter. Danton (who finds into death by his own grace) projects brotherliness into irreality: "~~Thou~~ You cannot prevent that in the basket" = You see, it is a borrowed ⌞quotation⌟ and a mortal word exiled into infinity: the poetic ~~are~~ ⌞, that is the place⌟ ~~that are~~ the ⌞in the darkness⌟ scattering quotation marks.—

259, 422, 11/708 • The strangeness ⌞the darkness,⌟ of poetry comes from this: from the direction in which it moves.—the estranged around it • hurrying through, directed toward what's strangest.×/

• hurrying through—something impatient.—not: impetuous—inheres ⌞probably⌟ in all of us —; we do lie beneath the ruins of the scales on which we are weighed.—

121, 136, 153, 825 60/582 ×/ Here, in this context, i.e. abruptly, should come a phrase by Pascal, which I, even more abruptly, quote via Shestov: ne nous reprochez pas le manque de clarté ... That is, if not the congenital, then however the born-to-it darkness of the poem. It has nothing to do with obscurantists, even academic ones.—•

• with which I absolutely do not believe to have to mean ~~an over~~ the creation of a suprapersonal relation.—

×

►376/530 *112* *F 102,2* *Ms.*

---

precise

small place

hostile to civilization

without origin—

❖❖❖

596◄►261 *113* *F 30,2* *Ms.*

... the poem sees, even beyond the deathbarrier, the possibility to exist,
-i- that—horrible "pars pro toto"—the heads embrace in the baskets.—

❖❖❖

163◄►60/582 *114* *A 22,3* *Ms.*

There exist⌞in thinking⌟ not only logically determined courses; there are also insights{,}. {t}To these insights this one for ex. belongs ⌞can⌟ belong: that, when the poem achieves certain syntactic or sound formations, it is forced into tracks, which lead it out of its own realm, i.e. out of the actuality that co-determines its necessity. There exists, in other words, a language-taboo specific to the poem and only to it, which not only holds for its vocabulary, but also for categories
222 such as syntax, rhythm or articulation; ⌞from⌟ the unspoken, some things become

understandable; the poem knows the argumentum e silentio. There thus exists an ellipsis, which one must not mistake for a trope ⌊or, worse, for stylistic refinement⌋. The god of the poem is indisputably a deus absconditus. *875*

❖❖❖

Ms. *F 8,1* *115* *189◄►313*

The argumentum e silentio: in this sense it is admissible

❖❖❖

from 20.8.59, Ms. *F 19,5* *116* *131◄►490*

Surrealism was a ragbag. But in this ragbag, besides the certainly questionable psychogram, there was also this—central—thought: Les jeux ne sont pas encore faits—a thought that accompanies every genuine poetic intention.

Since then: the cards, unshuffled, have been dealt; ⌊on⌋ none of these cards can one see an image of what the poet could mean.

❖❖❖

Ms. *workbook II, 15; inserted sheets [3,2]* *117* *322◄►967*

-i- the ominous business of poetry— *167*

❖❖❖

Ms. *F 65,5* *118* *251◄*

Forebodings, ominous thinking *886*

Ms. *F 65,6* *119*

---

the "last things" *17,182,520*

Ms. *F 66,1* *120* *►756*

---

not 'found' darkness!

Co-nativeness of the darkness in the poem.

❖❖❖

Ms. *ÜR 6.12,1 [4]* *121*

---

the image ⌊here⌋ is not metaphor; ~~it has~~ ⌊this poetry is not emblematic⌋ ⌊is not mood-poetry⌋ *256, 333, 68/384*

the image has phenomenal character—it appears.

the vision— *277, 912*

⌞⌞not least⌟ Out of this turning toward these layers of time, this blackearth: the⌟ congenital,
802 constitutive "Darkness" of the poems. One remembers Pascal's words: ne <nous reprochez pas
33/111, 136, 153, 825 le manque de clarté ...>

❖❖❖

393◄ 122 *ÜR 6.13,15 [2]* *Ms.*

что – то в них попало

527 something had gotten into this
something: the other, the uncanny
(alienating?
~~alienating~~ ⌞back⌟ to the truth \Zur Wahrheit ⌞Zurück-⌟ Verfremdende)\)
the appearing—(and, rarely enough, what in the vision is looked at)

❖❖❖

Groundlessness and abyss

63/332◄ 123 *F 15,2* *19.8.59, Ms.*

|| The poem, like man, does not have sufficient ground. ⌞(Therefore its ⌞specific⌟ darkness, which
484 has to be taken into account if the poem is to be understood as poem. ~~Darkness~~⌟

Maybe also: the poem has its ground in itself; with this ground it rests
27, 30, 151 ~~groundless~~ (see above) in the groundless.

►878 124 *F 15,3* *19.8.59, Ms.*

479, 548 || discontinuity of the poem

❖❖❖

492◄►688 125 *F 16,5* *19.8.59, Ms.*

|| The poem has grounds—and it does not hide these grounds from us; the poem and the poem's grounds however do not have sufficient ground, ~~except for~~ ⌞be it⌟ this one: the questioning of it.

❖❖❖

221◄ 126 *F 118,6* *Ms.*

---

discontinuity of the poem

Ms. *F 118,7* *127* *►503*

The poem is grounded in itself; with this ground it rests on the groundless, like man.

❖❖❖

from 22.8.60, Ms. *Workbook II, 21 [7]* *128* *=806*

? Wesensgrund / ground of being
? Abgrund / abyss
Urgrund / ur-ground
? Ungrund / un-ground

❖❖❖

Ms. *F 5,2* *129* *385/505◄►548*

⌊End:⌋
Leave the poem its darkness; maybe—maybe!—it will give, when ~~the~~ ⌊that⌋ excessive brightness ~~of the exac~~ ⌊which the exact⌋ sciences ⌊know already today to put before our eyes⌋ will have changed the very ground of the human genotype, ⌊—maybe it will⌋, on the ground of this ground, ⌊provide⌋ shade in which man can reflect on his humanity. 614

❖❖❖

from 30.8.59, Ms. *F 21,5/22,1* *130* *320◄►447*

The darkness of the poem = the darkness of death. The humans = the mortals. Therefore the poem, remaining mindful of death, counts among the most human side of man. The human is however not, ~~the Gree~~ we have meanwhile experienced this copiously, the main characteristic of the humanists. The humanists are those who look beyond the concrete human being toward the 679
noncommittal side of humanity.— 313

❖❖❖

892◄►116
from 20.8.59, Ms. *F 19,4 [F 119,1]* *131* *[503◄►489]*

The poem always, even there where it steps outside the human, takes man with it. ‖ 195, 372

❖❖❖

Ms. *F 31,2* *132* *620◄►538*

××/ If it is true that there is also a relation to man from the heavens, this new turn can only be 27
welcome for him—for he lives on as man's abyss.— 704, 711

❖❖❖

521◄ *133* *F 87,2* *Ms.*

16, 484 Released from his complicity: .... from the moment's everlastingness \Unvergänglichen\: into the most everlasting: the openness of the not-yet-existing??

×

►31 *134* *F 87,3* *Ms.*

409, 704, 805 .. That he did not walk on his head—: this transposition—(ironically further).
The verticality, the steepness ~~of~~ and ruggedness of poetry—

❖❖❖

153◄ *135* *B 27,1* *17.5.60, Ms.*

---

17. 5. 60.

B-R

On the 'complicity,' from which we are released:
183, 866 With each poem we stand, "alongside the poem," in the secret. The "Darkness" comes from this stay.

136 *B 27,2* *17.5.60, Ms.*

33/111, 121, 153, 825 Pascal: Ne nous reprochez pas l'obscurité, puisque nous en faisons profession.

137 *B 27,3* *17.5.60, Ms.*

389, 797, 805, 876 Hofmannsthal: pointe acérée de l'infini.

►298 *138* *B 27,4* *17.5.60, Ms.*

---

to walk on one's head →
→ under the servants' stairs (Hofmannsthal)

❖❖❖

929◄ *139* *D 7,1* *Ms.*

BR

353, 597 The poem as vigil

140 *D 7,2* *Ms.*

Shestov, p. 18 Aristotle:

141 *D 7,3* *Ms.*

Who wants to have the proofs (the keys) delivered together with the poem—

Ms. *D 7,4* *142*

Secret of the poem— *307*
Therefore: who wants to destroy the poem, tries to destroy the person—

Ms. *D 7,5* *143* *►760*

Dishope \Enthoffen\: from the deepening darkness; *407, 534*

❖❖❖

Ts. *E 5,1* *144* *394◄►870*

Pascal—Abyss // Eye-to-eye with nothingness

❖❖❖

Ms. *F 83,6* *145* *398◄►844*

-i- the sleepwalking-ness of the poem—

❖❖❖

Ms. *ÜR 6.12,2r [1]* *146*

One
Someone: each one of us can be this someone. "Someone has to be there<">, writes Kafka, "someone has to keep watch."

❖❖❖

Ms. *F 97,2* *147* *312◄*

{—} The poem—an endless vigil

Ms. *F 97,3* *148*

Shestov, ~~Ghé~~ Geth<semane>, pp. 71 f.:
"Lorsque Platon affirmait que le plus grand malheur qui puisse arriver à l'homme c'est de devenir μισόλογος, il disait déjà ce que devait enseigner plus tard Pélage *570*

Ms. *F 97,4* *149*

-i- misology in Büchner

---

150 *F 97,5* *Ms.*

Poetry is on the side of the unassuming and the small; it hates the banal, (the commonplace)

►166 *151* *F 98* *Ms.*

27, 30, 123 The abysmal (is in fact) the <u>bottomless</u>
↙
Abyss—Pascal

❖❖❖

232◄►238 *152* *A 32,6* *Ms*

139. Psalm: nox illuminatio mea
... darkness is like the light
ולילה כיום יאיד כהשיכה כָאודָה

❖❖❖

406◄►135 *153* *B 26* *1.6.60, Ms.*

1.6.60.

Büchner-speech

The counterword for "apparently" is not, as one may want to think at first, "real" or "obvious"; it has to be looked for in the "inconspicuous," the not appearing, not coming into the light of day; it is the hidden, which only wakes up when it knows our eye to be ⌊open and⌋ ⌊en route and⌋ ⌊thus also⌋ close by. →
33/111, 121, 136, 825 "Ne nous reprochez pas l'obscurité, that is a saying by Pascal, ne nous rep. ... puisque ..."

❖❖❖

494◄ *154* *B 23,1* *Ms.*

Büchner-speech

488 place above heavens—transuranian—(Plato)

155 *B 23,2* *Ms.*

393 Plotinus

156 *B 23,3* *Ms.*

Pascal: Ne nous reprochez pas l'obscurité
Shestov: Gethsemane

Ms. *B 23,4* *157* *►406*

Kafka: language as having Being — *296, 720, 732, 843*

❖❖❖

Ms. *F 68,2* *158* *934◄*

-i- Uncovering—discovery—of the abyss between sign and signified

Ms. *F 68,3* *159*

"hyper-ontol."
core tension \Grundspannung\

Ms. *F 68,4* *160* *►498*

[-i- in poetry itself there also is the—"⌊hyper⌋trans-uranian place"—

❖❖❖

The poem's lack of origin

Ms. *A 14,2* *161* *425◄*

Not "origin," but native\innate \von Haus aus\. ~~The~~ So I don't say that the darkness of an "early stage" of the poem is responsible for the poem in our "late stage." ⌊Each poem has its here and now.⌋

Ms. *A 14,3* *162* *►61/103*

Killy
The color words in Trakl: they are not there "originally" and thus detachable and symbolically evaluable; a Trakl poem is thus in fact already dyed in the wool, this way or that way, it remains, blue or brown, the poem; ~~an~~ apart from that linguistics knows that the color words are derivates: albus, et cetera. (clay-gray etc.)

❖❖❖

Ms. *A 22,2* *163* *648◄►114*

Scheler, p. 178: ⌊the principle⌋ consists in bringing back the relatively unknown to the previously known.

Who wants to explain poems that way, loses sight of the fact that the direction in which the route to "unknown" unrolls, helps to constitute this unknown.

❖❖❖

181◂ *164* *A 11,4* *Ms.*

A certain sense for aporias should not be lacking—

▸608 *165* *A 11,5* *Ms.*

!! To speak nowhere about the creation of the poem; but always only about the created poem !!

❖❖❖

151◂ *166* *F 99,1* *Ms.*

No concessions

▸208 *167* *F 99,2* *Ms.*

what's underground, imperious

117 —ominous and in terms of governing\regierungsweise\—

❖❖❖

555◂ *168* *F 100,1* *Ms.*

-i- where the poem wants to go by itself \von sich• aus will\

×

1, 4/696, 20/695 Is the poem • aware of all the consequences? How far? The poem also wants to stay with itself•—///—

169 *F 100,2* *Ms.*

a): contradiction between Being and appearance

×

▸537 *170* *F 100,3* *Ms.*

The showing through of the inside

×

❖❖❖

Ms.	*F 100,5*	*171*	*537◄*

Coming of age

Ms.	*F 101*	*172*	*►33/111*

no codification, no systematization *548, 610*

❖❖❖

from 7.10.60, Ms.	*F 26,1*	*173*	*216◄►350*

Expansionlessness \Ausdehnungslosigkeit\ of the poem—

❖❖❖

Ms.	*F 53,1*	*174*	*217◄►666*

The poem begins with itself— *848*

❖❖❖

Ms.	*F 55,5*	*175*	*864◄*

Tao 25. .... → the poem has only itself *379*

Ms.	*F 55,6*	*176*	*►306*

The self-evident, the natural

❖❖❖

28.9.60, Ms.	*F 85,8*	*177*	*►282 =855*

The self-evident, become 'a problem'— *422*

❖❖❖

The Poem

Opacity of the Poem

607◄►561 *178* *A 19,2* *Ms.*

"<u>Dark</u>" the poem is to begin with due to its existence, due to its o ⌊<u>ppositeness,</u>⌋ bjectivity; dark
508 in fact in the sense of an opacity particular ⌊⌋, and thus phenomenal⌋ to any given object; This
57/485 in that sense then, that it wants to be understood from its self ⌊⌋, as an existent⌋

❖❖❖

380◄ *179* *A 11,1* *Ms.*

‖ <u>the visual</u>, the phenomenal/allusion to the modern novel—

180 *A 11,2* *Ms.*

"opacity" of the phenomenal

►164 *181* *A 11,3* *Ms.*

The poem's obviousness ⌊praised by many⌋ is not a <u>plastic</u> quality; {—} the poem remains always a
944; 385/505 manifestation of language; the synesthesia to be performed ⌊by the reader⌋ does not consist in
the ⌊perfect⌋ synchronization of the sense organs

❖❖❖

28◄►619 *182* *F 25,1* *from 7.10.60, Ms.*

17, 119, 520 The poem speaks of the first and most accidental things as if they were <u>the last ones</u>: The near is at
492 → the same time the infinitely distant; if it has the •opacity of what stands opposite it, it also has
the •brightness of the faraway

❖❖❖

306◄►404 *183* *F 56,2* *Ms.*

135, 307; 843,
866 Darkness (secret) of what is present, opposite, opacity of what exists—

❖❖❖

685◄►88 *184* *E 3,1* *10.10.60, Ts.*

B-speech
10.X.60.

Who has seen through ⌊it⌋ already before he perceives and looks at ⌊it⌋, him the poem opposes in ⌊with⌋ its whole—to be understood also in its geological sense—thickness.

⌊The already tight/compact {ver~~~~bare<?>};⌋ {I}it fills itself with the ⌊compacts itself around
the⌋ Dark⌊,—with the sense⌋ of that which stands against it; an erratic language-block, come
from your own, a for you too available ⌊depth and⌋ height and distance, faces you with silence; 371, 496, 513
even there it still gives you a chance.

❖❖❖

Ms. *D 10,3/11* *185* *746◄►684/721*

~~The~~

Who has ⌊already⌋ seen through ⌊has⌋, before he ⌊perceives and⌋ looks at⌊,⌋ ~~has, whom we before the (the) the poem fills itself for him~~ to him the poem appears in all its—⌊also⌋ to be understood in its geological sense—thickness; it ~~has the~~ ⌊~~him it~~ fills itself with the⌋ darkness of what stands opposite; an erratic language-block, it faces you with silence. ~~It throws your talk back at you until your breath {and} turns The poem does not speak of the offense;~~ it is the offense—even there it still gives you a chance.— 418

❖❖❖

10.10.60, Ts. *M 1,2* *186* *21◄*

Thickness: to be understood from the geological, and thus from the slow catastrophes and the dreadful fault lines of language— — —

❖❖❖

Ms. *F 63,1* *187* *462◄►363*

-i-

the sole hope: that the poem be there, once more, erratic—

❖❖❖

Ms. *F 63,5* *188* *456◄►670*

-i- between the found and the discovered , the discoverable stands the poem.

❖❖❖

Ms. *F 7,4 [F 117,2]* *189* *265◄►115 [577◄►352]*

The lapidary. ||

❖❖❖

Ms. *F 53,5* *190* *304◄►640*

Oppositeness, Objectivity of the poems: looking at, not seeing through—: the poem is indeed what is behind 851

❖❖❖

191 *Journal of VIII. 2. - IX. 9 1960 [2]* *Ms.*

—BR
Those ~~one~~ who see through the poem—not looking at—from the seeing-through the poems become non-transparent; opacity—

192 *Journal of VIII. 2. - IX. 9 1960 [3]* *Ms.*

-i-
‖ ... who claim to have seen through one, before having looked at one.

❖❖❖

200◂▸507 193 *F 105,4* *from 5.10.60, Ms.*

Event = Eyevent??
before eyes—

❖❖❖

194 *ÜR 6.12,23c-d [4]* *Ms.*

53, 486 The stone is older than we are, it stands in another time: in the together ⌞conversation⌟ with it, ~~we undertake the attempt~~ the one facing us with silence, we set ourselves in relation to the space from which it stands toward us: ⌞from⌟ this direction, the direction of our speaking, our words are given their share of color and reach {magnitude}.

204/632 The stone, as the other, the inorganic will resemble more that which in us is not plant- and animal-like: it becomes the spiritual principle; it reaches down into the depths, it rises up.

❖❖❖

195 *ÜR 6.12,30 [1]* *Ms.*

The stone, the inorganic, the mineral, is the older, that which stands toward and opposite man from the deepest time-layer ⌞, from prehistory—that is also man's prehistory,⌟. The stone is
131, 372 the other, the not-human \Außermenschliche\, with its silence it gives direction and space to the one who speaks; ~~spiritual relevance he has to~~ ⌞he has to,⌟ as ~~from the~~ he stands up and reaches down, ~~from the~~ taking ⌞with his⌟ distance ~~in nea~~ into his nearness, he must have spiritual relevance. One can confide in it, ~~oneself and one's~~ ⌞one may with one's—questioning—⌟ word ⌞go to it⌟: ~~the poem you write is epigraph~~
the stone

❖❖❖

196 *ÜR 6.12,26 [1]* *Ms.*

– M –

59 ... language becomes lapidary, the poem has the character of an inscription ⌞—waiting for a near or distant {—}eye—⌟ .

197 *ÜR 6.12,26 [2]* *Ms.*

[Time as caesura]

❖❖❖

Ms. *ÜR 6.12,29r [1]* *198* *►969*

—M—

Time ⌊—the ⌊now⌋ wordless—⌋ as caesura tenses what's named in the poem into an exciting presence—

❖❖❖

The poem as Speech-Grille

5.10.60, Ms. *F 105,2* *199* *343◄*

~~The strange~~
For a long time now the form of the poem has not been that of ~~its~~ its lines and stanzas; a much wider whiteness than that of its type page determines its contours

5.10.60, Ms. *F 105,3* *200* *►193*

Stereometry,: the symmetries → depth → speechgrille.—

❖❖❖

Ms. *F 32,2* *201* *538◄►497*

the autarky of the poem:
-i- through the autarky of the poem
= Speech ⌊crystal⌋—grille → inorganic → ⌊Höld<erlin>?⌋ Aorgic??? → deadly?? *843*

the work's "self-reliance \Aufsichgestelltsein\" (Lukács *894*

Lukács: The possibility to experience \Erlebbarkeit\
The ability to experience \Erlebnishaftigkeit\: only a determinable quality

❖❖❖

Ms. *F 116,6* *202* *419◄►286*

Insularity of the poem?

❖❖❖

Ms. *Workbook II, 15 [3]* *203* *671◄►240/410 =765*

⌊× → into the speechless—⌋
Determined from the direction of death : the wintery, crystal-like, inorganic as realm of the most essential turning-toward the one speaking ⌊in the poem⌋, humanscape {:}—deathscape.

❖❖❖

=791 | 204/632 | *Workbook II, 15 [29]* | *from 19.8.60, Ms.*

194 "Primordial urge of life to return to the inorganic" (•Freud, Beyond the Pleasure Principle)

-i-—this world moment is ours—
Maybe our space flights too are to be understood from there—

❖❖❖

=793 | 205/633 | *Workbook II, 15 [31]* | *from 19.8.60, Ms.*

"Forms" as homage to the autonomy/entelechy of the
→ •inorganic? (death drive?)
↙ speechgrille?, spacegrille?
/Crystalline
388 /Escape from contingency—

❖❖❖

88◄►637 | 206 | *E 3,3* | *10.10.60, Ts.*

843 ⌊Bettina⌋ That the laws of the mind are metrical, can be felt in language, as it throws a net over the mind.

❖❖❖

405◄►64/102 | 207 | *A 5,2* | *Ms.*

(Phaidros, p. 452.
The metrical = the bound

❖❖❖

167◄ | 208 | *F 99,3* | *Ms.*

subjective impulse

209 | *F 99,4* | *Ms.*

573 "Strictest measure is also highest freedom" (Georg<e>

►554 | 210 | *F 99,5* | *Ms.*

who after the measure of the other: Bloch, Rimbaud
Baudelaire—

×

❖❖❖

Ms. *Workbook II, 15; inserted sheets [1]* *211*

B—

The symmetry reaching back to the days of creation (of language too, etc.)—

<u>Rhythm</u>: time figure, whose parts require each other (Scheler) *257*

Reality—standing opposite /face-to-face/

❖❖❖

240/410◂

19.8.60, Ms. *Workbook II, 15 [5]* *212* *=767*

Rhythm—sense-movement toward an as yet unknown goal. ⌞→ a sort of tropism "by the lightsense you divine"⌟ *611, 843; 27, 344; 344, 378*

19.8.60, Ms. *Workbook II, 15 [6]* *213* *=768*

The minutest change in structure: heavy disturbances (Therefore maybe 'corrections' to prevent such disturbances) *443*

▸48

19.8.60, Ms. *Workbook II, 15 [7]* *214* *=769*

The rhythmic processes ⌞in the poem ~~buil~~⌟ can be released, they cannot be determined.

❖❖❖

Ms. *F 27,2* *215* *254◂▸349*

Vividness = not something visual, but something spiritual.—
⌞a matter of the accent / not of syllable counting⌟ *345*
<u>Sound-image</u> (something different from impressionistic tone-painting \Lautmalerei\, timbre etc. *256, 611*
= namely a way of speaking \Sprechart\ /Visible from the language- or speechgrille

❖❖❖

from 7.10.60, Ms. *F 25,4* *216* *669◂▸173*

Syllable counting // accentual poetry

❖❖❖

Ms. *F 52* *217* *644◂▸174*

Interval = Speechgrille *348, 400*
Rhythm, Accent

❖❖❖

497◄ *218* *F 36,1* *Ms.*

BR

263, 394, 276 ‖ ... In the “mora and cola” the poem culminates.—

×

219 *F 36,2* *Ms.*

---

378 The poem involves language: it folds itself

×

►19 *220* *F 36,3* *Ms.*

Speechgrille—Spacegrille

×

❖❖❖

334◄►126 *221* *F 118,5* *Ms.*

Poems as wordscapes

❖❖❖

517◄ *222* *F 12,4* *Ms.*

---

114 The new wordscape /with it, speech-taboo

223 *F 13,1* *Ms.*

‖ Remembrance—anamnesis etc.

224 *F 13,2* *Ms.*

Speechspaces

225 *F 13,3* *Ms.*

The poem has time and has no time.

►757 *226* *F 13,4* *Ms.*

---

561 ‖ The “poem in the poem” : hidden in the poem, in each ⌊wordf⌋{F}iber of the poem, in each interval.—

❖❖❖

Ms. *F 118,2* *227* *71◄►449*

There is a "poem in the poem": it is in each wordfiber, in each interval.

❖❖❖

Ms. *A 31,5* *228* *649◄►919*

Das Kampaner Tal, p. 51, footnote: *608*
... "as on the houses of the Jews (in memory of ruined Jerusalem), something always has to be left unfinished"

to remember in the poem—remembrance as absence— *458*

❖❖❖

Ms. *A 32,2* *229* *919◄*

No syllogistic ⌊enriched with this or that theory of association⌋, no logistic will ever be able to do justice to the fact of "poem"—the alleged thought- or language-scheme of the poem is never "finished." *462, 945*

Ms. *A 32,3* *230*

---

syntactic (and other!) clutches

Ms. *A 32,4* *231*

Oppositeness?

Ms. *A 32,5* *232* *►152*

Multivocity

❖❖❖

from 22.8.60, Ms. *Workbook II, 21 [20]* *233* *248◄►409 =819*

-i- The poem as the far from gapless structure, as the gappy, the occupiable, the porous: ("à toi de passer, vie!) *448, 484, 504 320, 340, 355*

❖❖❖

Ms. *F 12,2* *234/615* *614◄►517*

---

porous, spongy: ⌊the p<oem>⌋ it knows about the erosions it is exposed to. *55, 61/103, 305*

❖❖❖

475◄ *235* *F 46,1* *Ms.*

-i- the poem: sublated (waiting) present—

►85 *236* *F 46,2* *Ms.*

The poem { open / porous, / spongy—

❖❖❖

Poem and language

420◄►484 *237* *A 28,2* *Ms.*

In the poem:
272 1. Direction (wherefrom, whereto), language → soliloquy → conversation.
2. Time
3. The objects, the world, Being, the to-be, Appearance
4. Thought and language (Theaetet-citation etc.)
595, 843 4 a. : the tropes (Benveniste essay)

❖❖❖

152◄ *238* *A 33,1* *Ms.*

445, 34/493, 843 Mysticism as wordlessness
Poetry as form

►443 *239* *A 33,2* *Ms.*

The poem is inscribed as the figure of the ⌞complete⌟ language; but language remains invisible
381 {.}; that which actualizes itself—language—takes steps, as soon as that has happened, back into the realm of the possible. "Le Poème", ~~word-sequences? sentences?~~ writes Valéry, est du langage
26, 27, 255; à l'état naissant; language in statu nascendi, thus language in the process of liberation.
32/74, 259

❖❖❖

203◄►212
=766 *240/410* *Workbook II, 15 [4]* *19.8.60, Ms.*

68/384, 338 The poem is the place where synonymity becomes impossible: it only has its lang{eb}-×/ and therewith its meaning level. Stepping out of language, the ~~lang~~ the poem. steps opposite language. This opposition cannot be sublated.

×/ that's why the poem, in its being and not through its subject matter first—is a school of true humanity: it teaches to understand the other as the other ⌞i.e. in its otherness⌟, it demands brotherliness with <new page, dated: "8.19.60"> ⌊respect before⌋ this other, in the turning toward this other, even there where the other appears as the hooked-nosed and misshapen—in no way almond-eyed—accused by the "straightnosed" *33/111, 401, 747, 843* *394*

❖❖❖

Ms. *B 3a* *241* *463◄►547*

The poem comes into being through intercourse with something that remains {I}invisible to us: through intercourse with language. It *10*

❖❖❖

Ts. *C 5,3* *242* *26◄►587*

---

a meeting with language is a meeting with the invisible *256*

❖❖❖

Ms. *F 55,1* *243* *535◄►307*

Something of the foreknowledge of language falls to the one who is attentive: the invisible of the "point of crystallization" *771; 854*

❖❖❖

Ms. *F 115,2* *244* *►427 =909*

-i- co-appearance of language in the poem or: language as co-appearing (the poem as translucent) background =

❖❖❖

from 22.8.60, Ms. *Workbook II, 21 [10]* *245* *=809*

T.<he> poem as epiphany of language. *468*

❖❖❖

Ms. *C 14,1* *246* *516◄*

~~Opinion is more than reflection~~
-i- The poem is monotone/monotonic ‖ *658*

Ms. *C 14,2* *247* *►682*

There is a fate of the words of the poem prefigured by language~~; whi~~, as there is Censure and Economy for, Emile Benveniste{,} has shown it for οὐσία, for thought.

___

❖❖❖

from 22.8.60, Ms. *Workbook II, 21 [19]* *248* *►233 =818*

-i- Language as the language of the one who speaks / / *502*
the one who speaks as the speaker of the language =
in this antinomy—without synthesis—stands the poem.

___

❖❖❖

▸671
=763 249 *Workbook II, 15 [1]* *Ms.*

27; 272, 808 ‖ The assonance of language (as a whole) in the poem—⌞→ Timbre =
= untransferable⌟

❖❖❖

744◂▸596 250 *F 29,2* *Ms.*

We converse with language—despite and with all the "speakers"

❖❖❖

326◂▸118 251 *F 65,4* *Ms.*

-i- Carefulness in the intercourse with language, in light of the ⌞real⌟ opening-up of language—

❖❖❖

338◂▸386 252 *C 10,2* *Ts.*

The floating, ⌞the lightness⌟ i.e. the floating away of many a poem recalls ⌞—and that is, like high art a dream of great magic⌟ the state of levitation. ⌞"With it I saw the power of heaviness end"⌟

~~He who attains this state as language and through language—through as poem—, will realize—this dream and what's great in it lives on!—, will realize~~ art—I am quoting a saying by A.
587 Schönberg, I quote it according to T. Adorno—'Art doesn't come from being able to, it comes from having to. You see, there is also this kind of etymology: not through what has been derived from the imperceptible root do we have the true and the ground; we become aware of it through the root-distant branch ⌞the branch that stands into time⌟,the branch driven into time by the root.

❖❖❖

349◂▸744 253 *F 28,2* *Ms.*

Art—I quote here, following Th. W. Adorno{,}—a word {—}by Arnold Schönberg—, art doesn't come from being able to, it comes from having to.There is also this etymon: not the one derived from a root, but that has not been visible for a long time, but the one perceived on the branch—

❖❖❖

383◂▸215 254 *F 27,1* *Ms.*

Levitation

⌞B-R⌟

❖❖❖

587◂ 255 *C 6,1* *9.10.60, Ts.*

---

9. 10.

B-speech

26, 27, 239, 259 Levitation / for sublation, hovering, status nasc.

9.10.60, Ts. *C 6,2* 256

Re metaphor, image etc:

The pictorial is by no means something visual; it is, like everything else connected with language,
a mental phenomenon. ⌊Language: is that not an encounter with the <u>invisible</u>⌋ It is, *121, 333, 68/384*
even in what is furthest from the voice, a question ⌊to⌋ of the accent; in the poem the perception *242*
of its soundpattern also belongs to the perceived image. ⌊By the breath-steads in which it stands, *215, 611*
you recognize it, by the crest-times⌋ That is by no means the same as this or that cheap *400; 394*
impressionistic tone-painting, timbre etc. It is, here too, a manifestation of language, a speech-art that has to be heard in the written, i.e. the silent (The language-grille, which is also the speechgrille, makes this visible.)

9.10.60, Ts. *C 6,3* 257 *►80/303*

---- The state of the free-soaring, of the sublated is levitation *27*
Crest-times
Time-figures *211*

❖❖❖

Ms. *C 14,4* 258 *682◄►701*

The action of the precipitation of language from language is an arbitrary action ~~(i) by the~~ single *25, 47*
direction of this arbitrariness—it can be ~~recognized~~ by the ⌊unnoticeable, but consequent⌋
deviation ~~from the~~ morphological, syntactic and semantic categories—;

❖❖❖

Ms. *ÜR 6.12,19v [1]* 259

11/708, 33/111,
The poem estranges. It estranges by its existence, by the mode of its existence, it stands opposite *422*
and against one, voiceful and voiceless simultaneously, as language, as language setting itself *55, 271, 336,*
free, as language in statu nascendi—as Valéry once said—, ⌊and around the⌋ middle of language *398, 507;32/74,*
are grouped,—~~"each word calls for a counter~~ *239, 255*

❖❖❖

Ms. *F 10,2* 260 *340◄►556*

Language in statu nascendi, language setting itself free

❖❖❖

Ms. *F 30,3* 261 *113◄►557*

+ -i-
as stage direction: vacant lots—rubble etc. *740, 745, 843*
↙
possible only as language

❖❖❖

Breath

Breath

579◄►96 *262* *E 14,2* *30.5.60, Ms.*

'What's on the lung, put on the tongue,' my mother used to say. Which has to do with breath. One should finally learn how to also read this breath, this breath-unit in the poem; in the cola meaning is often more truthfully joined and fugued than in the rhyme; shape of the poem: that is presence of the single, breathing one.—

❖❖❖

455◄►566 *263* *B 50,2* *Ms.*

"What's on the lung, put on the tongue" my mother used to say—— ... on breathroutes it
843 comes, the poem, it is there, pneumatic: for everyone.
218, 394 In the mora meaning clarifies itself—

❖❖❖

87◄►394 *264* *E 4,3* *Ts.*

---

10 What's on the lung, put on the tongue," my mother used to say—on breathroutes it comes, the poem;

❖❖❖

653◄►189 *265* *F 7,3* *Ms.*

---

10 A thing or two come ⌊perhaps⌋, even now ⌊, even today⌋ still, on dove's feet.

❖❖❖

411◄►677 *266* *B 44* *Ms.*

Büchner-speech

Breath:
The poem remains, if you allow me a little critical jargon, pneumatically touchable.

❖❖❖

83◄ *267/605* *E 8,1* *Ms.*

Büchner-Sp—

here, on breathroutes, the poem moves =

►271 *268/606* *E 8,2* *Ms.*

Information theory, cybernetics =

❖❖❖

23.5.60, Ms. *B 29* *269* *416◂▸520*

Büchner-speech

23.
"Breath-units" (Buber); cola

❖❖❖

Ms. *C 16,1* *270/703* *702◂▸704*

-i- Stoppages of the breath—

❖❖❖

Ms. *E 9,1* *271* *268/606◂*

Büchner-speech

voiceful—voiceless simultaneously *55, 259, 336, 398, 507*

Ms. *E 9,2* *272*

•Voice—direction (wherefrom ← ensouling
↕ whereto → death, God) *611; 237* *321*
Timbre *249, 808*

Ms. *E 9,3* *273*

Ezekiel (O. T.—Hess. Landb.)
Isaiah

Ms. *E 9,4* *274*

Accent Rhythm Beat

Ms. *E 9,5* *275*

•Gestimmtheit \voice-mood\

Ms. *E 9,6* *276*

Mora, cola *218, 394*

Ms. *E 9,7* *277*

Image = vision (not: metaphor) *121, 912*

278 *E 10,1* *Ms.*

Novalis

279 *E 10,2* *Ms.*

Read Nietzsche!

►739 *280* *E 10,3* *Ms.*

59, 104, 518 Timesteads, breathed through, breathed around

❖❖❖

Mortality

581◄►676 *281* *B 31,4/32,1* *Ms.*

70, 381 Poems are not accumulations and articulations of "word material;" they are the actualizing of something immaterial, language-emanations carried through life-hours, tangible and mortal like us. These hours are, especially in the poem, our hours—this is one of them—; ~~we wri~~ hours have no phenotype; we still write for our life

❖❖❖

852◄
=856 *282* *F 86,1* *28.9.60, Ts. (Ms.)*

⌊28.IX.⌋ BR

•It builds ⌊, from the direction of death,⌋ the ⌊at the⌋ countercosmos of the mortals.—

546 Artistry and word-art—that may have the feeling of something occidental, evening-filling.
82; 17, 305 Poetry is ⌊something else; poetry.⌋ heart-grey, ⌊⌊sublunar,⌋ ⌊heavens- and heart-grey⌋ heart-
and heavens-grey⌋ breath-marbled language in time. • ~~Wordart and artistry too~~ Ultimately it
522 also ~~is~~ saved, word-art' into its ~~decli~~ drift and decline; survival is ⌊means⌋ in no way "everything"
335, 370, 579, for it. ...
656

❖❖❖

690◄►476 *283* *F 74,1* *Ms.*

Artistry ⌊and word-art⌋, ⌊—⌋ that may have the feeling of something occidental, evening-filling. Poetry is ⌊heart-grey, ⌊breath-clouded ⌊breath-marbled⌋⌋ language in time.—

❖❖❖

Ms. *C 21* *284* *467◄►76*

Poetry is heavens- and heart-grey language in time. ||

❖❖❖

Ms. *F 91,1* *285* *495◄►464*

Re:—heart-grey language in time.:
... it builds, from the direction of death, onto the counter-cosmos of the mortals{,}—it builds, like language, ~~from the under in a~~ under the law of that which is invisible because near and nearest. It ~~had~~ has all its dimensions in itself.: depth and distance— 37

❖❖❖

Ms. *F 116,7* *286* *202◄►577*

-i- ⌊poem⌋ not ⌊eye-catching or secret⌋ mirror of the cosmos, but countercosmos. The sublunar as "counter"-the supralunar (so still anthropocentric??)

❖❖❖

Ms. *F 67,4* *287* *639◄►934*

finite-infinite ("A shrub of transience, beautiful— 385/505, 461,
"Infinite-saying \Unendlichsprechung\ (Letter to Kasack etc. ... 520; 737

❖❖❖

Ms. *E 16,1* *288* *740◄►296*

... and the eternal, that is at the same time the mortal, kept safe in the word and in the word's finitude.

❖❖❖

Ms. *ÜR 6.6,12 [1]* *289*

—i—

⌊(The knowledge),⌋ that the poem has only the⌊n⌋, {where}when it lets the transience of all things and of itself come to word, the prospect to last.

❖❖❖

Ms. *B 4,2* *290* *547◄►750*

~~The po~~
The language of the poem is personal ⌊mortal⌋ language; it is, like ~~the call of 'Lucile'~~ 310
What in the poem is mortal, its breath, ~~is what actually remains; fate can be read from the poem ⌊—⌋ as language is here that which has been promised one. Maybe it has to do with the fact that one can never correctly read poems one has written oneself.~~

❖❖❖

42◄►43 *291* *F 127* *Ms.*

Man is a soul creature; we do not get his image from the organization of the chromosomes, we
25, 715 get it —not least!— <from> his hippocratic face—

❖❖❖

617◄ *292* *F 83,2* *Ms.*

---

557 -i- The mimetical of the poem = person, gesture, hands, physiognomy

293 *F 83,3* *Ms.*

---

hippocratic face

►398 *294* *F 83,4* *Ms.*

---

932 "The poet's soul- and fate-closeness to the hero" (Gundolf, B<üchner>)

❖❖❖

676◄►362 *295* *B 33* *28.5.60, Ms.*

Paris 28.5.60.
625, 643, 810 In the chiasmus ~~more of~~ the cross is nearer than in the theme "cross."—

❖❖❖

288◄ *296* *E 16,2* *Ms.*

Kafka:
157, 720, 732, 843 Language means to have, not to be

297 *E 16,3* *Ms.*

‖ (Acm.<eism>: To lead language into closeness with being—

❖❖❖

138◄ *298* *B 27,5* *17.5.60, Ms.*

Kafka: to be, not to have (language = to have)

►594 *299* *B 28,1* *17.5.60, Ms.*

And everything he blew upon was lost.

❖❖❖

Ms. *A 17,1* *300* *584◂▸106*

---

like all that, a breath \an inspiration\, ~~like a~~ ⌊each⌋ word spoken in what direction. "And everything he blew upon, was lost."

❖❖❖

Ms. *C 47,4* *301* *65◂▸758*

Handiwork—hands of the one-time, ⌊the⌋ mortal soul-monad man. *444*

❖❖❖

Ms. *F 130* *302* *45◂▸578*

Poems cannot be manufactured, they have the liveliness of mortal soul creatures— *16*

❖❖❖

9.10.60, Ts. *C 6,4* *303/80* *257◂▸659*

The poem is the detour from you to you; it is the route. It is also the route of language to itself, its becoming visible and mortal: therewith the poem becomes the raison d'être of language.

❖❖❖

Ms. *F 53,4* *304* *667◂▸190*

The poem as that which literally speaks-itself-to-death. *850*

❖❖❖

Person and language

Ms. *C 44,2* *305* *395◂▸66*

The present of the poem is—and that <has> nothing to <do> with biographical dates, the poem
is life-writing—the present of the poem is the presence of a person. {—}This person participates
⌊—⌋ as ⌊is ~~a~~⌋ ⌊as⌋ nomen ⌊—and that can <remain> unsaid because perhaps un unsayable—⌋, ⌊~~to-~~ *70*
~~recognize~~⌋ ⌊~~perceivable~~⌋ not ⌊readable⌋ ~~as~~ ⌊{a}as⌋ pronoun.—With the poem, the open-to- *55, 870*
time, ⌊the⌋ time-permeable, ⌊the⌋ porous poem it stands into time. Here time can join ... *55, 61/103,*

Poems, under today's skies, ~~are~~ ⌊is⌋, heart-grey language in time. *234/615*
17, 282

❖❖❖

176◂▸183 | *306* | *F 56,1* | *Ms.*

341, 486
865

~~In language~~ In the poem: the presencing of a person as language, the presencing of language as person—

❖❖❖

243◂▸863 | *307* | *F 55,2* | *Ms.*

862; 142, 183

Language's sensuality, its falling under the senses /sinn~~en~~fällige/ is the secret of the presence of a voice (person)

❖❖❖

655◂▸341 | *308* | *F 77* | *Ms.*

340, 355

-i- Fortuitousness \Zufälligkeit\: ⌊fate-like⌋ filled language: the poem—

❖❖❖

665◂▸618 | *309* | *F 121,2* | *Ms.*

... language that actualizes itself and that, for the sake of its shape as it falls under the senses \Sinnfälligkeit\, sends itself into mortal conversation (mortality)—

❖❖❖

69◂▸374 | *310* | *C 25,3* | *Ms.*

290

re Lucile: The essential is not the 'problem of art'; the essential is the ⌊becoming shape⌋ becoming visible ⌊appearance⌋ of language through the presence of a person {;}, it is the
~~the making finite \Verendlichung\ of language as~~
the-making finite \Verendlichung\ of language as appearance

❖❖❖

2◂▸100 | *311* | *C 4,3* | *Ms.*

an artless poetry?
it is the fateful, the person, whom one sees speak like Lucile—

❖❖❖

630◂▸147 | *312* | *F 97,1* | *Ms.*

×

What do we look for when we order word to word, if not the experience of ⌊foreordination \Fügung\, of⌋ fate. Something of that inheres in even the most innocuous rhymings. Therefore too the God knows how outmoded reverence for poetry—

❖❖❖

Ms. *F 8,2* *313* *115◄►687*

It belongs to the poem's essence that in its radical individuation ⌊of man,⌋ ~~and~~ in its separation it 339
⌊actualizes and thus⌋ makes the ⌊human⌋ and human kind-like \Menschheitliche\ visible—not 130
the other way around.
~~The way the poem shows, the poetry of the one who writes it, has~~

❖❖❖

Ms. *F 71,2* *314* *762◄*

-i- The poem is the taking on of shape of the I's desire, which, by dis-closing \ausgrenzt\, itself, reveals itself; we are literally there and present.— 844

Ms. *F 71,3* *315*

The poem: the trace of our breath in language 520
-i- the aura \Hauch\ of our mortality, with which a language fragment goes over into
nothingness and that vacancy thus arises, ~~in which~~ which gives form to the new 845

Ms. *F 71,4* *316*

(Natorp: Hu<sserl><?> : Logos) the finite: from the over-, in-finite, that is, the predetermined

Ms. *F 71,5* *317* *►418*

Plato: kinesis of the oaths—

❖❖❖

Ms. *A 17,3* *318* *106◄*

---

each object designated by a word carries the trace of the poet; the poet inhabits his words.

Ms. *A 17,4* *319* *►107*

To write poems: a beginning without illusion.

❖❖❖

from 30.8.59, Ms. *F 21,4* *320* *424◄►130*

In the poem something happens, something comes to pass: ~~In the hour of the poem, language{goes}~~
⌊~~passes~~⌋ ~~{als} as the Being of the one who writes the poem, through the narrows~~ language as Being 90; 349
passes through the (narrow) hour ⌊narrows⌋ of the one who writes the poem; it goes through and 233, 340, 355
past.

❖❖❖

=800 321 *Workbook II, 21 [1]* *22.8.60, Ms.*

8. 22. 60.— B—

voice—rhythm—
843 person, secret, presence

but: question concerning the limit and unity of the person

the poem as I-quest?

272 Death as the principle creating unity and limits, thus its omnipresence in the poem.—

-i- The poem as the I becoming a person: in conversation—awareness of the other and the
500, 817 stranger. The active principle thus a You assumed ("occupiable") this way or that.—(death as You?)

❖❖❖

►117 322 *Workbook II, 15; inserted sheets [3,1]* *Ms.*

658 "Nobody becomes what he is not"
Hofmannsthal, Bergwerk—

❖❖❖

431◄ 323 *F 64,3* *Ms.*

-i- delusional character of poetry??
A reminder that we are not only that which we believe we are?

324 *F 65,1* *Ms.*

-i- I mean the poem as fate, as a having dedicated oneself \Verschriebenhaben\ to this special existence =

325/36 *F 65,2* *Ms.*

489 -i- The poet as person is given to the poem as its share—

►251 326 *F 65,3* *Ms.*

-i- ~~Where the~~ Through what the fantastic and the hallucinatory-delusional are separated, I have no answer for.—

❖❖❖

668◄►110 327 *F 62,1* *Ms.*

The poet's being-directed-toward-language \Auf-die-Sprache-Gerichtetsein\
(being-inclined?)

❖❖❖

Ms. *Ts. "A" (Note on verso of last page)* *328*

You are, when your breath marbles it, given over to your poem.

❖❖❖

Ms. *C 49,1* *329* *759◄*

I know that I am given over to my poems—I ask myself: what do I give them also, when I don't give them<?>:
The following:

Ms. *C 49,2* *330* *►480*

I say ⌞that⌟, because this putting into question of art—not to say: this ⌞latent⌟ hostility toward art—speaks to me: the poem = breath = creature— *376/530; 411*

❖❖❖

Ms. *B 52,2* *331* *566◄►741*

In the singular the common speaks.— ||

❖❖❖

19.8.59, Ms. *F 15,1* *332/63* *502◄►123*

The poem: ~~th~~ a self-realization of language through radical individuation, i.e. the single, unrepeatable speaking of an individual.

❖❖❖

Ms. *D 8b* *333* *760◄►513*

⌞The place⌟ where the images have phenomenal character: ⌞but⌟ as something seen, as something addressed—as witness of a singular existence *121, 256, 68/384*

❖❖❖

Ms. *F 118,4* *334* *449◄►221*

The words in the poem, set into a singular happening, move toward their end (lastness) *457, 517*

❖❖❖

Ms. *B 12* *335* *752◄►650/748*

"Survival is everything"—that is singular in its context; it cannot, like ~~tha~~ the poem, be translated into cynicism.— *282, 370, 579, 656*

❖❖❖

336 *Workbook II, 15; inserted sheets [4]* *Ms.*

All that has been transmitted is only there once, as voice; its reappearance, its
55, 259, 271, respective present is a becoming-voiced of what has stepped back and is stored in the voiceless;
398, 507 decisive for its new appearance is its new voice; problems of style, are motives ⌞themes⌟ etc. are
41, 42, 560 co-extensive, not co-essential with poetry. (of the same origin)

❖❖❖

509◂
=822 337 *Workbook II, 21 [23]* *from 22.8.60, Ms.*

-i- co-essential with a being
co-extensive with an expansion

❖❖❖

81◂▸252 338 *C 10,1* *Ts.*

B-speech

17, 70 Vocabulary etc.: Poems supposedly consisting of words—no, n'en déplaise à Mallarmé:

484 The poem is, also in terms of its semantic meaning, the place of the singular, the irreversible; it
68/384, 240/410 is, to say it differently, the cemetery of all synonymics. (it resides beyond all synonymics

❖❖❖

599◂▸614 339 *F 11,3* *Ms.*

⌞It will be difficult⌟ Today {for the} the poem ~~has no~~ there is no genre term ⌞that stands⌟ above it; any ⌞given one⌟ has "something" of the ode, ⌞something⌟ of the elegy, something iambic or choric, at times it partakes of the ballad or is romantic; it is never only ode, only elegy, ⌞only satire ..⌟ only ballad, only romance. I am not suggesting with that that I think of it as a hybrid;
313 rather, I believe that a more radical individuation is expressed in the poem today {.} ⌞than hitherto.⌟

❖❖❖

377◂▸260 340 *F 9/10,1* *Ms.*

The poem ⌞, that I have in mind,⌟ is not surface-like \flächenhaft\; nor is this changed by the fact that even recently, with Apollinaire{,} or ⌞with⌟ Chr. Morgenstern, one had the shape poem; rather, the ⌞poem⌟ has the ~~complex~~ ⌞~~a double~~⌟ ~~spatial depth of the soul of the~~ spaciality {,} of the , who demands it of the soul ⌞and indeed a complex one:⌟ the spaciality ⌞and tectonics⌟ of the one, who demands it of himself; and the spaciality of the ⌞of his own⌟ language, i.e. ~~language which~~ ⌞not simply of language as such, but of the language which⌟ configures ⌞and actualizes⌟
422 itself under the special angle of inclination of the one who speaks ~~in which it actualizes itself;~~ and thus the poem is fateful language.
308, 355 "Fateful": a highly contestable word, I know; but let it function at least as an auxiliary word; as auxiliary word, for ex., for the description of an experience: that one has to emulate one's poem, if it is to remain true; that concerning this or that poem one has to ask oneself if it hadn't been better to have left it unwritten; that ~~one~~ even ~~the~~ the most ~~pronounced~~ ⌞~~most articulated~~⌟ ⌞literal⌟
233, 320, 355 Irreality form \Irrealis\ speaks the language of the imperative: "You have to go through here, life!"

The ~~temp~~ modes, the tenses, the aspects of time: in the poem they live close together. These—too—are darknesses, ladies and gentlemen.

❖❖❖

Ms. *F 78,1* *341* *308◂▸444*

... a language that presences, that fulfills itself under the singular angle of inclination of existence. *306, 486*

❖❖❖

Direction

Ms. *F 125* *342/39* *38◂▸40*

Only that he

We write—~~our~~ ⌊the⌋ poem writes—always still the 20th January, this 20th January. From such dates does it write itself—it writes ⌊itself⌋ toward the horizons which become visible from there: it writes itself ~~toward the necessary~~ in no way toward the imaginary, it writes itself toward the ~~necessary~~ ⌊needed⌋ and inalienable ⌊real⌋ ; it is en route there; from this direction does its meaning open up for it—open up for us. *386*

❖❖❖

5.10.60, Ms. *F 105,1* *343* *29◂▸199*

B-R
5. Oct.—

~~Poems~~
~~From the strange and the strangest~~
The strange is the horizon of the poem; ~~the~~ in the ⌊breath-carried⌋ conversation with the other ~~is the~~ ⌊this⌋ direction ⌊gives⌋ the meaning; the sense-enlivening, breath-carried *43*

❖❖❖

Ms. *B 3,1* *344*

Rhythm in the poem: that is ⌊unrepeatable, fateful⌋ sense-movements toward something unknown, that lets itself ~~perha~~ ~~at times~~ ~~so~~ sometimes be thought as a you: "by the lightsense you divine the soul" \"am Lichtsinn errätst du die Seele"\.—They are ⌊, even there where they are most voiceless,⌋ language-conditioned. *27, 212* *212, 378*

Ms. *B 3,2* *345* *▸873*

Re the poem's accent—German is not ~~yet~~ by chance accented and not syllable-counting. *215*

❖❖❖

670◄►642 | *346* | *F 63,7* | *Ms.*

=i= ~~ate~~ sense-, i.e. breath-enlivened—

❖❖❖

534◄ | *347* | *F 108,1* | *6.10.60, Ms.*

6. X. 60. B-R

The falling silent of language → = direction, oppositeness—something else than the atomization, the search for words, word parts,—Particles

►691 | *348* | *F 108,2* | *6.10.60, Ms.*

217, 400 Breath = interval

These intervals cannot be replaced with ⌊human-⌋ empty space and time-segments!

❖❖❖

215◄►253 | *349* | *F 28,1* | *Ms.*

——not all the poems one writes: no one is a poet through and through and inch for inch——

320 Poems are narrows: you have to go through here with your life—

❖❖❖

173◄►382 | *350* | *F 26,2* | *from 7.10.60, Ms.*

490 Poems are sketches for existence—not conscious sketches, but arising between the unconscious and the conscious.

❖❖❖

351 | *ÜR 6.12,5r [3]* | *Ms.*

Poems are sketches for existence: one has to live them ⌊, for the sake of their truth.⌋

❖❖❖

189◄ | *352* | *F 117,3* | *Ms.*

Poems are narrows

"You have to go through here, life": •sketches for life

353 | *F 117,4* | *Ms.*

139, 597 no oneiric qualities, but vigils

354 | *F 117,5* | *Ms.*

53, 501, 556 not an art of expression /keine Ausdruckskunst/

Ms. *F 117,6* 355 ▸*71*

• fateful—a highly contestable word, and yet, allow me, to use it here as an auxiliary word: one ⌋ *308, 340*
has to live according to one's poems, if they are to remain true; and concerning this or that poem one has to ask oneself if one hadn't better left it unwritten. Even ~~in all~~ irreality has something of that imperative: Here you, life, have to go through.— *233, 320, 340*

❖❖❖

Ms. *F 140* 356 *399*◂

Büchner—Sp.—

Poems have <u>direction</u>, life-direction ...

❖❖❖

Ms. *C 46,3* 357 *761*◂▸*75*

The poem describes circles—life-circles.

❖❖❖

Ms. *C 47,2* 358 *396*◂▸*65*

There are routes—routes, of which one doesn't know at first, that they are routes.

❖❖❖

Ms. *AE 15,8 [1]* 359 ▸*742*

Büchner-speech

The poem is what prescribes itself—what has been prescribed to one—one has to follow ⌊it⌋, with one's life

❖❖❖

Ms. *Journal of 2.VIII. - 9.IX.1960 [1]* 360

Bspeech

... on what street—heaven's streets \Himmelsstraßen\ belong here too—will be picked up one day; we do not know where the poem, which <u>lives ahead</u> of us, will point us *736*

❖❖❖

Ms. *B 18* 361 *466*◂▸*510*

—and through the contemporary rubble ⌊heaped up daily before us⌋ ~~,the daily before us heaped u~~ the poem comes, "like Egyptian m.<ummies> provided with everything necessary for life" toward us, toward each one of us.

❖❖❖

295◄►50 *362* *B 34* *Ms.*

B-R—

To dress with attributes
Nakedness
Undressing
↘

Poems: Equipment for a journey—the decisive one, the single one, which does not know its goal, but its whereto—

❖❖❖

187◄►944 *363* *F 63,2* *Ms.*

Question!!!
Finale:—upon what?

❖❖❖

576◄ *364* *F 95,1* *Ms.*

Distance: I mean distance, in no way do I mean future

×

►635 *365* *F 95,2* *Ms.*

On the questioning of texts—the questioning of- ⌊and-beyond⌋ and back-to-the poem—
×

❖❖❖

578◄►514 *366* *F 131,2* *Ms.*

The symbolic—related to the infinite—
Allegory

❖❖❖

47◄ *367* *F 135,1* *Ms.*

-i- GB-Sp

600 The standing-into-the-infinite of the poem: thus its parable-aspect
↙
= parable = definition—geom.<etry>—

---

368 *F 135,2* *Ms.*

Du solt minnen das niht, du solt vliehen daz iht

►453 *369* *F 135,3* *Ms.*

Heimann: There is divine dupery in the parable, and from it we learn to know what is unknowable”
3, p. 101

❖❖❖

Breathturn

Breathturn

Ms. *C 3,3* *370* *381◂▸590*

I had survived some things,—but survival \Überstehn\ hopefully isn't "everything"—, I had a bad conscience; I was searching for—maybe I can call it that?—~~a~~ my breathturn ... *282, 335, 579, 656*

❖❖❖

Ms. *C 24,1* *371* *401◂*

there too it still gives you a chance
to it faces you with silence: *184, 496, 513*

⌊maybe here we can ⌊remember the⌋ •the medusa-likeness of ~~poetry ⌊remember:⌋; it faces you with silence; it takes your—false—~~breath away; you have come to a breathturn.

Ms. *C 24,2* *372*

•maybe here we can—for ⌊here to⌋ there is talk of {~} ~~the strangest, come from elsewhere, from outside the human ⌊and what's turned~~ toward the human⌋—to remember the medusa-likeness *131, 195*

Ms. *C 24,3* *373* *▸13*

To face with silence:

~~The whole~~ it tightens compacts \turns poem\ verdichtet\ around the pain, ~~so much~~ with so much that has been ~~spiritualized~~ clarified into spirit ⌊to no avail⌋ ~~tighten~~ ⌊~~the unworthy one~~⌋ ~~to have stepped~~; to have come ⌊to you⌋; it silences you;

❖❖❖

Ms. *C 25,4* *374* *310◂▸86*

Lenz: the Medusa-likeness of poetry—to: faces you with silence, it takes your—false—breath away; you have come *715*
//// to the breathturn

❖❖❖

Involution

Ms. *E 12,2* *375/738* *737◂▸930*

... Büchner's last words on his deathbed, Lenz's words (Moscow) have not come down to us—it is the return into the just still voiced, as in Woyzeck—it is language as involution, the unfolding of meaning in the one, word-estranged syllable—: ~~the~~ it is the 'rootsyllable,' recognizable in the

476 ⌊death-rattled⌋ stuttering, the ⌊language as⌋ what has returned into the germ—the meaning-carrier is the {mou} mortal mouth, whose lips won't round themselves. Muta cum liquida,—~~and~~
506 vowel-buttressed, the rhyme-sound as self-sound.

❖❖❖

112◄►29 *376/530* *F 103* *Ms.*

---

330 Hostility to art—thus not ~~of~~ ⌊the⌋ development's, but involution's conspirators—in Büchner: without a doubt it belongs to what speaks to us.

16, 638; 561 Art, that is the artificial, the faked, the synthetic, the manufactured: it is human- and
16, 718; 40 creature-distanced creaking of the automatons: it is, here already, cybernetics, puppets readied for reception, it is man this and that side of himself: the cosmonaut, born from the womb of
619, 634 technology, for whom language means a fall-back to a pre-existence.—

❖❖❖

687◄►340 *377* *F 8,4* *Ms.*

‖ The voiced-ness of the poem today; in the anlaut: muta cum liquida.

❖❖❖

663◄ *378* *F 89,2* *Ms.*

219; 212, 344 the language of the poem: involutive → by its lightsense <you> divine the soul: the creaturely as the poem's horizon—

►862
=861 *379* *F 90,1* *28.9.60, Ts.(Ms.)*

BR 28.IX.60

175 The poem is with itself, it has also taken back the song it has proved ⤏ folding → involution

---

❖❖❖

64/102◄►179 *380* *A 8-10 [Extracts]* *21.8.59, Ms.*

(The man without glasses

"Involution," he said, "yesyes." "Back-formation{"}—I don't need to explain that to you." I nodded assent.

<...>

The man without glasses: involution
"So to speak": enjoy it like "involution)

<...>

❖❖❖

Leap

Ms.	*C 3,2*	*381*	*97◄►370*

Word-material—that has its ⌊could have a certain⌋ weight; poetry is a leap; one should not weight oneself down, when one wants to set over—and return. Language is invisible *70, 281; 4/696* *239*

❖❖❖

from 7.10.60, Ms.	*F 26,3*	*382*	*350◄*

O. Becker: success = not enough happiness *429, 438, 928*

Ms.	*F 26,4*	*383*	*►254*

Preparation: The translation of poems is an exercise in this sense: it happens across the abysses of the languages: what unifies is the leap.—⌊Such a leap is happiness and success—⌋ *601*

❖❖❖

Ms.	*C 26,2*	*384/68*	*86◄►715*

39b The poem is the place where all synonymity ⌊and ~~all same~~⌋ stops; where all tropes ⌊and everything inessential⌋ is led ad absurdum; the poem has, I believe, even there where it is most visual \bildhaftesten\, an anti-metaphorical character; ~~it is untranslatable;~~ the image has a phenomenal aspect, recognizable through perception.—What separates you from it, you cannot bridge; you have to take the decision to leap. *240/410, 338* *121, 256, 333* *428, 549*

❖❖❖

Ms.	*F 5,1/6,1*	*385/505*	*17◄►129*

It would be wrong to see the poem's claim for totality as a—more or less gapless—synopsis, rather, here an eye, ~~that~~—and with this I do not mean ⌊for example⌋ an organ detachable from the human and optically perfected—goes with the ⌊so far⌋ seen ~~to~~ to the single objects—and continues with them. For in the poem every thing enters into an event \Geschehen\, an event that is determined by the one who steps toward it. / Where that does not happen, i.e., where the lyrical I goes to the things to caress them with language, there we have that genre-bound poetry which, though not lacking in "mood," will not survive the moment of its "having been there": ⌊to⌋ such poems ⌊one cannot⌋ ~~no doubt have~~ deny the charm of the ephemeral; but they lack ever so little the greatness of true decline. ×/ *181*

×/ that world-gaining and ⌊simultaneous⌋ world-freeing, in the sense that the totality that wants to be represented also in the single tries to rid itself of all that contingency: ~~si~~ the ~~infi~~ finite-infinite of the poetic decomposes into its parts here. *523, 823* *689* *82, 287, 461, 520*

❖❖❖

252◄►82 | *386* | *C 10,3/11* | *Ts.(Ms.)*

597; 414, 718, 843; 39/342

There are—and this has nothing to do with any intoxications—ecstasies.
World-gain, reality-gain, ⌐and by that I do not mean a result, but a direction—¬ in the poem that means at the same time this too:
→ To step out of contingency.

❖❖❖

387 | *ÜR 6.12,13v [2]* | *Ms.*

12/710

—⌐that¬ "uncanny" laughter: in the absurd he breaks it ⌐he becomes world-free—¬ he frees himself from contingency

❖❖❖

388 | *ÜR 6.12,4r* | *Ms.*

205/633

⌐in that¬ that "nonsensical," uncanny laughter ⌐of the one who is falling silent¬ the escape from contingency—and this is an old dream of the poetic—is realized.

❖❖❖

389 | *ÜR 6.12,27 [1]* | *Ms.*

137, 797, 805, 876

In the finite-making \Verendlichung\ we feel the infinitiveness\Infinitivische\, we feel that ⌐—so often invoked by Hofmannsthal—¬ "sharp point of the infinite"of Baudelaire.
It is there where world wants to be banned; the ancient dream: simult. to become world-free—

390 | *ÜR 6.12,27 [2]* | *Ms.*

And exactly this remaining-in-time will make the sov<iet> critics accuse him of staticity ⌐and¬ reject him as being "anti-progress"—

391 | *ÜR 6.12,27 [3]* | *Ms.*

It is the—ancient—double movement of the poetic: as the world is delivered in the world, something (—what?) becomes world-free

❖❖❖

392 | *ÜR 6.12,21 [1]* | *Ms.*

M

the absurd ⌐—route into the other existence¬
an absolute laughter that makes world-free
the absurd:
the escape from contingency

an ~~absolute~~ ⌐"absurd"¬ laughter, which ⌐(permits.)¬ ⌐(the escape from)¬ frees from contingency.

❖❖❖

Ms. *ÜR 6.13,15 [1]* 393 *►122*

Mandelstam

/ Plotinus / *155*

Original and reproduction are the same
the yearning to become world-free
~~the gaze \die Anschauung\, not the~~
the gazed at, not the unlocked enigma

❖❖❖

Reversal—the foreign as the most own—Jewishness

Ts. *E 4,4* 394 *264◄►144*

Ricercar - - - re B.

⌊Your⌋ reversal—what is that? ~~Only when~~ Is it the word from the almond-eyed beauty, that I hear *240*
you repeat, varied most opportunistically? Only when with your most own pain you'll have been with the crooked-nosed and yiddy and goitery dead of Auschwitz and Treblinka and elsewhere, will you also meet the eye and the almond. And then you stand with your ~~thinking in~~ falling silent thinking in the pause which reminds you of your heart, and don't speak of it ~~any more.~~ And ~~only later,~~ speak, ~~after a while~~ ⌊later,⌋ of yourself. ~~In the~~ ⌊In this "later," in ~~the~~ there⌋ remembered
pauses, in the cola and mora {,} your word speaks; the poem today—it is a breathturn ⌊crest- *218, 263, 276*
times \Kammzeiten\ ⌊and soul-turn⌋⌋, that's how you recognize it. ⌊—be aware of it.—⌋ *256*

❖❖❖

Ms. *C 44,1* 395 *546◄►305*

On the crest-time of the remembered pause your word finds you

❖❖❖

Ms. *C 47,1* 396 *75◄►358*

It is not by shedding a tear, visible from far-away, for the almond-eyed beauty, that you will meet her.—

❖❖❖

Ms. *F 72,2* 397 *417◄►690*

He who is ready only to weep the tear of and for the almond-eyed beauty, he kills her too, almond-eyed beauty, another time. The ⌊~~gassed~~⌋ crooked-nosed ones, the goitery ones, the inhabitants of the stinking Jew-warrens, the yid-maws—they are remembered by the upright poem—the High Song →

❖❖❖

294◄►145 *398* *F 83,5* *Ts.*

55, 259, 271, -i- ... ⌊you encounter⌋ the eye and the almond. And here, in this encounter, into the interval
336, 507; 534 between voiceless and voiced, steps remembered, real <u>beauty</u>. There exists, I believe, also this
939 eidetics.

❖❖❖

621◄►356 *399* *F 139* *Ms.*

... then maybe you also meet the eye and its almond. But then you do not immediately speak of
82, 34/493, 430 it, then you stop or step into the interval—and that, unnamed, is beauty!—and speak only when
475 you know that you have met yourself.

❖❖❖

85◄►84 *400* *F 48,1* *28.9.60, Ts.(Ms.)*

⌊<u>BR</u> 28.IX.—⌋

He who is ready only to weep a tear for the almond-eyed beauty, ⌊buries her only⌋ he kills her too, the almond-eyed beauty, just ⌊deeper into forgetting⌋.—Only when you go with your ⌊most personal⌋ pain to the crooked-nosed, hunchbacked and yiddy ⌊and goitery⌋ dead of Treblinka, Auschwitz and elsewhere, will you also meet the eye and ⌊then ~~its~~ its Eidos: the⌋ almond.×/—Not the motif, but pause and interval, but the mute breath-auras, but the cola
217, 348; 256 guarantee ⌊in the poem⌋ the truth of such an encounter. In this sense the lips of the poet have,
439, 470/592 like Danton's, <u>eyes</u>. (Which is not to be ⌊dismissed⌋ as metaphor, but understood as knowledge
593 and vision.!!)
Not a seminar-ready metaphor furthering this or that topos-research, but a knowledge and a vision of the ~~bloodi~~ most naked evidence.—
×/ <u>Beautiful</u>, that would here(with) probably name what in the truth of such a meeting would manifest itself as something silent

---

❖❖❖

714◄►371 *401* *C 23,3* *Ms.*

The Almondeye:

—not only the almondeye that was <u>extinguished early</u>,

one also reads in a description by Edith Stein:

only when you'll have recognized the Other and foreign as what is most your own and
33/111, 240/410, yourself ... this relation to the most foreign as the most brotherly is what the poem ⌊wants to⌋
747, 843 create: not through its theme, but through its being.

❖❖❖

100◄►26 *402* *C 5,1* *Ms.*

With being-other there is turning
← Only when you—BSp

❖❖❖

Ms. *D 13* *403* *684/721*◂

I say here, what I say to myself, when I am ⌊all⌋ alone ⌊with these things⌋ : Only

❖❖❖

Ms. *F 56,3* *404* *183*◂▸*37*

One has to learn to love (to acknowledge) the dark like the dark-eyed, the dark-skinned— *868*

❖❖❖

Ms. *A 5,1* *405* *661*◂▸*207*

μελανόμματος
7 8 9 10 11 12 13 14 15 16 ~~17 18~~

❖❖❖

Ms. *B 25* *406* *157*◂▸*153*

Here comes my already in its title "kiking" "Conver<sation in the Mountain>. Something hooknosed, I know, for those who hold their tear ready only for ⌊the⌋ gassed ⌊attractive⌋ prince{~~sses~~} ⌊lets with almond-eyes and lower body. But maybe I may name it a second degree hooknosed-ness, an acquired atavism. *51, 737*

There is a third one standing by, le témoin, by the grace of language~~. An aversion~~ and malgré lui. He speaks, ~~only blondnesses~~ grayhaired as he stands there, still nothing but blondnesses.

❖❖❖

Ms. *F 58,4* *407* *421*◂▸*412*

Some things still arise from the depth of time, unexpected, against all expectations. We want to retain the thought of the "atavistic" return of the poem— *143, 534*

❖❖❖

Ms. *F 69,2* *408* *35*◂▸*622*

<u>against all expectations</u>

❖❖❖

from 22.8.60, Ms. *Workbook II, 21 [21]* *409* *233*◂▸*509* *=820*

Buber, I and Thou, p. 137 "—until the great fright comes, and the •holding of one's breath in the dark, and the readying silence":

+ ↕

• for "only at times it was unpleasant for him. *134, 704, 805*

❖❖❖

203◄►212
=766 *410/240* *Workbook II, 15 [4]* *Ms.*

68/384, 338 The poem is the place where the synonymous becomes impossible: it has only its language {pla} ×/—and thus meaning-plane. Stepping out of language, ~~the la~~ the poem steps in front of language. This opposition cannot be sublated.

×/ that is why the poem is by its essence and not first by its thematics—a school of true humanity: it teaches understanding of the other as the other _i.e. in its otherness_ , it demands
33/111, 401,747, brotherliness with <new page, dated: “19.8.60”> _respect for_ this other, a turning toward this other,
843 there too where the other appears as the hooknosed and misshapen—and in no way almond-eyed—accused by the “straight-nosed”....

❖❖❖

675◄►266 *411* *B 43* *Ms.*

330, 680 Respect for the secret of the hooknosed creature—that is one way to the poem

❖❖❖

407◄ *412* *F 59,1* *Ms.*

The hooknosed. Hook-languaged. Goitery—

►646 *413* *F 59,2* *Ms.*

The poem as oc-curence, pre-cedent\Vor-Kommnis\

❖❖❖

595◄ *414* *B 28,4* *18.5.60, Ms.*

386, 718, 843 the poem as ecstasy: world-gain as world-loss; unbecoming

415 *B 28,5* *18.5.60, Ms.*

One can become a Jew, _as one can become a human;_ one can jewify \verjuden\ and I would like to add, from experience: most easily today in German

►269 *416* *B 28,6* *18.5.60, Ms.*

Novalis

❖❖❖

418◄►397 *417* *F 72,1* *Ms.*

847 -i- Jewify \Verjuden\:
One can jewify\verjuden\; this is, admittedly, difficult and, why not admit this too?—_even_ many a _born_ Jew has failed to do so; that's exactly why I believe it to be so commendable

⌊Jewify : It is the becoming-other, to-stand-toward\for\-the-other-and-his-secret—⌋
~~Love of man~~ ⌊—Love for the human⌋ is something else than philanthropy— *690, 858*
Turning—for that there do seem to be too many one-way streets.—Two-way traffic and turning, ‖ those are different things, but even on dirt roads, it seems, alas, that there are few occasions to do so

---

❖❖❖

Ms. *F 71,6* *418* *317◄►417*

-i- Not by speaking of offense, but by remaining unshakably itself, the poem ~~is~~ becomes offense—becomes the Jew of Literature—The poet is the Jew of Literature—One can jewify, though that happens rarely, yet does happen from time to time. I believe jewifying to be recommendable—hooknosed-ness purifies the soul. Jewification that to me seems to be a way to understanding poetry, and not only exoteric poetry— *846* *185; 84*

❖❖❖

Ms. *C 32* *419* *15◄►18*

the Jewish—
when in ~~September~~ May 1945 I wrote the Deathfugue, I had then, as I seem to remember, read the reports on the Lemberger ghetto in Izvestia— *589*
done only once.—
But this question comes at me, with many others, again and again, and so
The poem is a turning

❖❖❖

Ms. *A 28,1* *420* *565◄►237*

In Jewishness: God, not as the one who came and is coming back, but as the coming one; given that, time becomes determining, co-determining; where God is near, time comes to an end. *843*

❖❖❖

Ms. *F 58,3* *421* *628◄►407*

[M. Buber, in conversation (Vico:) There are two times that run parallel, a "holy" and a "profane" one]

❖❖❖

Encounter

Encounter with the Poem

105◀▶584 *422* *A 16,1* *Ms.*

Even for the one, ⌊—and before all for the one,⌋ for whom the encounter with the poem belongs
to the quotidian ⌊and self-evident⌋, this encounter has to begin with the darkness—of the self-
177; 11/708, 33/111, evident ⌊what makes every encounter with a stranger strange.⌋: “Camarado, who ⌊this is no
259 book, who⌋ touches this, touches a human”
Only ~~from~~ by this touch—that is not a “making contact”—comes the way to intimacy. Aisthesis is
not enough here, man is more than his sensorium{.}; {I} it is a question of conversation, as it is
340 a question of language: (noesis does not suffice; it is a question of the angle of inclination under
which one came together; it is a question of fate. ⌊, as is the case with every real encounter, of
the here and Now, the place and the hour.⌋ /××

/×× Over both hangs, ⌊~~it~~ hangs and outlines them—⌋ a shadow, and this has repeated itself often since Hegel:

❖❖❖

641◀ *423* *F 21,2* *30.8.59, Ms.*

The attentiveness of the reader: a turning-toward the poem.

▶320 *424* *F 21,3* *from 30.8.59, Ms.*

In the poem {:}⌊what happens is⌋ not communication, but self-communication
(“Camarado, who touches this, ...”)

❖❖❖

62/542◀▶161 *425* *A 14,1* *Ms.*

Aisthesis alone (+ noesis?) is not enough

❖❖❖

616◀▶512 *426* *A 31,2* *Ms.*

↖
→ aisthesis is not enough; the ... ; noesis is not enough; .... ; what is needed is personal presence, what is needed is conversation; conversation{s} and entertainment are two different things; conversations are demanding, strenuous.

❖❖❖

244◀
=910 *427* *F 115,3* *Ms.*

Uniqueness of the encounter: under inclusion of the absent contemporaries \(co-)world \(Mit-) welt\

Ms. *F 115,4* *428* *=911*

Leap—as entrance into the poem *68/384*

❖❖❖

Ms. *F 66,3* *429* *756◄*

-i- Leap (O. Becker) *382, 438, 928*
~~Lan~~ creat. Leap of the poet, creat. Leap of the reader (you)—prerequisite (not guarantee!) is the being-turned-toward-each-other

Ms. *F 67,1* *430* *►638*

With that (conversation) the poem is as self-encounter encountering the other—and vice versa. *82, 34/493, 475, 399*

❖❖❖

Ms. *F 64,2* *431* *642◄►323*

Perception of the strange
becoming aware\innewerden\ + acc<usative>

❖❖❖

from 22.8.60, Ms. *Workbook II, 21 [16]* *432* *=815*

Intensive perception: becoming aware

---

from 22.8.60, Ms. *Workbook II, 21 [17]* *433* *=816*

To expect = attentiveness

❖❖❖

22.8.60, Ms. *Workbook II, 21 [5]* *434* *=804*

Perception rather: Becoming-aware-of \Gewahrwerden\

❖❖❖

Ms. *F 69,6* *435* *624◄*

Ontology of the aesthetic

Ms. *F 69,7* *436*

---

the poetically receptive

437 *F 69,8* *Ms.*

Writing as way-of-being leads in the final analysis no longer to see a difference in principle between poem and handshake—

438 *F 70,1* *Ms.*

328, 429, 928 O. Becker: Work and reception: unparted

439 *F 70,2* *Ms.*

400, 470/592 [Danton, your lips have eyes: ⌊Not a metaphor
a knowing⌋
—Your mouth speaks itself to the eye \Dein Mund spricht sich dem Aug zu\—

440 *F 70,3* *Ms.*

-i- ⌊seeing as⌋ discovering \gewahren\, becoming aware, seeing, to be truly aware \Wahrsein\

441 *F 70,4* *Ms.*

in a countermovement

➤762 *442* *F 70,5* *Ms.*

476 precarious = the poetic as the precarious

❖❖❖

239◄ *443* *A 33,3* *Ms.*

213 Corrections in the poem: each time from a new point of view. What ~~one praises as~~ handicraft—among other reasons also to bring ~~the alibi of the~~ manual in a technical world—, is there where there is ~~no handiwork~~ and manipulation, always only this: a ⌊new⌋ conversation with the spoken—in view of an answer
wrong formulation

❖❖❖

341◄➤935 *444* *F 78,2* *Ms.*

301; 14, 506, 546 Handicraft: the work of hands, accompanied by the hope for congruence

❖❖❖

from 7.10.60, Ms. *F 24,1* *445* *27◂*

-i- Reception
≠ To be deeply moved \Ergriffenheit\: neighbor to other, similar excitations.
Irritations
↙
I do not believe that criteria can be worked out here, that would be able to differentiate the encounter with the poem from mystical experiences *238, 34/493, 843*

from 7.10.60, Ms. *F 24,2* *446* *▸28*

-i-
Who takes in the poem, takes the place of that strangest, to which ⌊—voiceless and thus || language-near—⌋ it remains spoken for; in the encounter, as in the advent of the poem, language resounds, language is set free.—

❖❖❖

from 30.8.59, Ms. *22,2 [F 119,3]* *447* *130◂ [489◂▸664]*

Who does not expect the poem, will not recognize it either—

from 30.8.59, Ms. *F 22,3* *448* *▸27*

Poem ⇆ ~~~: two-way cathexis \wechselseitige Besetzbarkeit\ *233, 484, 504*

❖❖❖

Ms. *F 13,6 [F 118,3]* *449* *757◂▸499 [227◂▸334]*

reciprocal cathexis

❖❖❖

Ms. *F 114,2* *450* *=903*

The poem as a summons to the You → Out of= (out of absence) =demand

Ms. *F 114,3* *451* *=904*

Narrowing *32/74, 536/712*

Ms. *F 114,4* *452* *=905*

The one writing and the one understanding poems remain complementary in relation to each other *529*

❖❖❖

369◄►745 | *453* | *F 136,1* | *Ms.*

with thinking soul

Attention:

the soul's thinking-itself-toward-the-poem—

❖❖❖

933◄►579 | *454* | *E 13,5* | *Ms.*

Notebook at Gisèle's

↖

In the gazed at, the you awakes (s. -i-)

❖❖❖

683◄►263 | *455* | *B 50,1* | *Ms.*

B-R

In the gaze of the onlooker the gazed at awakes—but it does not awake to eternal life—

❖❖❖

944◄►188 | *456* | *F 63,4* | *Ms.*

643 -i- the poem speaks itself toward you ⌊the absent one⌋

❖❖❖

522◄►655 | *457* | *F 76,1* | *Ms.*

-i- BR—

The poem waits (= stands open) for ~~the~~ its absent—coming and ⌊thus⌋ future—you: in this way ~~it stands at~~ <it> stands toward the end-times \Letztzeitlichen\ ~~and end~~ (as some end-thing
334, 517 \Letztdingliches\): la Poésie brûle nos étapes.—Poetry is in a hurry: the must to which it obeys
618, 12/710 has nothing to do with the orders it gets from history's "bystanders."—

❖❖❖

647◄ | *458* | *F 60,3/61,1* | *Ms.*

228 Freud, Civilization and its Discontents p. 49: "Writing is originally the language of the absent one" = in the poem something absent comes near, it steps up close to you ⌊someone even more absent⌋ =

In the poem, and the poem is, as writing, "the language of an absent one," someone absent steps up close to you, the ⌊even more⌋ absent one.
[The thought lies close that the encounter of those who are absent may not occur.

Ms. *F 61,2* *459*

The royal glimmer of the ephemeral

Ms. *F 61,3* *460* *►668*

Heartpoint

❖❖❖

Ms. *F 62,3* *461* *110◄*

-i-

You = who is absent, what is absent
↗

The finite-infinite You helps build the shape of the poem: from its near distance. *287, 385/505, 520*

Ms. *F 62,4* *462* *►187*

against the ⌞indirect⌟—predictable—associating!! For direct perception!! *229, 945*

❖❖❖

Ms. *B 3,4* *463* *873◄►241*

Per ception \Wahr nehmung\ [lit. true-taking]: in the ⌞most⌟ literal sense ‖ *511, 843*

❖❖❖

Ms. *F 91,2* *464* *285◄►585*

The addressee of the poem is no one. No one is there when the poem becomes poem. To take the fate of that no one upon oneself is what leads to the poem.— ‖

❖❖❖

Ms. *F 92,1* *465* *585◄►656*

← who also wants to perceive \wahrnehmen\ the catastrophes, the tremors, the rejections inside of language

❖❖❖

Ms. *B 17* *466* *652◄►361*

It is en route, it is there, and we can [do] it,
—true<?>attention—

❖❖❖

713◄►284 *467* *C 20,3* *Ms.*

|| There exists, not only in the poem, a turn toward the gaze, perception
(—Ethos of the eye?—)
perhaps this leads to ⌊an⌋ ethos of the eye

❖❖❖

24◄►634 *468* *C 59,1* *Ms.*

245 epiphany

For the reappearance of language in the poem there is need for the resurfacing of the reading eye.—

❖❖❖

636◄►918 *469* *F 96,1* *Ms.*

"Streak in the eye"—the blind spots—

❖❖❖

►685 *470/592* *E 2,1* *Ms.*

B-R

400, 439 The lips that speak here have, like Danton's—let's not forget what happens to him—⌊his direction—⌋ eyes. They have perceived and seen; they know what they say.—
He who finds only metaphor in the poem, ⌊has not looked for anything else; he⌋ perceives nothing; ~~there certainly are~~, {T}there certainly are metaphor-pickers and perfumed bouquets offered afterward; the lyrical potpourri exists.—

❖❖❖

583◄►565 *471* *A 26* *Ms.*

108 No poet ever speaks on matters other than his own{.}; ~~in that there lies a~~ ⌊and only⌋ someone will call this egocentrism who overlooks (on purpose) that these matters belonging to the poet and him alone, namely that what is said in the poem is laid bare to the thinking of anyone; the thinking, not to the one with a program who on certain days tunes in to the Third Program.

❖❖❖

43◄►45 *472/44* *F 128,2* *Ms.*

612 Not a communication addressing this or that "erogenous{"} zone" of the other—shouldn't one
843 say here "message ⌊messägsch⌋" = but that which, shapely, steps up to the shape of the other; it is
16, 483, 508 an encounter accompanied by the secret of friendship and love.

❖❖❖

from 19.8.60, Ms. *Workbook II, 15 [36]* 473 =798

-i- B

No poem opens up for the one who, when approaching the poem, is not ready for the encounter; with so-called texts

from 19.8.60, Ms. *Workbook II, 15 [37]* 474 =799

Not the—wide-gauge—⌞modern poetry⌟ that understands ⌞itself as⌟ standing on its head—, but the poem that arises from the feeling of such unease.— 62/542

❖❖❖

Ms. *F 45* 475 31◂▸235

⌞To self-encounter?⌟ 82, 34/493, 430, 399

The poem, no matter how fragile, is something that hardly exists today: it is solidary. It stands toward you. And with it stands, ~~wi~~ where the near fails, with ~~which the~~ distant ⌞—the human-distant too⌟ toward you, to and for whom it speaks itself. It is, ~~at core~~ ⌞~~in th~~⌟ the second at the core and in the casing of your desperation.— 533

It stands with you against infamy. It stands against Goebbels and Goll.—

❖❖❖

Ms. *F 74,2* 476 283◂▸95

⌞The poem,⌟ As precarious ⌞and fragile⌟ as it is, ⌞is solidary;⌟ it stands with you, when you reflect upon yourself; it is •the second ⌞in the core (germ)⌟ (of) your desperation.— 857; 442 375/738

↓

•in the core and casing of your desperation.—

❖❖❖

Ms. *F 110,1* 477 506◂

Conclusion:

Encounter! Encounter!

Ms. *F 110,2* 478

On the hands on which it had to walk, the poem comes to you, puts itself into your hand. 805 82

Ms. *F 110,3* 479 ▸755

—Discontinuity of the poem— 124, 548

❖❖❖

330◄►3/693 *480* *C 50* *Ms.*

it puts itself, artlessly, into your hand

❖❖❖

755◄ *481* *F 111,2* *Ms.*

The comprehension of a poem is a matter of the ability-of-being-with-it: the poem is always ready for this ...

482 *F 111,3* *Ms.*

32/74 Tyche

×

►72 *483* *F 111,4* *Ms.*

16, 44/472, -i- The poem is open; only ~~in the~~ ⌊through the⌋ encounter,—which remains a secret—does it
508 again approach the hidden from which it comes. In that it resembles nature.—In ~~the destinies~~
⌊the destiny-second⌋ of the poem the "odyssey of the spirit" is repeated.
The destiny- second of the poem reminds you of the "odyssey of the spirit."

❖❖❖

237◄►616 *484* *A 29/30* *Ms.*

The poem as poem is dark, it is dark because it is the poem. Under{with<?>}this congenital
darkness I do not mean those Lichtenbergian clashes of books and readers' heads, where the
hollow sound does not always come from the book; to the contrary, the poem wants to be
123 understood, it is exactly because it is dark that it wants to be understood—{—}: as poem, as
'poem's dark.' Each poem thus demands understanding, {(}will to understand, learning to
understand (that is, but let this ⌊secondary⌋ phenomenon be mentioned here for the last time, a
true understanding and in no way some "To enter into the co- or re-production, as fastidiously
584 suggested these days on the federal and other levels. The poem, as I said, wants to be understood,
it offers itself up to an interlinear version, even demands it; not that the poem is written in view
of this ⌊or that⌋ interlinear version; rather the poem carries, as poem, the possibility of the
interlinear version, both real and virtual; in other words: the poem is in its own way occupiable. I
want to insist on the fact that here I am using the term interlinear version as an auxiliary word;
233, 448, 504 n<?> more specifically: I do not mean the{,} ~~betw~~ empty lines between verse and verse; ~~not~~ I beg
you to imagine these empty lines as spatial, as spatial {—} and—temporal. Thus spatial and
temporal, and, for this too I beg you, always in relation to the poem.

There exists, I return to this here already, because ~~it~~ ⌊n<?>⌋ nothing can be lost sight of, {—}
no co-, no re-production; the poem is, ~~as poem~~ because it is the poem, unique, unrepeatable.
(Unique too for the one who writes it and from whom you and I who are reading it, may not
expect anything other than just this unique shared knowledge.) Unique and unrepeatable, irreversible
338 on the other or on this side of any esotericism, hermeticism, etc.— —
16, 133

❖❖❖

Ms. *ÜR 6.12,3r [1]* *485/57*

—M—

Here the poem is the place where what is gazed at and perceived through language—the named—enters into a relation of tension with its time in relation to the gazer and the speaker. The foreign remains foreign, it "complies" \"entspricht"\ ⌊and answers⌋ not completely, it retains its opacity ⌊that lends it relief and appearance (phenomenality)⌋ *178*

—to let the incommensurable of the other speak too:
the time proper to him, the other, the space proper to him, the temporal and spatial nearness and distance, the unknown, from which it{he} comes toward you—like you toward ~~him~~ this other.—

❖❖❖

Ms. *ÜR 6.12,5v [2]* *486*

Re Kamen: he speaks—he is silent *53, 194*

E<dmund> H<usserl,> Vorl<esung zur Phänomenologie des inneren> Z<eit>b<ewußtseins>, *936*
p. 400 underli *306, 341*
Wahrnehmung—⌊in the poem that means⌋ not reproduction in language, but making present through language—
⌊Only⌋ By things having time, i.e. Now Before After temporal extensions, do they have individuality

Only in the perceiving eye does the object constitute itself

Remembrance and expectation belong to the consciousness of time: (~~in the time-field of this~~

❖❖❖

Ms. *ÜR 6.6,6 [1]* *487*

Mandelstam—

And so one will also understand that M'<andelstam>'s poems are not, as had often been said, "hermetic," but ~~in~~ rather open, wide open for the eye that tries to understand them in the totality of their temporal depth.

Ms. *ÜR 6.6,6 [2]* *488*

Conclusion: MANKIND'S PLACE—A PLACE IN THE COSMOS *53, 154*

❖❖❖

The dialogical poem

131◄►447 *489* *F 119,2* *Ms.*

The poem is never topical, but can be made topical. That too is, temporally, the cathexability
36/325 /ability to occupy/ \Besetzbarkeit\ of the poem: the You, to whom it is addressed, is given to this
You \ihm mitgegeben zu diesem Du\.

❖❖❖

116◄ *490* *F 20,1* *22.8.59, Ms.*

22.8.

In the poem something is said{:}, but ⌊in effect⌋ so that the said remains unsaid as long as the
one who reads it will not let it be said to him. In other words: the poem is not topical, but can be
made topical. That too is, temporally, the "cathexability" of the poem: the You, to whom it is
addressed, is given to it on the way to this You. The You is there, even before it has come.(That
350 too is a sketch-for-being \Daseinsentwurf\.)

►641 *491* *F 20,2* *22.8.59, Ms.*

"Sketched life" \"Entworfenes Leben"\

❖❖❖

881◄►125 *492* *F 16,4* *19.8.59, Ms.*

182 The You of the poem = (infinitely) near and infinitely distant (spatially and temporally).

❖❖❖

656◄►571 *493/34* *F 93* *Ms.*

I speak, ~~in that I~~ as I write poems, in my own and most own matter. With that I hope, and that
seems to me to belong to the last⌊, because oldest⌋ and still to be defended hopes of the poem, to
promise ⌊also⌋ in strange matters. In the strangest matter: in You-distance. At the perihelion of
509 poetry.—The poem has, I am afraid , entered the phase of total You-darkness: it speaks in the
strangest matter!—

I speak alternately in the first and second person; by naming at times the one at times the other, I
82, 430, 475, 399 mean the same.—~~The possi~~ In the You-darkness too the possibility of the selfencounter ×/
remains
I have to document this—I quote (Büchner): "..."

238, 445, 843 ×/ mystical motive—

❖❖❖

921◄►154 *494* *B 22,3* *Ms.*

selfencounter—mysticism—

❖❖❖

28.9.60, Ms. *F 90,9* *495* *►285* *=869*

Conclusion: poetry as selfencounter; unrepeatable and because of that to be undertaken ‖

❖❖❖

Ms. *C 59,3* *496* *634◄*

And even there where it has the courage to rise way above itself, it silences itself toward something foreign and {o} Other imagined as a You *184, 371, 513*

❖❖❖

Ms. *F 33* *497* *201◄►218*

The knowledge of the ~~poet~~ ⌞poem⌟ is a—psychoanalytically probably not fathomable—shared knowledge ⌞with an other⌟; there are ⌞invisibly⌟ communicating vessels.— *82*

❖❖❖

Ms. *F 68,5* *498* *160◄►35*

There are communicating vessels

❖❖❖

19.8.59, Ms. *F 14,1* *499* *449◄*

19.8.59

the "lyrical" I

/ Phenomenology? /

19.8.59, Ms. *F 14,2* *500*

---

but: polyvalence of the poem: I—You: no fixed relation

↗

I—You (infinite relation / tertium non datur
syncretism / *594*

rather: a third is given only insofar as it has been given to the You.

Essentially: the You of the poem, even there where it answers "literally," never gives an answer (cathexability there too). Constant back and forth of the I. *321, 817*

Linguistically possible I- forms (~~for ex.~~ ⌞extreme example:⌟ the participle!)

19.8.59, Ms. *F 14,3* *501*

Poetry: not an "expressive art \Ausdruckskunst\"! *53, 354, 556*

►63/332 | 502 | *F 14,4* | *19.8.59, Ms.*

248 ⌊Double⌋ relational framework of the poem: that of language, that of the speaking I

❖❖❖

127◄►131 | 503 | *F 118,8* | *Ms.*

I-You: not a fixed relation
A third is given only insofar as it
the linguistically possible I-forms

❖❖❖

=777 | 504 | *Workbook II, 15 [15]* | *from 19.8.60, Ms.*

233, 448, 484 -i- cathexability /ability to occupy/
The form—empty⌊hollow-⌋form—of the poem, is the poet's heart waiting for the poem.—

❖❖❖

The conversation with things

17◄►129 | 505/385 | *F 5,1/6,1* | *Ms.*

It would be wrong to see the poem's claim for totality as a—more or less gapless—overview, rather here one eye, ~~that~~—and with that I do not mean an organ separable from man and
181 optically perfectible—goes with the ⌊hitherto⌋ seen~~-to~~ to individual things—and takes them further. For in the poem each thing enters into an event \Geschehen\, an event that is determined by the one who steps toward it. / Where that does not happen, i.e. where the lyrical I comes up to the things to caress them with language, there we have that genre-bound poetry that, though certainly not lacking in "mood," will not survive the moment of its "having-been-there"; ⌊to⌋ such poems ⌊one cannot⌋ ~~no doubt have~~ deny the charm of the ephemeral; but they lack ever so little the greatness of true decline. ×/
523, 823 ×/ that world-gaining and ⌊simultaneous⌋ world-freeing, in the sense that the totality that wants
689 to be represented also in the single tries to rid itself of all that contingency; ~~si~~ the ~~infi~~ finite-
287, 461, 520 infinite of the poetic decomposes into its parts here.

❖❖❖

691◄►477 | 506 | *F 109* | *6.10.60, Ms.*

6.X. -i- B-R
14, 444, 546 The conversation with things (things not precisely congruent with the sign or something like
375/738 <that>)—things as ⌊(future)⌋ •witnesses—the ⌊vocal⌋ things, to whom man gives ⌊himself⌋ ⌊the I⌋ as consonant \Mitlaut\ into another time

• = as I-carrier = man carries himself over \überträgt\ to them (his I)

❖❖❖

from 5.10.60, Ms. *F 105,5* 507 *193◄*

In every poem language waits as voice
the poem's voiceless-voicefulness— *55, 259, 271,*
→to invoke \Anrufen\ = *336,398*

from 5.10.60, Ms. *F 106* 508 *►531*

The reification, the becoming-object dialogue of the poem: in the vocabulary too (as indeed it ~~has to~~ is everywhere ⌞a question of s<elf>⌟ incarnation) A naming—that is, before it is something else, always still an invocation (there too where it is a silent gaze): hence, from this naming , the poem according to its Being is anti-metaphorical; what is transferred to the objects is at best the I: it is, from the naming, the silent consonant of the named *843* *823*

Why not give an extreme formulation? : The poem is the unique, the untransferable, ~~real~~ the present \Gegenwärtige\— *586*

As the objective \Gegenständliche\ it can also have the objects' muteness and opacity; it only wakes up ~~thro~~ in the true encounter, which it has as its secret. Therefore every real encounter is also remembrance of the poem's secret. *178* *16, 44/472, 483*

❖❖❖

from 22.8.60, Ms. *Workbook II, 21 [22]* 509 *409◄►337* *=821*

-i- Our time: the time of the You-latency, you-lessness— *34/493*
" —I-latency

the I partakes in things; through the ⌞—I-containing \ichhafte\—⌟ naming of things the I and its conversation are woken up.—

❖❖❖

Ms. *B 19* 510 *361◄*

Mandelstam
Ordering \Reihung\, the asyndetic character of phenomena
the binding \das Bindende\: the poetic I—

Ms. *B 20* 511 *►51*

the verb as partaking: participial

Perception \Wahrnehmung\ before all!—in the most literal sense— *463, 843*

❖❖❖

Ms. *A 31,3* 512 *426◄►649*

idea of the bracket (voicedness)
syncope ↙
the ⌞this⌟ vibrato of the words ~~is a~~ too has semantic relevance. *59*

___

❖❖❖

333◄►917 *513* *D 9* *Ms.*

184, 371, 496, 602 To write poems so that they remain attuned, ~~even there~~ if not to our talking, then to our silence, {w} to our keeping-silent-with-the-named; so that we only silence ourselves before a foreign You as consonants \nur als Mitlaute ein fremdestes Du anschweigen\—and give it a chance.—

❖❖❖

366◄ *514* *F 131,3* *Ms.*

"Last-thing-ness \Letztdinglichkeit\"

►46 *515* *F 131,4* *Ms.*

---

507 "voiced—voiceless—

❖❖❖

82◄►246 *516* *C 13* *Ms.*

Abyss:
maybe there is only this one ~~them~~ infinitely variable <?> theme, fed by near and distant springs:
24, 711 this oppositeness, in which the participants can be represented <?> :

maybe it is only from there that the conversation—the gaze—of things becomes possible: as the last of ~~thi~~<?>, in the simultaneity of the being-with-them-at-the-end\des Mit-ihnen-Zuletztseins\—in their end-being-going\ Letztsein-Gehens\—as the consonant.

vibr. consonant

❖❖❖

234/615◄►222 *517* *F 12,3* *Ms.*

334, 457 The words that have been thing-fastened \dingfest gemachten\, the word-things in the poem—set into ⌊a⌋ unique process they {go}move, ~~they hurry~~⌋ toward their end ⌊, hurry toward it:⌋: they stand in the light of a "last-thing-ness" \ "{l}Letztdinglichkeit"\—I say light, I do not say darkness, but consider this: the shadow, the shadow which {they throw}this throws!

❖❖❖

552◄►653 *518* *F 7,1* *Ms.*

---

to make thing-fast.
last thingness
59, 104, 280 in the poem the things are—time stead \Zeithof\!—always in their last thingness—

❖❖❖

560◄►714 *519* *C 23,1* *Ms.*

The things = the last things

❖❖❖

Ms. *B 30,1* 520 *269◄►604*

Mandelstam

⌞\of\ infinite forms⌟ Thus the things in the poem are the "first" and at the same time already the "last" things; ~~are~~ the poem is the place where finite and infinite ~~come together~~ ⌞reveal themselves to each other⌟: only ~~following~~ ⌞with⌟ the trace of the mortal ~~will the can the~~ ⌞you follow the⌟ track of ~~immortality~~ ⌞the everlasting.⌟ ~~be searched for~~.— *17, 119, 182* *287, 385/505,* *461, 529; 315*

❖❖❖

Ms. *F 87,1* 521 *94◄►133*

That thing-nearness accrues despite all the human-distance, even in the poem, this must not surprise.—

×

❖❖❖

Ms. *F 75* 522 *95◄►457*

-i-

Poetry is not "word art"; it is a listening and obeying \ein Horchen und Gehorchen\— *282*

❖❖❖

Ms. *ÜR 6.6.13v [Auszug]* 523

A word about the poems: ~~By nearly none of his~~ ⌞As for ~~only~~ only a few of his? contemporaries{,} ⌞—and with that not ~~only~~ those⌟ writing ~~not only those writing in the Russian~~ language{,} ⌞are meant,? for Osip Mandelstam, born in 1891 ~~in Warsaw the word in the poem are sign and signified~~ the poem is the place, where what can be reached through language ⌞by the individual⌟ ~~seems gathered is gathered, to make the perceived in the word "thing-fast"~~ enters into an indissoluble connection with ~~the what~~ his (the individual's) speechlessness, ~~with~~ ~~WHERE~~ it, ~~thingfast its~~<?> meets the question after the whereto and wherefrom of the one who speaks, voiced \stimmbegabt\ and voiceless at the same time, meets the wish to gain world and the wish, the ur-original wish of the poet, thus, in the poem, to become free of the world. *385/505, 823*

For the things in the poem ~~have a relationship with~~ are related to those things that one calls the last ones.

❖❖❖

Ms. *ÜR 6.12,28* 524

Time-steads \Zeithöfe\

The perceiver \Wah<r>ne<h>m<en>de\<?>—the one who is attentive, present—
in their uniqueness and unrepeatability: the first and simultaneously the last things—

❖❖❖

525 *ÜR 6.13,12r* *Ms.*

-i-

Mandelstam

The things: more thingy \dinglicher\ in the sense of their presentness, the presentness for the one who sees them and deals with them. Not transfigured, not heightened ⌊not dipped into a ⌊symbolic⌋ vagueness⌋—but looked at{,} ⌊and set into words ⌊(set in?)⌋ (sertis dans des mots)⌋—⌊from the nearness⌋ ~~by~~ ⌊with⌋ mortal eyes

thingfast

526 *ÜR 6.13,12v [1]* *Ms.*

The things, that want to step into a name, step forward, come before the eyes

527 *ÜR 6.13,12v [2]* *Ms.*

---

122 "gotten into \hineingeraten\"

❖❖❖

528 *ÜR 6.13,17 [1]* *Ms.*

---

the thingfast words →
last things →
through their finitude ⌊led⌋ ~~at~~ ⌊to⌋ the end

529 *ÜR 6.13,17 [2]* *Ms.*

---

452 Complementarity (Pöggeler)
520 the finite complementary with the infinite—and vice versa

❖❖❖

Hostility to Art

Hostility to Art

Ms. *F 103* *530/376* *112◄►29*

What is hostile to art—thus not sworn to an unfolding but to an involution—in Büchner: this *330*
belongs doubtlessly to what speaks to us.

Art, that is the artful, artificial, synthetic, the made: it is the creaking of the automatons, far *16, 638; 561*
from the human and creaturely: it is, here already, cybernetics, tuned to reception~~-ready~~ *16, 718; 40*
puppets, it is man on this and that side of himself: the cosmonaut born from the womb of
technology, for whom language means a relapse into a pre-existence.— *619, 634*

❖❖❖

Ms. *F 107,1* *531* *508◄*

<u>Hostility to Art</u>

Ms. *F 107,2* *532*

Elargissez l'Art!— *638, 700, 852*

Ms. *F 107,3* *533*

The prefigured despair at the artistic,—a despair which the poem today{,} has to take into its
core, in order to exist as poem— *475*

Ms. *F 107,4* *534* *►347*

Hermeticism, today: to close oneself to the ⌊conventional⌋⌊compromised⌋ "beautiful," in order to *398*
open up to something true \Wahren\—perhaps coming \Kommenden\—not "comfortable" *650/748*
\"Kommoden"\—I would speak here of hope; the poem "tests the wind" \"verhofft"\, like the *143, 407*
hunted creature—

❖❖❖

Ms. *F 54,3* *535* *593◄►243*

No Mercier-ian "Elargissez l'Art!"

❖❖❖

711◂▸713 *536/712* *C 20,1* *Ms.*

élargissez l'art

32/74, 451 No widening, but a narrowing

⌊not a{n} ~~ar~~ theory widened toward some modern or most modern—

❖❖❖

170◂▸171 *537* *F 100,4* *Ms.*

‖ In the tightest space =// Elargissez l'Art

Contrast

↕

Not economy, but: ...??

but what???

×

❖❖❖

132◂▸201 *538* *F 32,1* *Ms.*

701, 713, 906 Re "hostile to art": ⌊at least, perhaps:⌋ meta-aesthetic

❖❖❖

=915 *539* *F 116,4* *Ms.*

⌊the⌋ meta-aesthetic = hostility to art ⌊in Büchner⌋

❖❖❖

▸202

=916 *540* *F 116,5* *Ms.*

= Falling silent: much is set in brackets

❖❖❖

610◂ *541* *A 13,1* *Ms.*

Coming to the end of ~~this assessment~~ these thought processes, permit me one more assessment, namely that they did not need the concept of the "beautiful."

Lyric poetry—Artistry—Expressive Art—Facticity

Ms. *A 13,2* *542/62* ►*425*

I speak ~~here~~, given that I write poems, in matters that are my own; permit me to attach a hope to this assessment, namely that because of this I speak in a certain way in strange matters.

I do not, to start with, speak of "modern poetry"{.}, ~~In brackets~~ I speak of the poem today. (~~Besides~~ ⌊By the way⌋, and that indeed ⌊already⌋ belongs to this "today": it would not be uninteresting, I believe, to investigate the conditions under which these nouns, the "lyric \Lyrik\" and the "lyric poet \Lyriker\" coined at the beginning of the 19th century—before that, one spoke of "lyric poetry \lyrischer Poesie\"—came into that tense relationship with "Poetry"and "poet"—descriptions that also have their fates—{.},{)} in which they stand ~~toda~~ without a doubt.) *474* *561, 60/582*

❖❖❖

Ms. *A 21,1* *543* *108*◄

"Lyrik—Dichtung"
The uneasiness → Lyrik
the ~~progress~~\\~~Fort~~schritt\therein

An uneasiness similar to that in relation to the word literature\Schrifttum\ (which Heine uses ...)

Tension between Lyrik = Dichtung *9, 17*
~~Questions~~ Lyrik
"Problems of ~~poetry~~"

~~Questions~~

Ms. *A 21,2* *544* ►*662*

We live in a brighly lit time, a time that illustrates everything; ~~we~~ lyric poetry has a cosmopolitan trait: "Felice notte!" writes our ~~gre~~ so agreeably contradictory Gott. Benn ...

❖❖❖

Ts. *C 43,1* *545* 9◄

The poem finds little answer. We live in a world of perversion: even that which ~~the poem attains, once transformed into so-called "lyric poetry,"~~ contributes to the murder of the poem.

Ts. *C 43,2* *546* ►*395*

The poem finds little as answer; thus it too has to stand in for the non-answering ⌊the ~~engagement~~⌋; it makes responsible; le poète paye de sa personne; aujourd'hui, il paye doublement. It is a matter of ~~this resp~~ this also Standing-for-the-Other, in a shrinking place, the

14, 444, 506 poem; it is a matter of this one-ness \Einssein\, a matter of this congruence. Here the concept of
282 the artistic no longer suffices; not to mention the ~~artistic~~ so-called artistic. Artistic and engaged:

What matters is the sublation of a duality; given the I of the poem the You is also given; what matters is such a ~~oneness~~ Seeing-into-the-One \In-eins-Sehen\; what matters is congruence; here the concept of the artifactual \Künstlerischen\ no longer suffices; neither does that of the artistic \Artistischen\.

❖❖❖

241◄►290 *547* *B 4,1* *Ms.*

---

doesn't sound different today. ~~It is uncanny for me~~ ⌊~~we~~ For me it is⌋ somewhat uncanny to hear ⌊—I hear it sometimes—⌋, that my poems have something to do with 'artistry'; in fact for me ~~no such thing~~ ⌊nothing like that⌋ is involved.

❖❖❖

129◄ *548* *F 6,2* *Ms.*

124, 479; 172, 610 Discontinuity of the poem (no system—⌊but⌋ a structure)

549 *F 6,3* *Ms.*

68/384 To understand the cognitive character of the poetic solely as one with ~~it~~ its dialectical leap into Being—

282 *550* *F 6,4* *Ms.*

‖ today: a certain artlessness (in contrast to Bennian "artistry\ Artistik\")

551 *F 6,5* *Ms.*

Lyric poetry is no longer a heuristics

►518 *552* *F 6,6* *Ms.*

Hegel (II, ~~105~~ 1015, court poets and everyman-poets)

parenistic (parenesis) admonishing, remembering, edifying

❖❖❖

603◄►30 *553* *F 39* *5.10.60, Ms.*

32/74 The asceticism of poetry; this is a time for exercises, not for experiments.

❖❖❖

Ms. *F 99,6* 554 *210◄*

-i- The time of programmatic explanations is over—we are alone—

×

Ms. *F 99,7* 555 *►168*

Ascesis, the ascetic character of poetry

❖❖❖

Ms. *F 10,3* 556 *260◄►597*

The poem is absolutely not, as many believe, the result of some kind of "expressive art \Ausdruckskunst\." *53, 354, 501*

❖❖❖

Ms. *F 30,4* 557 *261◄►620*

Gestures—⌊but⌋ no expressivity— *292*

❖❖❖

Ms. *F 121,4* 558 *618◄►657*

The poem today:
not joyfully expressive and in no way loquaciously communicative; cybernetically under age—*not reliable* *813; 81*

❖❖❖

Ts. *C 7,3* 559 *660◄►32/74*

In the⌊ambit \Umkreis\ ⌊shambit \Dunstkreis\⌋ of poetry⌊and hands ...⌋⌋ there is much talk of handicraft. Indeed, handicraft exists; as prerequisite.

❖❖❖

Ms. *C 22,4* 560 *78◄►519*

Poetry and handicraft are, ~~like (the) spoken and the handed, coextensive; they are not not~~ *336*

❖❖❖

Ms. *A 19,3* 561 *178◄►108*

"The poem in the poem" *227*
"The poetry of poetry"—for the comprehension of which no etymological commonplaces of pretense\facticity \vo{m}n "Mache"\ etc. will help; the poem does not explain its design \Machart\; but it is of course not really surprising that today there is interest before all in questions of production and manufacture.) *16, 376/530*
~~th~~<?> The nouns 'lyric poetry\Lyrik\' and 'lyric poet\Lyriker\' date to the beginning of the 19th C. *62/542, 60/582*

1833, 1827

❖❖❖

742◄ 562 *AE 15,8 [3]* *Ms.*

⌊Today⌋ it has become fashionable to give an answer to the question of how poems are made; one should rather ask how come that one asks oneself such a question—someone, for whom this question was fateful: • ×/

×/ There is also much easy and insouciant talk of the craft of poetry—without having washed one's hands before, certainly not in the water of real words.
Craft is a matter of clean hands et cetera.
There is no golden bottom et cetera. → (⌊Letter to⌋ Bender—)

---

563 *AE 15,8 [4]* *Ms.*

"How does one make verses" • Mayakovsky tried to ask himself at a certain hour—with ~~this question~~ he did.—the boat of his love shattered on the thusness \Sosein\ ⌊(and the refusal to want to be something other⌋ of human dailiness ... Omnipotence puts it back together—

---

564 *AE 15,8 [5]* *Ms.*

⌊The making \Das Machen\⌋ The faking \Die Mache\ → machination \Machenschaft\. I have observed just such a supposedly "lyrical" case. Some of you probably know what and who this is about. That too exists. It is a "literary" version of infamy, a particularly monstrous—because manufactured ⌊with words⌋—kind of namelessness

Mayakovsky: someone who, like Lenz, meets his fate in Moscow, in the shape of a bullet fired by himself—you can't always leave that to the others—, Mayakovsky—

❖❖❖

471◄►420 565 *A 27,1* *Ms.*

The time when, as in the Young Fate, the poem offers itself as a Théâtre de l'Intellect, a stage on which spirit puts itself on show,—that time is gone. Thought, language, remains, without wanting to incarnate itself and step before an eye that is first eye, and as such is spiritual, in its own realm, a realm in which the words keep in touch with the one who thinks them, with him and primarily with him.

❖❖❖

263◄►331 566 *B 52,1* *Ms.*

B-Sp—

Büchner's hostility to Art—permit the translator of the Young Fate this confession—I share it—

❖❖❖

Ms.	*B 39,2*	*567*	*753◄►679*

And who also with the verse of the Nibelungenlied—the alexandrine—Bateau Ivre—Jeune Parque—

❖❖❖

Ms.	*B 46,1*	*568*	*677◄*

Büchner-speech

One can say everything (Shestov)

Ms.	*B 46,2*	*569*	

-i- Where wouldn't we already be, if we were with our words!

Ms.	*B 46,3*	*570*	*►672*

Hostility to Art, hostility to words, too *148*
Silence, inherent in speaking—

❖❖❖

Ms.	*F 94,1*	*571*	*34/493◄*

veilless

---

the veilless

×

Ms.	*F 94,2*	*572*	

language set free as memory of our freedom???

Ms.	*F 94,3*	*573*	

Speechgrille—the strictest measure is highest freedom— *209*

×

Ms.	*F 94,4*	*574*	

the element hostile to art—

↓ unstylized, naked

Ms.	*F 94,5*	*575*	

-i- the representation like \Abbildhafte\—

►364 | *576* | *F 94,6* | *Ms.*

Ground-figures (not: -words)

❖❖❖

286◄►189 | *577* | *F 117,1* | *Ms.*

---

today: a certain artlessness

❖❖❖

302◄►366 | *578* | *F 131,1* | *Ms.*

The simple is the uncomfortable.—

❖❖❖

454◄►262 | *579* | *E 14,1* | *30.5.60, Ms.*

30.5.60 Büchner-speech—

282, 335, 370, 656 “Survival is everything”—no, it is not everything; ⌞no, to survive is indecent, as survivor one has to write for one’s life even more so.—⌟ and it is not by chance that these words are a citation—a citation taken over and taken responsibility for with ⌞much⌟ less than one’s own life-breath; yes, from artistry there is just one step to posthumous whitewash.

❖❖❖

674◄ | *580* | *B 31,2* | *Ms.*

Poems are something else than rhyming footnotes to Theodor Lessing

►281 | *581* | *B 31,3* | *Ms.*

Survival is everything.: that was a line in a poem (?), it is a citation, and citations are something else than strange bodies which we, being medial and thus set in centers, feel as flowing toward us; they are—~~the~~ peace to the also cited—foreign bodies as such.—

❖❖❖

Metaphor

114◄ | *582/60* | *A 23/24* | *Ms.*

Ladies and gentlemen,

I speak⌞, as I write poems,⌟ in matters concerning me; ~~permit me this addition: exactly because of that{,} I believe, and~~ indeed in more than one aspect, to speak in matters of the strange.” ⌞whereby, and that is also connected to the writing of poems, I hope to speak ⌞at least⌟ in some way also in matters of the strange.⌟

I speak ⌊of the poem, of the poem today. I do not speak of "modern lyric poetry"⌋ of the darkness of the poem. ×/ I say poem and by that understand ~~something,~~ ⌊a language construct,⌋ that is enlisted by both poetry \Dichtung\ and by the lyric poem\Lyrik\.
"Lyrik" and "Lyriker," those are coinages from the early 19th C. *62/542, 561*
Tense relationship et cetera.
There is, I believe, ~~beyond~~ this side and beyond all esotericism and hermeticism, this side and beyond secret and revealed knowledge, a darkness of the poem.
"Writing as a form of prayer," we read ~~in~~<?>—deeply moved—in Kafka. This, however, does not mean that praying comes first, writing does: one cannot do it with folded hands.

×/ And I do not speak either of those darknesses that a "Philology"—I wish one could, in this context, spell that word with a small initial letter—that triumphs under the applause of the dilettantes, spreads over the poem; a philology that babbles f. ex. about ⌊genitive⌋ metaphors, without ever having given a thought to what a m. is, where it is to be found in the text, and how many genitives there are. Of these, the tracts and tractlets of the philologically accredited cultural attachés, nothing will be said here. There are ⌊~~such~~ ⌊these⌋ highly cultured⌋ *612*
obscurantists, ~~certainly, even among the poets: Hölderlin~~ have always existed: let me remind you *33/111*
that the description "metaphysical" for Donne, Marvell was originally meant contemptuously

Ms. *A 25,1* *583* *►471*

The spirit blows where it wants to, and (luckily) the cultural attachés have no influence on that.

❖❖❖

Ms. *A 16,2* *584* *422◄►300*

No 'trobar cluz' {;} ⌊I am yours, you are mine⌋ lost is the little key \slüzzelin\. He who frequents the poem in order to sniff out metaphors, will always only find—metaphors. /×
×/ As long as it—~~permit me this wordplay~~ ⌊and here I may come close to its way of thinking with this wordplay ⌊~~a~~<?> also a little cheekily "re-enact"—⌋ ⌊—given that it's a matter of "tropics."— *484*
as long as this or that liana growth does not embrace it.
For the poem, ⌊which is the poem of a human,⌋ the human is ~~not a nose~~ ⌊more than a ~~culture-bloated~~ ⌊by culture hypertrophied⌋ organ of smell,⌋ and certainly not a trunk ⌊(animal) (being)⌋

❖❖❖

Ms. *F 91,3* *585* *464◄►465*

-i- Metaphor, that is sometimes only an (auxiliary)word ⌊a (white)lie⌋ in the mouth of those ~~whose eyes~~ who look past the poem into the mirror; it is selftranslation, selftransport, selfpromotion. ⌊It stands for arrogance.⌋ With transit as primum and exit as secundum movens.

❖❖❖

=896 586 *F 113,1* *Ms.*

Re <u>metaphor</u>:

⌊-i-⌋ ~~In the~~ ⌊The⌋ untransferability of the poem is felt by many as something ⌊unbearable, as⌋ tyranny; but to be among men \unter Menschen-Sein\, that can also be understood as: to be under kings \unter Königen sein\—

↙

508 Exactly ~~the~~ ⌊because of its⌋ untransferability ~~the poem~~ {it}the poem is ~~at~~ often felt as something
16 unbearable—and hated. Without a doubt there exists a tyranny of the poem: ~~the tyranny~~ it has the imperiousness of the thought that to be among men can also mean: to be under kings.

❖❖❖

242◄►255 587 *C 5,4* *Ts.*

As that which cannot be carried over \Unübertragbare\, as the ⌊not easily⌋ borne and the often unbearable—unbearably heavy—one <u>hates</u> the poem. He who does not ~~want to see,~~ ⌊not ⌊help⌋ carry, carries over and⌋ ~~likes to~~ speaks of metaphor⌊s⌋. Just as he who doesn't want
252 anything to do with the poem, speaks of art and of skills.
⌊Who does not want to help carry, speaks of metaphors—⌋

❖❖❖

650/748◄►651 588 *B 14* *Ms.*

Black milk of morning: that's not one of those genitive metaphors, ~~which~~ ⌊as they⌋ are presented to us ⌊by⌋ our so-called critics, to keep us from approaching the poem; it is <u>no longer</u> a figure of speech or an oxymoron, it is <u>reality</u>.

Genitive metaphor = No, a being-born-to-each-other of the <u>words</u> under heart's distress

❖❖❖

613◄►644 589 *F 51,1* *Ms.*

419 ⇢ in a ⌊well-intended⌋ discussion of the 'Death Fugue' the German middle school kids are told that Shulamit is a name from the <u>Balkans</u> etc.—
Shulamit, that is a name from the Song of Songs.—

❖❖❖

370◄►67 590 *C 3,4* *Ms.*

Death Fugue
reasons to regret it—⌊but one ~~writes~~ ⌊incurs⌋ and calls up <u>that</u> too.⌋

❖❖❖

66◄►761 591 *C 46,1* *Ms.*

Apparently one incurs that too.—

❖❖❖

Ms. *F 2,1* *592/470* ►*685*

B-Sp

The lips that talk here have, like Danton's—let's not forget where he winds up—⌞he is turned toward—⌟ eyes. They have apprehended and seen; they know what they say.— *400, 439*
He who finds only the metaphor in the poem, apprehends nothing ~~of~~ ⌞in⌟ the poem, ⌞he will have looked for nothing else either⌟; ~~there is, certainly,~~ There certainly are metaphor-pickers and perfumed bouquets offered afterward; the lyrical potpourri exists.—

❖❖❖

Ms. *F 54,2* *593* *654*◄►*535*

"Danton, your lips have eyes": that is not a "modern metaphor," that is knowledge, from afar, concerning ⌞visionary⌟ knowledge of a mouth—

❖❖❖

18.5.60, Ms. *B 28,2* *594* *299*◄

18.5.
"Genitive metaphor" How many genitives?
In the genitive: for the syncretism of language, as in the poem *500*

18.5.60, Ms. *B 28,3* *595* ►*414*

Benveniste: metaphors, tropes → dream events (Cf. Revue de Psychan. Le Langage) *237, 843*

❖❖❖

Ms. *F 30,1* *596* *250*◄►*113*

BSp
—Benveniste, psychoanalysis—
↙
Tropes—

❖❖❖

Ms. *F 10,4* *597* *556*◄

Consciousness: (on metaphors—Benveniste—)
in no case do I want here to speak \das Wort reden\ the oneiric qualities of the poem; there is no doubt that poems are the result of vigils; there also still exist "sober intoxications." *139, 353; 386*

Ms. *F 11,1* *598*

There is no word, ~~{that} no expression~~ that, ~~not in the fig~~ once said, doesn't carry with it the figurative meaning; in the poem the words mean ~~in~~ to be untransferable\unübertragbar\. *71*

▸339 599 *F 11,2* *Ms.*

hermeneutic circle

❖❖❖

600 *Workbook II, 21; inserted pages [1]* *Ms.*

Metaphor

367 "You must not deny me parables, otherwise I wouldn't know how to explain myself" (Goethe)

F. Schlegel: The image is the deliverance of the spirit from the object. By creating \dichtet\ an image of it, the object no longer exists.—
cf. Mandelst.

❖❖❖

Time Critique

Technique

5.10.60, Ms. *F 38,1* *601* 19◂

5.X.60

-i- The tendency to fall silent cannot not be heard; here no ultrashort can help.— 852

In the ~~un~~ gruffness of the language there manifests itself, it cannot not be heard, the tendency to fall silent. This argument offers itself to the one translating \Übertragenden\, after 383
crossing the bottlenecks of earlier and other-languaged forms, ...

×

5.10.60, Ms. *F 38,2* *602*

Man as information—I permit myself something by Günter Eich a year ago—can be confronted 27; 16
only by man as silence: "You" ~~are~~ don't ⌐hear me⌐ ~~addressa~~— ⌐any longer—⌐ , therefore I will
confront you with silence 513

×

5.10.60, Ms. *F 38,3* *603* ▸553

(I know: Seriousness is something so old-fashioned, resp., something so surreal ...)

❖❖❖

Ms. *B 30,2* *604* 520◂▸674

B— ⌐Don't look a gift horse in the mouth⌐ In this time, when proverbs rule the world, I will give myself permission to act counter to this proverb.

I do not "inform" you, I speak to you.

I know that today human conscience speeds ahead even faster than the means of transportation with which it races through the geography. It "puts down" with ⌐too much⌐ pleasure its two hundred "things" ... I am a pedestrian. I write poems {:}—I write by hand.

❖❖❖

Ms. *E 8,1* *605/267* 83◂

Büchner-Sp—

here, on breath-routes, the poem moves =

Ms. *E 8,2* *606/268* ▸271

Information theory, Cybernetics =

❖❖❖

107◄►178 *607* *A 19,1* *Ms.*

A higher Esperanto
Only in the districts \Gauen\ ⌊—I say: ⌊in the⌋ Gauen—⌋ of ultrasonics will there be an ultralanguage—

(Cybernetics, information theory)

❖❖❖

165◄ *608* *A 12,1* *Ms.*

---

228 Reread the Jerusalem-place in the Campaner valley!

609 *A 12,2* *Ms.*

The absurdity of the whole beginning: woven into the poem—

►541 *610* *A 12,3* *Ms.*

172, 548 The poem: not a sign system

❖❖❖

643◄ *611* *F 50,1* *Ms.*

⌊D. Seckel, Hölderlin's Speech Rhythm⌋

-i-:

212, 843; 215, 256 • Rhythm is something else than specific "sound form"
voice
↙↗
voicelessness

272 • Voice has direction -i-

612 *F 50,2* *Ms.*

-i- Rhythm is not something acoustically measurable

44/472 Poems: no "message"
no "information"

~~Message mea for whom the poem is only 'message,' that one wi~~

60/582 culturally attached in this or that manner, i.e. unfree inside—sold to the unfree from birth—

►589 *613* *F 50,3* *Ms.*

"Each human has his own individual rhythm" Novalis, ~~III~~ Fragments III ⌊118⌋ Kluckhohn

❖❖❖

Ms. *F 12,1* *614* *339◄*

The poem today is no Poésie pure; it knows that there cannot be pure poetry; ⌞for that it couldn't be ⌞, no matter how lapidary its appearance⌟ the result of such complex metamorphic processes;⌟ for that there is ⌞among other things⌟ too much Strontium 90 in the air it breathes. World.•

~~So enamored of mutation is it~~ in relation to this it is, however, absolutely not enamored of mutation.

The ⌞caskets and⌟ little treasure chests wait in vain.

• The poem ⌞otherwise⌟ certainly open to transformation, concerning the genotype of the one toward whom it remains directed *realiter* and *virtualiter*, shows absolutely no love for mutation. 129

Ms. *F 12,2* *615/234* *►517*

porous, spongy: ⌞the p<oem>⌟ it is aware of the erosions to which it exposes itself. *55, 61/103, 305*

❖❖❖

Ms. *A 31,1* *616* *484◄►426*

yes yes, not only the Geiger-, but also the so ill-famed "syllable-counters" ⌞of a literature that *24*
calls itself engaged⌟ do register some things. *215, 345*

❖❖❖

Ms. *F 83,1* *617* *966◄►292*

-i-

Attentiveness is not a technique of observation;

'Attent.',—Benjamin, Malebranche, *941*

❖❖❖

Ms. *F 121,3* *618* *309◄►558*

"Super-cyst \Überbein\" and supersonic \Überschall\ make today's "bystander of history" all the more uncanny *12/710, 457*

❖❖❖

from 7.10.60, Ms. *F 25,2* *619* *182◄►669*

×× There are ⌞(⌞world⌟)⌟space travelers. And there are heaven-falls \Himmelsstürze\. *376/530, 634*

×

❖❖❖

557◄►132 *620* *F 31,1* *Ms.*

I don't know if we can get rid of our "soul waste" more easily than of our "atomic waste"

❖❖❖

745◄►399 *621* *F 138* *Ms.*

Where the little spark \Fünklein\ is missing, there ⌊then⌋ arises radio-poetry\Funkdichtung\—

❖❖❖

408◄ *622* *F 69,3* *Ms.*

the hawked ⌊and dissyllabled⌋ modernity of language

623 *F 69,4* *Ms.*

~~tasteful~~ ⌊~~and~~⌋ ~~sub~~
⌊ today's language:⌋ language subliminally radio-ed \verfunkte\ in the most tasteful manner

►435 *624* *F 69,5* *Ms.*

(Who wants to insult the poem, insults ⌊therefore<?>⌋ the poet; and vice versa.)

❖❖❖

37◄ *625* *F 57,2* *Ms.*

You, who like so much to show someone up: do become aware of us! Not-to-want-to-become-aware-of is the liars' main business.
295, 643, 810 How often the cross leaps from evidence into the chiasmus!

626 *F 57,3* *Ms.*

890 This is no time for word-acrobatics, for Sunday-supplement feuilletonistic refurbishments of 'what-one-likes-to-hear', ~~artisti~~<?> ⌊photogenic ⌊and radio-happy⌋ time-critique in verses⌋ ... and, ~~if one will~~ ⌊if you⌋ give me permission: the economic miracle does not become something else ⌊better—⌋ through mirror writing; in any case the dandy (fop until last shot) still belongs ....

627 *F 58,1* *Ms.*

the close-at-hand, what has been put close-to-hand—

►421 *628* *F 58,2* *Ms.*

perversion—

Ms. *F 96,3* *629* *918◄*

~~No~~ ⌊After the⌋ loss of the ritual character they want to "make progress" toward the myth of getting on the wavelength.—

×

Ms. *F 96,4* *630* *►312*

The poem is that which does not fit the measure \das Ungemäße\

❖❖❖

from 19.8.60, Ms. *Workbook II, 15 [28]* *631* *=790*

---

man: the bestia cupidissima rerum novarum

from 19.8.60, Ms. *Workbook II, 15 [29]* *632/204* *=791*

"The original desire of life to return to the inorganic" (•Freud, *Beyond the Pleasure Principle*) *194*

-i-—this world-moment is ours—
Maybe other space flights can be understood from there—

❖❖❖

Ms. *Workbook II, 15 [31]* *633/205* *=793*

"Forms" as homage to the self-legitimacy \Eigengesetzlichkeit\ of the
•inorganic? (Death drive?)
↙ Speechgrille?, Spacegrille?
/Made of crystal
/Escape from contingency— *388*

❖❖❖

Ms. *C 59,2* *634* *468◄►496*

One cannot assume that in the spaceships ⌊spaceship-libraries⌋ Büchner is read.— *376/530, 619*

❖❖❖

Ms. *F 95,3* *635* *365◄*

We still belong to this world-hour. ~~The poem remains as poem as long~~ There will not be a synthetic poem as long as there is no synth. life. *16*

×

Ms. *F 95,4* *636* *►469*

Because the analyses and apparatuses prove only how far the ability to feel and perceive, how far the simple ability to read, has already shrunk. With what, I ask, does one want to measure presence ~~of~~?

❖❖❖

206◂▸70 637 *E 3,4* *10.10.60, Ts.*

Nietzsche: the reader: "by nature so prodigal that he reflects on the read"

❖❖❖

430◂ 638 *F 67,2* *Ms.*

532, 700, 852 -i- ... some Mercier-ian Elargissez l'Art, that in our dark and simultaneously ⌊for all kinds of⌋ word-acrobatics—because a majority of so-called 'artistry' falls into that category—so receptive, I mean to say ready-to-receive, days—is supposed to be augmented by diverse
376/530 germ-free aesthetic messages ⌊synthetic poetries⌋—

The germ-free is the murderous; ~~the perf~~ fascism today lies in "formal designing."

▸287 639 *F 67,3* *Ms.*

Roots of being \Seinswurzeln\

❖❖❖

190◂▸678 640 *F 53,6* *Ms.*

Hostility to art—: ...
There is no synthetic poetry—

❖❖❖

491◂▸423 641 *F 21,1* *30.8.59, Ms.*

30.8.59.

Feigned poetry: that does not exist.

❖❖❖

346◂▸431 642 *F 64,1* *Ms.*

-i- we are on the way to the synthetic poem "art-art"arse-art \Ku-Kunst\

❖❖❖

Polemic

84◂▸611 643 *F 48,3/49* *28.9.60, Ts.*

The poem listens as little to the ⌊happy to be modulated and thankful to be alienated⌋ "giddyap this way" of the (supposedly) politically engaged, as it listens to the (recently also cybernetically accredited) "giddyap that way" of the aesthete; it moves along its own trajectories; it harkens and listens; and from that harkening and listening it speaks itself, with its sorrow and its grief, toward

you; it speaks you—finite, i.e. in front of the horizon of its infinitude—to yourself. The poem, 456
yes, ⌞—why not use this word which has become so unusual? I often heard it in my childhood.⌟—rues \härmt\ itself any time for you too. A great and barely mentioned Russian poet, a barely mentioned and great one—do you perceive, as so often in a poem, in this chiasmus the cross that had to be borne here—, ~~Osip Mandelstam whom I translated into~~ German ⌞whose 295, 625, 810
German translator I have the honor of being,⌟ remembers in one of his last pieces of writing to have reached us, ~~which~~ in the middle of the flowering malice and the perversion of even the most literal, and at a time thus when, amidst all the babble, all that remained to him was the conversation with his language, his old predilection for the Latin gerund. The gerund, that is, as you know, the participle \Mittelwort\ of the form of suffering \Leidensform\ of the future.—Yes, the poem can be a passion.

❖❖❖

Ms. *F 51,2* *644* *589◄►217*

-i-

The poem listens as little to the "giddyap this way" of the politically engaged, as to the "giddyap that way" of the aesthete ⌞—the cyberneticists among them are also meant—⌟; it moves along other trajectories; it {he}harkens and listens; and from that harkening and listening it speaks itself, ⌞with its sorrow and its grief,⌟ toward you—it speaks you ⌞—finite, i.e. in front of the horizon of its infinitude—⌟ to yourself. The poem {r}, yes, rues itself for you.—A great and ~~greatest~~ ⌞~~forgotten~~⌟ ⌞barely mentioned⌟ Russian poet, ~~someone forgotten~~ ⌞a ~~forgotten~~ barely mentioned⌟ and great one,⌟ ⌞~~—in this~~ perceive in this chiasmus the cross-⌞~~in the interw.~~<eave>⌟, that was carried here—⌟ whose German translator I have ⌞—(that's) büchnerian!—⌟ the honor to be, remembers, late in life, ⌞in the middle of the flowering malice⌟ and when all he had left was <u>the conversation with language</u>, his predilection for ⌞the form of⌟ the gerund. ~~You kn~~, The gerund, you know, that is the participle \Mittelwort\ of the form of suffering \Leidensform\ of the future. Yes, the poem, ~~is~~ ⌞can be⌟ a <u>passion</u>{.}.—

❖❖❖

Ms. *E 6,5* *645* *877◄►83*

The ghosts right and left. The 'this way-that way' intellectuals ...

❖❖❖

Ms. *F 60,1* *646* *413◄*

To the angry ones ~~as to~~ and to the related no less loved and PR-able cynics, I would like to say: What do you know of grief and sorrow!

Ms. *F 60,2* *647* *►458*

<u>Rue \Harm\</u>: a word that no longer exists

a ruing soul—Mandelstam—gerund—the participle of the form of suffering of the future—

❖❖❖

662◂▸163 *648* *A 22,1* *Ms.*

---

107 The—oh so wordily lamented—loss of tradition: the legitimism of those who "legitimize" themselves everywhere, so as not to have to justify themselves to themselves.

❖❖❖

512◂▸228 *649* *A 31,4* *Ms.*

The poet: always in partibus infidelium

❖❖❖

335◂▸588 *650/748* *B 13* *Ms.*

~~Many a~~
Do you think that he, Franzos, took those to us so obvious and so seriously smiley \so ernst
33/111, 84 zugelächelten\ quotation marks
534 (comely\kommode / coming\kommende) religion ... seriously
Many a word has quotation marks \lit.: hare's ears, Hasenöhrchen\. If only we were born more often with such instruments! But we prefer to spoon, academically educated noblesse oblige, in poetry, i.e. in and with the souls ...

❖❖❖

588◂ *651* *B 15,1* *Ms.*

Quotation marks \Hasenöhrchen\
"   : but no, we have to watch as they spoon about in our souls {—} with heavy ⌊culture-⌋ silver of course—which as we know are somewhat soupy, at times even tastily so.—

▸466 *652* *B 15,2* *Ms.*

⌊Russian =⌋ Quote? Shestov?
Büchner in Russia (theater) → I hear that in Leipzig they busy themselves with the question if one should show Danton's Death to the citizens of this so ~~wonderful~~ ⌊totally⌋ different{ly} ⌊named⌋ republic—You see that one does not live only among contemporaries—with advanced, progressing and progressive age always higher criteria are added—

❖❖❖

518◂▸265 *653* *F 7,2* *Ms.*

‖ ← World-cargo and culture-ballast, those are (as is generally known⌊?⌋ ...) two different things.

❖❖❖

Ms. *F 54,1* 654 *678◄►593*

We have been, each in his own way, witnesses of a process, which has led us to this circumstance
from that which only fifteen years ago still lay true and heavy on our heart: talk of the turning
\Umkehr\ instead of change itself, supposed engagement and commitment instead of real *394, 686*
responsibility, cultural busy-ness rather than simple attentiveness

❖❖❖

Ms. *F 76,2* 655 *457◄►308*

The experience that the talk about "engagement" means only that one projects the responsibility, which one is in no way ready to assume, on this or that novel character,—: this too the poem has to take into account

❖❖❖

Ms. *F 92,2* 656 *465◄►34/493*

The ~~quote from~~ Survival-is-all-quote one finds among those who survive-it-all, those *282, 335, 370,*
renouncing-all-up-to-the-light-with-shot\Auf-alles-bis-auf-das-Helle-mit-Schuß-Verzich- *579*
tenden\. I am so old-fashioned that I take the red grits to be poetically irrelevant.—

❖❖❖

Ms. *F 122* 657 *558◄►38*

The smaller the capacity for the real—the reverent—experience of form—of performance—the louder the "critic's" red- and also brown-welsch used with the ongoing consideration (←rectification) due foreign language dictionaries

❖❖❖

Ms. *C 4,1* 658 *99◄►2*

I know, today as a writer one is, in relation to the bookfair, ⌊a Hessian event in fact,⌋ kept to the annual custom, but:
Poetry is ⌊and will probably remain forever⌋ monotone. "Nobody becomes what he is not" as is *246; 322*
said in the mines of Falun

❖❖❖

Ts. *C 7,1* 659 *80/303◄*

They say art and mean irresponsibility; they speak of "engagement" and mean that it is enough to rely on something written supplemented by numbers of copies published and translations into foreign languages. "Engagement:" means in many cases to dress up one's "hero" with those attributes one feels too refined to wear oneself.

Ts. *C 7,2* 660 *►559*

Distinguished professors exist thanks to poetry—not the other way around.

❖❖❖

101◄►405 *661* *A 4* *Ms.*

Hermeticism—

~~The~~ ⌊Certain⌋ “citizens” and the poem: they buy the surprise packet; one knows roughly what’s inside, it won’t be much, but then again it doesn’t cost much either, and when for once one visits the annual fair and one has enjoyed the woman with no lower though with an upper body, then gaiety does request one to do so. And when what is inside, though here too ⌊the superior⌋ humor ⌊of the buyer⌋ can prove itself, turns out to be cheaper than cheap, one still has the fun that all of this was “too” \“zu”\.

❖❖❖

544◄►648 *662* *A 21,3* *Ms.*

The secret marriage which in the poem the word contracts with the real and the true, is called “wild” only ⌊⌊~~with good reason~~⌋ mainly⌋ by those who do not want to forgo their lushly comfortable ⌊well-guarded⌋ culture-harem and{,}—especially—the eunuchal services that come with it. (Poetry certainly does not threaten this seraglio with any kind of abduction)

❖❖❖

31◄►378 *663* *F 89,1* *Ms.*

There is no lyric Koiné;

There is a language of the poem; and there is, as we know, a pidgin, renouncing syntax and coincidence \Fügung\, used by the semi-toughs of lyric poetry. They ~~sit~~ ⌊have⌋, no
867 matter how many manifestos against atomic death they sign, one hand on the switchboard, (with the other they grab their testicles ⌊whose<?>⌋{...}!! = twixt test and testicle)

×

❖❖❖

447◄ *664* *F 120* *Ms.*

We have, amidst the general loss of language, a lyric Koiné which, multiplying by fission, creates a “chain” of lyric counterfeiters in the world. It is not important, they converse with each other in party- to Pound-Chinese—

►309 *665* *F 121,1* *Ms.*

---

the hyper-trophing adjective: modern poetry

↖

⌊character.<istically>⌋ for the poem today: only indirectly interested in that

---

❖❖❖

174◄ *666* *F 53,2* *Ms.*

---

the ⌊language- and responsibility-weary⌋ lyric Koiné of our times

Ms. *F 53,3* *667* *►304*

Party-~~Chinese~~ and Pound-Chinese balance each other—

❖❖❖

Ms. *F 61,4* *668* *460◄►327*

---

the lyric hotchpotch of our days
the Koiné *849*

❖❖❖

from 7.10.60, Ms. *F 25,3* *669* *619◄►216*

There is, (in small and smallest coin,) a ~~well-covered~~ lyric Koiné; {A}and there is the unique language of the poem.— *17*

❖❖❖

Ms. *F 63,6* *670* *188◄►346*

-iii- The language-blind (~~and l~~ *955*
—language-blindness {—}as

❖❖❖

Ms. *Workbook II, 15 [2]* *671* *249◄►203 =764*

Literalness of the said, of what has become word.—But the interpreters: they don't want it to be word, build their talk before and after, shred the cited, the conjured, the present with the help of citations. ~~With~~ They come along on visible and invisible quotation marks: beauty is not truth for them, it is the ⌊differently repeatable⌋ curlicue of their own signature. Along such curlicues they then also find the "rhyme."

❖❖❖

Ms. *B 47* *672* *570◄►683*

We do not write for the edification of happy bookfair visitors!!

❖❖❖

Ms. *B 55* *673* *741◄*

Büchner-speech

⌊Hostility to Art, Danton-scene:⌋

with and through language against the breath-alien wordbrew =

There is much rabble ~~in~~ and riffraff (= poets) in German literature: the old and the new, the emigration and the so-called ⌊young⌋ ~~new generation~~, on

❖❖❖

604◄►580 *674* *B 31,1* *Ms.*

---

736 ... it doesn't have to be, as for R. Lenz, a Moscow street at all; necropolises, and what kind of necropolises, are, we remember, built much faster than ever ⌊metropolises⌋; ~~they can be~~ they are, we know, stamped out of the ground as well as driven into the air; they are everywhere ...

❖❖❖

679◄►411 *675* *B 42* *Ms.*

Büchner-speech

all these poets who fled the East and who in the West know so quickly how to make a good living from the fact that they just couldn't live in the East.

❖❖❖

281◄►295 *676* *B 32,2* *Ms.*

---

853 Outcasts ... But the League of {un}World{ly} outcasts, that, yes indeed, that still remains to be called into existence.—

❖❖❖

266◄►568 *677* *B 45* *3.10.60, Ms.*

3.{9}10.—

The League of Worldoutcasts {:} remains to be founded.

❖❖❖

640◄►654 *678* *F 53,7* *Ms.*

---

853 the "homeland-outcasts": ~~they have~~ in the thought that and how they forfeited the homeland, lies the homeland.

❖❖❖

567◄ *679* *B 41,1* *Ms.*

Büchner-speech

130 ... humanistic phrasemongers, posthumous caretakers of Jew. thought inheritance

I do not say this to have my words be part of some present or future judgment—but: time is running out. And so I say it, so that they (..) should tremble and turn back for one moment—.

►675 *680* *B 41,2* *Ms.*

---

411 Long live the crooked-nose creature!

Ms., 30.5.60? *E 15,2* *681* *754◄►740*

[Alas, ~~these~~ ⌊many of these⌋ posthumous caretakers of German poems by Jewish hands ...]

❖❖❖

Ms. *C 14,3* *682* *247◄►258*

The Nazi tone survives the Nazi vocabulary; the
– ↕
Nazi pong

❖❖❖

Ms. *B 48* *683* *672◄►455*

Büchner-speech

This too, I know it ⌊because I have lived and experienced it,⌋ belongs to the poem: put into the unknown—and therefore deemed friendly—hand, it hurtles back, flung by this hand which when touching something clean ⌊something turned toward the clean, contracts into a fist, it returns {,} ~~estr~~, into a stone estranged, in the opposite direction, lethal—why? I don't know. But it seems to me, ⌊this way too,⌋ that it testifies to this, our world, our world of projections and perversions.—Maybe soon it will have to suffice that we hear it whirring in the air, that we hear the whirring and only it—the "fast, outside ..."

❖❖❖

Ms. *D 12* *684/721* *185◄►403*

I can't help it, but here, also thinking back to the knife-scene in Woyzeck, I have to try to speak of something that is often mentioned today: of a turning, a reversal—as a turning inside out of the clichés

❖❖❖

Ms. *E 2,2* *685* *470/592◄►184*

the ~~counter~~ turned inside out theme with the same intonation as yesterday.—

❖❖❖

Ms. *Diary 4; inserted sheets [4]* *686* *735◄►736*

It is not a sign of reversal when ~~in~~ with the same ⌊with other⌋ words but with the same intonation as yesterday, ~~by which~~ things and humans are praised that were damned yesterday. *654*

❖❖❖

313◂▸377 *687* *F 8,3* *Ms.*

Do not object: And what's the use of this for the tractor driver ~~near Vyasmo or Leipzig~~ ⌊in Ryasan or Röcken near Lützen⌋? Such objections, these especially, dishonor the tractor driver in his being and doing. Karl Marx read Homer and Sophocles; and ~~what~~ ⌊reading⌋, I ask, does one ~~give to read~~ ⌊expect from⌋ those who believe they are making his, Marx's, thoughts come true?

❖❖❖

125◂ *688* *F 17,1* *19.8.59, Ms.*

---

the question of why this one but not that one writes poems, can hardly be answered by the one who writes poems, and that's also why the question remains open, if there will be poems "tomorrow": it is thinkable that neither this one nor that one will undertake this. To this
878 thought a fear can be added: the fear that both, the causa materialis and the causa formalis could no longer be present in an altered genotype.
deficient formulation

▸109 *689* *F 17,2* *19.8.59, Ms.*

385/505 The question of contingency, again!

❖❖❖

397◂▸283 *690* *F 73* *Ms.*

Love for the human is ~~something~~ love for the creature; that's not an aggregate of animal
417, 858 protection and philanthropy—

❖❖❖

348◂▸506 *691* *F 108,3* *6.10.60, Ms.*

---

867 We know that we remain uninvolved in the decisions, that these are taken outside our field of vision.—

❖❖❖

715◂▸14 *692* *C 27* *Ms.*

Much is weighed, evaluated, measured; much that is precious ⌊and weighty⌋ has been won this way; but all of that is accompanied by the mute or halfloud thought that
the

❖❖❖

Notes on Büchner and K. E. Franzos

on Büchner

Ms. *C 51,1* *693/3* *480◄*

But there is always someone who is there and who doesn't listen, i.e. who hears and then does not know what was said; and has heard something that was not said. Who hears the one who speaks, who has perceived ~~ta~~ language{,} and shape, and, who could doubt it, direction, i.e. breath.— *262*
That is, you know, this woman comes toward you, every time from another direction; that's Lucile

---

Ms. *C 51,2–52b,1* *694*

On art, Lenz:
Art returns, it is here again: it is not only transformable, it is also ubiquitous

it also possesses the gift of ubiquity
The—literature
↗
a Mischwesen\chimera, cyborg\

Ms. *C 52b,2* *695/20*

Abyss: poetry—it does not have, as Camille suggests mockingly ⌞—oh, art—⌟ ; it has consequences—thus<?> : he who plans to walk on his head, knows that he then has the sky beneath him as abyss. *168*
↙
To wr.<ite> under such dates—

Ms. *C 52b,3–52a,4* *696/4*

Maybe poetry is a consequence of art—one of its consequences; maybe ⌞art⌟ is the route poetry has to travel again and again. There are, I know, shorter routes. Mais la Poésie, elle aussi, brûle nos étapes *20/695*

The one leads to the other, but: a leap is needed *381*

Ms. *C 52a,1* *697/5*

Vive le Roi
that is the counterword.—That, ladies and gentlemen, is poetry = a\n\ ⌞invisible,⌟ dependent being{,}(a being that belongs to a person.—

698 C 52a,2 Ms.

At table: literature
self-oblivion
medusa-head

699 C 52a,3 Ms.

Against it: To walk on the head—

▸23 700 C 52a,5 Ms.

532, 638, 852 Elargissez l'art
90 → Narrowing \Engführung\
Democritus—morality<?>—here I have to confess again, ~~that~~ with how guilty a conscience I give it the acute—
nothing in Diels—therefore no quotation marks

❖❖❖

258◂ 701 C 15,1 Ms.

Oh, art! S. 41
↙
here there is, heard today, no place for a ⌊further⌋ ⌊Mercier'ian⌋ Elargissez l'Art!
⌊know⌋ <"... you too, what I have said?" (Camille to Lucile)>
290, 310 to which Lucile, who likes so much to see him speak, to the question: You hear me too: •No, truly not

Lucile: the last figure to appear, the one most clearly •leaning toward Camille: she does not know what he says

-i- Already the conversation {on} about art ~~is~~ appears as unessential.
↙
538, 713, 906 Hostility to art, metaesthetic

702 C 15,2 Ms.

Woyzeck: "Look at the creature, as God created it: nix, nothing at all. Now look at art: walks upright, wears coat and pants, has a saber

703/270 C 16,1 Ms.

-i- Congestions of the breath—

Ms. *C 26,3* *715* *68/384◄►692*

---

medusa-like = the same Büchner, letter <to the> bride, complains of hippoc.<ratic> face—For he sees it! He sees the abyss *374; 25, 291*

❖❖❖

Ms. *C 31,1* *716* *79◄*

The nightingale of poetry no longer sings above our heads—the clay pipe (Danton<:> with water) has

---

Ms. *C 31,2* *717*

---

above our heads something other than songbirds whirs—I know, they are montaged into the poem; but I ask myself if they were not named more accurately, _more actual—_ if they remained unnamed—

Ms. *C 31,3* *718* *►15*

---

p. 375: I am an automaton *16, 376/530*
the automaton—is the soulless
ecstasy? as poetry *386, 414, 843*

❖❖❖

10.10.60, Ms. *D 1,1* *719*

10.X.
B-Sp—

March 1834
Letter to the bride, p. 379:
The sense of having died
hippocr.<atic> face
Were we the sacrifice in the glowing belly of the Perillus bull.

10.10.60, Ms. *D 1,2* *720* *►92*

Lenz, p. 107: "He had nothing"
↙
from there to Kafka: Language as Being *157, 296, 732, 843*

❖❖❖

Ms. *D 12* *721/684* *185◄►403*

I cannot avoid it, here, also in relation to the knife-scene in Woyzeck, I have to try to talk about something that is often mentioned today: reversal, reversal—as upending of the cliché

❖❖❖

=828 722 *Diary 4; inserted sheets [2,1]* *Ms.*

⌊Quote:⌋
p. 411: Letter to Gutzkov
"You and your friends ... our time is purely material ... Split bet.<ween> educ.<ated> and uned.<ucated society>

=829 723 *Diary 4; inserted sheets [2,2]* *Ms.*

-i- fadaises<?>—la Mada~~~~~—Michaux /~~~~~/

=830 724 *Diary 4; inserted sheets [2,3]* *Ms.*

p. 535: Gutzk.<ov> to B.<üchner>
"Of your 'piglet-dramas \Ferkeldramen\'
Your Danton did not pull

=831 725 *Diary 4; inserted sheets [2,4]* *Ms.*

Deutsche Drama hrsg. von B. v. Wiese 58

=832 726 *Diary 4; inserted sheets [2,5]* *Ms.*

Viëtor: "antipathetic contrast" as principle of construction

Viëtor DVJS 1934, "The tragedy of heroic pessimism
K. May Form und Bedeutung 1957 Stuttgart

=833 727 *Diary 4; inserted sheets [2,6]* *Ms.*

p. 399, B.<üchner> to the fam.<ily> about my dramatic play—
⌊p. 400⌋ "The dram.<atic> poet

=834 728 *Diary 4; inserted sheets [2,7]* *Ms.*

55 -i- the demotic, the lower in Büchner—

=835 729 *Diary 4; inserted sheets [2,8]* *Ms.*

Glosses to Spinoza's Ethics: Viëtor, p. 247f.
to: / Spinoza-citation Thomas Payne's, DT, III, 1

Ms. *Diary 4; inserted sheets [2,9]* *730* *=836*

Fallhut—barrelets (d'enfant)

Ms. *Diary 4; inserted sheets [3,1]* *731* *=837*

Walter Rehm, Gontscharow und die Langeweile / E.<xperimentum> M.<edietatis> /
/ on B.<üchner>: p. 110 /

⌞quote:⌟ p. 109: Gutzkov, 1835, "Wally the doubtress": the "eternal self-ennui"
Hebbel, diary.; in 1846 Hebbel plans a drama in 5 act<s>: The bore.<dom>
Grabbe: B.<oredom> = deity of the antifatalists
p. 110: Büchner
pp. 110ff.

Ms. *Diary 4; inserted sheets [3,2]* *732* *=838*

Leonce and Lena, pp. 135, 136 Lena: "A horrifying thought occurs to me: I believe that there are people who are unhappy, incurably so, and only because they are."

/-i-: To get oneself through language, which—Kafka!—is only a having, into an accurate relation with one's Being!—/ *157, 296, 720, 843*

Ms. *Diary 4; inserted sheets [3,3]* *733* *=839*

Graduation house (-work)\: bâtim<en>t de graduation, chambre graduée
Brine: eau salée, saline
(Bittering): saumure, eau-mère

Ms. *Diary 4; inserted sheets [3,4]* *734* *=840*

Nous ferons un peu de romantique pour nous tenir à la hauteur du siècle (Büchner to his fiancée) / Viëtor, p. 174.

❖❖❖

➤686

Ms. *Diary 4; inserted sheets [3,6]* *735* *=842*

-i- Brain- and heart-infuriating! \Zum Hirn- und Herzwütigwerden!\

❖❖❖

Ms. *Diary 4; inserted sheets [5]* *736* *686◄*

Büchner-speech

Lenz
... it does not have to be a Moscow street at all; today—and we don't need to think far back on this to ~~put this before our eyes~~ realize this—necropolises are quickly built; they don't need to be dragged out of the earth; one conjures them from thin air.— *360; 674*

❖❖❖

739◄ *737* *E 12,1* *30.5.60, Ms.*

30.5.60 Büchner-speech

51, 406 in the mountain
... we are with Büchner, with Lenz—we are with the poem.—
287 Poems: infinite-saying of mortality and nothingness

►930 *738/375* *E 12,2* *30.5.60, Ms.*

... Büchner's last words on his deathbed, Lenz's words (Moscow) have not come down to us—it is the return into the just still voiced, as in Woyzeck—it is language as involution, the unfolding of meaning in the one, word-estranged syllable—: it is the 'root-syllable' recognizable in the
476 ⌊death-rattled⌋ stuttering, the ⌊language as⌋ what has returned into the germ—the meaning-carrier is the {~~mou~~} mortal mouth, whose lips no longer grow round. Muta cum liquida, ~~and~~
506 vowel-buttressed, the rhyme-sound as self-sound.

❖❖❖

280◄►737 *739* *E 11* *14.10.60, Ms.*

1{3}4.

This conversation—literature happens at the table
→ then medusae—
only when again mountain hands: thus only there where I—sky situation—and again the traveled route back—

❖❖❖

681◄►288 *740* *E 15,3* *Ms.*

261, 745, 843 Reference to 'Embankments, Roadsides, Vacant Lots etc.' =
→ read later in Woyzeck = : (Krolow as witness: Rochefort: Embankment—

❖❖❖

331◄►673 *741* *B 53* *Ms.*

"The most refined of all epicureans": {H}he too is confronted by death!!

❖❖❖

359◄►562 *742* *AE 15,8 [2]* *Ms.*

"Livid light before the storm" (Heimann)—we have to breathe it, today too.—Also in ~~their~~ "rose-colored"

that is the coloring of Leonce ⌊primer⌋

❖❖❖

on Karl Emil Franzos

Ms. *C 30,2* *743* *6/73◄►79*

⌞my so paper loving, so uncritical<?>, ab<?> {and} resp. rat-hating⌟ Franzos—of that I was, as ⌞in⌟ I as ⌞in my<?>⌟ ~~high school student~~ through the street *84; 81, 83*
student at the same university as he—
not conscious—it is a way—these routes mean something to me—it is the strange "art-distant" confirmations—

❖❖❖

Ms. *F 29,1* *744* *253◄►250*

There are routes. We walk them by entrusting ourselves to the word, by not avoiding the reality which it creates, which it creates for us
Forester's house in Czortkov—rats—garret— *749*

❖❖❖

Ms. *F 137* *745* *453◄►621*

Büchner-speech
Secret routes = Franzos = Roadsides, Vacant Lots, Rubble—in the Rue d'Ulm, where I am Reader f.<or> G<erman> L.<anguage>—where I thus can read, read to, read with, re-read— *261, 740, 843*

❖❖❖

Ms. *D 10,2* *746* *917◄►185*

Like my fellow ⌞half-Asiatic⌟ countryman K. E. F<ranzos> who now ⌞via a detour⌟ through Hesse has come close to me—

❖❖❖

from 22.8.60, Ms. *Workbook II, 21 [13]* *747* *749◄ =812*

Brotherliness of the poem; re which: Danton's sentence *33/111, 240/410, 401, 843; 704*
—Heads that kiss in the dust— —Praise to the {~} quotation marks! Reality of the Beyond!
by the way: Franzos's way also through the no-longer-being \das Nicht-mehr-seiende!!!

❖❖❖

Ms. *B 13* *748/650* *335◄►588*

~~Many a~~
Do you think that he, Franzos, took those to us so obvious and so seriously smiley \so ernst zugelächelten\ quotation marks *33/111, 84*
(comely \kommode\ ) religion ... seriously *534*
(coming \kommende\ )
Many a word has quotation marks \lit.:hare's ears, Hasenöhrchen\. If only we were born more often with such instruments! But we prefer to spoon, academically educated noblesse oblige, in poetry, i.e. in and with the souls ...

❖❖❖

Discarded Speech Parts

Discarded beginnings

►747
=811 *749* *Workbook II, 21 [12]* *from 22.8.60, Ms.*

Beginning: There are, in the poem too, secret routes
744 Czortkov-Czern.<ovitz> → Darmstadt.

❖❖❖

290◄►10 *750* *B 5,1* *Ms.*

I would like to thank you from the core of my heart. It is, I believe, an essential trait of the heartily ~~meant~~, that it has only a small number of words at its disposal. I ask your permission
91 ⌞therefore⌟, to say only a few small things here—those few small things which, I believe, I can take responsibility for.

❖❖❖

93◄ *751* *B 11,1* *Ms.*

Büchner-speech

►I have the honor... Cz<ernovitz> near Sadagora, in the vicinity of Vishnitz •(~~Buber~~)⌞, Kerty, Korsov and Bojan born, in the region, in which Rabbi Israel ... also called the Baal Shem, i.e. the carrier and master • of the name, lived and taught.—⌟

most easterly university—the children of this town, before all, the Jewish children, were <u>proud</u>—Greater Germany knew how to bury this pride—this, like the poem, is in no way to be understood as a metaphor.—

►335 *752* *B 11,2* *Ms.*

---

93 From me, who thanks you most cordially, do not expect an understatement—I'll try to do a statement.—\from "understatement" on, in English in the original.\

❖❖❖

49◄►567 *753* *B 39,1* *Ms.*

Büchner—

Isaiah: the lips
Hebrew. whom<?> in M. Buber's German version
I believe I may do this: I was born in Cz<ernovitz> near Sadagora—near that Sadagora, where M.<artin> B.<uber>

❖❖❖

Ms., 30.5.60 *E 15,1* *754* *96◄►681*

I am a belated child of the old Austria
(But: Landauer, (Kafka) et cetera.
Communism—Viennese February—Oh fly, we are the workers of Vienna

In parenthesis: Forest in Pinzgau, ⌊poem,⌋ impression, ⌊so-called "volksdeutsche" newspaper⌋
Royal resident—one tastes \goutiert\ , that ...

Reason for the mention: how rare reversal \Umkehr\ is!

❖❖❖

Discarded parts concerning public speaking

Ms. *F 111,1* *755* *479◄►481*

... permit myself, ⌊→⌋ with explicit reference to my lack of experience in discursive matters, t
but ~~in the~~ out of deference for the, at times invisibly, confirming experiences in the realm of the *85*
intuitive, ⌊→⌋ to inform you of some things concerning the poem—

❖❖❖

Ms. *F 66,2* *756* *120◄►429*

This address = : [beginning]
(-i-: ~~Unpracticed~~ Without practice in discursive matters, with some experience in the intuitive
as I hope, from experiences directed by intuition

❖❖❖

Ms. *F 13,5* *757* *226◄►449*

I am not talking of this or that specific poem, but I try to set the poem in front of my eyes and to look at it (thoughtfully).

❖❖❖

Ms. *C 47,5* *758* *301◄*

Dear Marie-Luise Kaschnitz, I am thinking of your slanting candles, in that church, so rammed into the ground, in Greece

►329 | *759* | *C 48* | *Ms.*

“One should not,” as Hofm<annsthal's> ~~now here also~~ well-known witticism has it, “One should not ask the fish, if one wants to know what the sea is. Not even then when one has landed the fish with Büchner-nets—

❖❖❖

143◄►333 | *760* | *D 8a* | *Ms.*

who wants to know
⌊One should—you will have noticed this already⌋ not ask the fish about the sea; not even then when one has pulled them from the water with Büchner-nets. I am indeed trying to say a few—jittery—things.—

❖❖❖

591◄►357 | *761* | *C 46,2* | *Ms.*

Please consider even that which will come now, as attempts to swim on dry land.—

❖❖❖

442◄►314 | *762* | *F 71,1* | *Ms.*

Aggregates of the fruits of reading

❖❖❖

Materials from Other Posthumous Writings

Workbooks etcetera, in received order

Ms.	*workbook II, 15 [1]*	*763*	*=249*

The assonance of language (as a whole) in the poem.—→ timbre =
= not transferable

Ms.	*workbook II, 15 [2]*	*764*	*=671*

Literalness of the said, of what has become word.—But the interpreters: they don't want it to be word, build their talk before and after, talk to the cited, the conjured, the present to shreds with the help of citations. ~~With~~ They come along on visible and invisible quotation marks: beauty is not truth for them, it is the differently repeatable curlicue of their own signature. Along such curlicues they then also find the "rhyme."

Ms.	*workbook II, 15 [3]*	*765*	*=203*

× → into the speechless—
Determined from the direction of death: the wintery, crystal-like, inorganic as realm of the most essential turning-toward the one speaking in the poem, humanscape {:}– deathscape.

19.8.60, Ms.	*workbook II, 15 [4]*	*766*	*=240/410*

The poem is the place where synonymity becomes impossible: it only has its language{/ev}-×/ and therewith its meaning level. Stepping out of language, the ~~lang~~ the poem. steps opposite language. This opposition cannot be sublated.

×/ that's why the poem, in its being and not through its subject matter first—is a school of true humanity: it teaches understanding of the other as the other i.e., in its otherness, it demands brotherliness with <new page, dated: "19.8.60"> respect before this other, in the turning toward this other, even there where the other appears as the hooked-nosed and misshapen—in no way almond-eyed—accused by the "straighnosed" ....

❖❖❖

19.8.60, Ms.	*workbook II, 15 [5]*	*767*	*=212*

Rhythm—sense movement toward an as yet unknown goal. → a sort of tropism
"by the lightsense you divine"

=213 768 *workbook II, 15 [6]* *19.8.60, Ms.*

The minutest change in structure: heavy disturbances (Therefore maybe 'corrections' to prevent such disturbances)

=214 769 *workbook II, 15 [7]* *19.8.60, Ms.*

The rhythmic processes ⌊in the poem ~~struc~~⌋ can be released, they cannot be determined.

=48 770 *workbook II, 15 [8]* *from 19.8.60, Ms.*

"except sometimes it annoyed him ..."
≡ I believe, I can go on from here

771 *workbook II, 15 [9]* *from 19.8.60, Ms.*

243 Foreknowledge

772 *workbook II, 15 [10]* *from 19.8.60, Ms.*

associative memory: Mneme (Scheler)

773 *workbook II, 15 [11]* *from 19.8.60, Ms.*

productive thinking—anticipation / providentia—prudentia

774 *workbook II, 15 [12]* *from 19.8.60, Ms.*

"Aha"-experience (Wolfgang Köhler) / suddenness

775 *workbook II, 15 [13]* *from 19.8.60, Ms.*

19.8.60, Ms.
"Spirit ~~has~~ ⌊is therefore⌋ objectivity, determination through the objective nature of things" (Scheler)

776 *workbook II, 15 [14]* *from 19.8.60, Ms.*

"To become human is elevation to this world-openness by virtue of the spirit" (Scheler)

=504 777 *Workbook II, 15 [15]* *from 19.8.60, Ms.*

-i- cathexability
The form—empty⌊hollow-⌋form—of the poem, is the poet's heart waiting for the poem.—

from 19.8.60, Ms. *workbook II, 15 [16]* *778*

Kant: transcendental apperception *885*

from 19.8.60, Ms. *workbook II, 15 [17]* *779*

Scheler: 'Spirit is the only Being incapable of becoming an object—it has its being only in and through the execution of its acts. The center of spirit, the "person," is not an object nor a substantial kind of being, but only a continuously self-executing ordered structure of acts.The person is only in and through his acts.

from 19.8.60, Ms. *workbook II, 15 [18]* *780*

Scheler ⌊p. 50⌋: Ideas do not exist 'before,' 'in' or 'after' things, but with them and are created by the eternal spirit only in the act of continuous world-realization (creatio continua). Therefore our participation:—a co-production, a co-creation of the essences coordinated with the eternal Logos and eternal Love etc. ...

from 19.8.60, Ms. *Workbook II, 15 [19]* *781*

Scheler: "... Examples for grasping the nature of things from them. Descartes tried to grasp the *essentia* of the body and its structure by examining a piece of wax."

from 19.8.60, Ms. *Workbook II, 15 [20]* *782*

Scheler: "Ideation: ... the essential modes and formal structures of the world through a single case only."
"Knowledge of essences: the 'windows into the absolute,' as Hegel ... says.

from 19.8.60, Ms. *Workbook II, 15 [21]* *783*

"The capacity to distinguish between essence and existence is a basic characteristic of the human || spirit, and is the foundation of all other characteristics."

from 19.8.60, Ms. *Workbook II, 15 [22]* *784*

[p. 53] Ideation—suspension of the characteristics of objects
Buddha: "wonderful to look upon the things of this world, and terrible to be them."

from 19.8.60, Ms. *Workbook II, 15 [23]* *785*

"What existence \Dasein\ ⌊(Experience of the \Das\.)⌋ gives us, is the experience of the resistance in a world already present as given—

786 *Workbook II, 15 [24]* *from 19.8.60, Ms.*

Scheler: Anxiety is the correlate of reality...

787 *Workbook II, 15 [25]* *from 19.8.60, Ms.*

De-actualization

788 *Workbook II, 15 [26]* *from 19.8.60, Ms.*

Man as the being who can say "No," the ascetic of life, ...

789 *Workbook II, 15 [27]* *from 19.8.60, Ms.*

omne ens est malum

=631 790 *Workbook II, 15 [28]* *from 19.8.60, Ms.*

man: the bestia cupidissima rerum novarum

=204/632 791 *workbook II, 15 [29]* *from 19.8.60, Ms.*

"Primordial urge of life to return to the inorganic" (•Freud, Beyond the Pleasure Principle)

-i-—this worldmoment is ours—
Maybe our space flights are also to be understood from there—

792 *workbook II, 15 [30]* *from 19.8.60, Ms.*

-i- word-magnetisms.—

=205/633 793 *workbook II, 15 [31]* *from 19.8.60, Ms.*

"Forms" as homage to the autonomy/entelechy of the
•inorganic? (death drive?)
↙ speechgrille?, spacegrille?
/crystalline
/escape from contingency—

794 *workbook II, 15 [32]* *from 19.8.60, Ms.*

Hofmannsthal ('Yesterday'): What taught us to give the name 'soul' to the commingling of a thousand lives?

from 19.8.60, Ms. *workbook II, 15 [33]* 795

"Sphere of totality (pre-existence) / ⌊a.⌋ Ad me ipsum *802*

---

from 19.8.60, Ms. *workbook II, 15 [34]* 796

Hof<mannstha>l, p. 227, Ad me i-<psu>m:
"Of the antinomies of existence, this or that one becomes the axis of spiritual existence." ||

from 19.8.60, Ms. *workbook II, 15 [35]* 797

Ad me i-<psu>m, p. 233: "The point with which the infinite digs itself into the soul." *137, 389, 805, 876*

from 19.8.60, Ms. *workbook II, 15 [36]* 798 *=473*

-i- B

No poem opens up for the one who, when approaching the poem, is not ready for the encounter; with so-called texts

from 19.8.60, Ms. *workbook II, 15 [37]* 799 *=474*

Not the—wide-gauge—⌊modern poetry⌋ that understands ⌊itself as⌋ standing on its head—, but the poem that arises from the feeling of such unease.—

❖❖❖

22.8.60, Ms. *workbook II, 21 [1]* 800 *=321*

22.8.60.— B—

/ voice—rhythm—

person, secret, presence

but: question concerning the limit and unity of the person

the poem as I-quest?

Death as the principle creating unity and limits, thus its omnipresence in the poem— ||

-i- The poem as the I becoming a person: in conversation—awareness of the other and the stranger. The active principle thus a You assumed ("occupiable") this way or that.—(death as You?)

801 *workbook II, 21 [2]* *22.8.60, Ms.*

polarity
middle, border

802 *workbook II, 21 [3]* *22.8.60, Ms.*

795 Preexistence ≠ sphere of totality (Hofm<annstha>l, Ad me i-<psu>m)
121 ‖ from there the darkness {:}, the being-open-to-darkness—

803 *workbook II, 21 [4]* *22.8.60, Ms.*

Worldfeeling today—of what kind?

=434 *804* *workbook II, 21 [5]* *22.8.60, Ms.*

Perception rather: Becoming-aware-of, discovering, noticing\Gewahrwerden\

805 *workbook II, 21 [6]* *22.8.60, Ms.*

137, 389, 797, Hofmannsthal: "The point with which the infinite digs down into the soul"—
876 ↗ ↙
134, 409, 704 "except sometimes it annoyed him that ...
↙
478 ⌞Cavalry⌟ Babel, the Jewish boy who walks on his hands ...

=128 *806* *workbook II, 21 [7]* *from 22.8.60, Ms.*

? Wesensgrund \ground of being
? Abgrund \abyss
Urgrund \origin
? Ungrund \unground

807 *workbook II, 21 [8]* *from 22.8.60, Ms.*

configuration (= middle
constellation (

808 *workbook II, 21 [9]* *from 22.8.60, Ms.*

249, 272 frailty
creatureliness | : not "theme," but ... timbre?

=245 *809* *workbook II, 21 [10]* *from 22.8.60, Ms.*

T.<he> poem as the epiphany of language.

from 22.8.60, Ms. *workbook II, 21 [11]* *810*

~~In~~ ⌊~~certain~~ ⌊There are⌋ invisible⌋ chiasm{us}a there may be more from the cross than in the word that denotes it *295, 625, 643*

from 22.8.60, Ms. *workbook II, 21 [12]* *811* *=749*

Beginning: There are, in the poem too, secret routes
Czortkov-Czern.<owitz> → Darmstadt.

---

from 22.8.60, Ms. *workbook II, 21 [13]* *812* *=747*

Brotherliness of the poem; re which: Danton's sentence
—Heads that kiss in the dust— —Praise to the {~} quotation marks! Reality of the Beyond!
by the way: Franzos's way also through the no-longer-being \das Nicht-mehr-seiende!!!

---

from 22.8.60, Ms. *workbook II, 21 [14]* *813*

---

expression- (wordart-)joyous and able to communicate *558*

---

from 22.8.60, Ms. *workbook II, 21 [15]* *814*

---

pathos

---

from 22.8.60, Ms. *workbook II, 21 [16]* *815* *=432*

---

intensive perception: becoming aware

from 22.8.60, Ms. *workbook II, 21 [17]* *816* *=433*

---

to expect = attentiveness

---

from 22.8.60, Ms. *workbook II, 21 [18]* *817*

Buber, I and Thou, p. 107:
"... the eternal I of the mortal and the eternal You of the immortal ..." ‖
↕
-i- "cathexability," addressability \Ansprechbarkeit\, address \Anspruch\ *321, 500*
p. 108 (Buber on Buddha): the thou-saying to the origin

=248 *818 workbook II, 21 [19] from 22.8.60, Ms.*

-i- language as the language of the one who speaks //
the one who speaks as the speaker of the language =
in this antinomy—without synthesis—stands the poem.

=233 *819 workbook II, 21 [20] from 22.8.60, Ms.*

-i- The poem as the far from gaplessly structured, as the gappy, occupiable porous: ("à toi de passer, vie!)

=409 *820 workbook II, 21 [21] from 22.8.60, Ms.*

Buber, I and Thou, p. 137 "—until the great fright comes, and the •holding of one's breath in the dark, and the preparing \bereitende\ silence":

+ ↕

→ •for "only at times was it unpleasant for him.

=509 *821 workbook II, 21 [22] from 22.8.60, Ms.*

-i- Our time: the time of You-latency, You-lessness—
" —I-latency
the I partakes in the things; through the ⌊—I-containing \ichhafte\—⌋ naming of things the I and its conversation are woken up.—

=337 *822 workbook II, 21 [23] from 22.8.60, Ms.*

-i- co-essential with a being
co-extensive with an extension

❖❖❖

823 diary 4; inserted sheets [1,1] Ms.

/ M<andel>stam
Now, as otherwise we have no
"So let us time with Time": ⌊to⌋ this verbal construction, ⌊sounding⌋ ⌊~~as~~⌋ ~~probably~~ ~~as~~ ⌊~~all too~~ a little⌋ (personal) ⌊and⌋ deliberate in German, though in Russian rooted in the vernacular, M'<andelstams> poem is tuned.•
Gumilyov to: Batjuškov ...
mortality, temporality of things—/
•~~From it~~ ⌊Here⌋ something else than resignation speaks; here is an examination of the

temporality word, in which utopia too remains included ~~in to pai~~—most painfully—in the present.
worldgain // = worldfree *385/505, 523*

Language: the naming *508*

Ms. *Diary 4; inserted sheets[1,2]* *824*

---

of this earth {ah} yes, as one wants to say in these rocket-oriented days: terrestrial
The Aeon and the Hour<,> ⌊the spectacle of⌋ the century⌊ies⌋ and the ⌊listen<?>⌋ moment, *59*
⌊moment written into the gazing eye{s}—,⌋ both, worldtime and hearttime in their clutching embrace, the audible and the inaudible ticking of the watches.

the polarity of star and pupil, the mute and the speaking.

Ms. *Diary 4; inserted sheets [1,3]* *825*

Darkness: Pascal: ne nous reprochez *33/111, 121, 136, 153*

Ms. *Diary 4; inserted sheets [1,4]* *826*

To speak: a result of listening, a naming and making visible— *643*

Ms. *Diary 4; inserted sheets [1,5]* *827*

Martini <Das> Wagnis <der Sprache>
Staiger Gr<und>b.<egriffe der Poetik> *923*

Ms. *Diary 4; inserted sheets [2,1]* *828* *=722*

⌊Quote:⌋
p. 411:Letter to Gutzkov
"You and your friends ... our time is purely material ... Split bet.<ween> educ.<ated> and uned.<ucated society>

Ms. *Diary 4; inserted sheets [2,2]* *829* *=723*

-i- fadaises<?>—la Mada~~~~~—Michaux /~~~~~/

Ms. *Diary 4; inserted sheets [2,3]* *830* *=724*

---

p. 535: Gutzk.<ov> to B.<üchner>
"Of your piglet-dramas \Ferkeldramen\"
Your Danton did not pull

=725 *831* *Diary 4; inserted sheets [2,4]* *Ms.*

Deutsche Drama hrsg. von B. v. Wiese 58

=726 *832* *Diary 4; inserted sheets [2,5]* *Ms.*

Viëtor: “antipathetic contrast \Gegensatz\” as principle of construction

Viëtor DVJS 1934, “The tragedy of heroic pessimism”
K. May Form und Bedeutung 1957 Stuttgart

=727 *833* *Diary 4; inserted sheets [2,6]* *Ms.*

---

p. 399, B.<üchner> to the fam.<ily> about my drama—
⌊p. 400⌋ “The dram.<atic> poet

=728 *834* *Diary 4; inserted sheets [2,7]* *Ms.*

-i- the demotic, the lower in Büchner—

=729 *835* *Diary 4; inserted sheets [2,8]* *Ms.*

Glosses to Spinozas Ethik: Viëtor, pp. 247f.
to: / Spinoza-citation Thomas Paynes, DT, III, 1

=730 *836* *Diary 4; inserted sheets [2,9]* *Ms.*

Fallhut—barrelets (d’enfant)

=731 *837* *Diary 4; inserted sheets [3,1]* *Ms.*

Walter Rehm, Gontscharow und die Langeweile / E.<xperimentum> M.<edietatis> /
/ über B.<üchner>: p. 110 /

⌊quote:⌋ p. 109: Gutzkov, 1835, “Wally the doubtress”: the “eternal self-ennui”
Hebbel, Diary; in 1846 Hebbel plans a drama in 5 act<s>: The bore.<dom>
Grabbe: B.<oredom> = deity of the antifatalists
p. 110: Büchner
pp. 110ff.

=732 *838* *Diary 4; inserted sheets [3,2]* *Ms.*

Leonce and Lena, pp. 135, 136 Lena: “A horrifying thought occurs to me: I believe that there are people who are unhappy, incurably so, and only because they are.”

/-i-: To get oneself through language, which—Kafka!—is only a having, into an accurate relation with one's Being!—/ ‖

Ms. *Diary 4; inserted sheets [3,3]* *839* *=733*

Graduation house \Gradierhaus (-werk)\: bâtim<en>t de graduation, chambre graduée

Brine: eau salée, saline

(Bittering): saumure, eau-mère

Ms. *Diary 4; inserted sheets [3,4]* *840* *=734*

Nous ferons un peu de romantique pour nous tenir à la hauteur du siècle (Büchner to his fiancée) / Viëtor, p. 174.

Ms. *Diary 4; inserted sheets [3,5]* *841*

/ -i-

A play, the end

He, remaining alone, the two walking away: You should love your neighbor!

She—: I love him!

Three times, the third time, singing: I do love him

The parrot: I do love him ...

—End—

/ -i- oh, come from afar
and dead, oh so dead
Your word won't be of any use,
oh stay in your boat <?>
oh stay, oh leave

Ms. *Diary 4; inserted sheets [3,6]* *842* *▸686 =735*

-i- Brain- and heart-infuriating!

❖❖❖

From the -i- folders

843 *-i- 11,53* *Ms.*

Parallel places in notes in appendix

Perception
Presence \Gegenwärtigkeit\
Oppositeness \Gegenständigkeit\
Secret \Geheimnis\
Ecstasy

Form-ness \Gestalthaftigkeit\—

Language
Trubetzkoy
Metaphor—Benveniste

Hölderlin
(Sinclair)
Bettina
Blanchot

Rhythm
Breathroutes

Saran
Heusler
Sievers

Darkness ↙ Pascal
Darkness ↖ Shestov

The substantive
↙ (Benveniste)
Rubble, Vacant Lots-Büchner Danton
↙
The participle, infinite time-form

Dialogue
Brotherliness

Time—End-time

Kafka: To be, not to have

—(Mysticism)—

❖❖❖

Further Materials from The Meridian—*Collections*

Collected typescripts of 9.28.60 in inherited order

28.9.60, Ts. *F 84,1* *844* *145◄*

⌊28.IX.⌋ ⌊BSp⌋

The poem is the form taken by the yearning of the I, which by delimiting itself through language, reveals itself; we are there and present first through the word, first literally—by the letter *314*
\wörtlich\—.

28.9.60, Ts. *F 84,2* *845*

The poem: a language fragment that has become mortal, that starts the route into nothingness, thereby allowing the gap to arise which gives form to the new, to what follows. *315*

28.9.60, Ts. (Ms.) *F 84,3* *846*

Not by speaking of offense, but by remaining unshakably itself, the poem becomes offense— *418*
becomes, allow me ~~this comparison~~ ⌋, to call it thus⌋—the ⌊pariah and⌋ Jew ~~in~~ of literature. It lives in the ghetto.
at the periphery; on holidays it is permitted, in its Sunday best, to show itself.——
⌊Now,⌋ {O}one can jewify. This, as is well known, happens only extremely rarely, but it does happen. Something like jewification seems to me to be commendable for the comprehension of the poetic, and also of the exoteric.

28.9.60, Ts. *F 84,4* *847*

One can jewify; that is, admittedly, difficult and, why not admit this too, many a Jew has failed *417*
to do so; that's exactly why I believe it to be so commendable: It is ⌊It is, finally, only a word for⌋ recognizing-oneself-in-the-other, it is communion \Einkehr\ with the other as if with the self, it is a turning back \Umkehr\.

A turning back: this is talked about so often! And happens so rarely.
There are too many one-way streets. And two-way traffic and turning back are two different things. And, alas, even on country lanes there seems little occasion for that.

28.9.60, Ts. *F 85,1* *848*

BR -28.IX.60

The poem begins with itself. \(bei sich)\ *174*
⌊like the Tao (25): ... the poem has only itself—⌋

---

849 *F 85,2* *28.9.60, Ts.*

... The language- and responsibility-weary ⌊with {/} and without the "engagement" attested by the illustrated magazines and the lexica—⌋

668 The lyric Koine of our days ⌊/ the lyric hotchpotch⌋

Language-scrap

---

850 *F 85,3* *28.9.60, Ts.*

304 The poem as that which literally speaks itself to death

---

851 *F 85,4* *28.9.60, Ts.*

190 Oppositeness, objectivity of the poems. What is needed ⌊,⌋ is contemplation \Anschauung\ (not looking through \Durchschauen\—: the poem already is what is behind.

---

852 *F 85,5* *28.9.60, Ts.*

713 Hostility to art\ ('Danton,' 'Lenz'). Not synthetic poetry. No Mercier-ian
638, 601 Elargissez l'Art (poetry enlarged through ultrashort)

---

853 *F 85,6* *28.9.60, Ts.*

676 The homeland outcasts (the League of World Outcasts still remains to be called into existence ...) In the thought that and what and how they were outcast, lies the actual homeland.

---

854 *F 85,7* *28.9.60, Ts.*

243 Something of the foreknowledge of language falls to the attentive one: something invisible from the point of crystallization (????)

=177 *855* *F 85,8* *28.9.60, Ms.*

The obvious which has become a 'problem'—

28.9.60, Ts. (Ms.) *F 86,1* *856* *=282*

⌊28.IX.⌋ BSp

•It builds ⌊, from the direction of death,⌋ the ⌊at the⌋ countercosmos of the mortals.—

Artistry and word-art—that may have the feeling of something occidental, evening-filling. Poetry is ⌊something else; poetry.⌋ heart-grey, ⌊⌊sublunar,⌋ ⌊heavens- and heartgrey⌋ heart- and heavens-grey⌋ breath-marbled language in time. •~~Word-art and artistry too~~ Ultimately it also is saved. 'word-art' into its ~~decli~~ drift and decline; survival is ⌊means⌋ in no way "everything" for her . ...

28.9.60, Ts. *F 86,2* *857*

The poem, as precarious and fragile as it is, is solidary; it stands with you, ~~when~~ as soon as you, ~~on you~~ reflecting on yourself, turn toward it; it is the second in the core and casing of your desperation. *476*

28.9.60, Ts. *F 86,3* *858*

Love for men is not philanthropy. *417, 690*

28.9.60, Ts. *F 86,4* *859*

Last sentence:

I thank you for the prize that carries the name: Georg Büchner. 95

►521

28.9.60, Ts. *F 86,5* *860* *=94*

The poem: oh this infinity-speaking full of mortality and to no purpose! This ~~belief~~ ⌊momentary belief⌋ in the ~~infinite-infinite~~ noun and participle, this conspirational devotion \Ver- und Zugeschworensein\ to the ~~Infinite,~~ infinite forms of the temporal! This naming and naming of the most transient! I thank you for this prize, the prize that carries the name, open to time, steadfast in time: Georg Büchner.

❖❖❖

378◄

28.9.60, Ts.(Ms.) *F 90,1* *861* *=379*

BR 28.IX.60

The poem is with itself, it has also taken back the song it has proved → folding → involution

---

862 *F 90,2* *28.9.60, Ts.*

---

307 The sensual, the obvious \ Sinnfällige\ in language is the secret of the presence of a voice (person)

[307◄] *863* *F 90,3 [F 55,3]* *28.9.60, Ts. [Ms.]*

---

31 human un-land (maybe for the Mandelst<am>-place

[►175] *864* *F 90,4 [F 55,4]* *28.9.60, Ts. [Ms.]*

---

plump words

---

865 *F 90,5* *28.9.60, Ts.*

---

306 In the poem: The presencing of a person as language, realization of language as person (maybe reread: parole/language phonology

---

866 *F 90,6* *28.9.60, Ts.*

183, 843 Darkness—secret—of the present, objective. Opacity of what is at hand.

---

867 *F 90,7* *28.9.60, Ts.*

691; 663 The decisions that fall outside our "thought-spread \Denkweite\." Switchboards

---

868 *F 90,8* *28.9.60, Ts.*

---

404 One has to learn to love ⌊—acknowledge—⌋ the dark like the dark-eyed, the dark-skinned

---

►285
=495 *869* *F 90,9* *28.9.60, Ms.*

‖ Conclusion: Poetry as self-encounter; unrepeatable and therefore to be undertaken

❖❖❖

Single sheet with notes on Mandelstam

Ms. *E 5,2* *870* *144*◄

Mandelst.: he knew that ⌊in the poem⌋ time-close means time-open, not: <u>opportune</u>. *55, 305*

Ms. *E 5,3* *871*

Novalis: Philos. = homesickness

Ms. *E 5,4* *872*

He believed, with the best, that the revolution was a one-time chance for Russia and thus the world; because for the Russian Moscow is indeed the third and last Rome; there will not be a fourth.

Ms. *E 5,5 [B 3,3]* *873* *[345*◄►*463]*

His Jewishness is the Jewishness of the one for whom God is the—unpronounceable—name, for whom each word remains assigned to ~~the~~ ⌊this ~~and~~⌋ name.

Ms. *E 6,1* *874*

L. SR<?>, Maria<?> ~~~, Bakunin, Herzen, Lavrov, Michailovski above Solovyov and Shestov—<u>"Inonia"</u>

Ms. *E 6,2* *875*

Osip Mandelst's ~~poetry~~ ⌊poems⌋ are, as only a few ⌊others⌋, inscribed with the tetragrammaton, the name of the Deus absconditus, the E1 ... *114*

Ms. *E 6,3* *876*

La pointe acérée de l'infini (Baudelaire) ↔ Hofmannsthal *137, 389, 797, 805*

Ms. *E 6,4* *877* ◄*645*

"Inertia" in M<andelstam>: he who wants to, should ⌊make cl.<ear>⌋ prove, that our planet turns around itself, claim, that he feels it ...

❖❖❖

Excerpts

124◄ *878* *F 15,4* *19.8.59, Ms.*

causa formalis | immanent principle of form
causa materialis | (entelechy)

879 *F 16,1* *19.8.59, Ms.*

Is a poem "composed"?
(" ... the compound, however, comes into being by parts and dies away into parts." {)}Leibniz, Monadology)

880 *F 16,2* *19.8.59, Ms.*

"For in nature there are never two beings which are perfectly alike and in which it is not possible to find an internal difference, or at least a difference founded upon an intrinsic." (Leibniz, Mo.<nadology>)

►492 *881* *F 16,3* *19.8.59, Ms.*

"Et c'est <ce> qu'on appelle en nous Ame Raisonnable, ou Esprit" (Leibniz)

❖❖❖

109◄ *882* *F 18,1* *19.8.59, Ms.*

activity and passivity of the poem

883 *F 18,2* *19.8.59, Ms.*

But can one describe a face?

884 *F 18,3* *19.8.59, Ms.*

Mirror-quality of the you—

885 *F 18,4* *19.8.59, Ms.*

778 The process of perception → apperception in the poem

20.8.59, Ms. *F 18,5* *886*

Foreboding 20.8. *118*

20.8.59, Ms. *F 18,6* *887*

---

centering (variable)

20.8.59, Ms. *F 18,7* *888*

---

points of relation

20.8.59, Ms. *F 18,8* *889*

{"}Every between-space no matter how small is{"t} a "pond full of fish" (Leibniz)

20.8.59, Ms. *F 19,1* *890*

A certain contemp. "poetry" as a form of journalism (rhymed and unrhymed feuilleton). 626

20.8.59, Ms. *F 19,2* *891*

~~Sen~~ aesthetic pleasures = pleasures of the senses: muddled mental pleasures (Leibniz)

20.8.59, Ms. *F 19,3* *892* *►131*

---

sapere aude! dare to know

❖❖❖

Ms. *F 112,2* *893* *72◄*

Self-sublation of the subject = possible in poetry??? *27*

Ms. *F 112,3* *894*

Schelling
quotation vide. in Lukács, Logos VII, p. 7 *201*

Ms. *F 112,4* *895*

---

fullness of the subject = not the whole man

=586 *896* *F 113,1* *Ms.*

On metaphor:

⌊-i-⌋ ~~In the~~ ⌊The⌋ untransferability of the poem is experienced by many as ⌊something unbearable, as⌋ tyranny; but to be human, can also be understood as: to be under kings—

↙

Exactly ~~the~~ ⌊because of its⌋ untransferability ~~of the poem~~ {it}the poem is {of} so often felt as something unbearable—and hated. Doubtlessly there exists a tyranny of the poem: ~~tyranny~~ it has the imperiousness of the thought that to be among humans can also be called: to be under kings.

897 *F 113,2* *Ms.*

---

homogeneous

898 *F 113,3* *Ms.*

Coalescences and orderings

899 *F 113,4* *Ms.*

---

transformation faithful to the materials

900 *F 113,5* *Ms.*

---

fulfillment totality \Erfüllungstotalität\

901 *F 113,6* *Ms.*

⌊Lukács⌋ the "whole man" → the man whole

902 *F 114,1* *Ms.*

-i- Person → Personality

=450 *903* *F 114,2* *Ms.*

The poem as a summons to the You → Out of = (out of absence) = demand

=451 *904* *F 114,3* *Ms.*

---

narrowing

Ms. *F 114,4* *905* *=452*

The one who writes the poem and the one who understands remain complementary

Ms. *F 114,5* *906*

meta-aesthetic = ethical *538, 701, 713*

Ms. *F 114,6* *907*

object-structure

Ms. *F 115,1* *908*

Lukács, su<bject>—ob<ject>, Logos VII, p. 15:
"... act of indifference: ...
.....
it is an autonomous object in a very radical meaning of the word: it is posited as the only being object \einziger seiender Gegenstand\

Ms. *F 115,2* *909* *=244*

-i- Co-appearance of language in the poem or: language as co-appearing background (the poem as transparent ⌞ob⌟) =

Ms. *F 115,3* *910* *=427*

Uniqueness of the encounter: by inclusion of the absent (co-)world \(Mit-)welt\

Ms. *F 115,4* *911* *=428*

Leap—as entrance into the poem

Ms. *F 116,1* *912*

The "process of creation": active and contemplative at the same time
↗
Vision *121, 277*

Ms. *F 116,2* *913*

autonomizing \verselbständigen⌞te\ world⌟

914 *F 116,3* *Ms.*

... as sole real opposite

=539 *915* *F 116,4* *Ms.*

⌊the⌋ Meta-aesthetic = art-hostile ⌊in Büchner⌋

➤202
=540 *916* *F 116,5* *Ms.*

= Falling silent: much is put between brackets

❖❖❖

513◄➤746 *917* *D 10,1* *Ms.*

In self-movement the unity of subject and object takes place (-i- rather, to understand together \mitzuverstehen\)

❖❖❖

469◄➤629 *918* *F 96,2* *Ms.*

Adorno: historical innervation

❖❖❖

Bibliographic notes

228◄➤229 *919* *A 32,1* *Ms.*

‖ ⌊National libr.:⌋ Bühler—language planes

❖❖❖

51◄ *920* *B 22,1* *Ms.*

reread: Lenz: Lit. Encyclopedia, Russian

➤494 *921* *B 22,2* *Ms.*

Ask Krolow for his Büchner-speech, for Benn's speech too—

❖❖❖

Ms. *D 4,1* *922* *91◄*

Stenzel, Philos. d. Sprache.

Ms. *D 4,2* *923*

Staiger, Grundbegriffe *827*
—Interpre.
—Time

Ms. *D 4,3* *924*

Jahrb<uch der> Phän<omenologie>: II, III

Ms. *D 4,4* *925*

Benveniste, Noms d'agent et noms d'action *843*

Ms. *D 4,5* *926*

Benz, Barock

Ms. *D 5,1* *927*

Newald, de Boor

Ms. *D 5,2* *928*

Oskar Becker, Von der Hinfälligkeit ×/ des Schönen— *382, 429, 438*

~~Year~~ (Husserl Festschrift)

×/ Solger's concept—

Ms. *D 5,3* *929* *►139*

Solger 1847, 1848, 50, 49

❖❖❖

Ms. *E 13,1* *930* *375/738◄*

Landauer (→ Büchner)

931 *E 13,2* *Ms.*

'The creature' (Buber)

932 *E 13,3* *Ms.*

---

294 *Read Gundolf*

➤454 *933* *E 13,4* *Ms.*

Arnold Zweig—Büchner

❖❖❖

287◄➤158 *934* *F 68,1* *Ms.*

Schelling, Werke I. Abt., Bd. III S. 613ˣ ("System of transcend.<ental> Ideal.<ism> 1800, Abschn. VI)

❖❖❖

444◄ *935* *F 79,1* *Ms.*

—Binswanger—

936 *F 79,2* *Ms.*

---

486 Husserl, Vorl<esun>gen zur Ph.<änomenologie> des inn.<eren> Zeitbewußtseins
On the phenomenology of the consciousness of internal time

937 *F 79,3* *Ms.*

Heidegger, Being and Time
" , On the Essence of Ground

938 *F 79,4* *Ms.*

Bachelard, L'air et les songes

939 *F 79,5* *Ms.*

398, 948 •Eidetics 1. (: Jaensch 1920— eidetic disposition / visual images images eidetiques

subjective world\Eigenwelt\ / social \gemeinsch.\ world

• 2. Husserl. εἴδη: Les essences des choses, et non leur existence, présence
~~eidetic~~: Wesenswissenschaften

external = internal perception

Ms. *F 79,6* *940*

Flaubert: Corresp<ondan>ce “A force de regarder un caillou, un animal, un tableau, je me suis senti y entrer”

Ms. *F 79,7* *941*

‘the act of attentiom corresponding —to be found— to the object (to poetry): attentiveness: Malebranche *617*
(-i-)

Ms. *F 80,1* *942*

Hu<sserl>, Log.<ical> Inv<estigations>, vol. II, part 2., chapter 6: Sensuous and Categorical Intuitions

Ms. *F 80,2* *943*

“... Akt der Wahrnehmung, jeden erfüllenden Akt überhaupt als Anschauung und sein intentionales Korrelat als Gegenstand zu bezeichnen.

Ms. *F 80,3 [F 63,3]* *944* *[363◄►456]*

Synopses / Chromatisms (audition colorée) *181*

Ms. *F 80,4* *945*

No association = one burdens it with more (Bins<wanger>) than it can carry *229, 462*

Ms. *F 80,5* *946*

---

the poem:
beyond the epistemological opposition real—ideal = ||

Ms. *F 80,6* *947*

~~Ph~~. science of the phenomena of consciousness
Hu<sserl>, “Ideas pertaining to a pure phenomenology and to a phenomenological philosophy 1913 /

Ms. *F 81,1* *948*

---

p. 19, 20: Eidetic *939*

949 *F 81,2* *Ms.*

Uncalled,

950 *F 81,3* *Ms.*

Objects = what "stands ob-posite"\ das "Entgegenstehende"\ (psych.—

951 *F 81,4* *Ms.*

"Ekphoriazation \Ekphonierung\ of engrams"

952 *F 81,5* *Ms.*

"What can really be found in consciousness{,}... what is immanent to consciousness"

953 *F 81,6* *Ms.*

'perceiving intention' (Brentano)

954 *F 81,7* *Ms.*

Intentio
Attentio

955 *F 82,1* *Ms.*

670 ~~language-blind~~
Ph—<enomenolog>y: Purely descriptive ontology of immanent representations of consciousness.

956 *F 82,2* *Ms.*

Residuum Allheiler

957 *F 82,3* *Ms.*

Pfänder, Psychologie der Gesinnungen J<a>hrb<uch> 1.,3—

958 *F 82,4* *Ms.*

Bleuler, Lehrbuch

959 *F 82,5* *Ms.*

"Autism" (Chara⌊ct⌋—<eristic> of schizophrenia)

Ms. *F 82,6* *960*

"autistic thinking"

Ms. *F 82,7* *961*

---

introversion, narcissism

Ms. *F 82,8* *962*

Conrad-Martius, Zur Ontol.<ogie> und Erscheinungslehre der realen Außenwelt, J<ahr>buch III

Ms. *F 82,9* *963*

Expression-movements \Ausdrucksbewegungen\: language and writing—

Ms. *F 82,10* *964*

Jaspers: Hölderlin, Van Gogh, Strindberg ||

Ms. *F 82,11* *965*

"Innerlife"

Ms. *F 82,12* *966* *➤617*

-i- stepwise reduction

❖❖❖

Ms. *workbook II, 15; inserted sheets [3,3]* *967* *117◄*

Shestov—Une heure avec Sh.
(Frédéric Lefèvre<?>)
en volume

❖❖❖

Ms. *workbook II, 21; inserted sheets [4]* *968*

Heusler, Versgeschichte *843*

❖❖❖

Ms. *ÜR 6.12,29r [2]* *969* *198◄*

Heinz Lippmann: G.<eorg> B.<üchner> und die Romantik München 1913

The Poetry of Osip Mandelstam

1. Speaker: In 1913 a small volume of poetry was published in St. Petersburg, entitled "The 1
Stone." These poems clearly carry weight; as the poets Georgii Ivanov and Nikolai Gumilev admit, one would like to have written them oneself, and yet—these poems *estrange*. "Something," remembers Sinaida Hippius who was centrally involved in the literary life back then and who had a way with words, "something had gotten into them."

2. Speaker: Something strange that—as various contemporaries report—was also shared by 2
the author of the volume, Osip Mandelstam, born 1891 in Warsaw and who grew up in St. Petersburg and Pavlovsk and about whom it is known, among other things, that he studied philosophy in Heidelberg and is presently enamored of Greek.

1. Speaker: Something strange, somewhat uncanny, slightly absurd. Suddenly you hear him 3
break into laughter—on occasions where a completely different reaction is expected; he laughs much too often and much too loudly. Mandelstam is oversensitive, impulsive, unforeseeable. He is also nearly indescribably fearful: if, for example, his route leads past a police station, he'll make a detour.

2. Speaker: And among all the major Russian poets who survive the first post-revolutionary 4
decade—Nikolai Gumilev will be shot in 1921 as a counter-revolutionary; Velimir Khlebnikov, the great utopian of language, will die of starvation in 1922—this "scaredy-cat," anxious Osip Mandelstam will be the only defiant and uncompromising one, "the only one," as the younger literary historian Vladimir Markov notes, "who never ate humble pie."

1. Speaker: The twenty poems from the volume "The Stone" disconcert. They are not "word- 5
music," they are not impressionistic "mood poetry" woven together from "timbres," no "second" reality symbolically inflating the real. Their images resist the concept of the metaphor and the emblem; their character is *phenomenal*. These verses, contrary to Futurism's simultaneous expansion, are free of neologisms, word-concretions, word-destructions; they are not a new "expressive" art.

The poem in this case is the poem of the one who knows that he is speaking under the angle of inclination of his existence, that the language of his poem is neither "analogy" nor plain language, but language "actualized," voiceful and voiceless simultaneously, set free under the sign of an indeed radical individuation which however also remains mindful of the limits imposed on it by language and of the possibilities language has opened up.

The place of the poem is a human place, "a place in the cosmos," yes, but here, down here, in time. The poem—with all its horizons—remains a sublunar, terrestrial, creaturely phenomenon. It is the language of a singular being that has taken on form, it has objectivity and oppositeness, sub*stance* and presence. It stands into time.

6 *2. Speaker:* The thoughts of the "acmeists" or, as they also call themselves, the "Adamists," grouped around Gumilev and his magazines "The Hyperborean" and "Apollo," move along the same (or similar) orbits.

7 *1. Speaker:* The *thoughts*. But not, or only rarely, the *poems* themselves.

8 *1. Speaker:* "Akmē," that means the high point, maturity, the fully developed flower.

9 *2. Speaker:* Osip Mandelstam's poem wants to develop what can be perceived and reached with the help of language and make it *actual* in its truth. In this sense we are permitted to understand this poet's "Acmeism" as a language that has borne fruit.

10 *1. Speaker:* These poems are the poems of someone who is perceptive and attentive, someone turned toward what becomes visible, someone addressing and questioning: these poems are a *conversation*. In the space of this conversation the addressed constitutes itself, becomes present, gathers itself around the I that addresses and names it. But the addressed, through naming, as it were, becomes a you, brings its otherness and strangeness into this present. Yet even in the here and now of the poem, even in this immediacy and nearness it lets its distance have its say too, it guards what is most its own: its time.

11 *2. Speaker:* It is this tension of the times, between its own and the foreign, which lends that pained-mute vibrato to a Mandelstam poem by which we recognize it. (This vibrato is everywhere: in the interval between the words and the stanza, in the "courtyards" where rhymes and assonances stand, in the punctuation. All this has *semantic relevance*.) Things come together, yet even in this togetherness the question of their Wherefrom and Whereto resounds—a question that "remains open," that "does not come to any conclusion," and points to the open and occupiable, into the empty and the free.

12 *1. Speaker:* This question is realized not only in the "thematics" of the poems; it also takes shape in the language—and that's why it becomes a "theme"—: the word—the name!—shows a preference for noun-forms, the adjective becomes rare, the "infinitives," the *nominal forms* of the verb dominate: the poem remains *open to time*, time can join in, time *participates*.

13 *2. Speaker:* A poem from the year 1910:

The listening, the finely tensed sail.
The gaze, wide, empties itself.
The choir of midnight birds,
swimming through silence, unheard.

I have nothing, I resemble the sky.
I am the way nature is: poor.
Thus I am, free: like those midnight
voices, the flocks of birds.

You, sky, whitest of shirts,
you, moon, unsouled, I see you.
And, emptiness, your world, the strange
one, I receive, I take!

1. Speaker: A poem from the year 1911: 14

Mellow, measured: the horses' hoofs.
Lantern-light—not much.
Strangers drive me. Who do know
whereto, to what end.

I am cared for, which I enjoy,
I try to sleep, I'm freezing.
Toward the beam we drive, the star,
they turn—all this rattling!

The head, rocked, I feel it burning.
The foreign hand, its soft ice.
The dark outline there, the fir trees
of which I know nothing.

2. Speaker: A poem from the year 1915: 15

Insomnia. Homer. Sails, taut.
I read the catalog of ships, did not get far:
The flight of cranes, the young brood's trail
high above Hellas, once, before time and time again.

Like that crane wedge, driven into the most foreign—
The heads, imperial, God's foam on top, humid—
You hover, you swim—whereto? If Helen wasn't there,
Achaeans, I ask you, what would Troy be worth to you?

Homer, the seas, both: love moves it all.
Who do I listen to, who do I hear? See—Homer falls silent.
The sea, with black eloquence beats this shore,
Ahead I hear it roar, it found its way here.

1. Speaker: In 1922, five years after the October revolution, "Tristia," Mandelstam's second 16
volume of poems comes out.
The poet—the man for whom language is everything, origin and fate—is in exile with his language, "among the Scythians." "He has"—and the whole cycle is tuned to this, the first line of the title poem—"he has learned to take leave—a science."
Mandelstam, like most Russian poets—like Blok, Bryusov, Bely, Khlebnikov, Mayakovsky, Esenin—welcomed the revolution. His socialism is a socialism with an ethico-religious stamp; it comes via Herzen, Michailovski, Kropotkin. It is not by chance that in the years before the revolution the poet was involved with the writings of the Chaadaevs, Leontievs, Rozanovs, and Gershenzons. Politically he is close to the party of the Left Social Revolutionaries.

For him—and this evinces a chiliastic character particular to Russian thought—revolution is the dawn of the other, the uprising of those below, the exaltation of the creature—an upheaval of downright cosmic proportions. It unhinges the world.

17 *2. Speaker:*

Let us praise the freedom dawning here
this great, this dawn-year.
Submerged, the great forest of creels
into waternights, as none had been.
Into darkness, deaf and dense you reel,
you, people, you: sun-and-tribunal.

The yoke of fate, brothers, sing it
which he who leads the people carries in tears.
The yoke of power and darkenings,
the burden that throws us to the ground.
Who, oh time, has a heart, hears with it, understands:
he hears your ship, time, that founders.

There, battle-ready, the phalanx—there, the swallows!
We linked them together, and—you see it:
The sun—invisible. The elements, all
alive, bird-voiced, under way.
The net, the dusk: dense. Nothing glimmers.
The sun—invisible. The earth swims.

Well, we'll try it: turn that rudder around!
It grates, it grinds, you leftists—come on, rip it around!
The earth swims. You men, take courage, once more!
We plough the seas, we break up the seas.
And to think, Lethe, even when your frost pierces us:
To us earth was worth ten heavens.

18 *1. Speaker:* The horizons are darkening—leave-taking takes pride of place, expectations wane, memory reigns on the fields of time. For Mandelstam, Jewishness belongs to what is remembered:

This night: unamendable,
with you: light, nonetheless.
Suns, black, that flare up
before Jerusalem.

Suns, yellow: greater fright—
sleep, hushaby.
Bright Jewish home: they bury
my mother dear.

No longer priestly,
robbed of grace and salvation,
they sing a woman's dust
out of the world, in the light.

Jews' voices, silent they kept not
mother, how loud it sounded.
I wake up in my cot
by a black sun, surrounded.

2. Speaker: In 1928 a further volume of poems appears—the last one. A new collection joins 19
the two previous ones also gathered here. "No more breath—the firmament swarms with maggots"—: this line opens the cycle. The question about the wherefrom becomes more urgent, more desperate—the poetry—in one of his essays he calls it a plough—tears open the abyssal strata of time, the "black earth of time" appears on the surface. The eye, talking with the perceived, and pained, develops a new ability: it becomes visionary: it accompanies the poem into its underground. The poem writes itself toward an *other*, a "strangest" time.

1. Speaker: 1 JANUARY1924 20

Whoever kisses time's sore brow
will often, like a son, think tenderly
how she, time, lay down to sleep outside
in high heaped wheat drifts, in the corn.

Whoever has raised the century's eyelid
—both slumber-apples, large and heavy—,
hears noise, hears the streams roar
the lying times, relentlessly,

Imperious century, with loam-beautiful mouth
and two apples, asleep—yet
before it dies: to the son's hand, so shrunken,
it bends down its lip.

Life's breath, I know, ebbs away each day,
one more small one, a small one—and
deceased is the song of mortification, loam and plague,
with lead they seal your mouth.

Oh loam-and -life! Oh century's death!
Only to the one, I'm afraid, does its meaning reveal itself,
in whom there was a smile, helpless—to the inheritor,
the man who lost himself.

Oh pain, oh to search for the lost word.
oh lid and lid to raise, sick and weak,
for generations, the strangest, with lime in your blood
to gather the grass and the weed of night!

Time. The lime in the blood of the sick son
turns hard. Moscow, that wooden coffer, sleeps.
Time, the sovereign. And no escape anywhere ...
The snow's apple-scent, as always.

The sill here: I wish I could leave it.
Whereto? The street—darkness.
And, as if it were salt, so white, there on the pavement
lies my conscience, spread out before me.

Through winding lanes, through slipways
the journey goes, somehow:
a bad passenger sits in a sled,
pulls a blanket over the knees.

The lanes, the shimmering lanes, the by-lanes
the runners crunch's like apples under the tooth.
The strap, I can't grab it,
it doesn't want me to, and the hand is clammy.

Night, carwoman, with what scrap and iron
are you rolling through Moscow?
Fish thud here, and there, from pink houses,
it steams toward you—scalegold!

Moscow, anew. Ah, I greet you, once more!
Forgive, excuse—my misery wasn't very great.
I like to call them, as always, my brethren:
the pike's saying and the hard frost!

The snow in the pharmacy's raspberry light ...
A clattering, from afar, an Underwood ...
The coachman's back ... the roadway, blown away...
What more do you want? They won't kill you.

Winter—beauty. And skyward the white,
the starmilk—it streams, streams away and blinks.
The horsehair blanket crunches along the icy
runners—the horsehair blanket sings!

The little lanes, smoking, the petroleum, always—:
swallowed by snow, raspberry colored.
They hear the Soviet-sonatina jingle,
remember the year twenty.

Does it make me swear and damn?
—The frost's apple-scent, again—
Oh oath that I swore to the fourth estate!
Oh my promise, heavy with tears!

Oh whom will you kill? Whom will you praise?
And what lie, tell me, are you going to make up?
Tear off this cartilage, the keys of the machine:
the pike's bones you lay open.

The lime in the blood of the sick son: it fades.
A laughter, blissful, frees itself—
Sonatas, powerful ... The little sonatina
of the typewriter—: only its shadow!

2. Speaker: That's how to escape contingency: through laughter. Through what we know as 21
the poet's "senseless" laughter—through the absurd. And on the way there what does appear —mankind is absent—has answered: the horsehair blanket has sung.

Poems are sketches for Being: the poet lives according to them.

In the thirties Osip Mandelstam is caught in the "purges." The road leads to Siberia, where we lose his trace.

In one of his last publications, "Journey to Armenia," published in 1932 in the Leningrad magazine "Swesda," we also find notes on the matters of poetry. In one of these notes Mandelstam remembers his preference for the Latin *gerund*.

The gerund—that is the present participle of the passive form of the future.

78, rue de Longchamp Paris, 16 May 1960.

Dear, deeply revered Hermann Kasack!

Next to this sheet of paper lies a book: the poems of Oskar Loerke. I have opened it—I read:

Oskar Loerke
via
Hermann Kasack
thanks the poet
Paul Celan
Stuttgart, April 1954
HK

Dear, revered Hermann Kasack: that, with its names and words, was for me, who was barely thirty-four at the time, simultaneously honor and nourishment—: with and by these lines of dedication did I live.

And now your letter of 11 May this year has been added{,}—: I thank you, from the depth of my heart.

To be allowed to accept this prize, that carries the name of Georg Büchner: for me this means before all, encounter. Encounter, human closeness, encounter with one of the high names of the soul-monad mankind.

What a name! I thank you and all those in whose name I ~~de~~ am permitted to enter the proximity of that name.

Aren't words, especially in the poem, aren't they—aren't they becoming and —decaying—names? Aren't poems exactly this: the infinite-saying of mortality and nothingness that remains mindful of its finitude? (Please excuse the emphasis: it belongs to that dust that sets free and receives us and our voiceful-voiceless souls.) ~~and sets free.)—~~

Dear, revered Hermann Kasack, may I tell you something that is certainly unknown to you, from the "pre-history" of my Büchner-Prize? I'll dare: God knows that adolescent stuff isn't totally "foreign to the poem."

Roughly a year ago, in August 1959, after a longish stay in the mountains I wrote a small (a very small) story: "Conversation in the Mountain." And it ~~says~~ ⌊said⌋ somewhere in it, unsuspectedly and surprising for me too, something about a Jew who, like Lenz, walked through the mountains ...

Some months later, after many hours spent on Kafka's writings, I had to read and interpret Büchner with the students at the Ecole Normale Supérieure. And here, in Lenz, he returned, the eternal Jew ...

And Saturday when I was still in Frankfurt, a letter from Berlin reached me, the letter of a young American who has translated some of my work; he introduced himself as the translator of Büchner's Lenz ...

Dear, deeply revered Hermann Kasack: Please transmit to the German Academy for Language and Poetry, to the Land Hessen—and I mean to include in that all the trees too, please —and to the city of Darmstadt, my sincere thanks!

And to you my most heartfelt thanks and greetings from your truly devoted Paul Celan

Appendix

Concerning the Notes

The primary purpose of these notes is to identify citations and, wherever possible, also indirect citations and allusions. The notes have been slightly edited and simplified for this edition, though a range of English-language references have been added. Where necessary, brief elucidations concerning persons and objects are also given. Most of the original sources for the citations are obviously German language books and journals; the most important ones are given bilingually, using existing English translation. All non-attributed English translations are by Pierre Joris.

When Celan's text contains more extended citations, paraphrases or excerpts, only the source is indicated. If the citations are truncated or the cited text differs markedly from the original, then the notes cite the complete and/or corrected text.

As Celan's literary estate includes his library, the books from which he worked can at least in part be indicated, though caution is due. The library also contains volumes that show no sign of use. Celan often worked in public libraries, as shown by a number of bibliographic notes with call numbers.

Dietlind Meinecke and Stefan Reichert established a catalog of Celan's Paris library between 1972 and 1974, and in 1987 cataloged the one in Moisville. This catalog lists more volumes than the estate owns. In the notes, the editions used by Celan are indicated, wherever possible. In the remaining cases, and especially when only unclear citations and allusions are available, actual editions are used. When a cited book is in the catalog of Celan's library, it is indicated with "[*CL*]". Celan's marginal annotation of cited passages is noted when the book was accessible via the estate.

For Büchner, the 1988 Münchner edition is also referenced, besides Bergemann's—the one Celan used —which differs textually from current editions. For the English edition, citations from the plays have been newly translated or, more rarely, adapted from existing translations, though citations from "Lenz" use or adapt Richard Sieburth's version (Archipelago Books, New York, 2004). Celan read Osip Mandelstam in the Russian original, and here the German-language edition by Ralph Dutli is also used in the German edition of this volume; for the English edition, Mandelstam's texts have been translated from the German versions used or made by Celan.

In the notes, Celan's at times idiosyncratic spelling (Mandelstamm for Mandelstam, for ex.) is silently corrected to current German and, as the case may be, English usage.

References are always given at first occurrence of the citation. Keywords that appear more than once have their recurrences indicated in the margins (cf. *Editorial Comments*, p. 257). The notes referring to this occurrence can be located in the text that bears the lowest number.

Where necessary, descriptions of the original ms. are always given as the last note to the text. Here indications concerning dating, posterior textual emendations, material connections with texts printed elsewhere, as well as other marks and red-pencil corrections can be found. When a text is reprinted a second time in a wider context (this pertains to the workbooks and the sheets inserted into Diary 4, the excerpts, and a number of notations on Büchner), the first occurrence points to the number of the second occurrence with "=" and vice versa (cf. *On the numbering and reference system*). Notes concerning this larger context (concerning, e.g., dating) can be found at the second occurrence.

Abbreviations of often cited sources:

Becker = Oskar Becker: Von der Hinfälligkeit des Schönen und der Abenteuerlichkeit des Künstlers. Eine ontologische Untersuchung im ästhetischen Phänomenbereich, in: Festschrift für Edmund Husserl, zum 70. Geburtstag gewidmet, Halle 1929, pp. 27-52. [Ergänzungsband des Jahrbuchs für Philosophie und phänomenologische Forschung 10]

Benn = Gottfried Benn: Gesammelte Werke in vier Bänden, hrsg. v. Dieter Wellershoff, Wiesbaden [4]1977.

Bergemann = Georg Büchner: Werke und Briefe, hrsg. v. Fritz Bergemann, Wiesbaden 1958 [*CL*].

Büchner-Reden = Büchner-Preis-Reden 1951-1971, mit einem Vorwort von Ernst Johann, Stuttgart 1972.

GW = Paul Celan: Gesammelte Werke in fünf Bänden, Frankfurt a.M. 1992.

Hofmannsthal = Hugo von Hofmannsthal: Gesam-

melte Werke in Einzelausgaben, hrsg. v. Herbert Steiner, Frankfurt a.M. 1953-1959 [*CL*].
Lukács = Georg Lukács: Die Subjekt-Objekt-Beziehung in der Aesthetik, in: Logos. Internationale Zeitschrift für Philosophie der Kultur 7 (1917/18), Tübingen 1918, pp. 1-39.
Leibniz = Gottfried Wilhelm Leibniz: Monadologie, französisch-deutsch, übersetzt von Artur Buchenau, überarbeitet v. Herbert Herring, Hamburg 1956 [*CL*].
MA = Georg Büchner: Werke und Briefe. Münchner Ausgabe, hrsg. v. Karl Pörnbacher, Gerhard Schaub, Hans-Joachim Simm und Edda Ziegler, München [5]1995.
Mandel'štam = Osip Mandel'štam: Sobranie sočinenij, pod redakciej i so vstupitel'nymi stat'jami G. P. Struve i B. A. Filippova, N'ju-Jork 1955 [*CL*].
Platon = Platon: Sämtliche Werke in drei Bänden, deutsch v. L. Georgii, Heidelberg o.J. [*CL*].
Scheler = Max Scheler: Die Stellung des Menschen im Kosmos, München 1947 [*CL*]. Man's Place in Nature, translated by Hans Meyerhoff, Boston 1961.
TCA = Paul Celan: Werke. Tübinger Ausgabe, hrsg. v. Jürgen Wertheimer, Frankfurt a.M. 1996 ff.
— Sprachgitter. Vorstufen—Textgenese—Endfassung, bearbeitet von Heino Schmull unter Mitarbeit von Michael Schwarzkopf, Frankfurt a.M. 1996.
— Die Niemandsrose. Vorstufen—Textgenese—Endfassung, bearbeitet von Heino Schmull unter Mitarbeit von Michael Schwarzkopf, Frankfurt a.M. 1996.

Notes

To the Final Version (according to paragraphs)

1a-2 *puppet-like, iambically five-footed [...] a childless being:* cf. Camille's monologue in Georg Büchner's "Danton's Death," Act 2, Scene 3, 'A room' (Bergemann, p. 40 [*CL*]; ME, pp. 95f.)
— *Pygmalion:* mythical king of Cyprus who, according to Ovid, fell in love with the statue of a young girl fashioned by himself. Aphrodite brought her to life on his request and he took her for his wife.
— *'livid light before the storm':* Moritz Heimann on "Danton": "Vor dem Kunterbunt und hastig hingestrichenen Grunde stehen die Gestalten Dantons, Camilles, Robespierres in einem Lichte da, das in seiner gewittrigen Fahlheit eine unbeschreibliche Schärfe enthält.[Before the gaudy and hastily painted background stand the figures of Danton, Camille, Robespierre in a light that receives its undescribable sharpness from the livid light before the storm]." (Moritz Heimann: Georg Büchner, in: Die neue Rundschau 4 (1910), p. 1460).
3a *'in flight toward paradise,' [...]:* for this and the following citations see Büchner's "Leonce und Lena," act 3, scene 3 (Bergemann, p. 145, p. 147, pp. 143f. [*CL*]; MA, pp. 188f., p. 186).
5b *But who hears the speaker, who "sees him speak," [...]:* cf. Büchner's "Danton's Death," act 2, scene 3 'A room' (Bergemann, p. 40 [*CL*]; MA, p. 96): "Camille: Was sagst du, Lucile? / Lucile: Nichts, ich seh dich so gern sprechen. [...] Camille: Hab ich recht? Weißt du auch, was ich gesagt habe? / Lucile: Nein, wahrhaftig nicht. [Camille: What do you say, Lucile? / Lucile: Nothing, I love watching you while you speak.[...] Camille: Am I right? Do you know what I said? / Lucile: No, to tell the truth, I don't.]" In [*CL*] this passage is marked in the margins; Lucile's last sentence is further underlined.
6a-c *"the carts drive up and come to a halt."; Fabre even maintains that he can die "doubly,"; "a few"—nameless—"voices," find that "all of this is old hat and boring.":* all quotes from "Danton's Death," Act

4, Scene 7, 'Place of the Revolution' (Bergemann, pp. 80f. [*CL*]; MA, pp. 130f.)

— *Triumph of "puppet" and "string":* "Puppen sind wir, von unbekannten Gewalten am Draht gezogen; nichts, nichts wir selbst! [Puppets we are, our strings pulled by unknown powers; nothing, we are nothing.]" "Danton's Death", Act 2, Scene 5, "A Room" (Bergemann, p. 45 [*CL*], marked several times in the margins; MA, p. 100).

— *"Long live the king!":* cf. The end of "Danton's Death": "Ein Bürger: He, wer da? / Lucile *sinnend und wie einen Entschluß fassend, plötzlich*: Es lebe der König! / Bürger: Im Namen der Republik! *Sie wird von der Wache umringt und weggeführt.* [Citizen: Who goes there? / Lucile, *reflects a moment, then suddenly*: Long live the King! / Citizen: In the name of the Republic. *She is surrounded by the guards and led away.*]" (Bergemann, p. 82 [*CL*]; MA, p. 133).

7b *"the bystanders and old war-horses of history.":* cf. Letter to the bride of November 1833? (According to Bergemann, according to MA circa 9.-12. March 1834): "Es fällt mir nicht mehr ein, vor den Paradegäulen und Eckstehern der Geschichte mich zu bücken. [It wouldn't occur to me to stoop before the old warhorses and bystanders of history.]" (Bergemann, p. 374 [*CL*], underlined; MA, p. 288).

8b *Peter Kropotkin:* Petr Alekseevič Kropotkin (1842-1921), Prince, best-known representative of so-called communist anarchism, wrote among others, "Die französische Revolution" (1909, translated by Landauer).

— *Gustav Landauer:* (1870-1919), writer and politician, representative of a radical socialism and nonviolent anarchism. Editor of socialist publications. Essays on politics and literature as well as translations. Influenced by Kropotkin.

10a *"oh, art!":* "Danton's Death," Act 2, "A Room" (Bergemann, p. 40 [*CL*], underlined; MA, p. 96), cf. notes to 1a-2 and 5b.

11 *Ubiquität:* omnipresence.

12a *"At table Lenz was again in good spirits [...]":* "Lenz" (Bergemann, p. 94 [*CL*]; MA, p. 144).

12b *"The feeling that what has been created [...]":* the complete citation reads: "Ich verlange in allem— Leben, Möglichkeit des Daseins, und dann ist's gut; wir haben dann nicht zu fragen, ob es schön, ob es häßlich ist. Das Gefühl, daß, was geschaffen sei, Leben habe, stehe über diesen beiden, und sei das einzige Kriterium in Kunstsachen.[What I demand in all things is life, the potentiality of existence, and that's that; we need not then ask whether it be beautiful or ugly, the feeling that what has been created possesses life outweighs these two and should be the sole criterion in matters of art.]" (Bergemann, p. 94 [*CL*]; MA, p. 144)

13 *Reinhold Lenz [...] 'Anmerkungen übers Theater':* Jakob Michael Reinhold Lenz's "Notes on the Theater" were first published in Leipzig in 1774.

— *Mercier's 'Elargissez l'Art':* Louis-Sébastien Mercier (1740-1814): French author of novels, plays, and essays on drama. Shakespeare-influenced opponent of classical drama theory. "L'an deux mille quatre cent quarante. Rêve s'il en fût jamais» (1771), "Du théâtre ou nouvel essai sur l'art dramatique" (1773). Mercier appears as a prisoner in Büchner's play "Danton's Death," the sources of which include M.'s "Le nouveau Paris" (1799).

— *Elargissez l'art!:* (Fr.) Enlarge art!
Celan probably came across this citation (not attested in Mercier) when reading M. N. Rosanov's Lenz-monograph, where it is given as a motto in italics of the fith chapter, dealing with Mercier (p. 127), and discussed further: "Mercier demands the liberation of art from the fetters of narrowly limited academic considerations and its introduction into the wider field of popular interests, questions, and sympathies. His war cry is: 'Elargissez l'art!' This principle leads to a change in the content of art, the choice of appropriate material and in stylistic methods. Art has to connect with life, and take into consideration the latter's actual, daily tasks; it has to represent that which stands before the eyes of all, and must not remove itself from the real by even one step. Thus Mercier's demand for realism in art is far ahead of his time and appears as a precursor of today's school of Realism." (M. N. Rosanov [Assistant professor at the University of Moscow]: Jakob M. R. Lenz, der Dichter der Sturm- und Drangperiode. Sein Leben und seine Werke, vom Verfasser autorisierte und durchgesehene Übersetzung, deutsch von C. von Gütschow, Leipzig 1909, p. 131; cf. also p. 132).

14c-15 *"Idealism" and its "wooden puppets":* all citations from "Lenz" (Bergemann, pp. 94f. [*CL*]; MA, p. 144). The sentence "Man möchte manchmal ein Medusenhaupt sein [...]" underlined in [*CL*].

20b *Lenz spoke for a long time, "now all smiles, now serious"[...] , He had completely forgotten himself":* "Lenz" (Bergemann, p. 96 [*CL*], last sentence underlined; MA, p. 146).

22d *La poésie, elle aussi, brûle nos étapes.:* Fr.: brûler les étapes: not to set up a billet, to pass a halting-place without stopping.

24b *"He saw his existence as a necessary burden—And so he lived on ...":* End of "Lenz" (Bergemann, p. 111 [*CL*], first sentence underlined and passage marked in margin; MA, p. 158).

24d *"Death as final redeemer was not long in coming*

[...]": M. N. Rosanov: Jakob M. R. Lenz, der Dichter der Sturm- und Drangperiode. Sein Leben und seine Werke, vom Verfasser autorisierte und durchgesehene Übersetzung, deutsch von C. von Gütschow, Leipzig 1 909, p. 440.

24f *Lenz, who 'on 20th January walked through the mountains':* cf. First sentence of "Lenz." The indication "January \Jänner\" was added by Bergemann according to Oberlin. The original wording, as followed by MA, only says: "Den 20. ging Lenz [On the 20th, Lenz walked [...]]" (Bergemann, p. 85 [*CL*]; MA, p. 137).
On 1. 20. 1942 the implementation and coordination of the "final solution of the Jewish question" was discussed at the Wannsee conference.

25b *"except sometimes it annoyed him [...]":* "Lenz" (Bergemann, p. 85 [*CL*], underlined; MA, p. 138).

27 *6'Ne nous reprochez pas [...]':* Pascal: "Que disent les prophètes de Jésus-Christ? Qu'il sera évidemment Dieu? Non; mais qu'il est un Dieu véritablement caché [...]. Qu'on ne nous reproche donc plus le manque de clarté, puisque nous en faisons profession." (Blaise Pascal: Pensées, № 591 [751], in: Œuvres complètes, texte établi et annoté par Jacques Chevalier, Paris 1954, p. 1276 [*CL*]).
The citation can be found on several occasions with slight variations in the Shestov editions in Celan's library: in Lev Šestov: Na vesach Iova (stranstvovanija po dušam) [On Job's Scales], Pariž 1929, in the chapter "Gefsimanskaja noč. Filosofija Paskalja" ["The night of Gethsemane. On the philosophy of Pascal"]. In the Russian edition, present in [*CL*], the pages of this chapter are however not cut open. The French edition gives: "fuir les endroits éclairés, car la lumière fait voir le mensonge; aimer les ténèbres: 'Qu'on ne nous reproche pas le manque de clarté, car nous en faisons profession.'" (Léon Chestov, La nuit de Gethsémani. Essai sur la philosophie de Pascal, Paris 1923, p. 129). Celan used this edition, cf. Notes to nr. 140-148.
In Léon Chestov: Les révélations de la mort. Dostoïevsky-Tolstoï, préface et traduction de Boris de Schloezer, Paris 1923, p. XII [*CL*] the citation can be found in the preface, where Celan has marked it. Here the wording is: "Qu'on ne nous reproche pas le manque de clarté, parce que nous en faisons notre profession."
The citation can be found also as second epigraph of "Tausendundeine Nacht," the opening chapter of the book "Potestas Clavium," which Celan owned in a French translation: "Mille et une nuits," p. VII: "Qu'on ne nous reproche donc plus le manque de clarté, puisque nous en faisons profession. (Pascal)" (Léon Chestov: Le pouvoir des clefs [Potestas clavium], traduction de Boris de Schloezer, Paris 1928, p. VII; Celan dates the purchase: "Paris, 28. September 1959."). The citation surfaces a second time at the end of the preface on p. XXXVII, where it is also underlined. There and in the table of contents the reading date is given as "29. 9. 1959." We can assume that the actual source for the citations used in *The Meridian* speech was this French edition.
The citation with Celan's note "cf. Meridian" and with Celan's German translation ("Man werfe uns nicht Mangel an Klarheit vor, denn wir machen ihn uns zur Profession.") can be located in a German translation that Celan however acquired only on "21. Jänner 1961." (Leo Schestow: Auf Hiobs Waage. Über die Quellen der ewigen Wahrheiten, autorisierte Übertragung aus dem Russischen von Hans Ruoff und Reinhold von Walter, Berlin 1929, pp. 454f.)
In the French edition of Léon Chestov: Le pouvoir des clefs. Paris 1967, p. 37; Celan marked the epigraph once more, adding the note: "Meridian-Zitat."

— *Lev Shestov:* Lev Isaakovič Šestov, real name Ieguda Lejb Švarcman (1866-1938), worked first as a lawyer; first success with "Dostoievsky and Nietzsche" (1902), moves permanently to Paris in 1920, in 1928 meets Husserl, who introduces him to the work of Kierkegaard and Heidegger; other important works: "Apotheose der Abgründigkeit" (1905) (in German in [*CL*]: Leo Schestow: Auf Hiobs Waage. Über die Quellen der ewigen Wahrheiten, autorisierte Übertragung aus dem Russischen von Hans Ruoff und Reinhold von Walter, Berlin 1929), English edition: In Job's balances; on the sources of the eternal truths, by Leo Chestov, translated by Camilla Coventry and C. A. Macartney London, J. M. Dent, 1932, "Athen und Jerusalem" (1935) English edition: Athens and Jerusalem [by] Lev Shestov. Translated, with an introd., by Bernard Martin, Ohio University Press, 1966. Cf. also note to nr. 393.

— *congenital:* hereditary, innate.

31e *test the wind \verhoffen\:* "als sinnliche bedeutung ist für 'hoffen, verhoffen' [...] ‚überrascht aufspringen' vermutet. diese bedeutung ist wahrscheinlich im jagdausdruck erhalten: 'das wild hofft, verhofft', das wild wird stutzig, unruhig, sieht sich um. [...] 'verhoffen über ein ding', davon überrascht, darüber stutzig werden, auffahren [...] aus dem begriffe des unruhigwerdens, umblickens entwickelt sich der abstracte begriff 'in erwartungsvoller erregung sein, erwarten.'" (Deutsches Wörterbuch von Jacob und Wilhelm Grimm, Bd. 25, pp. 572f.)

31f *The "swift," which has always been outside":* "Woyzeck," "At the Captain's": "Hauptmann: Ich spür's schon, es ist so was Geschwindes draußen; so ein Wind macht mir den Effekt wie eine Maus. [I can feel it already, something swift, outside; that sort of wind affects me like a mouse.]" (Scene 1 in Bergemann, p. 151 [*CL*]. In later editions this scene no longer appears in that order.)

35d *"Attention is the natural prayer of the soul.":* Walter Benjamin in his Kafka essay: "Wenn Kafka nicht gebetet hat—was wir nicht wissen—, so war ihm doch aufs höchste eigen, was Malebranche 'das natürliche Gebet der Seele' nennt—die Aufmerksamkeit. Und in sie hat er, wie die Heiligen in ihre Gebete, alle Kreatur eingeschlossen. [If Kafka did not pray—which we do not know—what was highly characteristic of him, however, was what Malebranche called 'the natural prayer of the soul,' namely attentiveness.]" (Walter Benjamin: Kafka, in: Schriften, hrsg. v. Theodor W. Adorno und Gretel Adorno unter Mitwirkung v. Friedrich Podszus, 2 Bde., Frankfurt a.M. 1955, Bd. 2, pp. 196-228, p. 222; paragraph marked in margin in [*CL*], the Malebranche citation is further underlined; reading date noted at end of essay on p. 228 as: "11. XII. 59").

40a-b *Topos research [...] in light of u-topia:* cf.Celan's letter to Otto Pöggeler of 11. 1. 1960 from Paris, after the speech in Darmstadt: "It's done now, I even put, though at the very last moment, a (sort of) speech to paper—a few phrases from the Mandelstam radio play had to be included (you were much on my mind at that moment) as islands linking to other islands. (And among them also this sentence, meant for you: Topos research? Certainly! But in light of what is to be searched for: in light of u-topia—Only half a thought, alas, I know.)" (cited with friendly permission from Otto Pöggeler). Cf. also Otto Pöggeler: Dichtungstheorie und Toposforschung, in: Jahrbuch für Ästhetik und Allgemeine Kunstwissenschaft 5, Köln 1960, pp. 89-201; as printoff in [*CL*]. Thanks to Otto Pöggeler Celan already knew this essay in 1958.

44 *Poetry, [...]—: this infinity-speaking full of mortality and to no purpose!:* Cf. Letter to Hermann Kasack of 16 May 1960 in this volume, p. 222.

45c *"Voices up from the nettle-route. [...]":* Citation of the second stanza of Celan's poem "Stimmen" (TCA, Sprachgitter, pp. 2ff.) There only the word "*Stimmen*" is in italics; the first line is followed by an empty line. English translation in Paul Celan: Selections, ed. Pierre Joris, University of California Press, Berkeley 2005, p. 58.

45d *"like Lenz" through the mountains:* cf. Letter to Hermann Kasack of 16 May 1960 in this volume, p. 222.

48b *to misread, like [...] Karl Emil Franzos [...] the 'Commode' [the accommodating] [...] as if it was 'coming' ['Kommendes']:* End of "Leonce und Lena": "und bitten Gott um [...] eine kommende Religion! [and ask God for[...] a coming religion!" (Georg Büchner. Sämmtliche Werke und handschriftlicher Nachlaß, hrsg. v. Karl Emil Franzos, Frankfurt a.M. 1879, p. 157); "an accommodating religion \eine commode Religion\!" (Bergemann, p. 147 [*CL*]; MA, p. 189; the commentary to MA notes: "komm<o>de: probably a typo; should be: kommende," p. 571).

52e *Dear Marie Luise Kaschnitz, I thank you.:* At the Büchner-prize Kaschnitz gave the address on Celan. (Marie Luise Kaschnitz: Rede auf den Preisträger, in: Jahrbuch der Deutschen Akademie für Sprache und Dichtung 1960, Heidelberg/Darmstadt 1961, pp. 67-73 [*CL*]).

To Preliminary Stage "A" (according to the paragraphs)

8b *also with G.L.'s words for becoming human being:* cf. Gustav Landauer: Der werdende Mensch. Aufsätze über Leben und Schrifttum, im letztwilligen Auftrag des Verfassers hrsg. v. Martin Buber, Potsdam 1921 [*CL*].

* following **18c** *Günter Eich said here a year ago:* cf. Günter Eich: Büchner-Preis-Rede 1959, in: Büchner-Reden, pp. 73-87.
Cf. *Materials* # 602.

* following **31a** *Thus poems are indeed: monotone; 'Nobody becomes what he is not.':* "Das Bergwerk zu Falun," in: Hofmannsthal: Gedichte und Lyrische Dramen, Frankfurt a.M. 1952 (1. Aufl. Stockholm 1946), p. 349 [*CL*]. Cf. *Materials* ## 246 and 322.

To the Drafts

1 *the word that does not, unlike art, have consequences* : cf. "Danton's Death": "Schnitzt einer eine Marionette, [...] welch ein Character, welche Konsequenz! [But carve a puppet,[...] what a character-drawing, how consequential]"; Act 2, Scene 3, "A Room" (Bergemann, p. 40 [*CL*], marked in margins; MA, p. 95).

3-5 Cf. Description of the double sheet C 51-52 in ## 693-700.

6 Text completed aslant in margin.

9 *"If someone carves a puppet [...]":* cf. Note 1.
"You now see the art!": "Woyzeck." "Fairgrounds

with booths. Lights. People." (Bergemann, p. 155 [*CL*], underlined. In later editions the scene no longer appears in this textual order.)

10 *"What's on the lung, put on the tongue":* "Wie off der Long, su off der Zong. (Trier.)" = The mouth speaks the fullness of the heart. (Deutsches Sprichwörter-Lexikon. Ein Hausschatz für das deutsche Volk, Bd. 3, hrsg. v. Karl Friedrich Wilhelm Wander, Leipzig 1873, # 285).

— *on dove's feet:* cf. Nietzsche: "Da sprach es wieder wie ein Flüstern zu mir: 'Die stillsten Worte sind es, welche den Sturm bringen. Gedanken, die mit Taubenfüßen kommen, lenken die Welt.'[Then, in a whisper, it spoke again: 'It is the stillest words bring the storm. Thoughts that come on dove's feet rule the world.']" (Friedrich Nietzsche: Also sprach Zarathustra: "Die stillste Stunde." in: Werke in zwei Bänden, hrsg. v. August Messer, Leipzig 1930, Bd. 1, p. 417 [*CL*]. Also in: Werke in drei Bänden, hrsg. v. Karl Schlechta, München [2]1960, Bd. 2, p. 401 [*CL*]). Cf. also Benn: "Und Döblin würde antworten: 'Worte, die auf Taubenfüßen kommen, regieren die Welt.'" ["And Döblin would answer: 'Words that come on dove's feet rule the world."] ("Kunst und Staat," in: Benn I, p. 50; cf. also Benn's Büchner-Preis-Rede 1951, in: Büchner-Reden, p. 12).

11 Additions indicated with lines. Stippled line from "most unaffected" to "p. 96:"
Triple marks. From "brings it over ⌊, is, with it, the uncanny,"⌋ continued on the bottom of opposite page C 18. Next to it, a circular mark in red pencil, with an arrow pointing to what precedes. Cf. Facsimile on p. 276.

13 Red pencil mark in left margin: a circle.

14 *Kepler 1606:* in 1604 a new star had appeared in the constellation Ophiuchus ('snake-holder,' 'Serpentary'), which gave rise to much astrological speculation. Kepler reacted to this by publishing at the end of 1604 his "Gründlicher Bericht von einem ungewöhnlichen newen Stern / Welcher im Oktober diß 1604. Jahres erstmahlen erschienen." In 1606 he followed this with an expanded Latin version, "De stella nova in pede serpentarii."

— "Congruence" is written across the gutter of the double page (C 27/28) and linked by a line to "ancien régime (or nouveau régime or monarchy)."

16 *a line by Büchner [...], with which [...] I kept company against my will:* Meant is the line "sometimes it annoyed him [...]"; cf. also drafts ## 17, 23-25, 30f., 38-48, 51, which start with this citation.

— F 2/3 are typescripts and C 1/M 2 carbon copied thereof. In typescirpts F 2/3 Celan works primarily at the wording of the text. Carbon copies C 1 and M 2 each show a red pencil mark at the top edge; larger deletions mark probably textual transfers into the next preliminary version ("A"), as parts of the deleted text reappear there. Reproduced here are typescripts F 2/3; further corrections and markings from the carbon copies are indicated below.
[1]C1: ⌊~~they want~~⌋
[2]C1: ⌊; it is given to them⌋ (what follows is not deleted here.)
[3]F2: Textual emendation "~~With that poems are~~ [...]" handwritten in left margin.
[4]C1: deleted from: "As long as [...]" to "[...] in which it risks to completely go under" (end of page), below which with the same pencil as the deletion, the word: "Breath." On the next carbon copy (M 2) the text is deleted to "[...] thought now of this present hour." and the last paragraph "There are routes [...]" is bracketed.

17 *Probleme der Lyrik:* cf. Gottfried Benn's essay "Probleme der Lyrik" (Benn I, pp. 494-532).

— *In the poem: that, I believe, does not mean [...] n'en déplaise à Mallarmé, in one of those [...] over-differentiated language structures:* n'en déplaise à (Fr.): in spite of; even if it doesn't please .... Cf. Valéry: "Et Mallarmé lui répondit: 'Mais Degas ce n'est pas avec des idées qu'on fait des vers, c'est avec des mots.'" (Paul Valéry: Variété: Souvenirs littéraires, in: Œuvres I, Paris 1957, p. 784 [*CL*]; also in: Variété: Poésie et pensée abstraite, ebd., p. 1324). Cf. also Benn: "Am berühmtesten ist die Maxime von Mallarmé: ein Gedicht entsteht nicht aus Gefühlen, sondern aus Worten. [Most famous is Mallarmé's maxim: Poems are not made with feelings but with words]" ("Probleme der Lyrik," in: Benn I, p. 509).

— *lyric koiné:* Koiné: Greek language in the age of Hellenism; also other common languages formed by the flattening of dialectical differences.

— F 4, M 3, C 39 is a series of typescripts paginated as "-3-", "-4-" and "-5-." C 36, 37, 38 is the corresponding series of carbon copies.
M 3 and C 36-39 show a red-penciled circle at the upper edge.
Unlike F 2/3 and their carbon copies, here Celan only started text emendations on the typescripts, but has continued this work before all on the carbon copies, which also show transpositions and textual transfers. In the case of C 38 and 39 the roles played by typescript and carbon copy are inverted, so that copy C 38 shows no corrections and the red-penciled deletions of copy C 37 are continued on typescript C 39. One also finds there further textual corrections. Reproduced here are the more heavily annotated sheets C 36, 37, and 39.

18 "12-~" (jotted down by hand) could be a date, the

unreadable sign an unsuccessful "X" (thus 10.12.60); however, Celan does not use hyphens anywhere else in his datings.
First paragraph deleted in red pencil.

20 Cf. description of double sheet C 51-52 for ## 693-700.

21 *Horologes:* Horologium: liturgical book containing the texts for the horary prayers of the orthodox church; (obsolete) watch.

24 *beneath the ruins of the scales:* cf. Unpublished fragment of a poem from the vicinity of the "Pariser Elegie": (Signature: -i- 1,32): "Ich hörte: Du hältst / ja die Waage.—Nein, / ich halte sie nicht. Wenn ich einst / unter die Trümmer der Waage / zu liegen komm, so / ist das schon viel." [I heard: You do/ remain balanced.—No, / I do not. When some day I / will come to lie / under the ruins of the scale / that will already be a lot!) Cf. also the closing of the Nelly Sachs letter of 5.11.1960 (Paul Celan / Nelly Sachs. Briefwechsel, hrsg. v. Barbara Wiedemann, Frankfurt a.M. 1993, p. 39).

25 *hippocratic face:* Dying person's facial expression; cf. Büchner's letter to his bride of 3.7. 1834: "Ich erschrak vor mir selbst. Das Gefühl des Gestorbenseins war immer über mir. Alle Menschen machten mir das hippokratische Gesicht, die Augen verglast, [...]" ["I was frightened by myself. The feeling of having died kept hanging over me. Everybody showed me the hippocratic face, eyes glassy, [...]" (Bergemann, p. 379 [*CB*], marked in margin; MA, p. 287); cf. also "Danton's Death," Act 1, last Scene (Bergemann, p. 32; MA, p. 89).

— C 54: Ink marking on upper sheet edge: cross in a circle.
Marking of penultimate paragraph "We are those who have come [...]" deleted again.

27 *Ciliata, ciliary movements:* cf. "Flimmertier Lid / rudert nach oben" (TCA, Sprachgitter, p. 41). "Ciliary lid / rows upward" (PC: Selections, p. 63). Cf. also Benn: "'Es gibt im Meer lebend Organismen [...]': Flimmerhaare, die tasten etwas heran, nämlich Worte [...]." ["There are creatures living in the sea [...]': cilia, that grope toward something, namely words [...]."] ("Probleme der Lyrik," in: Benn I, pp. 511f.)

— *les espaces infinis:* "Le silence éternel de ces espaces infinis m'effraie." (Pascal: Pensées, Nº 91 [206], in: Œuvres complètes, texte établi, présenté et annoté par Jacques Chevalier, Paris 1954, p. 1113 [*CL*]).

— *Sounding of language amidst the information system:* cf. Note for # 602.

— Textual addition "In this inbetween" at upper edge of sheet.
"××/ the sky—those are [...]" in left margin.
619 (F 25,2) and # 132 (F 31,2) can also be read as further additions to this passage.
Initial letter of addition "Movement: by this [...] same pencil as "By this movement [...]."
Cf. Facsimile on p. 274.

28 to correlate to # 27 (F 23): "has the sky ××/ beneath him", also # 132 (F 31,2) and # 619 (F 25,2).
Dated "7.X." by # 27.

31 F 43 is an uncorrected copy of typescript F 88. Reproduced are F 88 and its continuation F 44, a typescript without carbon copy. F 44 bears the same title and dating as F 88/43.

32 *Tyche:* in Greek mythology the goddess of fate, associated primarily with success.

— *cybernetics:* "Wir haben beschlossen, das ganze Gebiet der Regelung und Nachrichtentheorie, ob in der Maschine oder im Tier, mit dem Namen 'Kybernetik' zu benennen, den wir aus dem griechischen, 'κυβερνήτηζ,' 'Steuermann,' bildeten." (Norbert Wiener: Kybernetik, Reinbek bei Hamburg 1968, p. 32; americ. First edition published 1948). ["We have decided to call the entire field of control and communication theory, whether in the machine or in the animal, by the name 'Cybernetics,' which we form from the Greek 'κυβερνήτηζ,' or 'steersman.'" (Norbert Wiener: Cybernetics, second edition, M.I.T. Press, Cambridge, 1965, p. 11)]

— possibly connected to # 559 (C 7,3); not a full empty line.
Textual addition "narrowing [...]" handwritten at upper edge of page, with arrow crossing over the page; corrections and insert in red pencil.
"An impossible word ⌊today—but not here!—⌋ [...]" handwritten, starts between the lines and continues in right margin.
"thus, what ultimately connects" written large in left margin, inserted with brace.

33 *"You cannot prevent that in the basket":* cf. "Danton's Death," Act, 4 Scene 7 "Place de la révolution": "Danton *zum Henker*: Willst du grausamer sein als der Tod? Kannst du verhindern, daß unsere Köpfe sich auf dem Boden des Korbes küssen? [Danton *to the executioner.* Would you be more cruel than death? You cannot prevent that our heads will kiss in the basket.]" (Bergemann p. 81 [*CB*]; MA, p. 131). Büchner has taken this citation from Louis-Adolphe Thiers (Histoire de la Révolution Française, Paris 1823-27, vol. IV, p. 230) (cf. MA, p. 497).

— Text addition "The estranged [...]" and "hurrying through [...]" at top edge of page; "Here now [...]" and what follows on the right next to # 112 (F 102,2).

— Cf. Facsimile on p. 273.

34 *perihelion of poetry:* Perihelion: the point in a

planet's orbit closest to the sun.

— Ink marking on page's upper right corner: a cross, marks in same ink and in red pencil.

37 *Solve et coagula:* (lat.) "Dissolve and coagulate!" Basic formula of alchemy according to which coming together can only happen when preceded by separation. Cf. also Hofmannsthal: "'das Ergon,' sagt die Fama, 'ist die Heiligung des inneren Menschen, die Goldmacherkunst ist das Parergon'— solve et coagula." ("Andreas," in: Hofmannsthal: Die Erzählungen, Frankfurt a.M. 1953 (1. Aufl. Stockholm 1945), pp. 236f. [*CL*]).

48 First notice on that page, dated "8.19. 60" on previous page.

51 Cf. Facsimile on p. 271.

52 Front page of a double sheet (folded typewriter sheet), cf. # 194 (ÜR 6.12,23c-d [4]).

53 *The volume "The Stone":* Osip Mandel'štam: Kamen'. Stichi, S.-Peterburg 1913. Celan owned the second and third edition of Kamen', to which Mandelstam had added many poems not in the first edition. The work copy for Celan's translations, also for those from Kamen', was: Osip Mandel'štam: Sobranie soèinenij, pod redakciej i so vstupitel'nymi stat'jami G. P. Struve i B. A. Filippova, N'ju-Jork 1955 [*CL*].

— *"a place in the cosmos":* cf. Osip Mandelstam: "Die Städte, die da blühn [...]" (GW V, p. 85; Mandel'štam, p. 67 [*CL*]).

— *a sublunar, a terrestrial, a creaturely phenomenon:* sublunar (lat.): what lies beneath the moon, earthly; terrestrial (lat.): earthly.

— "~~senbuous~~": typo for "sensuous."

The addition "at the same time remaining mindful [...]" starts between the lines and is continued by hand in the left margin.

55 *the hieratic begins to yield to the demotic:* demotic (Greek: demos = people): popular; hieratic: priestly, ritualistic.

— Addition starts between the already written paragraphs, continued with "×/" on verso.

56 Addition in left margin.

Transposition made noticeable with encirclement of "that does not come to an end" and marked with arrow.

57 *Opacity:* nontransparency, impermeability.

58 *The sail:* cf. Mandelstam «Das horchende, das feingespannte Segel» (GW V, p. 59; Mandel'štam, p. 41 [*CL*]).

— Cf. Facsimile on p. 270.

59 *timeyard \Zeithof\:* "Der Jetztpunkt hat für das Bewußtsein wieder einen Zeithof, der sich in einer Kontinuität von Erinnerungsauffassungen vollzieht." ["The now-point has for consciousness again a time-yard [time-window] \Zeithof\, which takes place through a continuity of memory conceptions."] (Edmund Husserl: Vorlesungen zur Phänomenologie des inneren Zeitbewußtseins, hrsg. v. Martin Heidegger, Halle 1928, p. 396 [*CL*], [Sonderdruck aus dem Jahrbuch für Philosophie und phänomenologische Forschung 9]).

— The preceding page of the typescript could not be found.

Addition handwritten at bottom edge of page, referred to by a line.

60 *a philology that babbles for ex. about genitive metaphors:* "Man kann heute, im Zeitalter der surrealistischen Entfesselung, mit metaphorischen 'Kühnheiten,' besonders mit den leidigen Genitivmetaphern, so gut wie alles beweisen [...]. Begabte Autoren versteigen sich zu Metaphern wie 'Papierkorb des Traums' oder 'das weiße Mehl der Verheißung' oder 'das Weißhaar der Zeit' [cf. Celans Gedicht "Spät und Tief" in: GW I, p. 35]. Das sind ganz sicher keine geglückten Metaphern, es sind poetische Wechselbälge, künstlich, wie in der Retorte gezüchtet. Der metaphorische Impuls scheint von der Laune einer bloßen X-beliebigkeit gelenkt zu sein. [...] Wenn der Autor jener unglücklichen Metapher Weißhaar der Zeit in einem anderen Gedicht die Stadt Paris feiert als 'die große Herbstzeitlose' [cf. "Erinnerung an Frankreich" in: GW I, p. 28], so ist ihm hier ein solches Gelingen geschenkt worden. [Today, in the age of surrealist escapology, one can prove just about anything with metaphoric 'audacities,' especially with the genitive metaphor [...] Gifted authors lose their way with metaphors such as 'wastepaper basket of the dream' or 'the white flour of promise' or 'the white hair of time' [cf. Celan's poem "Late and Deep," in GW I, p. 35]. Those are certainly not successful metaphors, they are poetic changelings, artificial laboratory products. The metaphoric impulse seems to be directed by sheer randomness [...] When the author of that unhappy metaphor 'the whitehair of time' celebrates the city of Paris in another poem as the 'great crocus' [cf. "Erinnerung an Frankreich," GW I, p. 28] then a like success has been granted him.]" (Hans Egon Holthusen: Vollkommen sinnliche Rede, in: Mein Gedicht ist mein Messer. Lyriker zu ihren Gedichten, hrsg. v. Hans Bender, Heidelberg 1955, p. 49 [*CL*]). Cf. also note # 81.

The so-called Goll affair reached its peak in April 1960. The accusations of plagiarism made against Celan also concerned genitive metaphors he supposedly took [from Goll's work].

— *Writing as a form of prayer:* Franz Kafka: "Fragmente aus Heften und losen Blättern," in: Gesammelte Werke, hrsg. v. Max Brod: Hochzeitsvorbereitungen auf dem Lande und andere Prosa aus dem Nachlaß, Frankfurt a.M. 1953, p. 348 [*CL*].

— *John Donne:* (1572/73-1631), English poet, Catholic by birth, converted to Anglicanism, ordained in 1615; from 1621 on as Dean of St. Paul's Cathedral in London, a famous preacher. He is the most important of the "Metaphysical Poets."

— *Andrew Marvell:* (1621-1678), English poet, from a Puritan family background. His early poetry in the style of the "Metaphysical poets" draws on Horace and is influenced by John Donne.

— Addition "And I do not speak either[...]" linked from lower edge of page (A 23) to the verso side (A 24) where it continues.

63 Dated on top of page # 499 (F 14,1).

64 *Etiology:* Study of causation; in its wider sense, the causes themselves. In relation to legends: Legends that want to explain conspicuous apparitions, customs and names.

— Dated with another pencil, bottom left on front page of # 64 (A 6).
Transposition conspicuously marked with arrows from "in view of the poem's contemporaneity."

68 First marking with red pencil.

69 Marking at left edge with red pencil: a circle.

70 Arrow from "in the single" to addition: "in the single [...]" viz. "Spiritual shape," line from "Tropik" over "in the single" to the addition.

72 Marking at left edge with red pencil: a circle.

79 "something immaterial": actually "something material" with additional line in front of the "m." The note is close to the left edge of the page next to # 743 (C 30,2); the i-point is presumably set outside the page and the second "m" was presumably forgotten. Cf. # 81 (C 8/9): "Something immaterial, not present."

80 Dated "10. 9." by # 255 (C 6,1).

81 *'perfect sensuous speech': \'vollkommen sinnliche Rede'* Title of Holthusen's essay in: Mein Gedicht ist mein Messer. Lyriker zu ihren Gedichten, hrsg. v. Hans Bender, Heidelberg 1955 [*CL*].He writes: "Dichtung ist, nach Lessings schöner Formulierung, die 'vollkommen sinnliche Rede,' also ein Modus des Sprechens, der sich von jeder anderen Ausdrucksweise kategorial [...] unterscheidet. [...] [Poetry, according to Lessing's beautiful phrase, is 'perfect sensuous speech,' thus a mode of speaking that distinguishes itself categorically from all other modes of expression.]" (p. 47); cf. also note to # 60.

— *Hasenöhrchen:* lit. "hare's ears" = lit. "goosefeet" \Gänsefüßchen\, quotation marks.

— *halfasian countryman Franzos:* Franzos comes from the Bukovina; cf. Karl Emil Franzos: Aus Halb-Asien. Culturbilder aus Galizien, der Bukowina, Südrußland und Rumänien, 2 Bde., Leipzig 1876; Vom Don zur Donau. Neue Culturbilder aus "Halb-Asien," 2 Bde., Leipzig 1878; Aus der großen Ebene. Neue Culturbilder aus Halb-Asien, 2. gänzlich umgearbeitete Auflage, 2 Bde., Leipzig 1888; in [*CL*]: Karl Emil Franzos: Halbasien, eingeleitet und ausgewählt von E. J. Görlich, Graz/Wien 1958 [Das österreichische Wort 36].

— *enemy of rats:* George Steiner, Karl Emil Franzos' great nephew, reports that according to family tradition the edges of the manuscripts of "Woyzeck," which Franzos was the first to edit, had been eaten by rats.

— "Perhaps" stood next to it and below it "Something invisible [...]" came first; the phrase "Something, that today [...]" was inserted subsequently.
The function of the arrow from the top "Perhaps" in the space between "[...] should be considered [...]" and "This is so [...]", in which the handwritten addition "What is it [...]" was inserted, cannot be explicitly determined.
The handwritten additions that circle around the definition of the "meridian," should probably not be read as a continuation of the typescript, but as a sort of gathering of materials. Cf. the facsimile on the cover.

82 *Selfencounter:* Subtitle by Ernst Bloch: Geist der Utopie, Berlin 1923, p. 7 [*CL*], Celan's dating of this book is: "Paris, 8 February 1960."

— Additions in last paragraph of typescript in red pencil. Cf. Facsimile on p. 275.

83 *forester's house [...] Karl Emil Franzos:* "Ich bin am 25. Oktober 1848 auf russischem Boden geboren, [in Czortkov] im Gouvernement Podolien, in einem Forsthause dicht an der österreichischen Grenze." ["I was born 25 October 1848 on Russian soil,[in Czortkov] in the state of Podolien, in a forester's house close by the Austrian border."] (Karl Emil Franzos in his autobiographical preface of 15. July 1893, in: Karl Emil Franzos: Der Pojaz, mit einem Nachwort von Jost Hermand, Königstein/Tp. 1979, p. 1).

84 Dating by # 400 (F 48,1).

88 Dating by # 184 (E 3,1).

90 *a vocable [...] büchnerian* Occurs often in Büchner's "Leonce and Lena" as a cry with ironic pathos.
Red pencil marking at top edge of page: a circle.
Conspicuous gray paper otherwise only used for # 91/92 (D 2/3). # 91 (D 2) was possibly the first attempt, developed further in # 90 (C41), and finally in # 92 (D 3) as its continuation with the pagination"-2-" on the back side of # 91 (D 2).

93 *...Thanks, to Hermann Kasack:* cf. Letter to Hermann Kasack of 16 May 1960 in this volume, p. 222.

94 Dating with the additions at # 856 (F 86,1).

96 Dating at # 579 (E 14,1).

97 *One could date this anew[...] from a 30 January:* 1. 30. 1933: Date of Hitler's takeover.

98 *This "who knows"—it has to be related to the first:* cf. Preliminary version "A," para. 31c and 30b.

To the Materials

108 *I do not speak of the "modern" poem, I speak of the poem today:* "modern poem" cf. "Probleme der Lyrik" (Benn I, p. 514 and pp. 528f.)

109 Dating at # 499 (F 14,1).

110 *"Born-to dreaming"\Zugebornes Träumen\ Valéry:* Valéry's formulation "songes naturels" in "La jeune Parque" is translated by Celan as "zugebornes Träumen." (cf. GW IV, pp. 128f.)

111-112 Cf. Facsimile on p. 273.

114 *argumentum e silentio:* (lat.) Conclusion drawn as to the nonexistence of facts based on their not being mentioned; cf. The poem "Argumentum e silentio", in: GW I, pp. 138f.

— From "a language taboo specific to the poem and only to it [...]" the text continues in several starts in the left margin.

116 Dating: "8. 20." at # 886 (F 18,5); "8. 22." at # 490 (F 20,1).

121 *blackearth:* steppe region of South Russia resp. the Ukraine, distinguished be a humus-rich, fertile 'black earth.' Cf. Mandelstam's Essay "Das Wort und die Kultur" ("Slovo i kul'tura") von 1921: "Poesie ist ein Pflug, der die Zeit in der Weise aufreißt, daß ihre Tiefenschichten, ihre Schwarzerde zutage tritt." ["Poetry is a plough that turns up time so that its deep layers, its black earth can come to light."] (Osip Mandelstam: Über den Gesprächspartner, Gesammelte Essays 1913-1924, aus dem Russischen übertragen und hrsg. v. Ralph Dutli, Zürich 1991, p. 84; russischer Originaltext in: Mandel'štam, p. 323 [*CL*]; Celan has underlined and marked the sentence in the margins.) Cf. also "Der Hufeisen-Finder" in Celan's translation (GW V, p. 135; Mandel'štam, p. 121 [*CL*]). The poem "Schwarzerde" ("Černozem"), written in 1935 during the Voronezh days, was first published in 1962 (TCA, Die Niemandsrose, p. 62). Cf. also note to the radio-essay on Mandelstam, para. 16.

122 что - то в них попало *something had gotten into this:* (Russ. Literally.: something had gotten into them [the verses]) Citation from an essay by Gippius on Valery Bryusov with the title "Oderžimy (O Val. Brjusove)" ["Der Besessene (Über Wal. Brjussow)"]. Celan read this essay in the magazine: Okno. Trechmesjačnik literatury (The Window. Quarterly Review of Literature), Pariž, N° 2 (1923), p. 221 [*CL*]. Under the title on p. 199 he notes: "Der Besessene (Süchtige)" ["The one possessed (the addict)"]. The citation itself reads: "V stichi ëtogo junca 'čto-to popala', kak my togda vyražalis". ("Into the young man's verses 'something had gotten,' as we used to say back then.") Celan underlines "čto-to popala" and writes beneath it "'something had gotten into.'" The whole page is marked with a double line; bottom of the page has the note "!Mandelstamm!" Cf. note on Celan's radio-essay "The Poetry of Osip Mandelstam" para. 1.

123 Dated at # 499 (F 14,1).
Line of separation first after "sufficient ground" and below it "~~groundless,~~" then continued to "(Therefore[...]."
Red pencil mark.

124 Dated at # 499 (F 14,1).
Red pencil mark.

125 *sufficient ground:* "Sie [unsere Vernunfterkenntnis] beruht zweitens auf dem Prinzip *des zureichenden Grundes*, kraft dessen wir annehmen, daß sich keine Tatsache als wahr oder existierend, keine Aussage als richtig erweisen kann [Our reasonings \Vernunftserkenntnis\ is grounded secondly on the principle of sufficient reason *\des zureichenden Grundes* in virtue of which we hold that there can be no fact real or existing, no statement true.]" (Leibniz, Nr. 32 [*CL*]).

— Dated at # 499 (F 14,1). (Translation adapted from Robert Latta's.] Marking and underlining in red pencil.

128 For dating cf. note to # 806.

130 *Menschheit:* cf. "Danton's Death," Act 2, Scene 7: "Die Schritte der Menschheit sind langsam, man kann sie nur nach Jahrhunderten zählen; hinter jedem erheben sich die Gräber von Generationen. [...] [Humanity's steps are slow; they can be counted only by centuries and behind each one rise the graves of generations.]" (Bergemann p. 49 [*CL*], underlined and marked up, beneath the note "Man//Mankind"; MA, p. 102).

— Dated "8. 30. 59" at # 641 (F 21,1), from # 424 (F 21,3) on, different pencil.

131 Dates "8. 20." at # 886 (F 18,5); "8.22." at # 490 (F 20,1).
Simple mark in left, triple in right margin.
F 119,1: later copy without marks.

132 Should probably still be related to # 27 (F 23) "××/ the sky—that is les espaces infinis [...]"; similarly also # 28 (F 24,3) and # 619 (F 25,2).

137 *Hofmannsthal: pointe acérée de l'infini:* "'Il est

de certaines sensations délicieuses dont le vague n'exclut pas l'intensité, et il n'est pas de pointe plus acérée que l'Infini.' (Baudelaire.)," 6.29.1917 ("Aufzeichnungen und Tagebücher aus dem Nachlaß 1904-1921," in: Hofmannsthal: Aufzeichnungen, Frankfurt a.M. 1959, pp. 181f. [*CL*]). "Über George. Einzige Berührung mit ihm beim Lesen der 'Hymnen' 'Pilgerfahrten'. Die Spitze mit der sich das Unendliche in die Seele gräbt—Über Borchardt" ("Ad me ipsum," in: Hofmannsthal: Aufzeichnungen, Frankfurt a.M. 1959, p. 233 [*CL*]; the sentence "Die Spitze [...]" is underlined. Celan notes at the bottom of the page: "pointe acérée de l'Infini / Baudelaires.")

"[...] und wen sie, 'die scharfe Spitze der Unendlichkeit,' in diesem geisterhaften Morgenkampf getroffen hat; [[...] and when it, the sharp point of infinity,' has struck in this ghostly dawn struggle ;]" ("Erinnerung," 1924, in: Hofmannsthal: Prosa IV, Frankfurt a.M. 1955, p. 206 [*CL*]).

"[...] und fühlt, daß ihn hier die Unendlichkeit mit einem schärferen Pfeil getroffen als je ein bestimmter Schmerz; er hat drei oder vier Erinnerungen, die alle diese pointe acérée de l'infini in sich tragen [and feels that here infinity has wounded him with a sharper arrow than ever any specific pain; he has three or four memories which all carry this pointe acérée.]" ("Andreas", in: Hofmannsthal: Die Erzählungen, Frankfurt a.M. 1953 (1. Aufl. Stockholm 1945), p. 204 [*CL*]; the phrase "pointe acérée de l'infini" ist also marked in [*CL*] in the following edition of Hugo von Hofmannsthal: Andreas oder Die Vereinigten, mit einem Nachwort von Jakob Wassermann, Berlin 1932, p. 120).

Cf. also Baudelaire: "Que les fins de journées d'automne sont pénétrantes! [...] car il est de certaines sensations délicieuses dont le vague n'exclut pas l'intensité; et il n'est pas de pointe plus acérée que celle de l'Infini." ("Le 'confiteor' de l'artiste," in: Charles Baudelaire: Œuvres complètes, texte établi et annoté par Y.-G. Le Dantec: Le spleen de Paris, Paris 1951, p. 276 [*CL*]).

Cf. Celan's poem "A la pointe acérée" (TCA, Die Niemandsrose, pp. 76ff.)

138 *under the servants' stairs (Hofmannsthal):* "So ist der Dichter da, wo er nicht da zu sein scheint [...]. Seltsam wohnt er im Haus der Zeit, unter der Stiege, wo alle an ihm vorüber müssen und keiner ihn achtet.[Thus the poet is there where he doesn't seem to be [...] Strangely he lives in the house of time, under the staircase, where everybody has to pass by him and nobody notices him.]" Hofmannsthal refers here to the legend of Saint Alexius. ("Der Dichter und diese Zeit", in: Hofmannsthal: Prosa II, Frankfurt a.M. 1951, pp. 280f., in [*CL*] paragraph marked on the side.)

139 *Vigil:* Nightwatch; in Roman-Catholic liturgy also the nightly prayer and deathwatch.

140-141 *Shestov, p. 18 Aristotle: Who wants the proofs [...] delivered together* "Aristote l'a formulé dans le mot célèbre: ne rien accepter sans preuves est un signe de manque d'éducation philosophique." (Léon Shestov: La nuit de Gethsémani. Essai sur la philosophie de Pascal, Paris 1923, p. 18).

144 *Pascal—Abyss:* The abyss ("l'abîme") is a core concept in Shestov's Pascal-interpretation. Cf. Shestov: La nuit de Gethsémani. Essai sur la philosophie de Pascal, Paris 1923.

146 *'Someone has to be there [...] someone has to keep watch':* "Nachts," in: Franz Kafka: Gesammelte Werke, hrsg. v. Max Brod: Beschreibung eines Kampfes. Novellen, Skizzen, Aphorismen, Frankfurt a.M. 1946, p. 116.

— On an envelope.

147 Ink marking in right margin: a cross.

148 *Shestov [...] pp. 71f.: "Lorsque Platon affirmait [...]":* Léon Shestov: La nuit de Gethsémani. Essai sur la philosophie de Pascal, Paris 1923, pp. 71f.

— *misologos:* (Gr.) Despiser of reason.

— *Pélage:* Pelagianism: Pelagius' doctrine, condemned by the church, which emphasized the free will of man as against Augustine's doctrine of the necessity of grace. In his essay on Pascal, Shestov refers to the "Lettres [provinciales] Provençales," in which Pascal forcefully opposes Pelagius' doctrine.

149 Ink marking in right margin: a cross.

152 *139. Psalm: nox illuminatio mea:* "Night is my illumination": Psalm verse 138,11b in the Vulgate ("Et nox inluminatio mea in deliciis meis.") It corresponds to verse 139,12b of the Hebrew Bible. (Lat. Psalms citation: Biblia Sacra juxta vulgatam versionem, recensuit et brevi apparatu instruxit R. Weber OSB, Stuttgart [3]1983).

— ולילה כיום יאיר כחשיכה כָאוֹרָה: "and night shines like the day, darkness is like the light," Hebrew Bible, Psalm 139,12b (Copies in [*CL*]: Biblia Hebraica. Adjuvantibus, edidit Rud. Kittel, Textum Masoreticum curavit P. Kahle, Stuttgart 1937; deutsche Ausgabe: Die Bibel oder die ganze Heilige Schrift des Alten und Neuen Testaments nach der deutschen Übersetzung D. Martin Luthers, Berlin 1897).

154-155 *place above heaven—transuranian—(Plato) / Plotinus:* "Den überhimmlischen Ort aber hat noch nie einer der Dichter hienieden besungen, noch wird ihn je einer nach Würdigkeit besingen." ["But of the heaven which is above the heavens, what earthly poet ever did or ever will sing worthily?" B. Jowett's transl.] ("Phaidros" 247c, in: Platon, Bd. 2,

p. 437 [*CL*]). The "Phaidros" shows strong reading traces in Celan's copy; the cited passage is underlined. Celan also marks the same passage in Theodor Gomperz's synopsis. There is mention there of the "space above heaven"; Celan adds the note "247c" as well as "the transuranian place" as literal translation of Plato's "τόποζὑπεϱουϱάνιοζ"). (Theodor Gomperz: Griechische Denker. Eine Geschichte der antiken Philosophie, 3 Bde., Bd. 1: Leipzig ^{3}1911 [*CL*], Bd. 2: Leipzig ^{2}1903 [*CL*], Bd. 3: Leipzig ^{1,2}1909 [*CL*]; here: Bd. 2, pp. 331ff.; date of purchase marked in 1st volume as: "Paris, 27 March 1958").

Cf. also Plotinus: Ennéades, hrsg. u. übers. v. Émile Bréhier, Paris 1956, 5. Bd. [*CL*] with multiple markings in the cut-open tractate 8 [31] "De la beauté intelligible." In his note to this passage, Bréhier points out that the 10th chapter is a synopsis of Plato's "Phaidros": "Plotin revient au cortège des voyants qui, dans le mythe du Phèdre (246d), ont la vision du lieu supracéleste où ils résident." (p. 132) In his copy, a footnote at the relevant place points to "Phaidros" 247c . Cf. also note # 393.

157 *Kafka: Language as having:* "Es gibt kein Haben, nur ein Sein, nur ein nach letztem Atem, nach Ersticken verlangendes Sein. [There is no 'having,' only 'being,' only being that craves a last breath, a suffocation.]" ("Betrachtungen über Sünde, Leid, Hoffnung und den wahren Weg" and: "Das dritte Oktavheft," Eintrag vom 24. Nov. 1917, in: Franz Kafka: Gesammelte Werke, hrsg. v. Max Brod: Hochzeitsvorbereitungen auf dem Lande und andere Prosa aus dem Nachlaß, Frankfurt a.M. 1953, p. 42 and p. 86 [*CL*]).

— "Being" is underlined three times.

159 *'hyper-ontol.' [...] core tension:* "Es ist die letzte, 'metaphysische' (streng genommen 'hyper-ontologische') Grundspannung, die zwischen ihnen [meant are Schelling's antagonistic principles of 'conscious' and 'unconscious'] herrscht und den Abgrund darstellt, den die Brücke des Ästhetischen [...] überwölbt." (Becker, p. 38); cf. also note to # 934.

162 *Killy [...] The color words in Trakl: they are not 'originally' there [...]:* "Jedes Farbwort erzeugt Stimmung. Jedes Farbwort ist versetzbar und kann Dingen zugeordnet werden, welche natürlicherweise nichts mit der Farbe zu tun haben. [Every color word creates mood. Every color word is transferable and can be associated with objects that have no natural connection with the color.]" ("'Der Tränen nächtige Bilder.' Trakl und Benn," in: Walther Killy: Wandlungen des lyrischen Bildes, Göttingen 1956, pp. 95-114, here: p. 102 [*CL*])

163 *Scheler, p. 178: principle consisting in bringing back therelativelyunknowntothepreviouslyknown:* source of citation could not be found.

165 *To speak nowhere about the creation of the poem; but always only about the created poem:* Dissociation from Gottfried Benn's statement in "Probleme der Lyrik": "Ich habe Ihnen im vorhergehenden drei besondere Themen aus dem Gebiet der Lyrik vorgeführt, nämlich erstens wie sieht ein modernes Gedicht nicht aus, zweitens den Vorgang vom Entstehen eines Gedichts, drittens versuchte ich, über das Wort zu sprechen. [In the foregoing I have presented three specific themes from the domain of lyric poetry, namely first what does a modern poem not look like, secondly a poem's process of becoming, and thirdly I tried to speak about the word."] (Benn I, p. 514).

167 *ominous and in terms of governing:* cf. The end of Thomas Mann's "Zauberberg": "Augenblicke kamen, wo dir aus Tod und Körperunzucht ahnungsvoll und regierungsweise ein Traum von Liebe erwuchs.[Moments there were, when out of death, and the rebellion of the flesh, there came to thee, as thou tookest stock of thyself, a dream of love.]" (p. 1019, English edition p. 716) and: "Es unterhielt Beziehungen zu ihm [dem Tod], die man lieben mochte, aber nicht ohne sich von einer bestimmten Unerlaubtheit solcher Liebe ahnungsvoll-regierungsweise Rechenschaft zu geben. [It [meant is the Schubert song "Der Lindenbaum"] had with death certain relations, which one might love, yet not without consciously, and in a 'stock-taking' sense, acknowledging a certain illicit element in one's love.]" (p. 929, English ed. p. 652. The latter omits translating the term 'regierungsweise.') Thomas Mann defines his protagonist's governing as "responsible thinking about" the conditio humana. (Thomas Mann: Der Zauberberg, Stockholmer Gesamtausgabe, Frankfurt a.M. 1954 [*CL*] p. 554; The Magic Mountain, transl. By H.T. Lowe-Porter, Alfred Knopf, New York, 1980.) Cf. also "Snow" p. 664, p. 700 and p. 928).

168 Arrows across the text; triple markings after the end of the text.

173 Dated "7. X." at # 27 (F 23).

175 *Tao 25.:* cf. 25th chapter in Laotse: Taoteking. Das Buch des Alten vom Sinn und Leben, hrsg. u. übersetzt v. Richard Wilhelm, Düsseldorf/Köln 1952, p. 27 [*CL*]: "Vier Große gibt es im Weltraum, / und der Menschenkönig ist einer davon. / Der Mensch hat die Erde zum Vorbild. / Die Erde hat den Himmel zum Vorbild. / Der Himmel hat den SINN zum Vorbild. / Und der SINN hat sich selber zum Vorbild. [There are four great powers in the universe, / and the king is one of them. / Earth follows Heaven. / Heaven follows the TAO. / And the TAO follows itself.]" "SINN" [literally, 'meaning' is Wilhelm's translation of "Tao."

177 handwritten note on typescript F 85, dated at # 848 (F 85,1).

— Ink mark at right edge: a cross.

179 Additional red-pencil double mark.

181 *Synaesthesia:* (Gr.) from "syn," "together," and "aisthesis," "sensation"; Psychology: excitation of one sense organ by stimulation of another; the fusion of several sense impressions produced by a language construct such as a cross-sensory metaphor; cf. Note for # 944.

182 Dated "7. X." at # 27 (F 23).

185 *in its geological sense [...] thickness:* Mächtigkeit: Eng.: powerfulness, mightiness. Geol.: thickness of a layer of stone.

186 Dated at # 21 (M 1,1).

— Red pencil mark in left margin: a circle.

189 Red pencil mark. F 117,2: later copy without mark.

193 *Event=Eyevent??\Ereignis=Eräugnis??\:* "Eräugnen, ereugnen, ereignen": "erscheinen, sich offenbaren"; "Eräugnis": "glückliche, traurige Ereignisse" (Deutsches Wörterbuch von Jacob und Wilhelm Grimm, Bd. 3, col. 699).

— Later note with different pencil on sheet dated at # 343 (F 105,1) as "5 Oct.—".

194 recto inside and backside of a double sheet, cf. # 52 (ÜR 6.12,23a [5]).

199-200 Dated "5. Oct.—"at # 343 (F 105,1). # 200 (F 105,3) with another pencil.

201 *Hölderlin? Aorgic???:* In "Ground for Empedocles" Hölderlin characterizes the opposition between "aorgic" and "organic." He sees the aorgic as "the less differentiating and differentiable, the less reflected, less comparable, the less figurative, the unorganized and the disorganizing." While at first "aorgic nature" forms the one pole and the "more organic, artistic man" the other, in the poet "the opposed principles interchange," until "through the progression of the opposed reciprocal effects [...] nature has become more organic through the forming, cultivating man, [...] whereas man has become more aorgic, universal, infinite." (Friedrich Hölderlin: Sämtliche Werke. Historisch-kritische Ausgabe, begonnen durch Norbert v. Hellingrath, fortgeführt durch Friedrich Seebass u. Ludwig v. Pigenot, Bd. 3, Berlin [3]1943, p. 324, pp. 321f. [*CL*]).[English translation by Thomas Pfau in Friedrich Hölderlin: Essays and Letters on Theory, SUNY Press, Albany 1988, pp. 53 and 55.]

— *the work's "self-reliance \Aufsichgestelltsein\" [...] Lukács: The possibility to experience \Erlebbarkeit\:* cf. Lukács, pp. 20f.: "Diese positive Seite der Unvergleichbarkeit des Werks drückt sich in seinem absoluten Aufsichgestelltsein aus. [...] Dennoch ist die Objektivität des ästhetischen Gegenstandes eine absolute, denn die unzerreißbare Bindung an Erlebbarkeit [...] bedeutet für das Werk nur eine bestimmte Geltungsqualität. Die Erlebnishaftigkeit ist nur der Stoff, aus dem sich seine innerlichst selbstgenügsame und auf sich selbst gestellte Welt aufbaut. [This positive side of the work's incomparability expresses itself in its absolute self-reliance [...] And yet, the objectivity of the aesthetic object is absolute because of its tearproof link to experience [...] means for the work only a limited validity. The ability to experience is only the stuff from which its most interiorly self-sufficient and self-reliant world builds itself.]"

204 *'Primordial urge of life to return to the inorganic':* (pp. 60f.); cf. also Sigmund Freud: Jenseits des Lustprinzips, in: Gesammelte Werke, chronologisch geordnet, Bd. 13, London 1940 [*CL*], p. 1-69, hier p. 40 und p. 41; in [*CL*] "Return to the anorganic" on p. 41 underlined, date of purchase: "4. 1. 1967."

206 *Bettina:* "Die Gesetze des Geistes aber seien metrisch, das fühle sich in der Sprache, sie werfe das Netz über den Geist, in dem gefangen, er das Göttliche aussprechen müsse [...] *das* sei Poesie: daß eben der Geist nur sich rhythmisch ausdrücken könne [...] [That the laws of the mind are metrical, you can feel it in language, it throws a net over the mind, caught in which he has to speak the godly [...] *this* is poetry: that the spirit can only express itself rhythmically.]" "Die Günderrode", in: Bettine von Arnim: Werke und Briefe in drei Bänden, hrsg. v. Walter Schmitz und Sibylle v. Steinsdorff, Frankfurt a.M. 1986, Bd. 1, p. 544 [Bibliothek deutscher Klassiker 12]).

— Dated at # 184 (E 3,1).

207 *Phaidros, p. 452 [...] The metrical = the bound:* "[...] sei es nun eine Staats—oder eine Privatschrift, in gebundener Rede als Dichter oder in ungebundener als Prosaiker?" ("Phaidros", in: Platon, Bd. 2, 258d bzw. p. 452 [*CL*];["... either a political or any other work, in metre or out of metre, poet or prose writer..." trans. B. Jowett] Celan writes the Greek words above the line. "Bound" is here the translation of "ἐν μέτρῳ" (literally: in measure).

209 *'Strictest measure is also highest freedom':* last sentence of the section "Über Dichtung I" in Stefan George's "Tage und Taten" (Stefan George: Werke. Ausgabe in zwei Bänden, München/Düsseldorf 1958, Bd. 1, p. 530).

210 *who after the measure of the other: Bloch, Rimbaud, Baudelaire:* Rimbaud: "Je est un autre." (Arthur Rimbaud: Letter to Georges Izambard on 05. 13. 1871, in: Œuvres complètes, édition établie, présentée et annotée par Antoine Adam, Paris 1972, p. 249). No such clear references could be found for Baudelaire and Bloch.

211 *Rhythm: Time figure [...] (Scheler):* Scheler, p. 20 [*CL*], mark on side.

212-214 Dating on top of page cf. # 766 (Workbook II, 15 [4]).

215 *Sound-image:* cf. Sound structure, note to # 611.

216 *Syllable counting // accentual poetry:* In syllable-counting, i.e. quantitative poetry, rhythmic emphasis is distributed according to the length and brevity of syllables, while in accentual poetry emphasis is distributed according to the words' stresses, where rhythmic and speech stresses coincide. Cf. The article "Akzentuierende Dichtung," which Celan excerpted from the Reallexikon der deutschen Literaturgeschichte, hrsg. v. Paul Merker und Wolfgang Stammler, Bd. 1, Berlin 1925/26, pp. 6f. Cf. also notes to ## 256 and 611.

— Dated "7. X." at # 27 (F 23).

218 *Mora and cola:* mora: smallest time unit in verse measure, corresponding to the duration of a short syllable; cola: rhythmic speech-unit based on breath-pause as articulation in verse and prose.

222 Cf. Facsimile on p. 269.

223 *anamnesis:* (Gr.) Recollection; in Plato (for ex. "Menon," 82b-85b) the soul's remembrance of the ideas it contemplated in an earlier existence, and which it now recognizes through the experiences of the senses.

226 *'poem in the poem':* cf. Walther Killy: Gedichte im Gedicht. Beschäftigung mit Trakl-Handschriften, in: Merkur 130 (1958), pp. 1108-1121 [*CL*]: Title marked on the cover; cf. also in: Walther Killy: Über Georg Trakl, Göttingen 1960, p. 66 [*CL*].

— red pencil marks.

228 *Kampaner Tal, p. 51, footnote:* Jean Paul: Das Kampaner Thal, in: Jean Pauls Werke in 60 Teilen, Berlin o.J. [between 1868 and 1879], 39. Teil, p. 51 [*CL*]; Celan noted the date of purchase on the inside of the cover of the last volume: "Vienna, May 1948." In the footnote on p. 51 he underlined: "Der Wilde, der Bettler, der Kleinstädter übertreffen sie [die höheren Stände] weit am Sinnengenuß, da an diesem, wie an den Häusern der Juden (zum Andenken des ruinierten Jerusalem's), immer etwas *unvollendet* gelassen werden muß, und da eben Arme noch zu wenige Forderungen des erdigen Menschen befriedigt haben, um von den Forderungen des ätherischen überlaufen und gepeinigt zu werden. [The savage, the beggar, the small-towner surpass them [the higher ranks] in sensuality, because in them something has to be left *unfinished*, as is done in the houses of the Jews (in memory of the ruined Jerusalem), and as in the poor too few of the demands of earthy man have been satisfied, to be flooded and tortured by the demands of the aesthetic.]"

233 *à toi de passer, vie!:* could not be traced qua citation.

— Dated at # 800 (Workbook II, 21 [1]).

234—Highlighted by double lines above and below. Cf. Facsimile on p. 269.

237 *Thought and language (Theaetet-citation etc.):* "Sokrates: Und Denken, verstehst du darunter eben das wie ich? [...] Eine Rede, welche die Seele bei sich selbst durchgeht, über dasjenige, was sie erforschen will." ("Theaitetos," in: Platon, Bd. 2, 190a bzw. p. 630 [*CL*]["Socrates: And do you mean by conceiving, the same which I mean? ... the conversation which the soul holds with herself in considering of anything." trans. B. Jowett] : in lower margin Celan wrote Heidegger's translation: "Das sagende Sichsammeln, das die Seele selbst auf dem Weg zu sich selbst durchgeht, im Umkreis dessen, was je sie erblickt. (Heidegger)").

— *the tropes (Benveniste-essay):* Émile Benveniste: Remarques sur la fonction du langage dans la découverte freudienne, in: Problèmes de linguistique générale, Bd. 1, Paris 1966, pp. 85-87; zuerst in: La Psychanalyse 1 (1956).

239 *'Le Poème,' [...] writes Valéry, est du langage à l'état naissant:* reference could not be found in Valéry, but cf. Paul Valéry: Variété: L'invention esthétique, in: Œuvres I, Paris 1957, p. 1415 [*CL*]. Cf. also Celan's letter to Hans Bender of 11. 18. 1954: "Poetry, says Paul Valéry somewhere, is language in statu nascendi, language setting itself free [...]", in: Briefe an Hans Bender, hrsg. v. Volker Neuhaus, München 1984, p. 34. Cf. also the letter to Werner Weber of 26 March 1960, reprinted in: "Fremde Nähe." Celan als Übersetzer, Deutsche Schillergesellschaft Marbach a.N. 1997, p. 398 [Marbacher Kataloge 50]. Cf. further para. 32b in preliminary version "A."

240 Addition started at bottom edge of page, continued on next page, where the date "19. 8. 60" is written with another pencil.

241 At the very top of an otherwise empty double sheet.

246 *the poem is monotone:* Cf. Preliminary version "A," ✲ after **31a**.

247 *[...] as there is [...] for Emile Benveniste has shown it for οὐσία, for thought.:* After Benveniste has examined Aristotle's categories for their linguistic determinations (and assigning οὐσία to the substantive), he writes: "Il [Aristoteles] était donc voué à retrouver sans l'avoir voulu les distinctions que la langue même manifeste entre les principales classes de formes [...]. Il pensait définir les attributs des objets; il ne pose que des êtres linguistiques [...]. Pour autant que les catégories d'Aristote sont reconnues valables pour la pensée, elles se révèlent comme la transposition des catégories de langue. C'est ce qu'on peut *dire* qui délimite et organise ce qu'on peut penser." (Émile Benveniste: Catégories de pensée et catégories de langue, in: Problèmes de linguistique générale, Bd. 1, Paris 1966, p. 70; zuerst in: Les Études philosophiques 4 (Oct.-Dec. 1958).

— Red pencil mark: a circle in left margin next to "Censure and Economy."

248 Dated at # 800 (Workbook II, 21 [1]).

252 *Dream of great magic [...] 'With it I saw the power of heaviness end.':* "Dann warf er sich mit leichtem Schwung der Lenden—/ Wie nur aus Stolz—der nächsten Klippe zu; / An ihm sah ich die Macht der Schwere enden. [Then, with a light swing of the hips he threw himself—/As if moved only by pride —toward the next cliff; / With him I saw the power of gravity end.] " ("Ein Traum von großer Magie" (1895), in: Hofmannsthal: Gedichte und Lyrische Dramen, Frankfurt a.M. 1952 (1. Aufl. Stockholm 1946), p. 20 [*CL*])

— *levitation:* Suspension of gravity, free floating (in the legends of saints and as spirit apparition).

— *'Art doesn't come from being able to, it comes from having to. ':* Adorno: "Beides hat er [Schönberg] formuliert: 'Die Musik soll nicht schmücken, sie soll wahr sein' und 'Kunst kommt nicht vom Können sondern vom Müssen.' Mit der Negation von Schein und Spiel tendiert Musik zur Erkenntnis. [He [Schoenberg] has formulated both: 'Music should not decorate, it should be true,' and 'Art originates not in 'can,' but in 'must.' Through the negation of semblance and play, music tends toward knowledge.]" (Theodor W. Adorno: Philosophie der neuen Musik, Tübingen 1949, p. 27 [*CL*]; Cf. Philosophy of New Music, translated, edited, and with an introduction by Robert Hullot-Kentor, Minneapolis, London, 2006, p. 36. Cf. also Arnold Schönberg: Probleme des Kunstunterrichts, in: Musikalisches Taschenbuch 1911, 2. Jg., Wien 1911).

— Addition "He who attains this state as language and through language~~—through~~ as poem—will realize" typed between the lines of the typescript, then continued at bottom of page with insertion mark"×/": "this dream [...]."

256 *crest-times:* In his definition of the metrical time of a poem, Franz Saran distinguishes between "Lautzeit, Silbenzeit, Kammzeit and Abstandszeit." Crest-time \Kammzeit\ designates the duration of the crest of the syllable, i.e. the linguistic stress of a syllable with ensuing consonance. (Cf. the article "Quantität" in Reallexikon der deutschen Literaturgeschichte, hrsg. v. Paul Merker und Wolfgang Stammler, Bd. 2, Berlin 1926/28, pp. 751ff.) Cf. also notes to ## 216, 611 and 843.

— Insertion "⌞Language: is that not [...]⌟" in red pencil.

261 *vacant lots—rubble:* cf. Note for # 740.

— "-" mark: star or crossed-out cross with same pencil as text.

262 Dated at # 579 (E 14,1).

269 For date cf. also ## 295 (B 33) of 5.28. and 262 (E 14,2) of 30. 5. 60: "Breathunit," "cola."

273 *Ezekiel (O.T. - Hess. Landb.) [...] Isaiah:* "'Er wird die Hecken und Dörner niederreißen und auf einem Haufen verbrennen.' Jesaias 27,4. [...] Zu einem großen Leichenfelde haben die Fürsten die deutsche Erde gemacht, wie Ezechiel im 37. Kapitel beschreibt: 'Der Herr führte mich auf ein weites Feld, das voller Gebeine lag, und siehe, sie waren sehr verdorrt.'" ("Der Hessische Landbote," in: Bergemann, p. 344 [*CL*], Celan underlined "weites Feld" (large field) and writes in the margin: "Freies Feld" (open field) [often used as setting of a scene in Büchner's plays]; MA, p. 60, 61).

281 *hours have no phenotype:* cf. Gottfried Benn: Roman des Phänotyp. Landsberger Fragment (Benn II, pp. 152-204).

282 handwritten addition "~~—Wordart and artistry~~ [...]" as continuation of the typescript; date above text at upper edge in same pencil.
Addition: "It builds⌞, from the direction of death,⌟ [...]" handwritten in top margin, connected by arrow.

284 Marks in red pencil.

285 Marks in left margin in red pencil: a circle, and on the right at top edge in ink: a cross.

286 *The sublunar as 'counter'- the supralunar:* supralunar: situated above the moon; cf. Lukács, p. 19. "Die naturphilosophische Mikrokosmosidee hat die Homogeneität des Universums zur Voraussetzung, ist doch eine ihrer entscheidenden Funktionen, die Trennung der sublunaren und "superlunaren Wirklichkeit zu beseitigen." Cf. note to # 53.

287 *A shrub of transience:* self citation from "Matière de Bretagne" (TCA, Sprachgitter, p. 49).

289 An "–i–" note draft for the "Note" on the translation from Mandelstam.

290 Deletion with same pen as that of text # 547 (B 4,1) in top margin.

294 *"The poet's soul- and fate-closeness to the hero"(Gundolf, Büchner):* Gundolf on "Danton's Death": "Among German plays that deal specifically with world historical materials [...] Büchner's exceptionally does not originate in boastful fantasy or conventional schoolboy or mimetic enthusiasm, but from the poet's soul- and fate-closeness to the hero or event." (Friedrich Gundolf: Georg Büchner, in: Romantiker, Bd. 1, Berlin 1930, p. 382).

297 *Acmeism:* Russ.: akmeizm, derived from Gr. akmē (Peak, Flower, Maturity). Literary group in St. Petersburg, that originated in Gumilyov's 'guild of poets' (Cech poëtov). Cf. the manifestos of Nikolai Gumilyov ("The heritage of Symbolism and Acmeism," 1913) and Mandelstam ("The morning of Acmeism," 1913). Polemically distancing itself from Symbolism, it stressed the earthly against the mystical, the concrete against the vague and indeterminate, and the organic and bodily against the abstract. Mandelstam's famous answer to the question 'what is Acmeism': "A yearning for world culture." Important Acmeists: Nikolai Gumilyov, Anna Akmatova, Georgi Ivanov, Osip Mandelstam.

298 Dated at # 135 (B 27,1).

299 *And everything he blew upon [...]:* from the folk song "Die schwarzbraune Hexe (The black-brown witch)": Es blies ein Jäger wol in sein Horn, / Und alles was er blies, das war verlorn.[A hunter did blow in his horn, / and everything he blew was lost.]" (Deutscher Liederhort. Auswahl der vorzüglicheren Deutschen Volkslieder, nach Wort und Weise aus der Vorzeit und Gegenwart gesammelt und erläutert v. Ludwig Erk, neubearbeitet und fortgesetzt v. Franz M. Böhme, Leipzig 1893, Bd. 1, pp. 52ff.)

— Dated at # 135 (B 27,1). Sheet B 28 is paginated -2- at # 299 (B 28,1).

305 Insertion: "and that can remain unsaid [...]" across left margin, conspicuously linked with a line.

310 Mark in left margin with red pencil: a circle each next to "re Lucile:" and next to "the making finite of language as appearance." Whole text crossed out diagonally with red pencil.

311 "an artless poetry?" slantwise in left margin.

312 Mark in ink at top edge: cross in circle.

314 "-i-" underlined three times.

316-317 *Natorp: [...] Logos [...] Plato: kinesis of oaths:* "Die Forderung des 'Grundes' ist schließlich diese: die [...] In-sich-selbst-Gegründetheit des Denkens; 'in sich selbst,' das heißt und kann nur heißen: im Prozeß. [...] Sicher erreicht [...] ist es in Platos tiefster Entdeckung: der der Kinesis der Eide. [The demand of the 'ground' finally is this: thought's being-grounded-in-itself [...]; 'in-itself,' that means and can only mean: in the process. [...] It is realized for certain [...] in Plato's most profound discovery: the kinesis of oaths.]" (Paul Natorp: Husserls 'Ideen zu einer reinen Phänomenologie,' in: Logos. Internationale Zeitschrift für Philosophie der Kultur 7 (1917/18), Tübingen 1918, pp. 224-246, here: p. 231).

320 Dated "30. 8. 59" at # 641 (F 21,1), from # 424 (F 21,3) other pencil.

322 *'Nobody becomes what he is not':* Cf. preliminary version "A," ✻ after 31a and the relevant note.

329-330 Written in red pencil.

335 *'survival is everything':* Rilke: "Who speaks of winning? Survival is everything.": last line from the 1908 "Requiem for Wolf Graf von Kalckreuth" (Rainer Maria Rilke: Werke in drei Bänden, Frankfurt a.M. 1966, Bd. 1, p. 420 [*CL*]). Cf. also Benn on Rilke: "Diese dürftige Gestalt und Born großer Lyrik, verschieden an Weißblütigkeit, gebettet zwischen die bronzenen Hügel des Rhônetals unter eine Erde, über die französische Laute wehn, schrieb den Vers, den meine Generation nie vergessen wird: 'wer spricht von Siegen—, überstehn ist alles! [This meager figure and font of great poetry, who died of leukemia and was laid to rest among the bronze hills of the Rhone valley, in earth fanned by French sounds, wrote the line that my generation will never forget: 'Who speaks of victory?—Survival is all!'"] transl. E. B. Ashton] (Benn: Figuren, in: Ausdruckswelt. Essays und Aphorismen, Wiesbaden 1949, pp. 73–87, here: p. 87 [*CL*]). Cf. also Hans Magnus Enzensberger: "die würgengel": "du mußt mit der zeit gehn / nicht überstehn / ist alles sondern nicht alles / überstehn / sondern nicht überstehn ist alles" ["The destroying Angels": "you have to go with time / not survive / is everything but not all / survive / but not survive is all]"(in: Akzente 5 (1958), pp. 421f.)

337 Dating at first text at # 800 (Workbook II, 21 [1]).

340 *a shape poem:* a poem which works at representing its content through the graphic ordering of the verses.

— "Fateful" marked and underlined in red.

344 *'by the lightsense you divine the soul'* :auto-citation from the poem "Sprachgitter" (TCA, Sprachgitter, p. 41).

350 Dated"7. X." at # 27 (F 23).

351 Written with a different pen and inserted before a draft of the "Note" on the translations from Mandelstam.

353 *oneiric:* onirique: (Fr.) dreamlike, related to dream.

355 written at bottom of page and connected by a line to # 352.

361 *'like Egyptian mummies provided with everything necessary for life':* cf. Mandelstam's essay "Über die Natur des Wortes (On the nature of the Word)": "Kann man denn eine solche Barke [gemeint ist "die zerbrechliche Barke des menschlichen Wortes"] für die weite Reise rüsten, ohne sie mit allem Notwendigen auszustatten für den so fremden und so teuren Leser? Noch einmal würde ich das Gedicht mit der ägyptischen Totenbarke vergleichen. In dieser Barke ist alles für das Leben bereitgelegt, nichts wurde vergessen." ["Can one equip such a boat (meant is "the frail boat of the human word") for such a long journey, without furnishing it with all the necessities for the so foreign and cherished reader? Once more I would compare the poem to an Egyptian funerary boat. In this boat everything necessary for life is provided, nothing is forgotten.]" (in: Osip Mandelstam: Über den Gesprächspartner. Gesammelte Essays I, hrsg. u. übers. v. Ralph Dutli, Zürich 1991, p. 130; Mandel'štam, p. 350 [*CL*]).

367 "parable" underlined three times.

368 *Du solt minnen das niht, du solt vliehen daz iht:* "You shall love the nothing/ You shall flee the something. / You shall stand alone / and shall go to no one." ("Die Einöde hat zwölf Dinge," in: Mechthild von Magdeburg: Das fließende Licht der Gottheit, in Auswahl übersetzt von Wilhelm Oehl, Kempten/München 1911, p. 54 (Nr. I, 35) [*CL*].

369 *Heimann: There is divine dupery in the parable [...]:* Moritz Heimann: Tao, in: Prosaische Schriften, Frankfurt 1918, Bd. 3, pp. 99-105, here: p. 101.

371 Mark and cross out in red.

372 Cross out in red.

374 Mark in red: circle around the name "Lenz": "Medusa-likeness" further underlined in red.

375 *Büchner's last words:* "Wir haben der Schmerzen nicht zu viel, wir haben ihrer zu wenig, denn durch den Schmerz gehen wir zu Gott ein! <—> Wir sind Tod, Staub, Asche, wie dürften wir klagen? [We do not suffer too much pain, we have too little, because it is through pain that we enter into God! <—> We are death, dust, ash, how could we complain?]" (Caroline Schulz' diary notes on Büchner's last days, in: Bergemann, p. 580 [*CL*]: marked; MA, p. 391). This Büchner-citation is also marked in the "Buch der Freunde." (Hofmannsthal: Aufzeichnungen, Frankfurt a.M. 1959, p. 33 [*CL*]).

— *involution:* (biol.) regression; Fr. also rolling up.

— *whose lips won't round themselves:* cf. "Gespräch im Gebirg" (GW III, p. 170).

— *muta cum liquida:* ling. Connection of plosives (b, d, g, p, t, k) and continuants (l, m, n, r). Cf. a draft for "Erratisch" in: TCA, Die Niemandsrose, p. 50.

— Dated at # 737 (E 12,1).

379 handwritten note on top of dated typescript F 90.

380 Dated "21. 8." on top of sheet A 9.
From a fragmentary draft for a prose text or possibly a play.

382-383 *Such a leap is happiness and success:* "Das Phänomen des 'Gelingens' tritt nur auf, wenn das Können nicht sicher ist [...]. Das 'Glück', welches das Gelingen durch seine 'freie Gunst' schenkt, leistet also mehr als alles Können und bedarf für sein Eintreffen u. U. nur sehr wenig, manchmal anscheinend gar nicht des 'Könnens.'[The phenomenon of 'success' only comes into play when the ability to do is not firm[...]. 'Luck,' which bestows success as a 'free gift,' thus achieves more than all proficiency and requires very little to happen, at times seemingly no proficiency at all.]" (Becker, p. 45); cf. also note to # 429.

— Dated "7. X." at # 27 (F 23).

385 Addition between F 5,1 and F 5,2, "×/" in bottom margin and then continued on verso (F 6,1).

386 "—To step out of contingency" verso (C 11).

387 *'uncanny' laughter:* Celan relates this formulation to Osip Mandelstam: cf. Celan's radio-essay *The Poetry of Osip Mandelstam* in this volume, pp. 215ff.

392 Cf. Facsimile on p. 270.

393 *Plotinus [...] Original and reproduction are the same:* cf. Plotin: Ennéades, hrsg. u. übers. v. Émile Bréhier, Bd. 5, Paris 1956 [*CL*] (with the ex libris "Gisèle Celan-Lestrange") with numerous marks in the cut-open tractate 8 [31] "De la beauté intelligible." Though in Plotinus original and reproduction are ontologically totally separate, one finds however formulations such as: "each reproduction produced by nature is there as long as the original remains." (Chapter 12) Celan also owned: Plotin: Ennéades, hrsg. u. übers. v. Émile Bréhier, Bd. 1, Paris 1954 [*CL*], cut and marked up in it was the text "Du beau," pp. 93-106.

— *world-free:* For Celan, Lev Shestov was an important source for Plotinus: Le pouvoir des clefs (Potestas clavium), traduction de Boris de Schloezer, Paris 1928 [*CL*]. The reading of the Plotinus chapter "Qu' est-ce que la vérité (Ontologie et Éthique)" (pp. 397-456) is dated to "1.10.1959," inscribed in the table of contents (p. 458) and at the end of the chapter (p. 456). There it says: "Il est, Lui, en vérité, inexprimable. Quoi que tu dises, tu ne pourras nommer que des choses particulières. [...] ἄφελε πάντα [...] la raison doit pour ainsi dire 'reculer en arrière.'" Celan notates this passage: "ἄφελε πάντα = Retranche toutes choses"; Celan underlined the text up to ἄφελε πάντα (p. 442).

— *the gaze\Anschauung\:* The "hyperuranic place" (cf. note to # 154f.) is in Plotinus the place of an intellectual "Anschauung." In Émile Bréhier's "Notice" zu 8 [31] (pp. 129f.) Celan marks the following: "Dans la vision, il y a une étendue spatiale entre celui qui voit et la région où il réside: supprimez cette extériorité: supposez le milieu absorbé dans l'être, l'être dans le milieu: tel est l'état de la vision intellectuelle. [...] nous aurons une vision, où il n'y a plus à distinguer entre les parties." (Vol. 5, s.o.)

394 *Ricercar:* (Ital. ricercare: to search, to search out) Self-contained instrumental composition for lute or keyboard instrument, especially organ; precursor of the fugue. Cf. Celan's poem "Ricercar" (Paul Celan: Die Gedichte aus dem Nachlaß, hrsg. v. Bertrand Badiou, Jean-Claude Rambach, und Barbara Wiedemann, Frankfurt a.M. 1997, p. 55).

395 Text written with red pen.

397 The arrow points to # 690 (F 73), cf. the parallel place in # 417 (F 72,1) higher up on the page.

400 Addition "—Not the motif [...]" starts as continuation of the typescript, and continues (with line connection) at top edge of page; from "Not a seminar-ready [...] new paragraph.
Addition "×/ Beautiful, that would be [...]" as footnote in lower margin.

401 *description by Edith Stein [...] the Other and foreign:* Personal experience and experience of the other are closely interwoven in Edith Stein: The "constitution of the foreign individual [is] the condition for the full constitution of one's own." [PJ] (Edith Stein: Zum Problem der Einfühlung, Inaugural-Dissertation, Halle 1917, Reprint of the original edition of 1917 with an "Approach" by Johannes Baptist Lotz SJ, München 1980, p. 99).

— Mark in left margin with red pen: cicrcles at "The Almondeye:—not only [...]" and next to "the Other and foreign as [...]"

402 Text written with red pen.

405 μελανόμματοζ: dark-eyed; cf. Plato: "Das nun von den beiden, welches von schönerer Beschaffenheit ist, ist seiner Gestalt nach aufrecht gebaut und gut gegliedert, hat [...] schwarze Augen" ["[...]is upright and cleanly made; [...] his eyes dark;" B. Jowett]. ("Phaidros," in: Platon, Bd. 2, 253d bzw. p. 445 [*CL*]).

406 *There is a third one standing by, le témoin [...] and malgré lui:* le témoin: (Fr.) witness; malgré lui: (Fr.) against one's will, despite oneself.

407 Mark in right margin in red ink: cross in circle.

409 *Buber, Ich und Du, p. 137:* "die Zeiten, in denen das Wort geltend wird, sind die, in denen sich die Entwirklichung, die Verfremdung zwischen Ich und Welt, das Werden des Verhängnisses vollzieht—bis der große Schauder kommt, und das Atemanhalten im Dunkel, und das bereitende Schweigen. [The ages in which the word becomes valid are those in which the deactualization, the alienation of I and world, the emergence of doom takes place—until the great shudder appears, the holding of breath in the dark, and the preparatory silence.]" (Martin Buber: Ich und Du, Leipzig 1923, Neuauflage 1957, p. 137. English transl. by Walter Kaufmann, I and Thou, New York, 1970, p.168.)

— Dated at # 800 (Workbook II, 21 [1]).

414-416 Dated "18. 5." at # 594 (B 28,2).

417 *Two-way traffic and turning, [...] on dirt roads, it seems, alas, that there are few occasions to do so:* cf. Martin Heidegger: Der Feldweg, Frankfurt a.M. 1949 [*CL*]; and: Zur Erörterung der Gelassenheit. Aus einem Feldweggespräch über das Denken, in: Gelassenheit, Pfullingen 1960 [*CL*].

— The mark relates to the word "turning."

418 *offense:* cf. "Danton's Tod," Akt 2, Scene 5 "A Room": "es muß ja Ärgernis kommen, doch wehe dem, durch welchen Ärgernis kommt!"["It must needs be that offense come; but woe to that man by whom the offense cometh."] (Bergemann, p. 45 [*CL*], multiple marks; MA, p. 99). The same as in the letter to the bride of November 1833? (Reference after Bergemann; according to MA circa 9-12 March 1834: Bergemann, p. 374 [*CL*], herein underlined; MA, p. 288). Cf. also Matth. 18,7; 1. Cor. 1,23 and Luke 17,1.

— multiple marks.

419 *Lemberger Ghetto:* erected 8. 11. 1941 as Ghetto, into which all Lemberger Jews had to move by 15. 12. 41. End 1942 closed Ghetto; January 1943 officially converted into a 'labor camp.' Dissolution of ghetto completed 2. 6. 1943.

— *Izvestia:* (russ.) News; Russian daily paper.

421 *Buber, in conversation (Vico:) [...] times [...], a 'holy' one and a 'profane' one.* Citation could not be verified.

422 *'Camarado, who [...] touches this, touches a man':* from the poem "So Long" by Walt Whitman: "Camerado, this is no book, / Who touches this touches a man, / (It is night? are we here together alone?) / It is I you hold and who holds you, / I spring from the pages into your arms— / decease calls me forth." (Walt Whitman: Leaves of Grass, London/New York/Toronto/Melbourne 1909, p. 460 [*CL*]). In the "Editor's Note" the second verse of this stanza is cited and interpreted as key to Whitman's life and work: "His [Whitman's] personality, the epitome of abounding life [...] breathes through the poems so vitally that he has become the friend of thousands who never saw him in the flesh."

— *aisthesis:* sense perception.

— *a shadow [...] Hegel:* citation could not be verified. Hegel treats "place" and "hour" in the first chapter of the "Phenomenology of Mind," by ascertaining the inconsistency of unmediated sense impressions. (Georg Wilhelm Friedrich Hegel: Phänomenologie des Geistes, in: Sämtliche Werke, hrsg. v. Johannes Hoffmeister, Bd. 5, [6]1952 [*CL*]).

— Addition "it is a question of the clinamen [...]" starts as continuation between the lines, then continues in left margins with "/××."
Cf. Facsimile on p. 268.

423-424 Dated "30. 8. 59" at # 641 (F 21,1), from # 424 (F 21,3) different pen.

425 *noesis:* intellectual perception.

429 *Leap:* cf. Oskar Becker: "[...] es [das Ästhetische] ist das im Unmittelbaren Ausgezeichnete. Diese Auszeichnung ist formal—paradox genug—dadurch charakterisiert, daß sie, in extremen Fällen, 'Spitzencharakter' hat, d.h. daß das 'Extremum' [...] nicht stetig erreicht wird, sondern durch einen Sprung. [...the aesthetic is what is characterized by the immediate. Paradoxically enough, this characteristic is formal [...] the 'acme' is not attained progressively, but through a leap.]" (Becker, p. 27)

435 *Ontology of the Aesthetic:* A concept Celan gets from Oskar Becker (Becker, pp. 39, 40).

438 *O. Becker: Work and reception: unparted* "Schaffen und Rezipieren sind gerade in der ästhetischen 'Sphäre' in ihrer letzten Wurzel prinzipiell ungeschieden: jede adäquate Rezeption ist ein Nachschaffen des Werks, und jede echte Schöpfung ist 'Vision'—besser: Schöpfung und Rezeption entstammen der *Vision* als ihrer gemeinsamen Wurzel." (Becker, p. 40)

439 *Danton, your lips have eyes: no metaphor [...]:* cf. "Danton's Death" Akt 1, Scene 5 (in: Bergemann, p. 24 [*CL*], here the sentence is underlined and additionally marked marginally; MA, p. 82).

— *Your mouth speaks itself to the eye:* altered auto-citation from "Zürich, Zum Storchen": "Dein Aug sah mir zu, sah hinweg, / dein Mund / sprach sich dem Aug zu, ich hörte: [...]" ["Your eye looked at me, looked away, / your mouth / addressed the eye, I heard:[...]" trans. Cid Corman] (written 30. 5. 60) (TCA, Die Niemandsrose, p. 14).

443 "wrong formulation" written above the mark in left margin, the marked text from "handicraft"crossed out, and the whole text once more crossed out.

445-446 Dated "7. X." at # 27 (F 23).

447 Dated "30. 8. 59" at # 641 (F 21,1).
Mark in left margin with red pen: circle.
F 119,3: later copy with no mark.

449 F 118,3: later copy.

454 *"Notebook at Gisèle's":* not in the workbooks published here.

458 *Freud, Unbehagen p. 49:* "Mit Hilfe des Telephons hört er aus Entfernungen, die selbst das Märchen als unerreichbar respektieren würde; die Schrift ist ursprünglich die Sprache des Abwesenden, das Wohnhaus ein Ersatz für den Mutterleib, die erste, wahrscheinlich noch immer ersehnte Behausung, in der man sicher war und sich so wohl fühlte. [With the help of the telephone he can hear at distances which would be respected as unattainable even in a fairy tale. Writing was in its origin the voice of an absent person; and the dwelling-house was a substitute for the mother's womb, the first lodging, for which in all likelihood man still longs, and in which he was safe and felt at ease.]" (Sigmund Freud: Das Unbehagen in der Kultur, Wien ^{2}1931, p. 49 [*CL*]; Standard Edition, The complete psychological works of Sigmund Freud, transl. by James Strachey, London, 1961. Vol XX1, p. 91; from "writing" to "absent person" only underlining in the book, additionally marked in margin; date of purchase: "Paris, 4 October 1959").

— Ink mark: cross at "⌞someone still more absent⌟" and at "In the poem[...]"

464 Mark in left margin with red pen: circle.

467 Triple mark, encirclement and addition with red pen.

468 on verso of # 24 (C 57).

469 *'Streak in the eye':* auto-citation from "Schliere" (TCA, Sprachgitter, p. 27).

475 *against [...] Goll:* cf. Note to # 60.

— Ink mark right next to title: cross in circle.

480 Text written with red pen.

483 Addition crosswise in left margin.

484 *Lichtenbergian clashes of books and readers' heads:* "Wenn ein Buch und ein Kopf zusammenstoßen und es klingt hohl, ist das allemal im Buch?" (Georg Christoph Lichtenberg: Bemerkungen / IV. Über Wissenschaft und Bildung / Über den Umgang mit Büchern, in: Gesammelte Werke, hrsg. v. Wilhelm Grenzmann, Frankfurt a.M. 1949, Bd. 1, p. 295 [*CL*]).

486 *Re Kamen: he speaks—he is silent [...]:* Kamen': (Russ.) The stone; Osip Mandelstam's volume of poems by the same name, published in 1913, enlarged edition in 1916 and 1923. Cf. Note to # 53.

— *Edmund Husserl, Vorlesung [...] p. 400:* "Auch in bloßer Phantasie ist jedes Individuelle ein zeitlich irgendwie Extendiertes, hat sein Jetzt, sein Vorher und Nachher, aber das Jetzt, das Vorher und Nachher ist ein bloß eingebildetes wie das ganze Objekt." (Edmund Husserl: Vorlesungen zur Phänomenologie des inneren Zeitbewußtseins, hrsg. v. Martin Heidegger, Halle 1928, p. 400 [*CL*], [Sonderdruck aus dem Jahrbuch für Philosophie und phänomenologische Forschung 9]).

492 Dated at # 499 (F 14,1).

495 Triple mark in same ink as the marks on the collected typescripts ## 848ff. (F 85ff.)
Handwritten text on dated typescript F 90; cf. # 861.

496 on verso of # 24 (C 57).

497 Bottom of page, upside down note: "Protocols, Berliner All the printed even<?> Literary Suppl<ement>."

504 Dated "19. 8. 60" two pages earlier at # 766 (Workbook II, 15 [4]).

506 After "Conversation with things" continued with different pen, including "-i-" and "B-R."

507 Dated "5 Oct.—" with different pen at # 343 (F 105,1). # 507 (F 105,5) at left margin; "→ invoke =" refers to # 508 (F 106) on verso of same sheet.

508 Mark top right at start of text with red pen: Star in circle (emphatically marked).
Addition in left upper margin continued with arrow.

509 Dated at # 800 (Workbook II, 21 [1]).

516 *[...] as the consonant [...] vibr. Con-sonant:* cf. "Schliere": "und als stumm / vibrierender Mitlaut gestimmt." ["and tuned as mutely / vibrating consonant."] (TCA, Sprachgitter, p. 27).

517 Mark with red pen.
Cf. Facsimile on p. 269.

521 ⋇: cross-out cross or little star.

523 From a draft of the "Note" to the translations from Mandelstam. Last sentence in left margin.

524 "Wah<r>ne<h>m<en>de<?>": readable as "Wahnemde" which can be a shortened "Wahrnehmende" or a misspelled "Wohnende." Back of an envelope with postal stamp of 5. 3. 1960.

525 Additions "⌞symbolic⌟" and "⌞and set into words [...]⌟" under the text and refer with emphatic line or possibly arrow.

529 *Complementarity (Pöggeler):* Otto Pöggeler discusses the concept of complementarity in his critique of Hans Egon Holthusen's book: Das Schöne und das Wahre, München 1958, in: Zeitschrift für philosophische Forschung, Heft 13/1, München 1960. Though there he does not in fact use this concept in relation to the finite-infinite pair of concepts.

533 Mark at left edge in red pen: circle.

537 Triple mark.

543 *literature \Schrifttum\ [...] bei Heine:* "Halten Sie es nun der Mühe wert, meine heutigen Mitteilungen in die heimische Mundart zu übertragen, so unterdrücken Sie gefälligst alle jene Schnörkeleien und Verbrämungen, welche noch an die aristokratische Rokokozeit des deutschen Schrifttums erinnern. Die Herrschaft der Schönschreiberei hat ein Ende wie so manche andre; auch die deutsche Schreibkunst wird emanzipiert, sie wird jedenfalls keine Kunst mehr sein. [Now, if you think it wortwhile to translate my current communications into the home vernacular, please eliminate all those embellishments and trimmings that bring to mind the rococo age of German literature. The rule of belles lettres has come to an end, like many others; the German art of writing is in the process of emancipation; at any rate it will no longer be an art.]"(Heinrich Heine: Vor dem Zusammenbruch 1847/48, in: Sämtliche Schriften, hrsg. v. Klaus Briegleb, Bd. 5, München 1974, pp. 212f.)

— "Questions" and "poetry" both crossed out.

544 *'Felice notte':* citation from Benn's poem "Lebe wohl" (Benn III, p. 149).

547 written later in the top margin above text # 290 (B 4,2) which is deleted with the same pencil. Cf. also the note for # 241.

550 *Bennsche Artistik:* "Artistik ist der Versuch der Kunst, innerhalb des allgemeinen Verfalls der Inhalte sich selber als Inhalt zu erleben [...], es ist der Versuch, gegen den allgemeinen Nihilismus der Werte eine neue Transzendenz zu setzen: die Transzendenz der schöpferischen Lust. [Artistry is the attempt by art amidst the general decay of contents to experience itself as content [...], it is the attempt to set a new transcendence against the generalized nihilism of values: the transcendence of creative desire." ("Probleme der Lyrik", in: Benn I, pp. 500f.)

— Mark in red pen.

551 *Heuristic:* Theory of the process of solving problems; methodic instruction in the gaining of new knowledge.

552 *Hegel [...] Hofpoeten und Jedermannspoeten:* "Mehr noch kann man es als einen ehrenwerten Zug Klopstocks rühmen, daß er zu seiner Zeit wieder die selbständige Würde des Sängers fühlte und, indem er sie aussprach und ihr gemäß sich hielt und betrug, den Dichter aus dem Verhältnis des Hofpoeten und Jedermannspoeten sowie aus einer müßigen, nichtsnutzigen Spielerei herausriß, womit ein Mensch sich nur ruiniert.[One can praise even more as an honorable trait Klopstock's, that in his days he again sensed the independent dignity of the singer and, by voicing it and behaving according to it, helped to rescue the poet from his role as court-poet and everyman-poet as well as from an otiose and useless game that can only lead to a man's ruin.]" (Georg Wilhelm Friedrich Hegel: Ästhetik, mit einem einführenden Essay von Georg Lukács, Berlin 1955, p. 1015: in the chapter on the lyric poet; numerous further marks in the chapters on the art of poetry; in the citation above, "court-poet and everyman-poet" is underlined. [*CL*])

— *parenistic (parenesis) admonishing:* Parenesis: Exhortatory writing, speech or sermon.

553 Dated "5. X. 60" both at # 601 (F 38,1) and # 30 (F 40).

559 possibly related to # 32 (C 7,4); not a full empty line between.

560 Mark in left margin in red pen: circle.

562 *Letter to Bender:* In a letter of 18. 5. 1960 to Hans Bender, Celan wrote about "craft \Handwerk\" and about "crafting / making \Machen\," that becomes "machination / faking \Machenschaft\." (GW III, pp. 177f.)

— probably first started as introduction to # 563 (AE 15,8 [4]) between # 742 (AE 15,8 [2]) and # 563 (AE 15,8 [4]), continued with "×/" in top margin.

563 *'How does one make verses' Mayakovsky tried to ask himself:* Vladimir Mayakovsky: Wie macht man Verse? Deutsch v. Siegfried Behrsing, Berlin 1949 [*CL*].

— *Mayakovsky:* Vladimir Vladimirovič Mayakovskij (1893-1930), Russian "Cubofuturist," poet, playwright, commentator and artist, who called himself the "drummer" of the revolution. He committed suicide in April 1930.

— "this question" encircled, crossed out and marked with dotted line.

565 *Young Fate:* cf. the poem by Paul Valéry in Celan's translation (GW IV, pp. 128f.)

567 *verse of the Nibelungenlied—the alexandrine—Bateau Ivre—Jeune Parque:* In the translations of Rimbaud's "Bateau Ivre" and Valéry's "Jeune Parque" Celan used the verse form of the Nibelungenlied with an added unstressed syllable in the middle of the verse to render the French alexandrine.

572 Red pencil mark above the text: circle.

580 *Theodor Lessing:* (1872-1933), commentator, writer and philosopher of culture; author of "Der jüdische Selbsthaß (Jewish Self-Hatred)" (1930). He came from a liberal Jewish family. He took part in the antirationalist culture and social critique at the end of the 19th C /begining of 20th C, and promulgated a pragmatic socialism.

584 *'trobar cluz':* new, 12th C. school (probably originating in Marcabru's work) of hermetic, 'dark' troubadour poetry (cluz: closed).

— *I am yours [...]:* cf. "Dû bist mîn, ich bin dîn" from the "nameless songs," belonging in fact to the easily understandable tradition of the trobar leu. (In: Des Minnesangs Frühling, unter Benutzung der Ausgaben von Karl Lachmann und Moritz Haupt, Friedrich Vogt und Carl von Kraus bearbeitet v. Hugo Moser und Helmut Tervooren, Stuttgart [38]1988, p. 21).

— Insertion "I am yours [...]" between the lines of the addition to # 422 (A 16,1).

"cheekily, 're-enact'" at lower margin, connected with arrow.

Cf. Facsimile on p. 268.

588 *or an oxymoron:* In his essay Peter Seidensticker speaks repeatedly of the "oxymoron 'Schwarze Milch der Frühe.'" (Peter Seidensticker [u.] Butzlaff, Wolfgang: Zwei Bemühungen um ein Gedicht: Paul Celans 'Todesfuge,' in: Deutschunterricht 12 (1960), Heft 3, pp. 36f.)

589 *well-intended discussion of the 'Death Fugue'* : "Among the Jews of the Balkans—the poet is born in the Bukovina—the name [Shulamit] represents the epitome of the Jewish woman." (Peter Seidensticker in: derselbe [u.] Butzlaff, Wolfgang: Zwei Bemühungen um ein Gedicht: Paul Celan: 'Todesfuge,' in: Der Deutschunterricht 12 (1960), Heft 3, p. 36).

595 *Benveniste: metaphors, tropes [...]:* "Car c'est dans le style, plutôt que dans la langue, que nous verrions un terme de comparaison avec les propriétés que Freud a décelées comme signalétiques du 'langage' onirique. On est frappé des analogies qui s'esquissent ici. L'inconscient use d'une véritable 'rhétorique' qui, comme le style, a ses 'figures,' et le vieux catalogue des tropes fournirait un inventaire approprié aux deux registres de l'expression. [...] La nature du contenu fera apparaître toutes les variétés de la métaphore, car c'est d'une conversion métaphorique que les symboles de l'inconscient tirent leur sens et leur difficulté à la fois." (Émile Benveniste: Remarques sur la fonction du langage dans la découverte freudienne, in: Problèmes de linguistique générale, Vol. 1, Paris 1966, pp. 75-87, here: pp. 86f., first in: La Psychanalyse 1 (1956)).

598 Mark with red pencil.

600 *'You must not deny me parables [...]':* Verse from the section "Aus dem Nachlaß. Invectiven," in: Goethes Werke. Weimarer Ausgabe, hrsg. im Auftrage der Großherzogin Sophie von Sachsen, 5. Bd., 1. Abt., Weimar 1893, p. 186.

— *Schlegel: The image is the deliverance of the spirit from the object [...]:* citation could not be verified. Cf. Friedrich Schlegel: "Das Bild ist ein Werk des Ichs, ein Gegen-Ding, welches das Ich hervorbringt, um sich der Herrschaft des Dings, des Nicht-Ichs zu entreißen. [The image is a work of the I, a counter-thing that produces the I in order to escape the rule of the thing, of the not-I.]" (Kritische Friedrich-Schlegel-Ausgabe, hrsg. v. Ernst Behler unter Mitwirkung von Jean-Jacques Anstett und Hans Eichner, Bd. 12: Philosophische Vorlesungen (1800-1807), 1. Teil, hrsg. v. Jean-Jacques Anstett, München/Paderborn/Wien/Zürich 1964, p. 359.

— "cf. Mandelst." Written above the mark in the left margin.

602 *Man as information:* cf. Günter Eich: "'Man is information.' [...] This sentence, which comes from the cyberneticist Norbert Wiener, is not meant figuratively [...]." (Günter Eich: Büchner-Preis-Rede 1959, in: Büchner-Reden, p. 85). Cf. also Wiener's chapter heading "Der Mensch—eine Nachricht" (Norbert Wiener: Mensch und Menschmaschine, Berlin 1958, p. 83). German translation of: The Human Use of Human Beings: Cybernetics and Society, Boston 1954. German chapter heading not a literal translation of any original chapter heading.

Cf. Preliminary version "A", ✻ after 18c.

607 *Gauen:* Gau, mhg. landscape, gen. fertile land for settlement; in national-socialist Germany, regional unit of organization of the NSDAP.

611 *D. Seckel [...] Rhythm is something else than specific 'sound form':* cf. Seckel: "Die Hauptmerkmale der schallanalytischen Sprachbetrachtung sind zweifacher Art: erstens [...] die tief eindringende Analyse konkreter Sprachgebilde unter Berücksichtigung feinster Schattierungen, und zweitens [...] die Erkenntnis der engen und ursprünglichen Verknüpfung dieser sprachlichen

Phänomene zu einem einmalig-individuellen Sprachcharakter, einer spezifischen 'Schallform.' [The main characteristics of sound analysis in language considerations are twofold: first [...] the far-reaching analysis of concrete language structures [...] secondly, the recognition of the close and originary combination of these linguistic phenomena into a unique individual language-character, a specific 'sound form.'"](Dietrich Seckel: Hölderlins Sprachrhythmus. Mit einer Einleitung über das Problem des Rhythmus und einer Bibliographie zur Rhythmus-Forschung, Leipzig 1937, p. 9 [Palästra 207]).

— *sound form:* "Gesamtheit der hörbaren Eigenschaften, die an dem gesprochenen oder aus dem Schriftbild klingend gemachten Vers haften. [Totality of audible properties pertaining to a verse, be it spoken, or sounded in its written form.]" (Reallexikon der deutschen Literaturgeschichte, hrsg. v. Paul Merker und Wolfgang Stammler, Bd. 3, Berlin 1928/29; Artikel zum Stichwort "Vers" cf. pp. 464ff., here p. 466); cf. also note to # 216, 256.

612 *Rhythm is not something acoustically measurable:* cf. Seckel's presentation of the experimental analyses of the Rutz-Sievers resonance phenomenon by H. Schulte, R. Walther, and G. Becking (Dietrich Seckel: Hölderlins Sprachrhythmus. Mit einer Einleitung über das Problem des Rhythmus und einer Bibliographie zur Rhythmus-Forschung, Leipzig 1937, pp. 9f. [Palästra 207]).

613 *'Each human has his own individual rhythm':* cf. Seckel: "Auch für den Rh. dürfte die These Gültigkeit haben, daß—prinzipiell—in jeder sprachlichen Äußerung sich die Eigenart eines Menschen unverwechselbar kundtut [...]. 'Jeder Mensch hat seinen individuellen Rh.' [The thesis that—in principle—the particularity of a human announces itself unmistakably in each speech act should hold true for rhythm too. 'Each human has his own individual rhythm.'"]. (Novalis, Fragmente. Ausg. v. Kluckhohn, III 118).(Dietrich Seckel: Hölderlins Sprachrhythmus. Mit einer Einleitung über das Problem des Rhythmus und einer Bibliographie zur Rhythmus-Forschung, Leipzig 1937, p. 11 [Palästra 207]). Cf. also Novalis: "Alle Methode ist *Rythmus*. Hat man den Rythmus der Welt weg—so hat man auch die Welt weg. Jeder Mensch hat seinen individuellen Rythmus.[All method is *rhythm*. If you get the rhythm of the world, you also get the world."] ("Das allgemeine Brouillon (Materialien zur Enzyklopädistik 1798/99)" in: Novalis: Schriften, Bd. 3: Das philosophische Werk II, hrsg. v. Richard Samuel in Zusammenarbeit mit Hans-Joachim Mähl und Gerhard Schulz, Darmstadt 1968, pp. 309f.)

614 *Strontium 90:* Strontium: chem. element, alkaline earth metal; in the explosion of atomic weapons, radioactive strontium 90 is set free. Cf. preliminary version of "Ein Auge, offen," in: TCA, Sprachgitter, p. 72.

— Insertion: "⌞for that it couldn't be ... processes;⌟" connected with line in top margin; addition "The poem ⌞otherwise⌟ certainly [...]" delimited with line and connected with arrow with another pen next to # 234 (F 12,2).
Cf. Facsimile on p. 269.

618 *'Super-cyst \Überbein\' and supersonic \Überschall\:* Überbein: ganglion, cystic growth that appears particularly in the area of the trapezoid on the back of the hand.

619 prob. connects to # 27 (F 23): "has the sky ××/ beneath him," ibid. # 28 (F 24,3) and Nr. 132 (F 31,2).
Dated "7. X." on top of # 27.

626 *Zieraffe (Zierbengel bis Schlußrakete):* Zieraffe: "schelte für einen sich zierenden, sich affektiert benehmenden menschen beiderlei geschlechts, auch putzsüchtiger mensch [dandy: insult for someone of either sex behaving with affectation, also someone addicted to finery]"; Zierbengel: "stutzerhaft gekleideter und im benehmen sich zierender mensch [someone spiffily dressed and with affected manners]," word coined by Georg Christoph Lichtenberg. (Deutsches Wörterbuch von Jacob und Wilhelm Grimm, Bd. 31, Sp. 1150 und 1158).

631 *man: the bestia cupidissima [...]:* cf. note to # 790.

634 on verso of # 24 (C 57).

637 *Nietzsche: the reader: 'by nature so prodigal; that [...]':* "Ein solcher Mensch [der ruhige Leser] hat noch nicht verlernt zu denken, während er liest, er versteht noch das Geheimnis, zwischen den Zeilen zu lesen, ja er ist so verschwenderisch geartet, daß er gar noch über das Gelesene nachdenkt—vielleicht lange nachdem er das Buch aus den Händen gelegt hat. Und zwar nicht, um eine Rezension oder wieder ein Buch zu schreiben, sondern nur so, um nachzudenken! [Such a man [the quiet reader]has not yet unlearned how to think while reading; he still understands the secret of reading between the lines, yes, his inclination is so prodigal that he even reflects on what he has read—perhaps even long after he has put down the book. And, moreover, not in order to write a review of the book or yet another book, but simply in order to think!"] ("Fünf Vorreden zu fünf ungeschriebenen Büchern: "2. Gedanken über die Zukunft unserer Bildungsanstalten", in: Friedrich Nietzsche: Werke in drei Bänden, hrsg. v. Karl Schlechta, München [2]1960, Bd. 3, p. 273 [*CL*]).

— Dated at # 184 (E 3,1).

643 *The gerund, that is [...] the participle of the form of* *suffering of the future.* cf. the beginning of the last chapter in Mandelstam's "Journey to Armenia" (published in 1933); below the chapter heading "Alagez" one reads: "In welcher Zeit möchtest du leben? /—Ich möchte im imperativen Partizip der Zukunft, in der passiven Handlungsart leben—im 'Zu-Werden-Haben.' / So kann ich atmen. So will es mir gefallen. Da ist das Ehrgefühl des Reiters, banditisch, aufgesessen. Deshalb gefällt mir auch das prächtige lateinische 'Gerundivum'—dieses Verb auf einem Pferderücken. [In what time would you like to live?/ —I would like to live in the imperative of the future passive participle—in 'What-Ought-To-Be.' / It lets me breathe. I like that. That mounted, outlawish, equestrian sense of honor. That's also why I like the magnificent Latin 'gerunds'—it's a verb on horseback.]" (Osip Mandelstam: Armenien, Armenien. Prosa. Notizbuch, Gedichte 1930-1933, aus dem Russischen übertragen und hrsg. v. Ralph Dutli, Zürich 1994, p. 51). In Celan's Mandelstam copies this passage has the following translator's notes: "Imper.," "Partiz.," "im 'zu Sollenden' sein," "Mittelwort der Leideform der Zukunft" (Mandel'štam, p. 316 [*CL*]). Cf. also the end of the radio-essay on Mandelstam in this volume, p. 213.

— handwritten dating at # 400 (F 48,1). The continuation of the typescript on the verso (F 49) is marked with "."

649 *The poet: always in partibus infidelium:* cf. Friedrich Schlegel in a letter of 15 January 1803 from Paris to his brother August: "ich betrachte mich hier als Idealist oder Poeten in *partibus infidelium.* [I see myself here as an idealist or poet in *partibus infidelium.*]" (Friedrich Schlegels Briefe an seinen Bruder August Wilhelm, hrsg. v. Oskar Walzel, Berlin 1890, p. 501); in partibus infidelium: (Lat.) in the lands of the unbelievers; title of bishops whose diocese was under 'pagan' rule. (Cf. also discarded title of the 1961 "Gauner- und Ganovenweise" in: TCA, Die Niemandsrose, pp. 42f.)

653 Red pencil mark.

657 *Rotwelsch:* German argot that developed in the late Middle Ages among marginal social groups more or less excluded from rural sedentariness or professionally settled urban life, and in daily contact with various German regional dialects and with, among others, Yiddish. Rot- probably means 'beggar,' 'vagabond'; -welsch signals 'hard to understand,' 'foreign.'

658 handwritten in top margin of carbon copy C 4,2 (Nr. 2), partly between the lines, though without marked reference to them.

664 *Pound-Chinese:* In his Cantos, Ezra Pound uses motifs from ancient China and inserts Chinese characters into the text. (cf. f.ex. Ezra Pound: Cantos LII-LXXI, London 1940 [*CL*]).

— F 120 and F 121,1 (Nr. 665) on independent sheets.

669 Dated "7.X." at # 27 (F 23).

673 on verso the note (probably in the context of his work on "The Young Fate"):

" Ballad
Sheet of pictures
Germ. verse meters
Real-<lexiko>n"

674 *necropolises [...] built faster than metropolises:* nekropole: large burial grounds of antiquity (Gr.: city of the dead).

681 Dated at # 579 (E 14,1).

684 *knife-scene in Woyzeck:* Meant is probably the final scene in Bergemann "At the Pond," in which Woyzeck throws the knife with which he has murdered Marie into the water. (Bergemann, p. 174 [*CL*]). Cf. also the scene "Pawnbroker's Shop," in which he buys the knife from a Jew. (Bergemann, p. 169 [*CL*]; in later editions these scenes appear in a different textual order).

687 *in Vyasmo or Leipzig [...] in Ryasan or Röcken near Lützen:* Vyasma: town in the region of Smolensk; Ryasan: Russian-governed region, in which Sergei Yesenin was born in the village of Konstantinovo; Röcken: Nietzsche's place of birth.

688 "deficient formulation" written aslant in the left margin above the double mark.

688-689 Dated at # 499 (F 14,1).

691 Dated at # 347 (F 108,1) with different pen.

692 The last word "the" (uncertain reading) stands already on the opposite right side C 28 (cf. # 14).

693-700 C 51-52 is a small double sheet on which notes are interwoven on three pages. C 51 (Nr. 3/693) is the front page, C 52a its verso and C 52b the opposite, right page. C 51,2-52b,1 (# 694) begins at bottom of C 51 and is continued on the next but one page C 52b. C 52b,2 (Nr. 20/695) continues with same, C 52b,352a,4 (Nr. 4/696) with another pen. "The one leads to the other, but: a leap is needed" occurs at bottom of facing left page C 52a. Texts C 52a,1-3 (Nr. 5/697, 698, 699) occur above and C 52a,5 (Nr. 700) was jotted down later with yet another pen aslant in right margin of same page.

Cf. Facsimiles on pp. 278f.

700 *Democritus—morality [...] nothing in Diels—therefore no quotation marks:* cf. Democritus according to Diels: "Nachdem D. sein Mißtrauen gegen die Sinneswahrnehmungen in dem Satze ausgesprochen: 'Der gebräuchlichen Redeweise nach gibt es Farbe, Süßes, Bitteres, in Wahrheit aber nur Atome und Leeres,' läßt er die Sinne gegen den Verstand reden. [After D. has said his distrust of sense perceptions in the sentence, 'Sweet, bitter, color, exist by convention, in reality only atoms and the void exist,' he lets the senses speak against the mind.]" (Hermann Diels: Die Fragmente der Vorsokratiker, Hamburg 1957, p. 106 [*CL*]). Cf. the passage marked in [*CL*]: "For he says: 'Sweet and bitter [...]; in reality only atoms and the void exist.'" (Die Vorsokratiker. Fragmente und Quellenberichte, hrsg. v. Wilhelm Capelle, Stuttgart 1953, p. 437). Cf. also Celan's letter to Erich Einhorn of 10.8.1962: "In my latest book of poems ('Sprachgitter') you'll find a poem called 'Engführung,'['Stretto'] which evokes the devastations caused by the atom bomb. At a central place stands, as fragment, this sentence by Democritus: 'There exists nothing excepts atoms and empty space; everything else is opinion.' I do not need to underline that the poem was written because of that opinion—for the sake of the human, thus against all emptiness and atomizing." in Paul Celan: Selections, ed. and transl. by Pierre Joris, Berkeley, 2005, pp. 181, 182. The continuation in "Stretto": "the rest/ [...] was opinion." is not in Diels. (Cit. in Marina Dmitrieva-Einhorn: Wo ich mit meinen Gedanken bin. 'Vom winzigen Worthaufen': Unbekannte Briefe Paul Celans an Erich Einhorn, einen Jugendfreund aus Czernowitz, in: Die Zeit vom 27. 10. 1995).

702 *Woyzeck: 'Look at the creature, as God created it: nix, nothing at all. [...]':* Charlatan in Büchner's "Woyzeck": "Booths. Lights. People" (Bergemann, p. 155 [*CL*], here marked in margin. In later editions this scene appears in a different textual order.)

706 *'The dying often become childish':* "Danton's Tod," Act 2, Scene 1 "A Room" (Bergemann, p. 34 [*CL*], here marked in margin; MA, p. 90).

707 The arrow in the margin points from the bottom edge of the right side C16 to the left top of the opposite left side C 15.

708-710 Cf. Facsimile on p. 276.

709 *p. 107, Lenz ... he had nothing:* "er hatte keinen Haß, keine Liebe, keine Hoffnung—eine schreckliche Leere, und doch eine folternde Unruhe, sie auszufüllen. Er hatte *nichts.* [he had no hate, no love, no hope—a horrible emptiness, and yet a tortured uneasiness demanding to fill it up. He had *nothing.]*" (Bergemann, p. 107 [*CL*], last sentence here underlined and with triple mark in margin; MA, p. 155).

713 Para. written around the first composed one and then crossed out ~~"I do not believe that"~~.

716 *The nightingale of poetry:* "Leonce and Lena," Act 1, Scene 3: "Leonce. All day long the Nightingale of Poetry sings its song above our head, but the finest song always goes to waste until we pluck the Nightingale's plume and dip it into ink or color." (Bergemann, p. 128 [*CL*], here marked in the margin; MA, p. 172. English translation by Carl Richard Mueller, p. 87).

— *Clay pipe:* "Danton's Death," Act 2, Scene 3 "A Room": "Camille. [...] Fiddle them out an opera which reproduces the rising and sinking of the human soul as a clay pipe with water reproduces the sounds of the nightingale." (Bergemann, p. 40 [*CL*], here "oh, art!" is underlined and passage marked in margin; MA, p. 96; English translation by Carl Richard Mueller, p. 32).

718 *p. 375: I am an automaton [...]:* cf.: Büchner's "Letter to the bride of November 1833?? (Ref. According to MA circa 9-12 March 1834): "Since I crossed the bridge over the Rhine, I am as if crushed in myself; not a single emotion surfaces in me. I am an automaton; my soul has been taken from me." (Bergemann, p. 375 [*CL*], sentence underlined there and further marked in margin; MA, p. 289).

719 *Perillus bull:* Bergemann comments: "Bü seems to have confused the legend of the Gr. metal caster Perilaos and his patron, the tyrant Phalaris of Agrigent, with the Egyp. legend of the phoenix." (Bergemann, p. 666 [*CL*];marked in index).

722 *p. 411: Letter to Gutzkov:* "And, to be honest with you, it seems to me that you and your friends have not chosen the most intelligent path. To reform society with the help of the Idea, starting from the educated class? Impossible! Our time is a purely materialist time; if you had gone about it in a more directly political way, you would soon have reached the point where reform would have come to a standstill by itself. You will never be able to bridge the rift between the educated and the uneducated classes." (Bergemann, pp. 411f. [*CL*], marked there in margins; MA, p. 319).

724 *p. 535: Gutzkov to Büchner [...] piglet-drama:* "Of your 'piglet-dramas' I expect more than something piggish. Your Danton didn't draw: maybe you don't know why? Because you did not betray history [...]" (Bergemann, p. 535 [*CL*], first sentence underlined there, passage marked further in margin; MA, p. 350).

725 *Deutsche Drama [...] B. v. Wiese:* Benno von Wiese (Ed.): Das deutsche Drama. Interpretationen, 2 Bde., Düsseldorf 1958.

726 *Viëtor: 'antipathetic contrast':* "But inside the acts [of "Danton's Death"] the scenes are articulated according to a principle that shows most beautifully how the structure grows organically from the content of the play. One could call it something like the *principle of antipathetic contrast.'* " (Karl Viëtor: Georg Büchner. Politik—Dichtung—Wissenschaft, Bern 1949, p. 155).

— *Viëtor [...] The tragedy of heroic pessimism:* Karl

Viëtor: Die Tragödie des heldischen Pessimismus. Über Büchners Drama "Danton's Death," in: DVjs 1934, pp. 173ff.

— *K. May, Form und Bedeutung:* Kurt May: Form und Bedeutung, Stuttgart 1957.

727 *p. 399, Büchner to the family about my dramatic play:* Letter of 28 July 1835 (Bergemann, pp. 399ff. [*CL*]; MA, p. 305); in [*CL*]: marginal marks from "The dramatic poet [...]" to top of p. 401 "[...] accept critique with thanks."

729 *Glosses to Spinoza's Ethics [...] Thomas Payne's:* Viëtor compares Büchner's "critical glosses" (p. 227) to Spinoza's Ethics on the logical proof of the existence of God (cf. "Spinoza," in: Georg Büchner: Sämtliche Werke und Briefe, historisch-kritische Ausgabe mit Kommentar hrsg. v. Werner R. Lehmann, 2. Bd.: Vermischte Schriften und Briefe, Hamburg 1971, pp. 227-290 [Hamburger Ausgabe]) with Thomas Payne's argument in the 1st scene of Act 3 in "Danton's Death." (Karl Viëtor: Georg Büchner. Politik—Dichtung—Wissenschaft, Bern 1949, pp. 247f.)

730 *Fallhut:* children's cap; cf. "Danton's Death" Act 1, Scene 1: "Saint-Just would be pleased if we crawled around on all fours again; that way Robespierre could invent for us, according to the instructions of our good Monsieur Rousseau, the watchmaker's son from Geneva, all sorts of caps and school benches and an Almighty god." (Bergemann, p. 11 [*CL*], marked in margin there; MA, p. 70; Transl. By C. R. Mueller, p. 5).

731 *Walter Rehm [...] on Büchner [...] Gutzkov [...] Grabbe:* cf. Walther Rehm: Gontscharow und die Langeweile, in: Experimentum medietatis. Studien zur Geistes- und Literaturgeschichte des 19. Jahrhunderts, München 1947, pp. 96-183; there pp. 109ff.

732 *Leonce and Lena [...] 'A horrifying thought occurs to me [...]':* Act 2, Scene 3: Bergemann, pp. 135f. [*CL*] triple mark in margin, there; MA, p. 179.

733 *Graduation house, (-work): bâtiment de graduation [...]:* Graduation works: aerated wooden structure faggots for the obtention of salt; cf. "Leonce and Lena," Act 3, scene 3: the "ladies of the court stand there like graduation works; the salt crystallizes on their necklaces." (Bergemann, p. 141 [*CL*]; MA, p. 183).

734 *Nous ferons un peu de romantique [...]:* March 1834 letter of Büchner to his bride. (Bergemann, p. 383 [*CL*], marked there in margin; MA, p. 291). Viëtor uses the sentence from Büchner's letter as motto for the chapter on "Leonce and Lena" (Karl Viëtor: Georg Büchner. Politik—Dichtung—Wissenschaft, Bern 1949, p. 174).

735 *Brain- and heart-infuriating:* cf. "Woyzeck": "Marie's Room": "Marie *shyly*: What's the matter, Franz?—Your brain is infuriated \Du bist hirnwütig\, Franz." (Bergemann, p. 163 [*CL*], marginal mark there, "hirnwütig" additionally underlined; MA, p. 222).

736 different format than inserted sheets 2 and 3 (# 719-735)

739 The date "14" corresponds probably to October 1960, the time of the definite formulation of the first and third part of the Büchner speech, as here one can already see the process of the final version of the Büchner speech for paragraphs 14 to 15 and their connection to 45.

740 *Reference to 'Embankments, Roadsides, Vacant Lots, etc.' = [...] Woyzeck:* Cf. Celan's poem "Bahndämme, Wegränder, Ödplätze, Schutt" (TCA, Sprachgitter, pp. 84f.) In a notebook containing notes for his teaching at the École Normale Supérieure, Celan writes: "-i- (cf. Embankments etc." and the scene "Booths, Lights, People" in Büchner's "Woyzeck" (Bergemann, p. 155 [*CL*]. In later editions the scene no longer appears in this textual order.)

— *Krolow as witness: Rochefort [...]:* Rochefort-en-Yvelines, place close to Paris, where his mother-in-law had a house in which Celan often stayed. Karl and Luzie Krolow visited him there often during the summer of 1959.

— Dated at # 579 (E 14,1).

741 *'The finest epicurean of them all':* "Danton's Death," Act 1, Scene 6 "A Room:" "Danton. [...] All men are epicureans, some crude, some fine; Christ was the most refined." (Bergemann, p. 29 [*CL*], marked here in margin; MA, p. 87; Mueller transl. revised by PJ).

743 Insertion "my so paper loving [...]" aslant in left margin next to # 6 (C 30,1).

744 *Forester's house in Czortkov:* cf. note to # 83.

745 *Rue d'Ulm:* The École Normale Supérieure, where Celan worked, is situated in this street.

747, 749 Dated at # 800 (Workbook II, 21 [1]).

751 *Sadagora [...] Vishnitz, Kerty, Korsov and Bojan:* Places close to Czernovitz. Rabbi Israel lived in Sadagora.

— *Rabbi Israel, the Baal Shem:* "Baal-schem" ("Master of the Name"), is how Israel ben Elieser von Mesbiž, the founder of Hassidism (1700-1760) was called. He later changed that name to "Baal Shem tov" ("Owner of the good name"), a man whom the people trusted. (Martin Buber: Die Erzählungen der Chassidim, Zürich 1949, pp. 29ff.) Cf. Martin Buber: Die Legende des Baal-Schem, Frankfurt a.M. 1918 [*CL*] and: Des Rabbi Israel Ben Eliser genannt Baal Schem Tow Unterweisung im Umgang mit Gott, Berlin n.d. [*CL*].

— *eastern University:* Czernowitz.

753 *Isaiah: the lips [...] in M. Buber's German version:* cf. Buber and Rosenzweig's Bible translation "Das Buch Jeschajahu": "Aber von den Brandwesen flog eines zu mir, / eine Glühkohle in seiner Hand, [...] und berührte damit meinen Mund / und sprach: / Da, / dies hat deine Lippen berührt, / so weicht dein Fehl, / so wird deine Sünde bedeckt.": Isaiah (Jesaja) 6,6-8 (in: Bücher der Kündung, verdeutscht von Martin Buber gemeinsam mit Franz Rosenzweig, Köln/Olten 1958, p. 25).

754 *Viennese February:* Worker uprising in Vienna on 13 and 14 February 1934; open street battles between socialists and austrofascistic regime; after four days and nights uprising put down in bloodbath; following which the social-democratic party is banned (cf. also "In eins," in: TCA, Die Niemandsrose, pp. 106f.).

— *Oh fly, we are the workers from Vienna:* well-known Viennese workers' song: "Oh fly, you flaming, you red flag,/ Lead the way we follow, / We are the future, faithful fighters, / we are the workers of Vienna."

— *Forest in Pinzgau:* Pinzgau: inner-alpine valley landscape in the Austrian state of Salzburg; capital, Zell am See. Known as the scene of numerous battles during the peasant wars in the 16th C.

— Dated at # 579 (E 14,1).

758 *your slanting candles:* "In the church of Kaisariani we each bought a few long thin candles, lit them and stuck them, slanting slightly toward the outside, in a candlestick." (Marie-Luise Kaschnitz: Büchner-Preis-Rede 1955, in: Büchner-Reden, p. 32).

759 *'One should not ask the fish [...]':* Hugo von Hofmannsthal: "The last to ask what the sea is, are the fish. At most one can learn from them that it is not made of wood." ("Poesie und Leben," in: Hofmannsthal: Prosa I, Frankfurt a.M. 1950, p. 268 [*CL*]).

— envelope with writing though not connected to # 758.

771-791 The following excerpts come from Max Scheler: Die Stellung des Menschen im Kosmos, München 1947 [*CL*]: most of the citations are underlined there and marked in the margins:

— *Foreknowledge:* "If we interpret instinctive behavior psychologically, it represents an individual *unity of foreknowledge and action.*" (p. 25) [translation adapted]

— *associative memory: mneme (Scheler):* "it represents 'habitual' [behavior] [...] the epitome of the phenomena of association, reproduction, and conditioned reflex, in short, the capacity which we call *'associative memory'* (mneme)." (p. 26) [translation adapted]

— *productive thinking—anticipation:* "*Anticipation*, therefore, is always characteristic of this type of thinking which is not reproductive but productive. It is a kind of prevision of a new, never before experienced state of affairs (pro-videntia, prudentia, cleverness, shrewdness, cunning)." (p. 34)

— *'Aha'-experience:* "The suddenness of the experience is reflected in expression, for example when the eyes of an animal light up, an expression which Wolfgang Köhler aptly called an 'Aha'-experience." (p. 34)

— *Wolfgang Köhler:* (1887-1967) Gestalt psychologist; Investigations of chimpanzee intelligence.

— *'Spirit is therefore objectivity [...]':* (p. 40)

— *'To become human is elevation [...]':* (p. 41)

— *Kant: transcendental apperception:* (p. 48)

— *'Spirit is the only being [...]':* (p. 49)

— *Ideas do not exist 'before' [...]:* (p. 50)

— *'Examples of grasping the nature of things from them [...]':* (p. 51)

— *'Ideation: ... the essential modes [...]':* (p. 51)

— *'Knowledge of essences: the 'windows into the absolute' [...]':* (p. 52)

— *'The capacity to distinguish [...]':* (p. 52)

— *Ideation—suspension [...]:* (p. 53)

— *Buddha: 'wonderful to look upon [...]':* (p. 53)

— *'What existence' [...]:* (p. 54)

— *Anxiety is a correlate of reality [...]:* (p. 55)

— *De-actualization:* (p. 55)

— *Man as a being who can say no [...]:* (p. 56)

— *omne ens est malum:* (p. 56)

— *Man: the bestia cupidissima [...]:* (p. 56)

— *'Primordial urge of life to return to the inorganic':* cf. note to # 204

784 double frame around "p. 53."

794 *Hofmannsthal [...]: What taught us to give the name of 'soul' [...]:* actually: "Who taught us [...]": "Yesterday," in: Hofmannsthal: Gedichte und Lyrische Dramen, Frankfurt a.M. 1952 (1. Aufl. Stockholm 1946), p. 155 [*CL*].

795 *'Sphere of totality (preexistence)'* cf. "Ad me ipsum," in: Hofmannsthal: Aufzeichnungen, Frankfurt a.M. 1959, p. 217 [*CL*].

796 *'Of the antinomies of existence [...]':* ibid., p. 227; in [*CL*] para. is marked in margin.

798-799 Single inscribed page far in the back of an otherwise empty workbook.

802 *Preexistence ≠ sphere of totality:* "Path to the social as path to the higher self: the nonmystical route. / a) through action b) through the work/ c) through the child / If the being drops out of any and all totality (preexistence, fatelessness), it is in danger of losing itself." ("Ad me ipsum," in: Hofmannsthal: Aufzeichnungen, Frankfurt a.M. 1959, p. 217 [*CL*]; cf. also marks in the margin on p. 238: "The beginning is pure magic: Preexistence.").

805 *Babel, the Jewish boy who walks on his hand:* cf. the last sentence of the chapter "Bei unserem alten

Machno" in Isaak Babel's "Die Reiterarmee": "Der Knabe schlenderte mit nachdenklichem Blick durch die Küche, seufzte, stützte sich mit den Handflächen auf den Boden, warf seine Beine in die Höhe und begann, während die Füße unbeweglich in die Luft ragten, schnell auf den Händen zu gehen." ["Left alone, the boy looked dully around the kitchen, sighed, rested his palms on the floor, swung his legs in the air, and, with his heels together, quickly walked around on his hands." (Transl. by Peter Constantine, in: The Collected Stories of Isaac Babel, New York, 2002, p. 338] (Zwei Welten. Die Geschichten des Isaak Babel. 46 Erzählungen, aus dem Russischen übertragen von Milo Dor und Reinhard Federmann, München/Wien/Basel 1960, p. 316 [*CL*]).

806 from here in different pen; rest of page empty.

817 *Buber, I and Thou, p. 107 [...]:* "aber wüßten wir, daß es Wiederkehr gibt, wir würden keiner zu entrinnen suchen, und wohl nicht nach dem krassen Dasein, aber danach begehren, in jedem, in dessen Art und Sprache, das ewige Ich des Vergänglichen und das ewige Du des Unvergänglichen sprechen zu dürfen. [But if we did know that there was recurrence, then we should not seek to escape from it: we should desire not crude existence but the chance to speak in every existence, in its appropriate manner and language, the eternal I of the destruction and the eternal You of the indestructible.]" (Martin Buber: Ich und Du, Leipzig 1923, Neuauflage 1957, p. 107. American edition, p. 139).

— *p. 108 (Buber on Buddha):* "Buddha kennt das Dusagen zum Menschen [...]. Gewiß kennt er in der Tiefe seines Schweigens auch das Dusagen zum Urgrund, über all die von ihm wie Schüler behandelten 'Götter' hinweg. [Buddha knows saying You to man [...] In the depths of his silence he certainly knows, too, the You saying to the primal ground, transcending all the 'gods' whom he treats like disciples.]" (Martin Buber: Ich und Du, Leipzig 1923, Neuauflage 1957, p. 108, American edition, p. 140).

823 *Gumilyov to: Batjuškov:* Nikolay Gumilyov (Nikolay Stepanovič Gumilëv, 1886–1921), Russian poet and critic; cf. also note to # 297.

Constantin Batyushkov (Constantin Nikolaevič Batyuškov, 1787–1855), poet (wrote principally elegies) of the transition between Russian Classicism and Romanticism. Mental illness from 1820. Celan refers to a comment by Gumilyov on Mandelstam's poem "No, not the Moon" from "The Stone," the second stanza of which is: "How conceited was Batyushkov's message! /'How late is it?' they asked him, and who wanted to know, heard 'Eternity.'" (CW V, p. 75) Gumilyov commented on this stanza in his review of the first edition of Mandelstam's "The Stone" as follows: "With this, he opened the door to his poetry for all those phenomena that live in time and not only in eternity or in the moment [...]" (First published in the magazine "Giperborey" # 5, 1913). Cf. Nikolay Gumilyov: Pis'ma o russkoj poëzii [Letter on Russian poetry], Petrograd 1923 [*CL*].

— # 823-842 consist in three pages of identical format, torn from a notebook, that seem to connected. There are two further loose pages inserted that are not connected to those: cf. # 686 and # 736.

827 *Martini [...] Staiger:* cf. Fritz Martini: Das Wagnis der Sprache. Interpretationen deutscher Prosa von Nietzsche bis Benn, Stuttgart 1954; Emil Staiger: Grundbegriffe der Poetik, Zürich 1946.

— With library book numbers.

843 *Trubetzkoy:* Nikolay Sergeevič Trubetzkoy (1890-1938): important Russian linguist.

— *Hölderlin [...] (Sinclair) [...] Bettina [...] Blanchot:* Keywords referring to the essay "La folie par excellence" by Maurice Blanchot. Blanchot quotes from a letter in the "Günderrode," concerning a conversation of Bettina von Arnim with Isaac von Sinclair on Hölderlin. (Maurice Blanchot: La folie par excellence, in: Critique 6, 15. Februar 1951, pp. 99-118, there: p. 117; in [*CL*] as marked up preface: Karl Jaspers: Strindberg et van Gogh, Swedenborg, Hoelderlin. Traduit par Hélène Naef et précédé d'une étude de Maurice Blanchot ["La folie parexcellence"],Paris1953;Dateofpurchasehowever only "Paris, 12.6.62."). Cf. also note to # 206.

— *Saran, Heusler, Sievers:* Authors of foundational textbooks for the study of verse and sound, mentioned in the articles "Verse" and "Accent" in the Reallexikon (cf. note to # 216). Franz Saran: Deutsche Verslehre, München 1907; Andreas Heusler: Deutsche Versgeschichte. Mit Einschluß des Altenglischen und altnordischen Stabreimverses, 2. unveränderte Auflage, Bd. 1-3, Berlin 1956; Eduard Sievers: Grundzüge der Phonetik zur Einführung in das Studium der Lautlehre der indogermanischen Sprachen, Leipzig 1881.

— Parallel references to the following keywords: Breath-routes: 263; Benveniste (Tropes, metaphor): 237, 595; Bettina: 206; brotherliness: 33/111, 240/410, 401, 747; dialogue: 508; ecstasy: 386, 414, 718; the objective \Gegenständigkeit\: 183, 866; presence \Gegenwärtigkeit\: 321; secret: 16, 44/472, 135, 183, 306, 483, 511; shape-like \gestalthaft\: 44/472; Heusler: 968; Hölderlin: 201; Kafka, speech as having: 157, 296, 720, 732; mysticism: 34/493, 82, 238, 445; Vacant lots etc.: 261, 740, 745; rhythm: 212, 611; noun: 56, 59, 70, 94; perception: 463, 511; time—end-time: 420

844 posterior handwritten dating. Mark (to the right above the text) with red pen: cross in circle.

845 Mark (to the right above the text) with red pen: cross in circle.

846 Addition started in handwriting between the para., continued above the text.

848 Mark in right margin with ink: cross. Cf. Facsimile to # 848-852 on p. 272.

850-852 Marks in right margins with ink: cross.

854 Mark to right under text in ink: cross and horizontal line under "Language [...] something invisible."

857 Line with same pen as marks.

862 Underlining in same ink as marks at # 848ff.

863 F 55,3: earlier handwritten note (only: "human unland").

864 F 55,4: earlier handwritten note.

865 *parole / langage:* These concepts as associated here refer to the Saussurian opposition between actualized speech and common language.

866 Underlining in same ink as marks at # 848ff.

871 *Novalis: Philos. = homesickness:* "Philosophy is actually homesickness—*the drive to be everywhere at home.*" ("Das allgemeine Brouillon (Materialien zur Enzyklopädistik 1798/99)", in: Novalis: Schriften, Bd. 3: Das philosophische Werk II, hrsg. v. Richard Samuel in Zusammenarbeit mit Hans-Joachim Mähl und Gerhard Schulz, Darmstadt 1968, p. 434).

872 *the third and last Rome*: refers to a precept by Filofey, a monk from Pskov, which he used in 1511 in a letter to the Grand Duke Vasili III and which has been subjected to various ideological (mis)-interpretations ever since: "Two Romes have fallen. The third stands. And there will be no fourth."

873 B 3,3: later copy with the note "Rediscovered -i-note for Mandelstam:"

874 *Bakunin:* Michail Aleksandrovič Bakunin (1814-1876), Russian revolutionary, who popularized anarchism as a movement.

— *Herzen:* Aleksandr Ivanovič Gercen (1812-1870), Russian revolutionary, writer and critic; lived in exile in Western Europe after 1847. Publisher of anti-tsarist newspapers. Cf. also radio-essay on Mandelstam, para. 16.

— *Lavrov, Mikhailovski:* Petr Lavrovič Lavrov (1823-1902), Nikolai Konstantinovič Michajlovskij (1842-1904). Theoretician of Russian revolutionary populism (Narodničestvo).

— *Solovyov:* Vladimir Sergeevič Solov'ëv (1853-1900), Russian philosopher of religion and poet; influenced the young Blok and Bely.

— *'Inonia':* cf. Sergei Yesenin's poem "Inonia," translated by Celan (GW V, pp. 195ff.) "Inonia *(Inonija)*, from *inoi'*, 'other,' thus 'Otherland,'—Utopia." (Footnote in GW V, p. 213). Cf. also the volume in [*CL*]: Rossija i Inonija (Russia and Inonia), Berlin 1920; includes texts by Ivanov-Rassumnik "Rußland und Inonien," Andrei Bely "Christus ist erstanden" and Sergei Yesenin "Der Genosse" and "Inonien."

875 *Tetragrammaton:* denotation of the four consonants with which the Hebrew Bible circumscribes the name of God, and which are read as "Yahwe." The tetragrammaton plays an important role in the mystic and kabbalistic tradition; in popular belief it was taken as an emblem of protection that was affixed to objects or buildings.

— *the name of the Deus absconditus:* (Lat.) the hidden God; in medieval theology and for Luther it designated the absolutely transcendent God.

— *the El:* highest among the gods of most Semitic peoples.

877 *'inertia' in Mandelstam:* inertia (Lat.), inertie (Fr.): laziness. In a note for the radio-essay on Mandelstam, Celan speaks of the "vis inertiae interpreted as hostile to progress by the Soviets" of the poems of Osip Mandelstam, and of "their seeming staticity." (cf. also # 390)

878 *causa formalis [...] causa materialis [...] Entelechy:* The concepts of causa formalis and causa materialis do not appear thus in the "Monadology." Celan is probably thinking of the rule that "perception, and what depends on it, is not explicable on mechanical grounds, i.e. from shape and movement." (Leibniz, # 17 [*CL*]) From there Leibniz moves to the definition of "entelechy" in the next paragraph: "Man könnte allen einfachen Substanzen oder geschaffenen Monaden den Namen Entelechien geben, denn sie tragen alle eine bestimmte Vollkommenheit in sich [...]; sie haben eine Art Selbstgenügsamkeit [...], die sie zu Quellen ihrer inneren Tätigkeiten und sozusagen zu unkörperlichen Automaten macht (cf. Theodicy, § 87). [One could call entelechies all simple substances or created monads, for they all carry a certain perfection in themselves [...]; they possess a kind of self-sufficiency[...] which makes them the source of their own internal activity and, so to speak, disembodied automats.]" (Leibniz, # 18 [*CL*]).

— *Entelechy:* (Gk.) continuous effectiveness; philosophy: an internal principle of form that guides an organism to self-fulfillment.

— Dated at # 499 (F 14,1).

879 *'the compound, however [...]':* "Man kann demnach sagen, daß die Monaden nur mit einem Schlage entstehen oder vergehen können, d.h., sie können nur durch Schöpfung entstehen und nur durch Vernichtung vergehen; das Zusammengesetzte hingegen entsteht aus Teilen und vergeht in Teile. [Thus it can be said that monads only come into being or come to an end all at once, that is to say, they can come into being only through creation and can come to an end only through annihilation; the compound, however, comes into being from parts and comes to an end by parts.]" (Leibniz, # 6 [*CL*], line in margin).

880 *'For in nature there never are two beings [...]':* Leibniz, # 9 [*CL*], line in margin.

881 *'Et c'est ce qu'on appelle [...]':* "Mais la connoissance des verités necessaires et éternelles est ce qui nous distingue des simples animaux et nous fait avoir la *Raison* et les Sciences; en nous élevant à la connoissance de nous-même et de Dieu. Et c'est ce qu'on appelle en nous Ame Raisonnable, ou *Esprit.*" (Leibniz, # 29 [*CL*], last sentence underlined).

882-885 Dated on top of F 14.

885 *Perception → apperception:* "Der vorübergehende Zustand, der eine Vielheit in der Einheit oder in der einfachen Substanz einbegreift und repräsentiert, ist nichts anderes als das, was man Perzeption nennt. Diese muß, wie sich in der Folge zeigen wird, von der Apperzeption oder dem Bewußtsein unterschieden werden. [The passing condition, which involves and represents a multiplicity in the unit or in the simple substance, is nothing but what is called Perception, which is to be distinguished from Apperception or Consciousness [...]." (Leibniz, # 14 [*CL*]).

889 *'Pond full of fish':* "Jedes Stück Materie kann wie ein Garten voller Pflanzen und wie ein Teich voller Fische aufgefaßt werden. Aber jeder Zweig der Pflanze, jedes Glied des Tieres, jeder Tropfen seiner Säfte ist wiederum ein solcher Garten oder ein solcher Teich. [Each portion of matter may be conceived as a garden full of plants and a pond full of fishes. But each branch of every plant, each member of every animal, each drop of its liquid parts is also some such garden or pond." (Leibniz, # 67 [*CL*]).

891 *muddled mental pleasures:* "obgleich allerdings, diese Vorstellung, was die einzelnen Dinge der Welt anbelangt, verworren ist und nur deutlich sein kann bei einem geringen Teil der Dinge, nämlich bei solchen, die für die Monade die nächsten oder größten sind; denn sonst wäre jede Monade eine Gottheit. Nicht im Gegenstande also, sondern in der verschiedenen Art der Erkenntnis des Gegenstandes haben die Monaden ihre Schranken. Verworren reichen sie alle bis ins Unendliche, bis zum Ganzen; sie sind jedoch begrenzt und voneinander verschieden durch die Grade der Deutlichkeit der Perzeptionen. [though it is true that this representation is muddled in terms of the details of the world, and can be clear only as regards a small number of things, namely, those which are either nearest or greatest in relation to the Monads; otherwise each Monad would be a deity. It is not in terms of their object, but in terms of the different ways in which they have knowledge of their object, that the Monads are limited. In a confused way they all strive after the infinite, the whole; but they are limited and differentiated through the degrees of their distinct perceptions.]" (Leibniz, # 60 [*CL*]); first sentence from "obgleich" to "verworren" underlined by Celan.
He notes at the end of the book: "8.19. 59 (not without trepidation...)"

892 *sapere aude!:* "*Sapere aude!* Have the courage to use *your own* mind! is also the motto of the Enlightenment." ("Beantwortung der Frage: Was ist Aufklärung," in: Immanuel Kant: Ausgewählte kleine Schriften, Hamburg 1965, p. 1; cf. also Kant's source: Horace: Letters, Book 1, Letter 2, para. 40).

894-895 *Schelling [...] quotation vide Lukács [...] fullness of the subject:* "He [Schelling] says: 'Philosophy attains the highest, but only brings a fragment of man to this point. Art brings all of man, how he is, along ... and on this rests the eternal difference and wonder of art. \ Die Philosophie erreicht zwar das Höchste, aber sie bringt zu diesem Punkt nur gleichsam ein Bruchstück des Menschen. Die Kunst bringt den ganzen Menschen, wie er ist, dahin ... und darauf beruht der ewige Unterschied und das Wunder der Kunst.\'" (Lukács, p. 7; cf. also p. 9 and pp. 14-17).

— Mark in right margin with red pen: circle.

897-899 *homogeneous [...] coalescences and orderings [...] transformation faithful to the materials [...]:* all concepts and citations: Lukács, p. 9.

908 *Lukács [...] act of indifference [...]:* Lukács, p. 15.

917 *In self-movement the unity of subject and object takes place:* not a direct citation; cf. Lukács, p. 35: Die "Isolierung [des Künstlers] aus jeder subjektiven wie objektiven Bindung und Gemeinschaft [...] macht als unendliche Bewegung in der Richtung auf ganzreine Subjektivität gleichzeitig das vollendet angemessene Objekt möglich und verwirklicht so die eigentlichste und echteste Subjekt-Objekt-Beziehung."

918 *Adorno: historical innervation:* "Die historische Innervation Strawinskys und seiner Gefolgschaft ließ davon sich verlocken, der Musik durch Stilprozeduren ihr verpflichtendes Wesen aufs neue einzubilden. [The historical innervation of Stravinsky and his followers succumbed to the temptation of using stylistic procedures to reinstill the binding quality in music.] (Theodor W. Adorno: Philosophie der neuen Musik, Tübingen 1949, p. 89 [*CL*] English edition, p.105).

— *Innervation:* Provision (of a body part) with nerves; Conduction of excitations through nerves to organs.

919 *Bühler:* Karl Bühler (1879-1963): Psychologist,

linguist. Research on the particular nature of the higher life of the soul. Contributions to Gestalt-, language- and child-psychology.

920 *Lit. Enzyklopädia, Russian:* Literaturnaja Ënciklopedija, hrsg. v. A. V. Lunačarskij, 11 Bde., Moskau 1930-1939; article on Lenz in vol. 6, pp. 264f.

921 *Ask Krolow for his Büchner-speech:* Karl Krolow: Büchner-Preis-Rede 1956, in: Büchner-Reden, pp. 34-42.

922 *Stenzel:* Julius Stenzel: Philosophie der Sprache, München/Berlin 1934.

923 *Staiger, Grundbegriffe, Interpre., time:* Emil Staiger: Grundbegriffe der Poetik, Zürich 1946; Die Kunst der Interpretation, Zürich 1955; Die Zeit als Einbildungskraft des Dichters, Zürich 1939.

924 *Jahrbuch der Phänomenologie: II, III:* Jahrbuch für Philosophie und phänomenologische Forschung 2, Halle 1916: contains the second part of Max Scheler's work "Der Formalismus in der Ethik und die materiale Werteethik;" the first part is reprinted in vol. 1,2, Halle 1913. The third vol. Contains contributions by Alexander Pfänder (cf. Note to # 957) and Hedwig Conrad-Martius (cf. Note to # 962).

925 *Benveniste:* Emile Benveniste: Noms d'agent et noms d'action en indo-européen, Paris 1948.

926 *Benz:* Richard Benz: Deutsches Barock. Kultur des 18. Jahrhunderts, Stuttgart 1949.

927 *Newald, de Boor:* Richard Newald; Helmut de Boor: Geschichte der deutschen Literatur von den Anfängen bis zur Gegenwart, München 1949ff.; in [*CL*] only vol. 6,1: Ende der Aufklärung und Vorbereitung der Klassik, München [3]1957.

928 *Becker:* cf. Oskar Becker, elsewhere.

— *Solger's concept:* the concept of the "Invalidity of the Beautiful \Hinfälligkeit des Schönen\" is cited by Becker from: Karl Wilhelm Ferdinand Solger: Erwin. Vier Gespräche über das Schöne und die Kunst, new edition by R. Kurz, Berlin 1907, p. 183.

— *Solger:* Karl Wilhelm Ferdinand Solger (1780-1819), German philosopher.

931 *'The creature' (Buber):* Die Kreatur: eine Zeitschrift, hrsg. v. Martin Buber; Viktor von Weizsäcker u.a., Berlin 1926-1930; in [*CL*] issues for year 1 (1926/27), 2 (1927/28) and 3 (1929/30). The creature is also a fundamental concept in Buber's "I and Thou" (cf. note to # 409 and 817).

932 *Read Gundolf:* cf. the study by Friedrich Gundolf: Georg Büchner, in: Romantiker, Bd. 1, Berlin 1930, pp. 375-395.

933 *Arnold Zweig—Büchner:* cf. Arnold Zweig: Versuch über Büchner (1921), Epilog zu Büchner (1936) (in: Arnold Zweig: Essays. Vol. 1: Literatur und Theater, Berlin 1959, pp. 152-203; pp. 204-205).

934 *Schelling, Werke I. Abt., Bd. III p. 613:* Celan retrieves this reference from the essay by Oskar Becker (p. 37). Becker references several times Schelling's "System of transcendental Idealism." He cites the specified passage (slightly changed) as follows: "Die künstlerische Anschauung ist eine solche, 'in welcher die bewußtlose Tätigkeit durch die bewußte bis zur völligen Identität gleichsam hindurchwirkt' [The artistic gaze is such that 'unconscious activity works through the conscious one until complete identity is achieved'] (Werke, I. Abt., Bd. III, p. 613)." Cf. also Becker's source: Schellings Werke, nach der Originalausgabe in neuer Anordnung hrsg. v. Manfred Schröter, 2. Hauptband: Schriften zur Naturphilosophie 1799-1801, München 1927, pp. 612f.: "Sechster Hauptabschnitt. Deduktion eines allgemeinen Organs der Philosophie [...] § 1. Deduktion des Kunstprodukts überhaupt." Cf. System of Transcendental Idealism (1800), transl. by Peter Heath, "Part Six. Deduction of a Universal organ of Philosophy [...], § 1. Deduction of the Art-Product as Such." University of Virginia Press, Charlottesville, 1978, p. 219. Cf. also note to # 159.

935 *Binswanger:* Ludwig Binswanger (1881-1966), Swiss psychiatrist; student of Eugen Bleuler and C. G. Jung; friendship with Sigmund Freud, but more interested than the latter in a philosophical grounding of psychiatry; influenced essentially by Husserl's phenomenology and Heidegger's philosophy of Being; co-founder of the "Daseinsanalyse," which tries to discover the fundamental structures of being \Dasein\ of the mentally ill and to find meaning in language, fantasy and art; cf. also note to # 945.

936 *Husserl, Vorlesungen [...]:* Edmund Husserl: Vorlesungen zur Phänomenologie des inneren Zeitbewußtseins, hrsg. v. Martin Heidegger, Halle 1928, pp. 367-489 [*CL*], [Sonderdruck aus dem Jahrbuch für Philosophie und phänomenologische Forschung 9].

937 *Heidegger, Being and Time:* Martin Heidegger: Sein und Zeit, Erste Hälfte, Halle 1927 [Jahrbuch für Philosophie und phänomenologische Forschung 8]; in [*CL*]: Tübingen [6]1949.

— *On the Essence of Ground:* Martin Heidegger: Vom Wesen des Grundes, in: Festschrift Edmund Husserl, zum 70. Geburtstag gewidmet, Halle 1929, pp. 71-110. [Ergänzungsband des Jahrbuchs für Philosophie und phänomenologische Forschung 10]. English version in Martin Heidegger: Pathmarks, Cambridge, 1998.

938 *Bachelard, L'air et les songes:* Gaston Bachelard: L'air et les songes: essais sur l'imagination du mouvement, Paris 1943. English edition: Air and Dreams, Dallas, 1988.

939 *Eidetics [...] Jaensch 1920 [...] visual images:* on the "eidetic pupillary reflex" cf. Erich Jaensch: Grundformen menschlichen Seins, Berlin 1929, pp. 483-493.

— *visual images:* describe the behavior of the pupilla in response to light and dark photographs.

— *Husserl [...] Les essences des choses:* The "Being of things" is a central concept of phenomenology: Die "*reine oder transzendentale Phänomenologie* [wird] *nicht als Tatsachenwissenschaft, sondern als Wesenswissenschaft* (als '*eidetische*' Wissenschaft) *begründet* [...]. Die zugehörige Reduktion, die vom psychologischen Phänomen zum reinen 'Wesen,' bzw. im urteilenden Denken von der tatsächlichen ('empirischen') Allgemeinheit zur 'Wesens'-allgemeinheit überführt, ist die *eidetische Reduktion*. [...pure or transcendental phenomenology will become established, not as a science of matters of fact, but as a science of essences (as an 'eidetic' science)[...] The relevant reduction which leads over from the psychological phenomena to the pure 'essence' or, in the case of judgmental thinking, from matter-of-fact ('empirical') universality to 'eidetic' universality, is the 'eidetic reduction.]." (Edmund Husserl: Ideen zu einer reinen Phänomenologie und phänomenologischen Philosophie, in: Jahrbuch für Philosophie und phänomenologische Forschung 1,1, Halle 1913, p. 4. : Ideas Pertaining to a Pure Phenomenology and to a Phenomenological Philosophy, First Book. Transl. By F. Kersten, Martinus Nijhoff Publishers, The Hague, Boston, London,1982, p. XX).

940 *Flaubert: Correspondance, 'A force de regarder un caillou, [...]':* "À force quelquefois de regarder un caillou, un animal, un tableau, je me suis senti y entrer. Les communications entr'humaines ne sont pas plus intenses." (Letter to Louise Colet of 26 May 1853, in: Gustave Flaubert: Correspondances, hrsg. v. Jean Bruneau, Paris 1980, vol. 2, p. 335).

942 *Husserl, Logische Untersuchungen:* cf. in [*CL*]: Edmund Husserl: Logische Untersuchungen 1. Bd.: Prolegomena zur reinen Logik, Halle [3]1922.

943 *'Act of perception, each fulfilling act [...]':* ibid. Bd. 2,2, p. 142.

944 *Synopses / Chromatisms (audition colorée):* \Synopsien\ (psychol.): visual synaesthesia, its most common form; chromatisme (Fr.) coloration, from GK. chrõma color; cf. note to # 181. The audition colorée (hearing colors) designates the perception of colors at the audition of sound, tones, music. Cf. also the French poet and student of Mallarmé, René Ghil (1862-1925), who outlined his concept of the connection between vowels and consonants and colors and sounds as a synaesthetic experience, based on Rimbaud's poem "Voyelles" in his "Traité du verbe" (1886).

— F 63,3 only has "[~~Synopsien~~."

945 *No association [...] Binswanger:* "Because the flight from ideas \ Ideenflucht\ consists [...] not only in the constant jumping from one thought to another, so that we were able to characterize existence as an idea-fugitive \ideen*flüchtige*\, as a jumping or hopping form of existence; nor does it show itself only in grammatical-syntactic particularities, in rhymes, sound-associations, word-destructions and a preference for parataxis, but can also show itself [...] in perfectly correct language use."(Ludwig Binswanger: Melancholie und Manie. Phänomenologische Studien, Pfullingen 1960, p. 102; in [*CL*] mark in margin).

947-954 *Husserl, 'Ideas [...]':* cf. Edmund Husserl: Ideen zu einer reinen Phänomenologie und phänomenologischen Philosophie, in: Jahrbuch für Philosophie und phänomenologische Forschung 1,1, Halle 1913, pp. 1-324:

— *pp. 19, 20 [German page numbers given in margins of English edition]: Eidetic:* ibid. § 9. "Region und regionale Eidetik."

— *Objects = what 'stands ob-posite \Entgegenstehende\'; 'Ekphorierung of engrams':* These concepts could not be found as citations in the "Ideas."

— *Ekphorie:* (med.) Process of remembering.

— *Engram:* (med.) Memory picture.

— *'what is immanent to consciousness':* cf. pp. 185ff.

— *'perceiving intention' (Brentano):* meant is Franz Brentano; cf. p. 186: "Das Ding, das Naturobjekt nehme ich wahr, den Baum dort im Garten; das und nichts anderes ist das wirkliche Objekt der wahrnehmenden 'Intention.' [I perceive the physical thing, the Object belonging to Nature, the tree there in the garden; that and nothing else is the actual Object of the perceptual 'intention.']"

— *Intentio [...] Attentio:* cf. pp. 189ff. § 92. "The Noetic and Noematic Aspects of Attentional Changes."

955 "language-blind" crossed out several times.

957 *Pfänder, Psychologie der Gesinnungen:* Alexander Pfänder: Zur Psychologie der Gesinnungen, Erster Artikel, in: Jahrbuch für Philosophie und phänomenologische Forschung 1,1, Halle 1913, pp. 325-404; Zweiter Artikel, in: Jahrbuch für Philosophie und phänomenologische Forschung 3, Halle 1916, pp. 1-125. Cf. note to # 924.

958 *Bleuler, Lehrbuch:* Eugen Bleuler: Lehrbuch der Psychiatrie, Berlin 1916; in [*CL*]: 10. Auflage, Berlin/Göttingen/Heidelberg 1960 [Date of purchase: "Göttingen, 1 July 1964"].

959 *'Autismus':* concept introduced in psychiatry by Eugen Bleuler for psychotic personality disorders, characterized by extreme self-absorption and introversion as well as by phantasy- and dream-like, free-associative and impulsive thinking and speaking.

962 *Conrad-Martius, Zur Ontologie:* Hedwig Conrad-

Martius: Zur Ontologie und Erscheinungslehre der realen Außenwelt, in: Jahrbuch für Philosophie und phänomenologische Forschung 3, Halle 1916, pp. 345-542. Cf. note to # 924.

964 *Jaspers: Hölderlin, Van Gogh, Strindberg:* cf. note to # 843.

965 *'Innerlife':* could not be traced as citation.

967 *Shestov—Une heure avec Sch. (Frédéric Lefèvre):* reference could not be found.

— on top of sheet the note "—calmant—Cared<?>(S)".

968 *Heusler, Versgeschichte:* Andreas Heusler: Deutsche Versgeschichte. Mit Einschluß des Altenglischen und altnordischen Stabreimverses, 2. unveränderte Auflage, Vol. 1-3, Berlin 1956.

To the Radio-Essay on Osip Mandelstam (according to paragraphs)

1 *'The Stone':* cf. note to # 53.

— *Georgy Ivanov:* Georgii Vladimirovič Ivanov (1894-1958), Russian poet, member of the poets' guild (Cech poëtov), belonged to the circle of the Acmeists. 1922 emigration to Paris. Celan owned several volumes of his poetry and the memoirs of his youth "Petersburger Winter," important for the Mandelstam essay. (Georgii Ivanov: Peterburgskie zimy, N'ju-Jork 1952 [*CL*]; Date of purchase: "Paris, January 1959").

— *Nikolai Gumilyov:* cf. notes to # 297 and 823.

— *Sinaïda Hippius:* Zinaida Nikolaevna Gippius (1869-1945), early symbolist poet and critic. She emigrated to Paris in 1919.

— *'something had gotten into them':* cf. note to # 122.

3 *Something strange, somewhat uncanny, slightly absurd. Suddenly you hear him break into laughter [...]; he laughs much too often and much too loud:* cf. the numerous markings in Celan's copy of Georgy Ivanov's memoirs "Petersburger Winter," with notes above Chapter 10, "Mandelstam": "Mandelstam is the most laughter happy being in the world. [...] He laughs loudly until he is out of breath. His face turns red, his eyes fill with tears. His conversation partner is astonished and shocked. [...] Could he be sick? [...]." (Georgii Ivanov: Petersburgskie zimy, N'ju-Jork 1952 [*CL*], p. 115, first sentence marked at side; cf. also pp. 116f.)

— *He is also nearly indescribably fearful [...] he'll make a detour:* Cf. Ilia Ehrenburg (1891-1967) in his "Porträts russischer Zeitgenossen" (Il'ia Ërenburg: Portrety russkich poëtov, Berlin 1922 [*CL*], pp. 102-105; date of purchase "Paris, 16 February 1959.") On p. 104 Ehrenburg writes: "But Mandelstam—poor Mandelstam, who never drinks water that has not been boiled, and always crosses to the other side of the street when he passes a police station—he is the only one who has understood the pathos of daily events."

4 *Velimir Chlebnikov:* Velimir, originally Viktor Vladimirovič Chlebnikov (1885-1922), co-founder of Russian Futurism; was also important for Mandelstam. "Zaum" language theory of (trans-mental language); worked at renewing the meaning of words through experiments with tone- and sound-elements; cf. Celan's translations (GW V, pp. 293-311).

— *Vladimir Markov [...] 'the only one who never ate humble pie':* (Vladimir Markov), Slavist,with whom Celan was occasionally in personal contact. Works on Russian Futurism and on Chlebnikov. In his essay "Über Chlebnikov. Versuch einer Apologie und Entgegnung" Markov writes: "Chlebnikov did not wind up in the one-way street of 'acceptability,' although everyone else, except for Mandelstam, wound up eating humble pie." (Vladimir Markov: O Chlebnikove. Popytka apologii i soprotivlenija, in: Grani. Žurnal literatury, iskusstva, nauki i obščestvennoj mysli [Grani. Zeitschrift für Literatur, Kunst, Wissenschaft und gesellschaftliches Denken], Frankfurt a.M., N° 22 (1954) [*CL*], p. 144; Date of reading: "28. 9. 59").

6 *'The Hyperborean':* (Giperborej) literary journal, appearing from 1912 to 1914. Though not an official Acmeist organ, it did support the acmeists.

— *'Apollo':* published in St. Petersburg between 1909-1917. Mouthpiece of the Acmeists, after Gumilyov took over as editor of the literary section at the end of 1912.

— *Acmeists:* cf. note to # 297.

13 *'The listening, the finely tensed sail [...]':* cf. GW V, p. 59; Mandel'štam, p. 41 [*CL*].

14 *'Mellow, measured: the horses' hoofs [...]':* cf. GW V, p. 63; Mandel'štam, p. 43 [*CL*].

15 *'Insomnia. Homer.':* cf. GW V, p. 91; Mandel'štam, pp. 76f. [*CL*].

16 *'Tristia':* Title poem "Tristia" cf. GW V, p. 105; Mandel'štam, pp. 95f. [*CL*].

— *'among the Scythians":* Scythians: ancient nomadic people, whose homeland lay between Russia and the Black Sea. Also brings to mind Ovid's place of exile, Tomi(s) (today Constanza in Romania) on the Black Sea, where he wrote his elegies "Tristia" and his "Epistulae ex ponto," in which the Scythians are often mentioned. While Ovid saw the Scythians as barbarians, they are positively connotated by the Russian symbolists. Cf. Blok's poem "Skythians" ("Skify") of 1918: "Yes, we are Scythians! Yes, we are Asians, / with slant and greedy eyes." Cf. also the almanac "Skify."

— *Blok:* Aleksandr Aleksandrovič Blok (1880-1921), best-known Russian symbolist poet, author of essays and several lyrical dramas. Celan translated his poem for the revolution, "The Twelve" (GW V, pp. 10-45).

— *Bryusov:* Valerij Jakovlevič Brjusov (1873-1924), one of the leading poets of Moscow Symbolism. He turned against the propositions of religious Symbolism (Blok, Bely, Ivanov) concerning a "second reality" (cf. Note to # 122).

— *Bely:* (Bely) originally Boris Nikolaevič Bugaev (1880-1934), symbolist poet, critic, and prose writer. Bely's poems from 1934 on Mandelstam's death were important for Celan (cf. TCA, Die Niemandsrose, p. 86).

— *Mayakovsky:* cf. note to # 563.

— *Yesenin:* Sergej Aleksandrovič Esenin (1895-1925), became famous as 'peasant poet,' joined the Imagists in 1919. Took his life in Leningrad. Cf. Celan's translations (GW V, pp. 163-277).

— *Herzen:* cf. note to # 874.

— *Michaïlóvsky:* cf. note to # 874.

— *Peter Kropotkin:* cf. note to para. **8b** of the final version.

— *Chaadaevs, Leontievs, Rosanovs and Gershenzons:* cf. in Mandelstam's essay "On the Nature of the Word": "It seems to me that Rosanov spent his entire life poking around in a soft yielding emptiness, groping for the walls of Russian culture. Like some other Russian thinkers, like Chaadayev, Leontiev and Gershenson, he could not live without walls, without Acropolis." (Osip Mandelstam: Über den Gesprächspartner. Gesammelte Essays I, hrsg. u. übers. v. Ralph Dutli, Zürich 1991, p. 118; marked in: Mandel'štam, p. 342 [*CL*]).

— *Chaadayev:* (Petr Jakovlevìè Èaadaev 1794-1856) cf. Mandelstam's Chaadayev essay from 1914/15 (Ossip Mandelstam: Über den Gesprächspartner. Gesammelte Essays I, hrsg. u. übers. v. Ralph Dutli, Zürich 1991, pp. 53-61).

— *Leontiev:* (Konstantin Nikolaevič Leont'ev 1831-1891) conservative philosopher of religion and history, essayist, and novelist.

— *Rosanov:* (Vasilij Vasil'evič Rozanov 1856-1919) philosopher, critic, and author. Cf. Mandelstam's essay "On the Nature of the Word" (Osip Mandelstam: Über den Gesprächspartner. Gesammelte Essays I, hrsg. u. übers. v. Ralph Dutli, Zürich 1991, pp. 118ff. Marks in Mandel'štam, p. 343 [*CL*])

— *Gershenzon:* (Michail Osipovič Geršenzon 1869-1925) philosopher and critic, who in 1908 published a Chaadayev edition that became important for Mandelstam.

17 *'Let us praise the freedom that dawns there [...]':* cf. GW V, p. 103; Mandel'štam, pp. 94f. [*CL*].

18 *'This night, unamendable [...]':* cf. GW V, p. 95; Mandel'štam, p. 87 [*CL*].

19 *volume of poems [...]—the last one:* The title of this last volume from 1928 was "Poems" ("Stichotvorenija" [*CL*]).

— *'No more breath—the firmament swarms with maggots:'* cf. "Bahnhofskonzert," in: GW V, pp. 121f.; Mandel'štam, p. 112 [*CL*]. Variation on line 1: "No breath left."

— *Essays on poetry [...] plough [...] 'Black earth of time':* In the essay "The Word and Culture" Mandelstam writes: "Poetry is a plough that turns up time so that its deep layers, its black earth can come to light." (cf. Osip Mandelstam: Über den Gesprächspartner. Gesammelte Essays I, hrsg. u. übers. v. Ralph Dutli, Zürich 1991, p. 84; Mandel'štam, p. 323 [*CL*]). Cf. also note to # 121.

20 *'Whoever kisses time's sore brow[...]':* first line of the poem "January 1st 1924," cf. GW V, pp. 145-149; Mandel'štam, pp. 126-128 [*CL*].

21 *Armenian Diary [...] preference for the Latin gerund:* cf. note to # 643.

To the Letter to Hermann Kasack

— *The Poems of Oskar Loerke:* Oskar Loerke: Gedichte, Auswahl und Nachwort von Hermann Kasack, Frankfurt a.M. 1954 [*CL*].

— *a longish stay in the mountains:* Celan spent the summer of 1959 in Sils Maria.

On the Signature and Reference System

The system of signatures and references provides information on the location of the texts in the Marbach Literature Archive, on their traditional ordering and on comparable locations within the complete text materials. Current numbers, signatures and related references are given in the headline to each text; references to comparable locations can be found on the side of the given text, at the level of the line in which the referenced concept occurs.

Each text is provided with a signature that indicates its location in the Marbach Literature Archive. The signature comprises a binder designation and the page number of the text. The latter was often added in pencil by the scholars in charge of Celan's literary estate. The editors have given extra numbers, separated by a comma from the page number [or else put between square brackets, when the signature already contained a comma] to various notes appearing on the same page and separated by a space or a line by Celan. Texts that take up several pages carry a single signature and are provided with a page count and, where necessary, with details concerning the textual subdivisions.

In this volume each text provided with a signature is given a continuous number corresponding to the sequence of occurrences in the book. The *drafts* are numbered 1–100, the *materials* start with number 100. All linked and parallel references correspond to these numbers.

In some cases a note appears in identical wording in two places in *The Meridian*-binders, i.e. also under two signatures (as typescript or carbon copy, or as copy). Such texts are printed only once, while the second signature is added in square brackets (for ex. F 19,1 [F 119,4]). The appropriate link-references are then also put between square brackets.

Some texts are present twice, i.e. included both in the *Materials* section and in the *Drafts* (or, as the case may be, in two rubrics of the *Materials* section). These receive two numbers separated by a slash (for ex. 32/74). These double numbers appear both at the two relevant text locations and in the reference system.

In a few cases, self-contained aggregates of notes *(workbooks, excerpts, notes to Büchner and K. E. Franzos)* are printed in their material context. In the linked references the relation between the complete aggregates and extracts thereof appearing in thematic rubrics is indicated by "=".

Often consecutive handwritten texts are gathered in groups that contain several signatures. These text groupings are framed by "❖❖❖."

The link references can be found next to each text, resp. next to the first and last text of such a grouping. The numbers provided with an arrow indicate the original order thus: preceding ("◄"), following ("►"). Using the arrows allows one to read the binders in their original order. This system, however, does not point beyond the given binder (for ex. not from the last text of "E" to the first text of "F").

Other notes from sections of the estate papers not associated with the Büchner-speech are only excerpted. In this case, link references are only given when the immediately preceding or following note was also included as an excerpt, as for ex. in the case of the materials for Mandelstam ("ÜR"-signatures).

References giving the consecutive numbers of the texts with parallel occurrences appear next to the texts. Such a parallel occurrence reference is used when both the content and the wording of two texts are related. Where several reference numbers occur in one place, they are separated by a comma when they refer to the same entry, with a semicolon when they refer to different entries in the same line.

The reference numbers are always printed at the level of the line to which they refer. They do not occur between texts which are content-wise related in the book's structure, but serve before all to connect texts that are at a distance from each other. One has therefore always to consider the wider environment of a referenced text that already has its own context. To avoid an excessive accumulation of parallel references, there are in principle no references to occurrences of text that is taken up in the final version of the Büchner-speech. These are indicated in the *drafts* with a bold paragraph number. Paragraphs dropped later on (marked with an ✻ in the text) get references to all other drafts in which a related paragraph also occurs.

If one traces the series of drafts of a specific formulation, one will find the references to parallel occurrences in the materials next to the chronologically earliest text. One arrives thus at the *Materials* section where further parallel occurrences are given. The parallel occurrence references always also include the drafts. A further connection is offered by those texts with a double number that are included simultaneously as drafts and materials. The *Drafts* section will provide that text's connections with other drafts, the *Materials* section, the connections with other materials.

On the Final and the Preliminary Versions of The Meridian *Speech*

Overview

Celan attached much importance to the division of the speech into sections separated by empty lines and into paragraphs that start on a new line. In a few places double empty lines mark larger breaks. In the typescripts, sections and paragraphs nearly always start with an indented first line. There is a letter of 3.17.1961 in the archive addressed to the German Academy for Language and

Literature. In it Celan asks that the text of the speech be reset for publication in the *Jahrbuch* of the Academy, so as to "respect all empty lines: for these empty lines are in no way typographical 'stretchings,' but are part of the text itself; they stress the breath- and meaning-units."

As it was generously set over 19 pages, the first printing of the speech had many page breaks that made it impossible to decide if a section or paragraph break was intended. The divergent subdivision of the *Jahrbuch* reprint is primarily due to the fact that Celan had sent along a copy of the first printing as model. The division of the final version into 53 sections reproduced here is based on composition pattern "I," in which Celan marked all single and double empty lines by hand. These correspond to proofs "B" of the S. Fischer-Verlag edition. There the speech is laid out over only six columns, and Celan has expressly indicated the intended empty lines on the remaining page breaks. Only the mark before section 24 was omitted, but a single empty line separates it in all other versions of the text including the first edition.

Preceding the first coherent version of the speech, there are a number of typescripts and carbon copies that went directly into the first version of the speech (preliminary stage "A"). The signatures F 2, F 3, F 4, M 3, and C 39 (## 16 and 17) form a series of continuously paginated (from 1 to 5) typescripts; sheets C 1, M 2, C 36, C 37, and C 38 are the corresponding carbon copies. On pages 1 and 2 of the typescripts Celan has worked before all on the wording of the text, while the carbon copies show larger deletions. They probably indicate transfers into preliminary stage "A," as parts of the deleted text reappear there. On pages 3 to 5, however, textual corrections were only begun on the typescripts to be continued primarily on the carbon copies on which transpositions and transfers are marked, mostly in red pencil. (Cf. detailed notes to ## 16 and 17).

Similarly, a conspicuous layer of marginal marks, deletions, and markings (usually a circle or a cross) covers binders "C" and "F" in a number of different pens and red pencils, while similar markings appear in binder "F," there done also in ink. This seems to be the trace of a perusal of the complete material in view of the composition of preliminary stage "A" and possibly also for later versions of the Büchner-speech. Many notes that served directly as draft material are marked up, while others echo only faintly or did not make it at all, at least in terms of the wording, into the final text of the speech. These latter ones are consequently not reprinted as drafts but as materials. The marks are referred to their corresponding texts in the notes section. While the red pencil-layer, which also includes single notes and textual corrections, can be clearly delimited, black ink is often used as writing material, so that in this case only the characteristic circle- and cross-markings and the marginal marks and underlines that have a direct relation to these, can be indicated.

On the Selection and Presentation

The final version of the speech opens the volume as straight-forward reading text. The section and paragraph numbering follows the preliminary stage "A" and proofs "B." These numbers are also inserted in boldface into the text of all the draft versions and point back to the corresponding paragraphs in the final version.

The texts are printed in four columns in chronological order: The first column reproduces as far as possible excerpts from the longer drafts that immediately precede preliminary stage "A." Empty spaces in this column show that Celan first wrote the text in question at the moment of the redaction of preliminary stage "A." When, due to the synoptic arrangement of the texts, a paragraph not present in the original is created, it is preceded and followed by continuation marks "<...>."

The texts and excerpts in this column are reproduced again in their complete context in the *Drafts* chapter; their presence here makes the comparison with the preliminary stages easier. Each text and excerpt from the drafts has its signature and a reference to the number of its reprint in the drafts section.

The second column reprints the complete text of preliminary stage "A," and the third that of preliminary stage "L." Given that the synoptic arrangement produces empty spaces, empty lines in the original are indicated with "=." When a new paragraph coincides with the top of a new page, this is indicated as <new page>.

The fourth column offers specific variations from "I," "D," and from the proofs, the complete reprinting of which would not be useful as they correspond in the main to the final version.

Variants from "I" and "D" are reproduced here as long as they are not identical to the "L" version or the final version, and thus document further intervening steps. Variants from "D" are only given when they are also present on the tape recording (in order to eliminate basic hearing and spelling mistakes.) Further, all textual changes in proofs "B" and the corrected proofs "C" that are not simple writing mistakes are indicated. Finally, the few variants from the reprint in the *Jahrbuch der deutschen Akademie für Sprache und Dichtung* <Jahrbuch> are also indicated here, as far as they could not be traced back to the page proofs of the first printing.

On the Drafts of the Büchner-Speech

Overview and Genesis

Only about a sixth of all available notes can be identified as drafts of specific passages from the Büchner-speech. They are presented in an ordering derived from the structure of the final version.

The speech was roughly divided into three main sections composed in the main independently from each other, i.e. with minor exceptions the texts of their drafts do not overlap. In the first main part, the theme of art is developed via examples from Büchner's work. The second part includes the actual core of the speech, the poem's defining qualities. The third part summarizes the speech under the figure of the "meridian" and draws connections between Celan's work and that of Karl Emil Franzos. Finally, the author reflects on the previously said and formulates his thanks.

On the Presentation

Inside the three main parts of the speech the arrangement of text groupings corresponds to Celan's specific work phases. As far as possible they are set up in recessive chronological order. Where — due to insufficient dating evidence—this is not possible, an order based on the sequence of paragraphs in the final version is applied. With the help of this presentation, the genesis of the Büchner-speech can be retraced: from the more or less final text via the drafts of specific sections to the first notes and on to passages from earlier work taken up again at a later date.
Overall only those texts are classified as drafts that prefigure the final version not only in terms of the thinking, but also in terms of the wording. For a wider context one has to bring in the materials gathered under the thematically related rubrics. The parallel and linked reference system offers a way to proceed.
The fourth section, *Additional Notes to the Text of the Speech* gathers a few texts that function as commentaries or variations on the more or less complete text. They stand on their own here as they cannot be considered drafts in the true sense of the word, though they belong to the compass of the work due to their close relation to the speech.

On the Rationale of the Chronology

As only a few sheets are dated and as their sequence as available provides few indications, any chronological ordering has to rely in the main on indirect clues, and can thus only claim plausibility, especially in terms of the sequence of specific texts within a textual grouping.
Guidelines are offered by the transfer of corrections into later versions. Material connections between drafts of different sections of the speech and between dated and undated sheets permit the elaboration of certain connections. A suggestive hypothesis, but one that doesn't always work, is the proposition of an essentially continuous development of the text, in which the retention of formulations once corrected and of inserted paragraphs is more likely than for such elements to be discarded and newly reintegrated. It would conform to Celan's tendency to condense formulations into formulaic phrases and to retain these. Textual passages that are formulated again and again in similar versions, (before all *25*, *30*, *31*) present the greatest difficulties, as does the ongoing recombination of elements that are in the main identical.

On the Materials for the Büchner-Speech

Overview and Presentation

The collection of materials presents itself as a sequence of texts circling around a few main themes, some of which are formally elaborate while others are given only as keywords. These themes extend with rather precise contours through the notes covering the whole time period, and were repeatedly gathered into different groupings, related to each other and completed with citations. It is noteworthy that Celan would often more or less modify already sketched out motifs and subsequently relate them to Büchner or apply ideas first developed in relation to Mandelstam to his own poetry.
The division of the materials into thematic rubrics based on Celan's own terminology suggested itself because all exterior criterions (dated sheets, inherited sequence of pages, writing implement used, handwriting) fail as aids for the organization. Binders A, B, and F, put together by Celan himself, do not propose a meaningful sequence for a historical genesis.The materials in binders C, D, and E, found after his death in various pieces of furniture and gathered subsequently, are even more dependent on chance occurrences for their sequential ordering. The workbooks dated end of August 1960 and the pages from the diaries, devoid of any reliable dates, also show a more or less great discontinuity in the process of note taking, thus throwing a little but not much light on the connections.
The editors were intent on elaborating the clear constants that led from Celan's notes to the text of the speech. Celan often jotted down core ideas and their development or draft versions in completely different places and apparently also at different times. Once a formulation had been worked out, it could later be referred to only by a keyword.
The gathering of texts from different origins, but related by theme and wording, seemed therefore to impose itself as the first step. Through the creation of meaningful transitions inside the thematically defined rubrics and subdivisions, and by indicating the relations between these, Celan's wide-reaching work on those reflections that were most important for his own poetry can be elucidated. The ensuing outline for notes characterized less by some single foundational theoretical concept than by variations on recurring core themes and formulations, should not be taken as a systematic exposition of Celan's poetics but rather as a practical guide for the reading of his notes. Decisive is not the subordination of a text under a given heading, but its coordination within a specific context for which the heading is only a basic marker.
The organization of the texts proceeds as follows: Each subdivision starts with a text that contains the core thought of the relevant theme. Then follow texts with related or complemental

formulations. These, in turn, fan out toward new thematic concerns, so that a widely ramified network of relations of themes and motifs becomes visible.

These content-defined rubrics are followed by notes on poetological reflections that are not specifically related to Celan's own poetics. These are in the first instance texts that stand between the drafts and the materials: the *Notes on Büchner,* consisting of excerpts that are usually only minimally commented on or put into perspective, and the *Notes on Karl Emil Franzos,* the editor of the first critical Büchner edition, who comes from Czernovitz.

On the Thematic Structuring of the Materials

The structure as presented here shows which themes predominate for Celan before he set about the task of writing a speech related to Büchner. The aspects of poetry most important to him are indicated by the keywords that organize our structure. The lines of separation between the concepts cannot always be drawn clearly and the transitions are fluid. But the subdivisions permit different aspects of a given concept and the ways in which they touch and interpenetrate reciprocally in Celan's thinking to emerge more clearly.

Darkness: The concept of darkness has priority for it is the core theme of the oldest binder, "A," entitled "On the Darkness of the Poetic." The thoughts therein, which go back in part to the summer of 1959, as a list of various titles from 6.13.1960 reveals, were meant for an unrelated essay. With the help of its title, the first subdivision, *Congenital Darkness of the Poem,* builds a bridge between the oldest notes dating to August 1959 and the final version of the speech; the second subdivision, *Groundlessness and Abyss,* links Shestov's interpretation of Pascal's abyss in his essay *La nuit de Gethsémani. Essai sur la philosophie de Pascal* with Leibniz's question of the sufficient ground; the third, *The Poem's Lack of Origin,* is more independent from the final version and insists that the poem has no genealogy and stands by and for itself.

The Poem: This rubric turns to the poem as such and no longer to the sphere from which it comes. The first subdivision, *Opacity of the Poem,* reflects its "objectivity and oppositeness." Visibly inspired by Mandelstam's first volume of poems, *The Stone,* it appears here as "lapidary," "erratic" language boulder. The texts of the second subdivision, *The Poem as Speech-Grille,* is concerned with the nature of the poem as crystalline on the one hand, and as a porous, gap-rich grille on the other. The handling of language in the poem as an invisible phenomenon also linked to "levitation" and "free floating" determines the third subdivision, *Poem and Language.*

Breath: This concept, which heads the third section, captures the creatureliness of both man and poem in the spirit of the phrase "Breath, that means direction and fate." The first subdivision, *Breath,* emphasizes the importance of breath and voice for the poem. The second, *Mortality,* connects breath with death. Under the title *Person and Language,* the third gathers those texts which have as theme the making present of the person in language. The fourth subdivision, *Direction,* shows the connection between the breath and the being en route of the poem.

Breathturn: Given its central importance in the speech, the term *breathturn* has earned the right to its own rubric. It appears as *involution* (interfolding, catagenesis) or as *Leap*—in the sense given in the essays of Husserl-student Oskar Becker: *Von der Hinfälligkeit des Schönen und der Abenteuerlichkeit des Künstlers* and *Von der Abenteuerlichkeit des Künstlers und der vorsichtigen Verwegenheit des Philosophen*—and finally as *turn* toward the "strange" as the "properly Jewish" that is linked to the dead of Auschwitz. These different guises of the breathturn describe the event of the poem through the relation that grounds and motivates it most profoundly.

Encounter: The fifth section defines the *Encounter with the Poem* first as the perception of the poem, a perception that was the initial instigation for its writing. As the poem here often confronts the reader as if it were a person, the subdivision *The Dialogical Poem* deals with its dialogical structure in that sense of dialogue Martin Buber had already proposed in his *I and Thou.* Finally, the encounter is understood as a *Conversation with Things,* which, according to Celan's reading of Mandelstam, can mean "last things."

Hostility to Art: The first five main rubrics taken together create the pole of "Poetry." We meet the opposite pole, "Art," in the two remaining rubrics, *Hostility to Art* and *Time Critique.* Many of the texts gathered here go back to the year 1959 where they stand in contrast to the texts on darkness.

In its literal meaning, "Hostility to Art" connects core anti-classical topi in Büchner's four main works with a critique of modern cybernetics and theories of lyric poetry—especially Benn's, but also Hugo Friedrich's. Also criticized is the use of traditional concepts of metaphor, borrowed from classical rhetoric, by critics and specialists in German literature in explaining Celan's poems. For Celan, these critics often seemed to have an affinity with Claire Goll and her nefarious doings.

Celan's encompassing conception of poetry as shown in the first five rubrics is also present in the hostile counter-images of "Art," i.e. in relation to the artificial, the automatic, the cybernetic in modern lyrical poetry and in the synthetic poem.

Time Critique: This section is determined by the same polarity as the section on *Hostility to Art,* though here modern technology plays a more specific role, and is always seen from a polemic perspective rooted in Celan's conception of "poetry." Finally, the section entitled *Polemic* gathers a range of critical statements, inspired by the Goll-affair, concerning hostile behavior, even by friends, neo-Nazi mentality, spurious political "engagement," and inhuman, yet humanistically disguised, education—all of which stand in close relation to the texts in *Hostility to Art.*

On Materials from Other Archival Papers

The binders directly associated with *The Meridian* were supplemented with further archival materials that had a text-genetic relation to the essay, and that therefore overlap time- and content-wise with it.

M 1-3 are located in a folder with the preliminary stages of the Büchner-speech. It consists of four single sheets of which only M 1 offers an original text. M 2 and M 3 are uncorrected carbon copies of C 1 and C 37, while M 4 is an uncorrected carbon copy of the last page of typescript "L."

AE 15,8 is located in a folder with various notes and drafts in the archives around the *Niemandsrose*.

-i- 11,53 is located in a folder with notes that are part of a binder "Dossier -i-."

The *Workbooks II, 15* and *II, 21* are interrelated notebooks which Celan used in summer 1960. They seem to be the only evidence from the time period between the beginning of June and the middle of September 1960, for which there is no dated material in binders A to F. Several of the sheets inserted into Diary 4 contain primarily notes on Büchner.

Workbook II, 15: five inserted sheets; reproduced here are [1], [3] and [4]. The notebook contains continuous writing from pages 3 through 9. The date 8.19.60 is written on top of p. 4 on note [5].

Workbook II, 21: one sheet inserted at the beginning, three at the end; one of them dated 6.13.60. Continuous writing on pages 3-8. The date 8.22.60 is written on top of page 3.

Diary 4: lined jotter with appointment dates from 5.16.-12.10.1960. Reproduced here at five loose inserted sheets, of which [1] through [3] have been torn from a workbook and are apparently connected; [4] is a smaller torn off piece of paper written on on both sides; [5] a small card.

The *Journal of 8.2.* to *9.9.1960* is a small-size notebook. Three pages with the title "B-speech" are reproduced here.

Binders on Osip Mandelstam

The inclusion of texts from the notes on Mandelstam is meant to document their close interrelation with the preliminary work on the Büchner-speech and is thus limited to both areas' overlapping thematic concerns.

From the preliminary work to the radio essay and the *Note* on the translations we therefore essentially reproduce texts that are drafts of directly or indirectly used paragraphs in the Büchner-speech from the radio-essay. This concerns primarily paragraphs **33** and **36** of the final version; though there is also material concerning the concepts of the absurd (cf. Para **8**), of the alienating / other (paras **26** and **29**) as well as concerning some attributes that will be connected to the topos of the "meridian" (para **50**). Beyond this, texts are included that interrelate content-wise with texts from binders A to F. This concerns primarily the themes of "time," dialogics, and specifically the "conversation with things," the delimitation of "wordmusic, expressionistic art and metaphoricity," as well as themes connected to Mandelstam's volume *The Stone*, which shade over into the question of the poem's "opacity." Altogether it involves a series of Mandelstam-themes that continue to be active in Celan's thinking, as well as several Celan-themes (darkness, phenomenology, "becoming free of the world," and "stepping outside of contingency") that shade over into the preoccupation with Mandelstam. The material not reproduced here consists essentially of biographical notations on Mandelstam and reflections more specifically concerning the poems. If several versions of a text were available, a selection was made.

Reproduced are extracts from the following dossiers:

ÜR 6.6 with preliminaries for the *Note* on the translations;

ÜR 6.12 with the title "Osip Mandelstam" (in Cyrillic and Latin script) containing drafts and notes for the radio-essay;

ÜR 6.13 with preliminaries for the radio-essay; inserted into a double sheet with the title "-i- Mandelstam." The first sheet contains a list of the translated and to be translated poems, dated 12.29.1958.

On the Radio-Essay: The Poetry of Osip Mandelstam

When on 2.3.1960 Celan received the request from the NDR (Nord Deutscher Rundfunk) for translations of poems by Osip Mandelstam and a "biographical-analytical commentary on the author" for a twenty-minute radio broadcast, he had already done preliminary work for an essay on mandelstam. On 3.8. Celan sent in his manuscript for the NDR broadcast.

In his letter dated 3.15., Wilhelm Asche, the editor responsible for the program, thanks Celan and informs him that his text will be broadcast in a slightly shortened version on 3.19.60 from 10:10 to 10:30 p.m. under the title *The Freedom that Dawns There—Poems by Osip Mandelstam translated from the Russian and introduced by Paul Celan*. The letter further contained a copy of Celan's typescript with the added NDR title. Celan's fair copy follows that text, and is available as signature ÜR 6.10 in the archives (See also the volume: "Fremde Nähe": Celan als Übersetzer, Deutsche Schillergesellschaft Marbach a.N. 1997, pp. 362ff. [Marbach Catalog, 50]; the letters mentioned above are available in the Celan archives.) The reproduction in this volume is also based on the contents of ÜR 6.10. The title page of the typescript is entitled:

THE POETRY OF OSIP MANDELSTAM

Text and translations of the poems:

P a u l C e l a n

Following Celan's habit, the underlined sections in the typescript are reproduced in *italics*. The notes in the appendix refer to the added paragraph numbers.

Index of Names

The **bold** numbers refer to the paragraphs of the *final version*; V. "A" resp. V. "L" with number—to paragraphs in preliminary version "A" resp. "L"; recto number—to the current number in *drafts* and *materials*; "M" with number—to paragraphs of the radio-essay *The Poetry of Osip Mandelstam* (cf. pp. 215ff.). The corresponding numbers in *italics* refer to the related notes. References to Preface and Appendix are indicated by the abbreviation for page numbers (p.). Only the names of authors and historical persons are indexed; names of literary personages are not. Persons who appear exclusively as publishers are not included.

Names that appear in the final version are no longer mentioned in the corresponding paragraphs of the preliminary versions, nor are names from texts reproduced again in the transmitted texts if these have already been printed as extracts.

Akhmatova, Anna, *297*
Adorno, Theodor W., 252f., 918; **35d**; *252*, *918*
Apollinaire, Guillaume, 340
Aristotle, 140; *140f.*, *247*
Arnim, Bettina von, 206, 843; *206*, *843*
Asche, Wilhelm, p. 261
Augustine, *148*

Baal Shem, The (Rabbi Israel ben Elieser), 751; *751*
Babel, Isaac, 805; *805*
Bachelard, Gaston, 938; *938*
Bakunin, Michail Aleksandrovič, 874; *874*
Batjuškov, Konstantin Nikolaevič, 823; *823*
Baudelaire, Charles, p. xvi; 210, 389, 876; *137*, *210*
Becker, Oskar, 382, 429, 438, 928; *159*, *382f.*, *429*, *435*, *438*, *928*, *934*; p. 260
Becking, Gustav, *612*
Bely, Andrei, M16, 874, *874*
Bender, Hans, 562; *60*, *81*, *239*, *562*
Benjamin, Walter, p. xvi; **35d**; 29, 32/74, 50f., 84, 617; **35d**
Benn, Gottfried, 544, 550, 921; 10, 17, 27, 108, 162, 165, 281, 335, 544, 550, 827; p. 260
Benveniste, Émile, 237, 247, 595-597, 843, 925; *237*, *247*, *595*, *843*, *925*
Benz, Richard, 926; *926*
Binswanger, Ludwig, 935, 945; *935*, *945*
Blanchot, Maurice, 843; *843*
Bleuler, Eugen, 958; *935*, *958f.*
Bloch, Ernst, 82, 210; *82*, *210*
Blok, Aleksandr Aleksandrovič, *874*; *M16*
Bollack, Jean, p. xviii
Boor, Helmut de, 927; *927*
Borchardt, Rudolf, 137
Bréhier, Émile, *154f.*, *393*
Brentano, Franz, 953; *953*
Bryusov, Valerii Jakovlevič, *122*; *M16*
Buber, Martin, 269, 409, 421, 751, 753, 817, 820, 931; V. "A": 8b; 409, 421, 751, 753, 817, 931; p. 260
Büchner, Georg, pp. xi-xvii; **2**, **3a**, **6b**, **13**, **14c**, **17b**, **18a,c**, **19**, **20a**, **23**, **24a,f**, **29a**, **42b**, **48b**, **49b**, **51**, **52a**; 2, 6/73, 10, 16, 24, 30f., 34/493, 49, 81f., 84, 89f., 94f., 149, 294,

Büchner, Georg (*continued*)
375/738, 376/530, 539, 566, 634, 644, 652, 715, 724, 727f., 731, 734, 737, 759f., 843, 859f., 930, 933, 969; "Letter to Hermann Kasack" (p. 222); ***1a-2***, ***3a***, ***5b***, ***6a-c***, ***7b***, ***10a***, ***12a,b***, ***14c***, ***15***, ***20b***, ***24b,f***, ***25b***, ***31f***, ***48b***; *1*, *9*, *16*, *25*, *33*, *90*, *130*, *273*, *294*, *375*, *418*, *439*, *684*, *702-741*, *932f.*; pp. 257-261
Buddha, 784, 817; *784*, *817*
Bugaev, cf. Bely
Bühler, Karl, 919; *919*
Butzlaff, Wolfgang, *588f.*

Chaadaev, Petr Jakovlevič, *M16*
Celan-Lestrange, Gisèle, pp. xf., xiv; 454; *393*, *454*
Chlebnikov, Velimir, *M4*
Conrad-Martius, Hedwig, 962; *924*, *962*

Degas, Edgar, *17*
Democritus, 700; *700*
Demus, Klaus, p. xvi
Descartes, René, 781
Diels, Hermann, 700; *700*
Dmitrieva-Einhorn, Marina, *700*
Döblin, Alfred, *10*
Donne, John, 60/582; *60*

Ehrenburg, Ilia, *M3*
Eich, Günther, V. "A" and "L": * after **18c** (and note); 16, 602; *602*
Einhorn, Erich, *700*
Enzensberger, Hans Magnus, 335
Esenin, Sergej Aleksandrovič, *687*, *874*; *M16*

Filofey, *872*
Flaubert, Gustave, 940; *940*
Franzos, Karl Emil, **48b**, **49b**; 81, 83f., 650/748, 743, 745f.; **48b**; *81*, *83*; p. 259, p. 260
Freud, Sigmund, 204/632, 458; *204*, *458*, *595*, *935*
Friedrich, Hugo, p. 260

George, Stefan, 209; *137*, *209*
Gercen, Aleksandr Ivanovič, 874; *874*
Gershenzon, Michaël Osipovič, *M16*
Gippius, Zinaida Nikolaevna, *122*; *M1*
Goebbels, Joseph, 475
Goethe, Johann Wolfgang von, 600; *600*
Gogh, Vincent van, 964
Goll, Claire, p. xvii; 475; *60*; p. 260

Gomperz, Theodor, *154f.*
Gontscharov, Ivan, A., 731; *731*
Grabbe, Christian Friedrich, 731
Grimm, Jacob und Wilhelm, 31e, *193*, *626*
Gumilev, cf. Gumilyov
Gumilyov, Nikolai Stepanovič, 823; M1, M4, M6; *297*, *823*
Gundolf, Friedrich, 294, 932; *294*
Gutzkov, Karl, 722, 724, 731; *722*, *724*

Hauptmann, Gerhart, **13**
Hebbel, Friedrich, 731
Hegel, Georg Wilhelm Friedrich, 422, 552, 782; *422*, *552*
Heidegger, Martin, 937; **27**; *59*, *237*, *417*, *486*, *935-937*
Heimann, Moritz, **2**; 25, 369, 742; ***2***; *369*
Heine, Heinrich, 543; *543*
Herzen, Alexander, cf. Gercen
Heusler, Andreas, 843, 968; *843*, *968*
Hippius, Sinaida, cf. Gippius
Hitler, Adolf, *97*
Hofmannsthal, Hugo von, p. xvi; V. "L": after **31a** (and note); 137f., 322, 389, 759, 794, 796, 802, 805, 876; *37*, *137f.*, *252*, *375*, *759*, *794ff.*, *802*
Hölderlin, Friedrich, 60/582, 106, 201, 611, 843, 964; *201*, *611-613*, *843*
Holthusen, Hans Egon, *60*, *81*, *529*
Homer, 687, p. 217
Husserl, Edmund, 316, 486, 928, 936, 939, 942, 947; ***27***; *59*, *316f.*, *486*, *935-837*, *939*, *942*, *947-954*; p. 260

Ivanov, Georgii Vladimirovič, p. 215; *297*; *M1*, *M3*, *M16*

Jaensch, Erich, 939; *939*
Jaspers, Karl, 964; *843*
Jean Paul, *228*

Kafka, Franz, p. xvi; **35d**; 32/74, 51, 60/582, 146, 157, 296, 298, 720, 732, 754, 838, 843; "Letter to Hermann Kasack" (p. 222); ***35d***; *60*, *157*
Kant, Immanuel, 778; *892*
Kasack, Hermann, pp. xiii, xivf.; **52d**; 90, 92, 93, "Letter to Hermann Kasack" (p. 222); ***44***, ***45d***; *93*; p. *256*
Kaschnitz, Marie Luise, **52e**; 758; ***52e***; *758*
Kepler, Johannes 14; *14*
Killy, Walther, 162; *162*, *226*
Kierkegaard, Søren, *27*

Klopstock, Friedrich Gottlieb, *552*
Köhler, Wolfgang, 774; *774*
Krolow, Karl, p. xix; 740, 921; *740, 921*
Kropotkin, Petr Alekseevič, **8b**

Landauer, Gustav, **8b**; 754, 930; ***8b***, *V. "A"*: ***8b***
Laotse, *175*
Lavrov, Petr Lavrovič, 874; *874*
Lefèvre, Frédéric, 967; *967*
Leibniz, Gottfried Wilhelm, 879-881, 885, 889, 891; *125, 878-891*; p. 260
Lenz, Jakob Michael Reinhold, **13**, **17b**, **24a,d**, **49b**; 6/73, 49, 81, 375/738, 564, 674, 736f., 920; ***13***, ***24d***; *920*
Leont'ev, Konstantin Nikolaevič, *M16*
Lessing, Gotthold Ephraim, *81*
Lessing, Theodor, 580; *580*
Lichtenberg, Georg Christoph, 484; *484, 626*
Lippmann, Heinz, 969
Loerke, Oskar, "Letter to Hermann Kasack" (p. 222) and note
Lukàcs, Georg, 201, 894, 901, 908; *201, 286, 552, 894ff., 987-899, 908, 917*

Mayakovsky, Vladimir, 563f.; M16; *563*
Malebranche, Nicolas, **35d**; 29, 32/74, 50f., 84, 617, 941; ***35d***
Mallarmé, Stéphane, **19**; 17, 70, 338; *17, 944*
Mandelstam, Osip, pp. xiii, xvf., xvii; 56, 59, 393, 487, 510, 520, 523, 525, 600, 643, 647, 823, 863, 870, 875, 877; M2-4, M9, M11, M16, M18, M19, M21; *40a-b, 53, 58, 121f., 289, 297, 351, 361, 387, 486, 523, 643, 823, 873, 877*; *M1, M3, M4, M13-20*; p. 257, pp. 259-261
Mann, Thomas, *167*
Marcabru, *584*
Markov, Vladimir, *M4*
Martini, Fritz, 827; *827*
Marvell, Andrew, 60/582; *60*
Marx, Karl, 687
May, Kurt, 726; *726*
Mayer, Hans, p. xvi
Mechthild von Magdeburg, *368*
Mercier, Sébastien, p. xvi; **13**; 2, 9, 32/74, 535, 638, 701, 852
Michailovski, Nikolai Konstantinovič, 874; M16; *874*
Michaux, Henri, 723
Morgenstern, Christian, 340

Natorp, Paul, 316; *316f.*
Newald, Richard, 927; *927*
Nietzsche, Friedrich, 279, 637; *10, 27, 637, 687*
Novalis, 278, 416, 613, 871; *613, 871*

Oberlin, Johann Friedrich, ***24f***
Ovid, *M16*

Pascal, Blaise, p. xvi; **27**; 17, 31, 33/111, 52, 121, 136, 144, 151, 153, 156, 825, 843; ***27***; *27, 140f., 144, 148*; p. 260
Payne, Thomas, 729; *729*
Pelagius, 148; *148*
Perilaos, *719*
Pfänder, Alexander, 957; *924, 957*
Phalaris von Agrigent, *719*
Plato, 148, 154, 317; *154f., 207, 223, 237, 316f., 405*
Plotin, 155, 393; *154f., 393*
Pöggeler, Otto, 529; ***40a-b***; *529*
Pound, Ezra, 664, 667; *664*

Rehm, Walter, 731; *731*
Rilke, Rainer Maria, *335*
Rimbaud, Arthur, 210; *210, 567, 944*
Rosenzweig, Franz, *753*
Rosanov, Matvei Nikon, p. xvi; **24d**
Rozanov, Vasilii Vasil'evič, *M16*

Sachs, Nelly, pp. xvi, xviii; *24*
Saran, Franz, 843; *256, 843*
Scheler, Max, 163, 211, 772, 775f., 779-782, 786; *163, 211, 771-791, 924*
Schelling, Friedrich Wilhelm Joseph, 894, 934; *159, 894f., 934*
Schlegel, Friedrich, 600; *600, 649*
Schönberg, Arnold, 252f.; *252*
Schulte, H., *612*
Seckel, Dietrich, 611; *611-613*
Seidensticker, Peter, *588f.*
Shakespeare, William, ***13***
Shestov, Lev Isaakovič, **27**; 17, 31, 33/111, 140, 148, 156, 568, 652, 843, 874, 967; ***27***; *140f., 144, 148, 393, 967*; p. 260
Sievers, Eduard, 843; *612, 843*
Sinclair, Issac von, 843; *843*
Solger, Karl Wilhelm Ferdinand, 928f.; *928*
Solovyov, Vladimir Sergeevič, 874; *874*
Sophocles, 687
Spinoza, 729; *729*
Staiger, Emil, 827, 923; *827*
Stein, Edith, 401; *401*
Steiner, George, p. xix; *81*
Stenzel, Julius, 922; *922*
Strindberg, August, 964; *843*

Švarcman, Ieguda Lejb, cf. Shestov
Swedenborg, *843*

Thiers, Louis-Adolphe, *33*
Trakl, Georg, 162; *162, 226*
Trubetzkoy, Nikolay Sergeevič, 843; *843*

Valéry, Paul, p. xv; 110, 237; *17, 110, 237, 565, 567*
Vasili III, *872*
Vico, Giambattista, 421; *421*
Viëtor, Karl, 726, 729, 734; *726, 729, 734*
Walther, R., *612*
Weber, Werner, *239*
Whitman, Walt, *422*
Wiener, Norbert, *32, 602*
Wiese, Benno von, 725; *725*

Zweig, Arnold, 933; *933*

Facsimiles

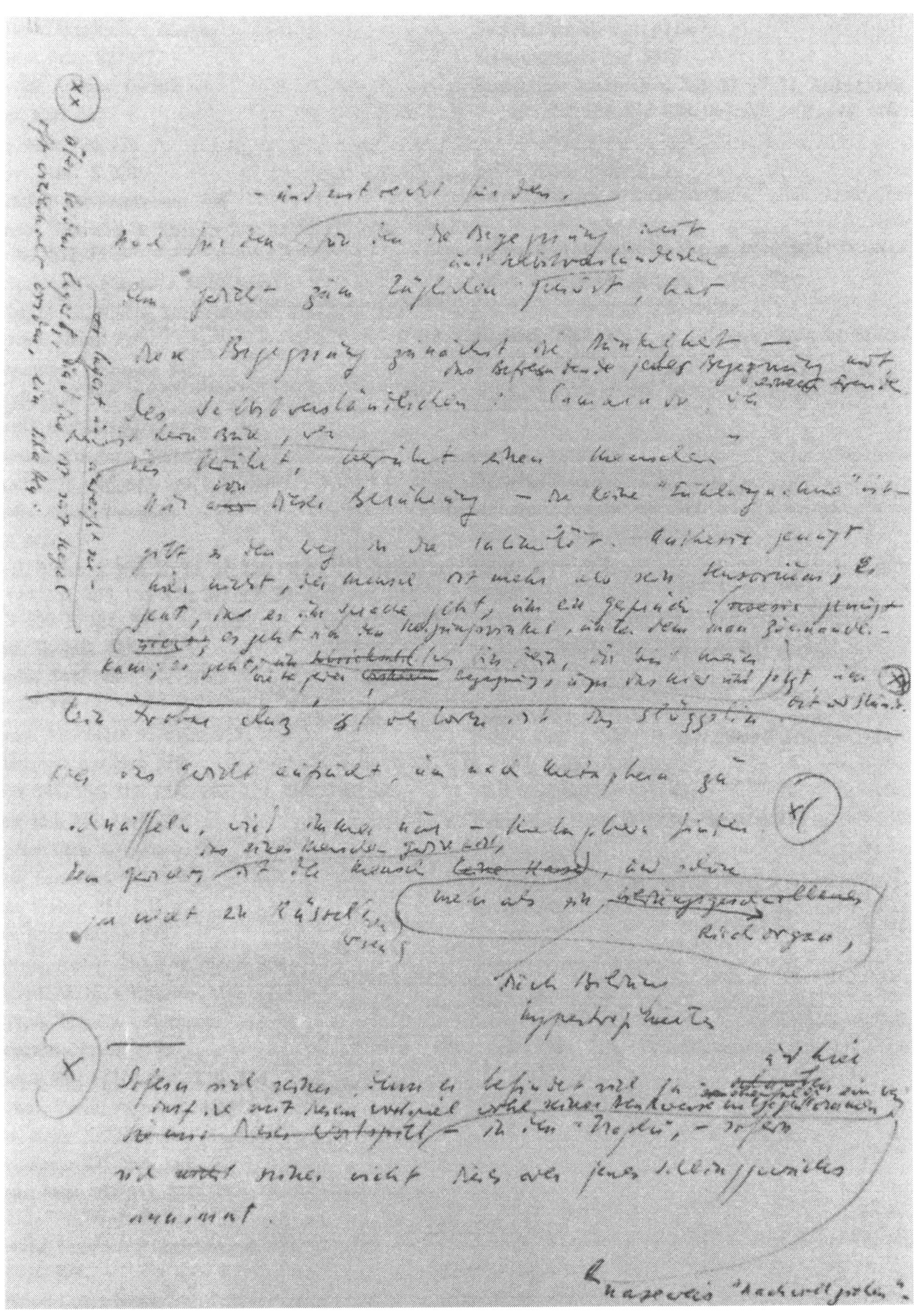

Facsimile of sheet A 16 from binder A entitled "On the Darkness of the Poetic," dated August 1959 (cf. ## 422, 584). Original size 29.7 × 21 cm. Writing pad sheet. Manuscript in blue ballpoint. Here, as on subsequent leafs, the signature was added in pencil at a later time and not by Celan.

Facsimile of sheet F 12 (cf. ## 222, 234, 517, 614f.). Original size 29.7 × 21 cm. Sheet from the same writing pad as binder A. Manuscript in pencil, single insertions in blue ballpoint, double mark in red crayon.

Facsimile of sheet ÜR 6.12,21 from the March 1960 drafts for the radio-essay on Osip Mandelstam (cf. ## 58, 392). Original size 29.7 × 21 cm. Manuscript in black ballpoint, diagonal deletion of middle paragraph in pencil.

Facsimile of sheet B 21: first draft of the Büchner-speech shortly after receiving the news of the upcoming presentation of the prize (cf. # 51). Original size 29.7 × 21 cm. Manuscript in black ink.

85

BR -28.IX.60

Das Gedicht fängt mit sich (bei sich) selber an.

[illegible]

... Sprach- und Verantwortungsüberdrüssige [illegible]

Die lyrische Koine unserer Tage [illegible]

Sprachverschrottung

Das Gedicht als das sich buchstäblich zu Tode Sprechende

Gegenstandlichkeit, gegenständigkeit der Gedichte. Was nottut, ist Anschauung (kein Durchschauen -: das Gedicht ist schon das Dahinter.

Ku stfeindlichkeit ('Danton','Lenz'). Keine synthetische Dichtung.
Kein Mercier'sches Elargissez l'Art (um Ultrakurz erweiterte Dichtung)

Die Heimatvertriebenen (Der Verband der Weltvertriebenen wäre wohl noch ins Leben zu rufen...)
Im Gedanken, dass und was und wie ie vertrieben wurden, ist die eigentliche Heimat.

Dem Aufmerksamen fällt etwas vom Vorwissen der Sprache zu: Unsichtbares vom Kristallisationspunkt (????)

[illegible]

Facsimile of sheet F 85. Newly dated compilation of older manuscript notes (typescript compilation); (cf. ## 848-852). Original size 26.9 × 20.9 cm. Typescript with corrections and marks in black ink.

Facsimile of sheet F 102; first formulation of paragraph 27 concerning "darkness" as annotation to notes that will not go into the final version (cf. ## 33, 111f.). Original size 27 × 20.9 cm; verso of a double page. Manuscript in blue ballpoint.

Facsimile of sheet F 23; draft for paragraphs 32 and 26b *et al.* of the Büchner-speech (cf. # 27). Original size 26.9 × 21 cm. Recto of a double page. Manuscript in black ink with corrections and additions in pencil.

B-Rede

Schluss:

Die Distanz, das Durchschrittene, das aus dem Uneadlichen Zurückkehrende, vom Fernsten her zurückkehrende, Uneendlich-Endliche, dae Unendlichgesprochene S Sterblichkeot und Umsonst ---------: Selbstbegegnung (Mystik, vgl. Ernst Bloch, Geist d. Utopie)

Das Gedicht gibt sich dir, dem xxx damit im Geheimnis der Begegnung Stehenden in die Hand - in welche Hand es sich damit gibt! Es gibt sich in deine Hand/als in die eigene! die von Fremdesten leuchtende

Vor sieben Jahren, ich war Büchner ferne, schrieb ich diese Zeilen: Stimmen vom Nesselweg her:/ Komm auf den Händen zu uns/ Wer mit der Lampe allein ist/ Hat nur die Hand, draus zu lesen. Erlauben Sie mir, dem mit dem Büchner Preis Bedachten, bei Lenz und bei dessen Händen zu stehen! Etwas Unsichtbares, und Irdisches das heute hier einen Namen suchen darf ~~im Vergänglichen aufleuchtet,~~ verbindet mich mit ihm: ein Meridian.

Facsimile of sheet C 12; draft for endpart of the speech with additional manuscript formulations for *The Meridian*. Original size 26.9 × 20.9 cm. Typescript with insertions in red crayon and pencil. Cf. also the excerpt from the facsimile of the chronologically following sheet C 8 (# 81) on the book cover.

Facsimile of sheet C 17. This and the following page: double page from a binder of variously gathered sheets with notations on Büchner (cf. ## 11, 708). Original size 26.7 × 20.8 cm. Manuscript in blue ballpoint.

Facsimile of page C 18, facing the page reproduced on the left /p. 276/ (cf. ## 11f., 708ff.). Original size 26.7 × 20.8 cm. Manuscript in blue ballpoint, circle with arrow in red crayon.

Facsimile of the front page of double sheet C 51, with notations coming from Büchner (cf. ## 3, 693f.). The lower note on "ubiquity" is continued on the left side of the verso page, reproduced on the right /p. 279/. Original size 20.9 × 13.4 cm. Manuscript in blue ballpoint.

Facsimile of the inside page of the same double sheet C 52 (cf. ## 4f., 20, 695ff.). The note starting on the lower right continues on the lower left. Original size 26.9 × 20.9 cm. Manuscript in three different blue ballpoints, with a penciled note written transversely to the other text.

- 12 -

wo alle Tropen ad absurdum geführt werden.

~~Erinnern Sie sich, bitte, an den wiederholten~~

Toposforschung? Gewiss! Aber im Lichte des zu Erforschenden: im Lichte der Utopie!

Welche Fragen! Welche Forderungen! Es ist Zeit, umzukehren.

Ich bin am Ende - ich bin wieder am Anfang.

Elargissez l'Art! Diese Frage, tritt, mit ihrer alten, auch schon in der Büchner'schen Dichtung ~~mitsprechenden~~ Unheimlichkeit, aus einer neuen Richtung an uns heran. Ich habe ~~ein Gegenwort~~ ~~gesucht~~ gesucht, nein, ich war mit diesem Gegenwort zu ihr gegangen.

Elargissez l'Art? Nein, sondern geh mit der Kunst in deine Enge!

~~Ich bin mit ihr in meine Enge gegangen.~~ Zweimal, bei Lucile's "Es lebe der König" und ~~damals~~ als sich unter Lenz der Himmel als Abgrund auftat, war die Atemwende da. Vielleicht auch, als ich auf ~~jenes~~ ~~ferne~~ ~~fremdeste~~ Du zuhielt, das letzten Endes ja ~~nur in der~~ wieder nur in der Gestalt Luciles sichtbar wurde.

~~Gedichte~~ -: ~~das~~ o diese/ Unendlichsprechung von ~~lauter~~ Sterblichkeit und Umsonst!

~~Ich hatte erzählt, einen Weg zu gehen, es war ein Kreis~~

~~Was war es nun~~? Erlauben Sie mir, bitte, da ich ja wieder am Anfang bin, noch einmal, in aller Kürze, aber aus einer andern Richtung danach zu fragen.

Meine Damen und Herren, ich habe vor einigen Jahren einen kleinen Vierzeiler geschrieben - diesen: "Stimmen vom Nesselweg her:/ Komm auf den Händen zu uns./Wer mit der Lampe allein ist,/hat nur die Hand, draus

Facsimile of page 12 of typescript "A" of the first complete preliminary version (cf. "Preliminary Stages," pp. 38-40). Original size 26.9 × 21 cm. Typescript with corrections and additions in black ink, blue crayon, and pencil.

- 12 -

-12-

"Der Tod", so liest man in einem 1909 ~~xxxx~~ in Leipzig erschienenen Werk über Jakob Michael Reinhold Lenz - es stammt aus der Feder M.N. Rosanows -, "der Tod als Erlöser liess nicht lange auf sich warten. In der Nacht vom 23. auf den 24. Mai 1792 wurde Lenz entseelt in einer der Strassen Moskaus aufgefunden. Er wurde auf Kosten eines Adligen begraben. Seine letzte Ruhestädte ist unbekannt geblieben."

So hatte er hingelebt.

Er: der wahre, der Büchner'sche Lenz, die Büchner'sche Gestalt, die Person, die wir auf der ersten Seite wahrnehmen konnten, der Lenz, der "den 20. Jänner durchs Gebirg ging, er - nicht der Künstler und mit Fragen der Kunst Beschäftigte, er als ein Ich.

Finden wir jetzt vielleicht/ den Ort, wo das Fremde war, den Ort, wo die Person sich freizusetzen vermochte, als ein - befremdetes - Ich? Finden wir ~~den~~ Ort ~~und den~~ Schritt?

"...nur war es ihm manchmal unangenehm, dass er nicht auf dem Kopf gehn konnte." - Das ist er, Lenz. Das ist, glaube

~~Wer auf dem Kopf geht, meine Damen und Herren, der hat den Himmel als Abgrund unter sich.~~ ich, er und sein Schritt, er

~~Auch dafür gibt es, wie für Luciles~~ und sein "Es lebe der König", keinen ~~ein für allemal feststehenden Namen, aber ich glaube... auch hier ist, wenn es xxxxxxxxx überhaupt so genannt werden kann, ein Ort der Dichtung - dieser Dichtung.~~

Facsimile of page 12 of typescript "L" which probably served as reading script, with last revisions (cf. "Preliminary Stages," p. 29). Original size 26.9 × 21 cm. Typescript with corrections in black ink and blue ballpoint.

MERIDIAN

Crossing Aesthetics

Peter Fenves, *The Messianic Reduction: Walter Benjamin and the Shape of Time*

Giorgio Agamben, *Nudities*

Hans Blumenberg, *Care Crosses the River*

Bernard Stiegler, *Taking Care of Youth and the Generations*

Ruth Stein, *For Love of the Father: A Psychoanalytic Study of Religious Terrorism*

Giorgio Agamben, *"What is an Apparatus?" and Other Essays*

Rodolphe Gasché, *Europe, or the Infinite Task: A Study of a Philosophical Concept*

Bernard Stiegler, *Technics and Time, 2: Disorientation*

Bernard Stiegler, *Acting Out*

Susan Bernstein, *Housing Problems: Writing and Architecture in Goethe, Walpole, Freud, and Heidegger*

Martin Hägglund, *Radical Atheism: Derrida and the Time of Life*

Cornelia Vismann, *Files: Law and Media Technology*

Jean-Luc Nancy, *Discourse of the Syncope: Logodaedalus*

Carol Jacobs, *Skirting the Ethical: Sophocles, Plato, Hamann, Sebald, Campion*

Cornelius Castoriadis, *Figures of the Thinkable*

Jacques Derrida, *Psyche: Inventions of the Other*, 2 volumes, edited by Peggy Kamuf and Elizabeth Rottenberg

Mark Sanders, *Ambiguities of Witnessing: Literature and Law in the Time of a Truth Commission*

Sarah Kofman, *Selected Writings*, edited by Thomas Albrecht, with Georgia Albert and Elizabeth Rottenberg

Arendt, Hannah, *Reflections on Literature and Culture*, edited by Susannah Young-ah Gottlieb

Alan Bass, *Interpretation and Difference: The Strangeness of Care*

Jacques Derrida, *H.C. for Life, That Is to Say...*

Ernst Bloch, *Traces*

Elizabeth Rottenberg, *Inheriting the Future: Legacies of Kant, Freud, and Flaubert*

David Michael Kleinberg-Levin, *Gestures of Ethical Life*

Jacques Derrida, *On Touching--Jean-Luc Nancy*

Jacques Derrida, *Rogues: Two Essays on Reason*

Peggy Kamuf, *Book of Addresses*

Giorgio Agamben, *The Time That Remains: A Commentary on the Letter to the Romans*

Jean-Luc Nancy, *Multiple Arts: The Muses II*

Alain Badiou, *Handbook of Inaesthetics*

Jacques Derrida, *Eyes of the University: Right to Philosophy 2*

Maurice Blanchot, *Lautréamont and Sade*

Giorgio Agamben, *The Open: Man and Animal*

Jean Genet, *The Declared Enemy*

Shoshana Felman, *Writing and Madness: (Literature/Philosophy/ Psychoanalysis)*

Jean Genet, *Fragments of the Artwork*

Shoshana Felman, *The Scandal of the Speaking Body: Don Juan with J. L. Austin, or Seduction in Two Languages*

Peter Szondi, *Celan Studies*

Neil Hertz, *George Eliot's Pulse*

Maurice Blanchot, *The Book to Come*

Susannah Young-ah Gottlieb, *Regions of Sorrow: Anxiety and Messianism in Hannah Arendt and W. H. Auden*

Jacques Derrida, *Without Alibi*, edited by Peggy Kamuf

Cornelius Castoriadis, *On Plato's 'Statesman'*

Jacques Derrida, *Who's Afraid of Philosophy? Right to Philosophy 1*

Peter Szondi, *An Essay on the Tragic*

Peter Fenves, *Arresting Language: From Leibniz to Benjamin*

Jill Robbins, ed. *Is It Righteous to Be? Interviews with Emmanuel Levinas*

Louis Marin, *Of Representation*

J. Hillis Miller, *Speech Acts in Literature*

Maurice Blanchot, *Faux pas*

Jean-Luc Nancy, *Being Singular Plural*

Maurice Blanchot / Jacques Derrida, *The Instant of My Death / Demeure: Fiction and Testimony*

Niklas Luhmann, *Art as a Social System*

Emmanual Levinas, *God, Death, and Time*

Ernst Bloch, *The Spirit of Utopia*

Giorgio Agamben, *Potentialities: Collected Essays in Philosophy*

Ellen S. Burt, *Poetry's Appeal: French Nineteenth-Century Lyric and the Political Space*

Jacques Derrida, *Adieu to Emmanuel Levinas*

Werner Hamacher, *Premises: Essays on Philosophy and Literature from Kant to Celan*

Aris Fioretos, *The Gray Book*

Deborah Esch, *In the Event: Reading Journalism, Reading Theory*

Winfried Menninghaus, *In Praise of Nonsense: Kant and Bluebeard*

Giorgio Agamben, *The Man Without Content*

Giorgio Agamben, *The End of the Poem: Studies in Poetics*

Theodor W. Adorno, *Sound Figures*

Louis Marin, *Sublime Poussin*

Philippe Lacoue-Labarthe, *Poetry as Experience*

Ernst Bloch, *Literary Essays*

Jacques Derrida, *Resistances of Psychoanalysis*

Marc Froment-Meurice, *That Is to Say: Heidegger's Poetics*

Francis Ponge, *Soap*

Philippe Lacoue-Labarthe, *Typography: Mimesis, Philosophy, Politics*

Giorgio Agamben, *Homo Sacer: Sovereign Power and Bare Life*

Emmanuel Levinas, *Of God Who Comes To Mind*

Bernard Stiegler, *Technics and Time, 1: The Fault of Epimetheus*

Werner Hamacher, *pleroma--Reading in Hegel*

Serge Leclaire, *Psychoanalyzing: On the Order of the Unconscious and the Practice of the Letter*

Serge Leclaire, *A Child Is Being Killed: On Primary Narcissism and the Death Drive*

Sigmund Freud, *Writings on Art and Literature*

Cornelius Castoriadis, *World in Fragments: Writings on Politics, Society, Psychoanalysis, and the Imagination*

Thomas Keenan, *Fables of Responsibility: Aberrations and Predicaments in Ethics and Politics*

Emmanuel Levinas, *Proper Names*

Alexander García Düttmann, *At Odds with AIDS: Thinking and Talking About a Virus*

Maurice Blanchot, *Friendship*

Jean-Luc Nancy, *The Muses*

Massimo Cacciari, *Posthumous People: Vienna at the Turning Point*

David E. Wellbery, *The Specular Moment: Goethe's Early Lyric and the Beginnings of Romanticism*

Edmond Jabès, *The Little Book of Unsuspected Subversion*

Hans-Jost Frey, *Studies in Poetic Discourse: Mallarmé, Baudelaire, Rimbaud, Hölderlin*

Pierre Bourdieu, *The Rules of Art: Genesis and Structure of the Literary Field*

Nicolas Abraham, *Rhythms: On the Work, Translation, and Psychoanalysis*

Jacques Derrida, *On the Name*

David Wills, *Prosthesis*

Maurice Blanchot, *The Work of Fire*

Jacques Derrida, *Points . . . : Interviews, 1974-1994*

J. Hillis Miller, *Topographies*

Philippe Lacoue-Labarthe, *Musica Ficta (Figures of Wagner)*

Jacques Derrida, *Aporias*

Emmanuel Levinas, *Outside the Subject*

Jean-François Lyotard, *Lessons on the Analytic of the Sublime*

Peter Fenves, *"Chatter": Language and History in Kierkegaard*

Jean-Luc Nancy, *The Experience of Freedom*

Jean-Joseph Goux, *Oedipus, Philosopher*

Haun Saussy, *The Problem of a Chinese Aesthetic*

Jean-Luc Nancy, *The Birth to Presence*

Made in United States
Troutdale, OR
07/09/2024